The Best of Art Culinaire

ISSUES 15-30

Photographs by Davide Biello, Dhanraj Emanuel, Roger Kramer,
Franz Mitterer, Mark Pampaloni

Published by Culinaire Inc.
PO Box 9268
Morristown, New Jersey 07963-9920
Distributed by Culinaire Inc.
973-993-5500
www.getartc.com

Library of Congress Cataloging-in-Publication Data
The Best of Art Culinaire, Issues 15-30 Culinaire Inc.
p. cm
Includes index.
ISBN 0-9623729-4-3
1. Cookery (The Best of Art Culinaire)
1. Title
TX 1174.T74 2001
Printed in Korea
Second Edition
2 3 4 5 6 7 8 9 10

The Best of Art Culinaire

Executive Editor: Christine L. Failla

Art Director: Tracy R. Jones

Graphic Artist: Christina Gille

Illustrator: Charles Perkalis

Editors: Anne Byrn, Russel Cronkhite, Mitchell A. Davis

Recipe Testing: Juliana Pascale, Steffani K. Smith-Lane

Culinaire Inc.
Morristown, New Jersey

CONTENTS

art culinaire

Preface

Issue 15 begins our second "The Best of Art Culinaire Magazine" Hong Kong's culinary scene was explored while it was still part of the British Empire. Roland Sager displayed Dim Sum such as Lotus Seed Flowers and Cheung Kam Chuen showed us Yellow Melon Soup with Bamboo Piths. Chris Northmore framed his talent of incredible desserts.

The spring of 1990 brought the next issue and started with a look at rhubarb with Philippe Reininger. An herb glossary and dishes followed from Christopher Hawver. Jean-Georges Vongerichten showed his flavored oil and changed the way chefs looked at a common ingredient. From Sweden, Jörgen Persson, Karl-Heinz Krücken, Sim Siik, and Christer Lingström gave an intimate view on their Nordic cuisine.

David Fye began Issue 17 with corn dishes and Daniel Boulud and Jacques Torres followed. Down south, Frank Stitt and Elizabeth Terry gave a taste of the south. Roland Liccioni and Joan Winters presented tempting caramel desserts.

Direct from Hawaii came the island dishes of George Mavrothalassitis, Roy Yamaguchi, and Amy Ferguson-Ota in Issue 18. David Burke and Don Woods showed that veal was more than just chops with dishes like Veal Tongue Ravioli with Sea Urchin. Jacques Torres brewed a strong cup for his coffee desserts.

The winter of 1990 warmed up with variations of Cassoulets and Ragoûts from Paul Bartolotta and Francis Drillien. André Jaeger gave an intimate view of the eating habits of Austria's royalty with Zander with Ginger Risotto. From the Big Apple came apple desserts with Richard Leach and Bruno Tison.

Issue 20 began in Italy's northeastern most corner of Friuli-Venezia Giulia with Roberto Cozzarolo, Toni Giacomini, and Gianni Cosetti. In Monte-Carlo Alain Ducasse walked in the markets to prepare for his dishes at Le Louis XV. Dishes like Gnocchi with Crayfish and Rooster Crowns, Herbed Cannelloni with Artichokes and Mascarpone Sherbet with Wild Strawberries filled the menu in his gold-clad restaurant.

On the line for issue 21 was Pacific seafood and California chefs Martin Woesle, George Mahaffey, and Mark Peel lead the way with fish such as King Salmon, Pacific Lobster, and White Sea Bass. Next was a bistro tour through France with Alain Dutournier, Michel Rostang, and Michel Cousin. It ended in California with Michel Richard at Citrus.

Patrick O'Connell opened the bottle and cooking with wine for Issue 22. Local Rabbit Braised in Pomerol was one of the results. Jimmy Schmidt took a new approach with wild rice and created Crayfish Cakes with Wild Rice Salsa.

Issue 23 set foot in Alsace. Paul Haeberlin, Jean Schillinger, Antoine Westermann, and Richard Riehm prepared dishes from one of the great food regions of the world. Jean-Louis Palladin and Dennis Foy took a look at wild game.

The spring of 1992 heated up with Gilbert LeCoze at Le Bernardin. David Burke took the confusion out of curry with his Roasted Monkfish with Moroccan Barbeque Sauce. Gray Kunz displayed his Cassoulettes and more at Lespinasse.

In Issue 25, Gérard Pangaud cooked with olives and summer fruits along with Peter Bührer. Spain shined and so did Spanish chefs Tomas Herranz, Pedro Larumbe, and Inaki Izaguirre with dishes like Codfish Rolls with Garbanzo Beans and Filled Apple Crêpes.

Jeremiah Tower and George Morrone toasted to cooking with Champagne in Issue 26. Michael Chiarello showed Italian food with a twist and Ken Hom displayed some of the dishes that come out of his kitchen. From New York's Russian Tea Room came Paul Ingenito new twists on Borscht and Caviar. Julian Serrano joined him for the caviar course.

Charlie Trotter and Douglas Rodriguez proved that grains were deserving of the spotlight in the winter of 1992. Potatoes were more that mashed after Joachim Splichal and Mark Baker finished cooking. Norman Van Aken, Allen Susser, and Jill Light puckered up to the sweetness of cooking with citrus.

Issue 28 posed the question of "why garden?" Sinclair Philip and Jan Birnbaum answered with dishes like Tuberous Begonia Petal Terrine. Stephen Levine began cooking with nut oils and then joined Emeril Lagasse and Lam Kam Shing for some barbecue. Brian Whitmer, Christer Larsson, and Christian Delouvrier proved that salmon is still king and Jean Joho varied Austria's Kugelhopf with great results.

Lamb was on the minds of Jean-Louis Palladin, Lydia Shire and Debra Ponzek in the summer of 1993. Jody Denton, David Walzog, and John Sedlar proved that tamales weren't limited to the traditional corn filling and spiced it up with combinations like Black Bean and Chorizo Tamale and Dark Chocolate Tamales. Dan Rundell, David Blom, and Dawn Rose chilled out with frozen desserts.

Issue 30 ends our second "Best of." Makoto Tanaka, Nobuyuki Matsushisa, Suser Lee showed Asian influences on American Cuisine. Vegetables took center stage and Hubert Keller, John Ash, and Ron Pickarski gave new life to "veg plates." Around the world to Greece and back to the States, Christoforos Veneris, Yiorgos Hatzyiannakis, Jonathon Fox, and Charles Bowman presented New Greek Cuisine that went beyond baklava, but didn't forget it.

"Beautiful soup! Who cares for fish, game or any other dish? Who would not give all else for two pennyworth only of beautiful soup?"

Lewis Carroll

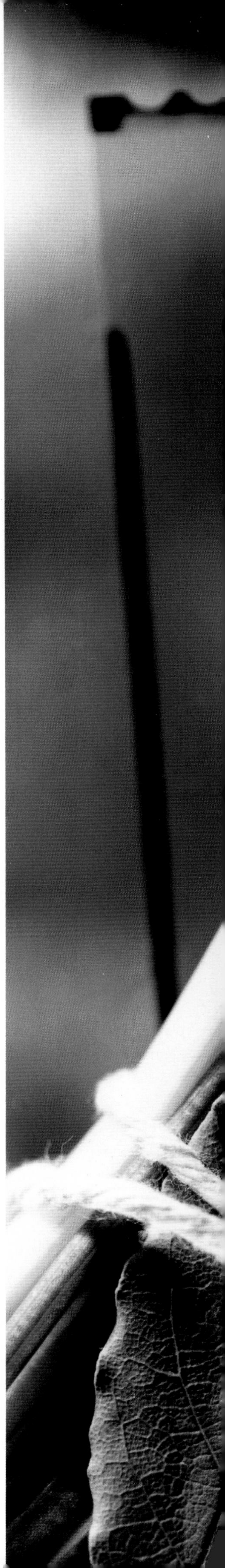

262 Yellow Melon Soup with Bamboo Piths
Cheung Kam Chuen

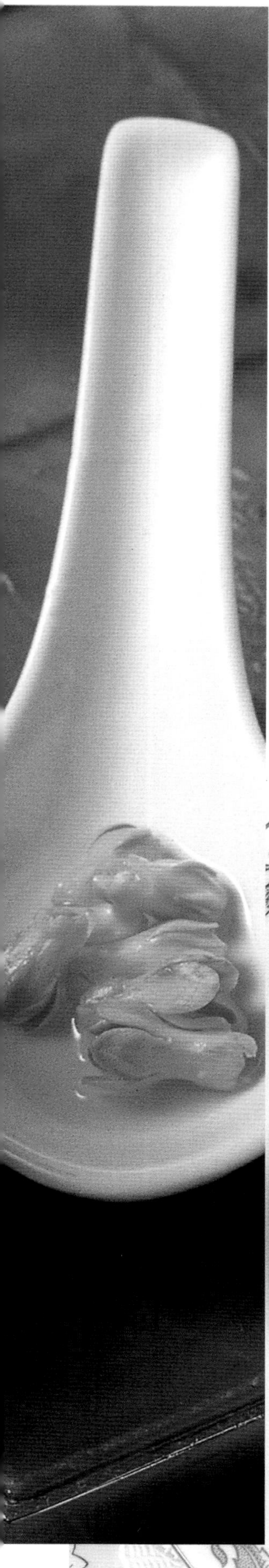

262 Cold Borscht
Paul Ingenito

262 Mussel Soup with Saffron
Jörgen Persson

263 | Sweet Corn Bisque with Lobster
David Fye

263 | Curried Pumpkin Soup with Shrimp Ravioli
Cheung Kam Chuen

264 Borlotti Bean Soup
Toni Giacomini

264 Soup of Shrimp with Couscous
Tomas Herranz

266 Butternut Squash Soup
Jan Birnbaum

265 Canadian Shellfish in a Pine Mushroom Broth
Sinclair Philip

266 Monterey Bay Salmon Soup
Brian Whitmer

266 Ginger Broth with Crab Dim Sum
Susur Lee

267 Avgolemono Soup with Roasted Lobster
Jonathon Fox

Salad

"Let first the onion flourish there,
Rose among roots, the maiden-fair,
Wine-scented and poetic soul
Of the capacious salad bowl."

Robert Louis Stevenson

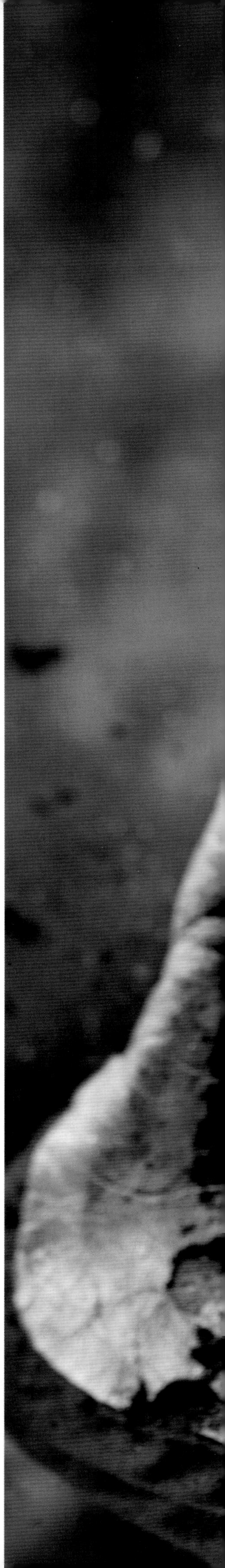

268 Warm Salad with Crisp Calves'Brain
Daniel Boulud

268 Warm Langoustine Salad
Alain Ducasse

269 Warm Salad of Octopus, Shellfish, and White Beans
Alain Ducasse

270 Warm Salad of California Crayfish
George Mahaffey

270 Tuna Niçoise
Mark Peel

271 Mixed Greens with Sweet Marjoram Vinaigrette
Sinclair Philip

271 Salad of Lobster with Sweet Potato
Joachim Splichal

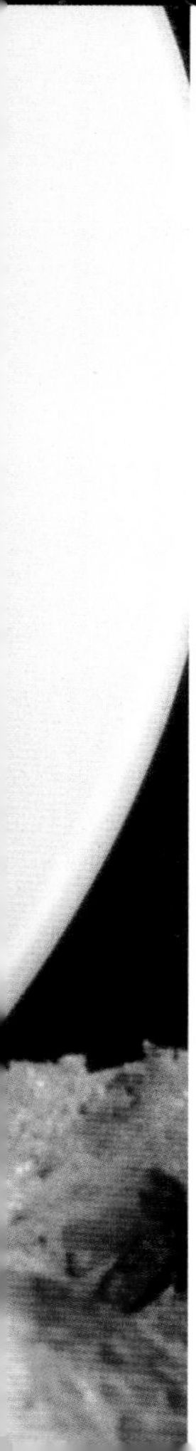

272 Rabbit Loin with Bulgur Salad
Charlie Trotter

272 Wild Mushroom Tamale Salad
Jody Denton

273 Feisty Salad of Lambs' Tongue
Lydia Shire

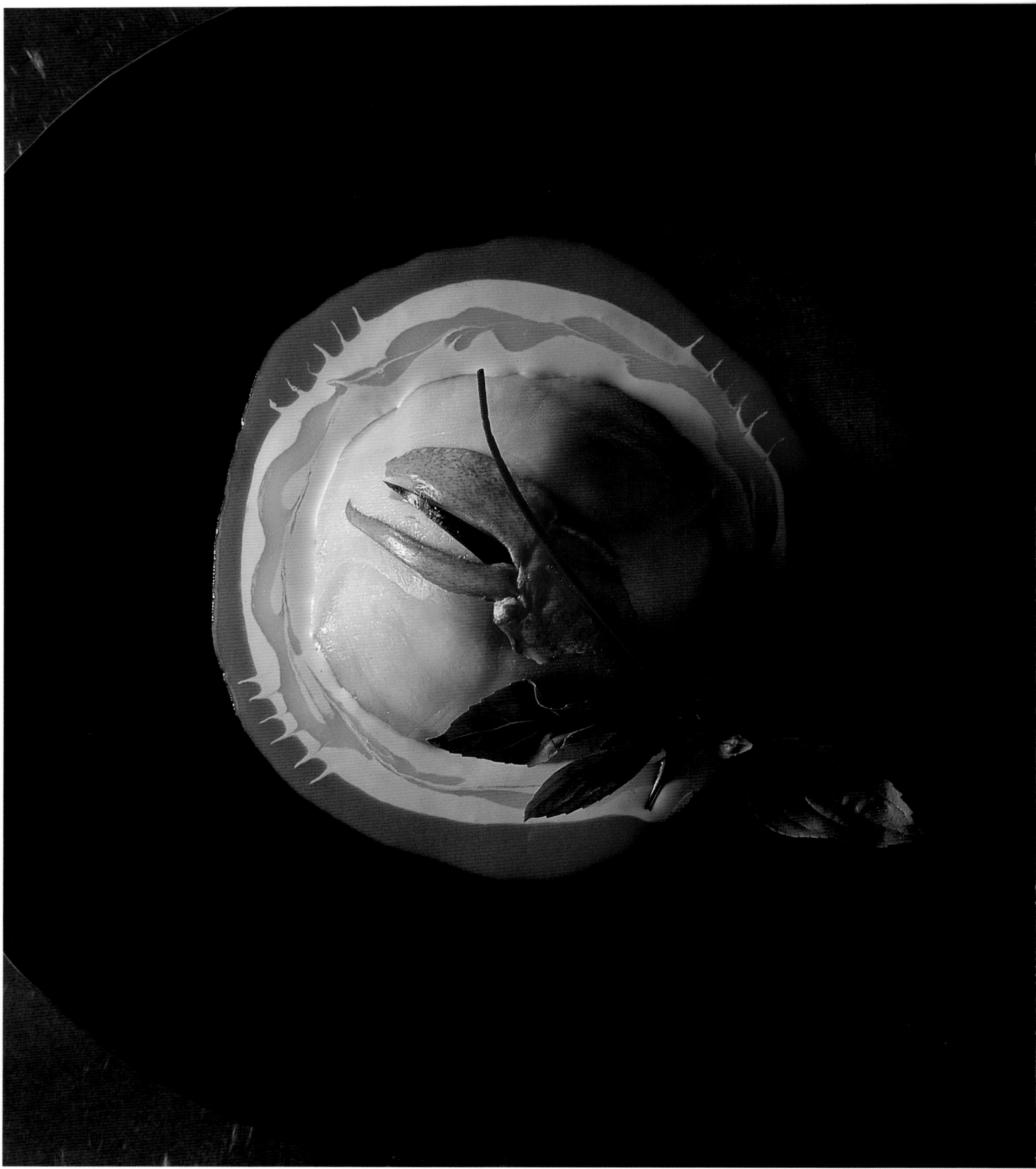

273 Lobster and Mango Salad with Lemon Grass
Susur Lee

274 Tempura Salad
Ron Pickarski

275 Olive Bread Salad
Jonathon Fox

"Appetizers are the little things you keep eating until you lose your appetite."

Joe Moore

276 Lotus Seed Flowers
Roland Sager

27G Pan-Fried Beef Cakes with Pine Nuts
Cheung Kam Chuen

27G Scallop Pockets
Roland Sager

277 Oysters with Shaved Sea Ice and Horseradish Oil
Jean-Georges Vongerichten

277 Five Warm Oysters
Jörgen Persson

278 Triangle Dumplings
Roland Sager

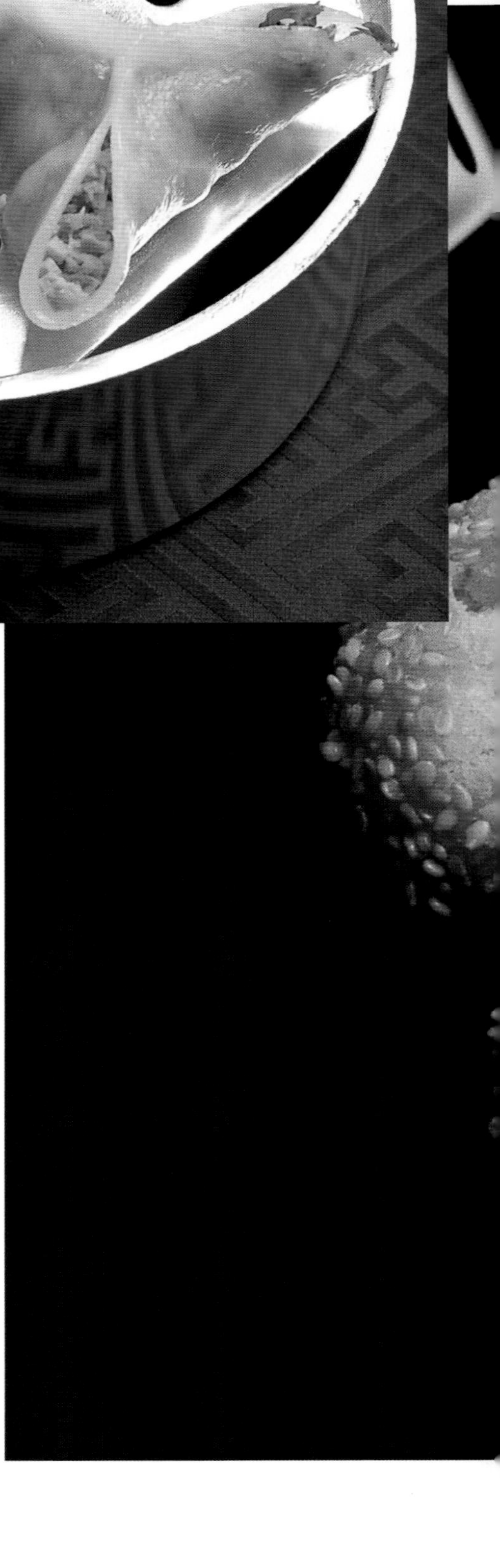

278 Sweet Flour Dumplings with Sesame Seeds and Lotus Paste
Roland Sager

279 Warm Oysters with Rhubarb
Christer Lingström

280 Asian Delicacies
André Jaeger

279 Veal Tongue Ravioli with Sea Urchin
David Burke

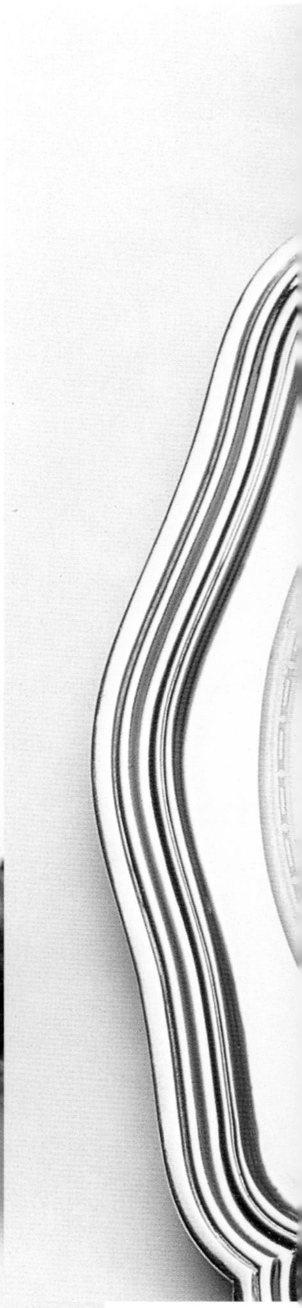

280 Friuli Cheese Crisp
Roberto Cozzarolo

281 Herbed Cannelloni with Artichokes
Alain Ducasse

281 Shrimp Dumplings with Bamboo Shoots
Roland Sager

282 Gnocchi with Crayfish and Rooster Crowns
Alain Ducasse

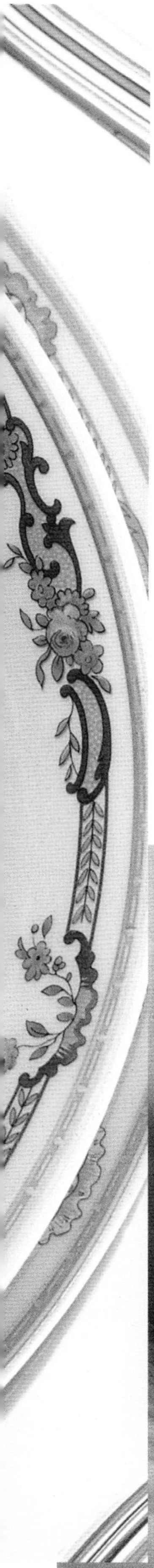

282 Oxtail Terrine
with Herb Vinaigrette
MichelRichard

283 Braised Snails with Mushrooms and Herbs
Paul Bartolotta

283 Pumpkin Gnocchi with Butter
Gianni Cosetti

284 Terrine of Pacific Fish with Saffron
Martin Woesle

284 Marinated Langoustines with Caviar
Jean Schillinger

285 Sea Snails in a Potato Crust
Michel Richard

285 Sea Urchin Medley with Shellfish Broth
Jean Schillinger

286 Terrine of Foie Gras, Leeks, and Pears
Patrick O'Connell

286 Marinated Anchovies
with Red Pepper Vinaigrette
Michel Rostang

297 Asparagus with Pickled Beets and Quail Eggs
Patrick O'Connell

288 Carpaccio of John Dory and Salmon
Jean Schillinger

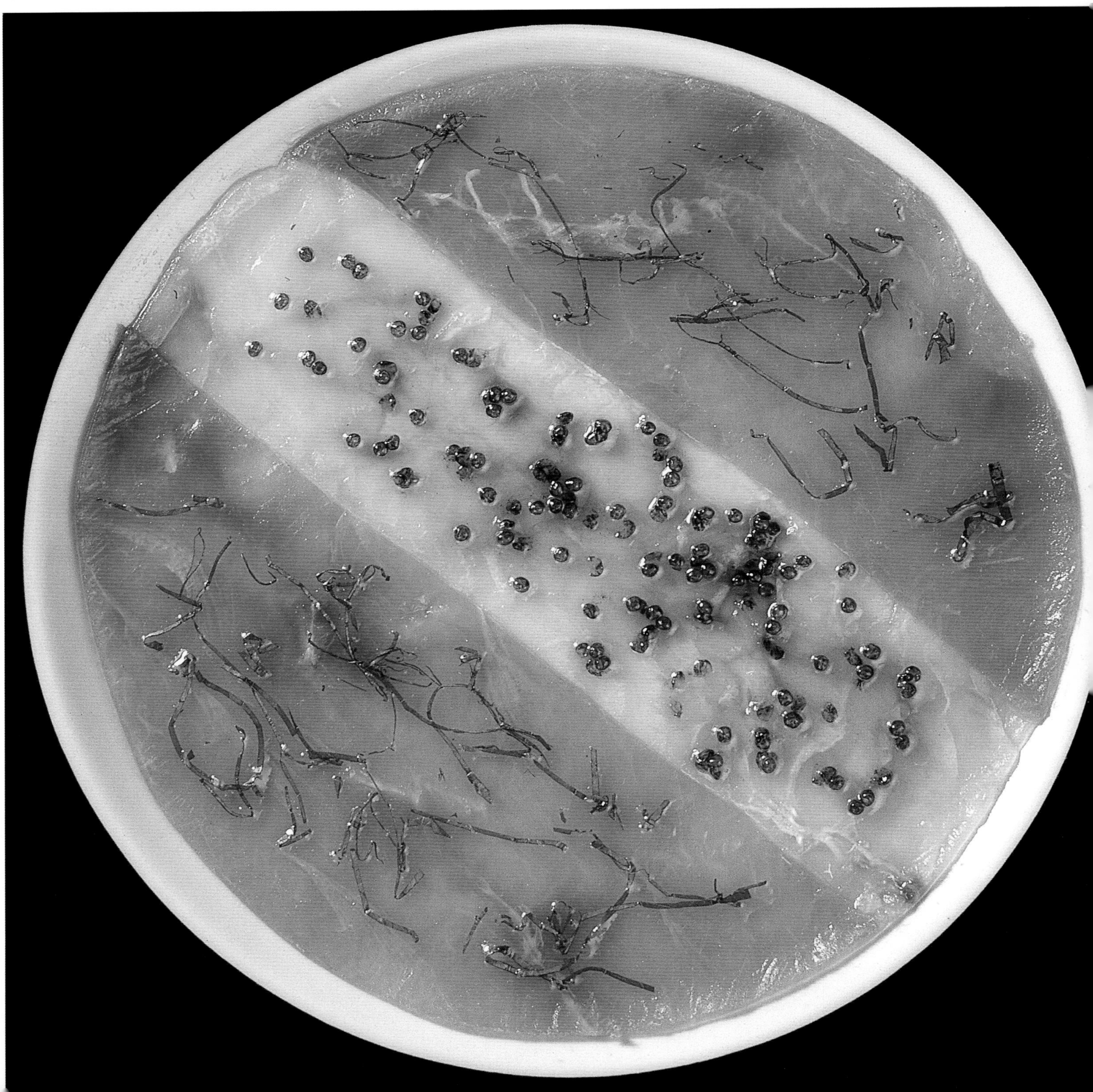

288 Truffles in Potato Crust
Paul Haeberlin

288 Potato Risotto
Michel Richard

289 Spicy Tuna Tartare with Wild Rice Blini
Charlie Trotter

289 Lemon Grass Crust Island Ahi with Ginger Rémoulade
Roy Yamaguchi

290 Couscous Stuffed Yellow Tomato with Tomato Essence
Charlie Trotter

290 Chicken Sun-Dried Tomato Spring Rolls
Ken Hom

290 Polenta and Scallop Terrine with Mustard Oil
Charlie Trotter

291 Tuna Carpaccio
Gilbert LeCoze

291 Sea Scallops with Couscous
David Burke

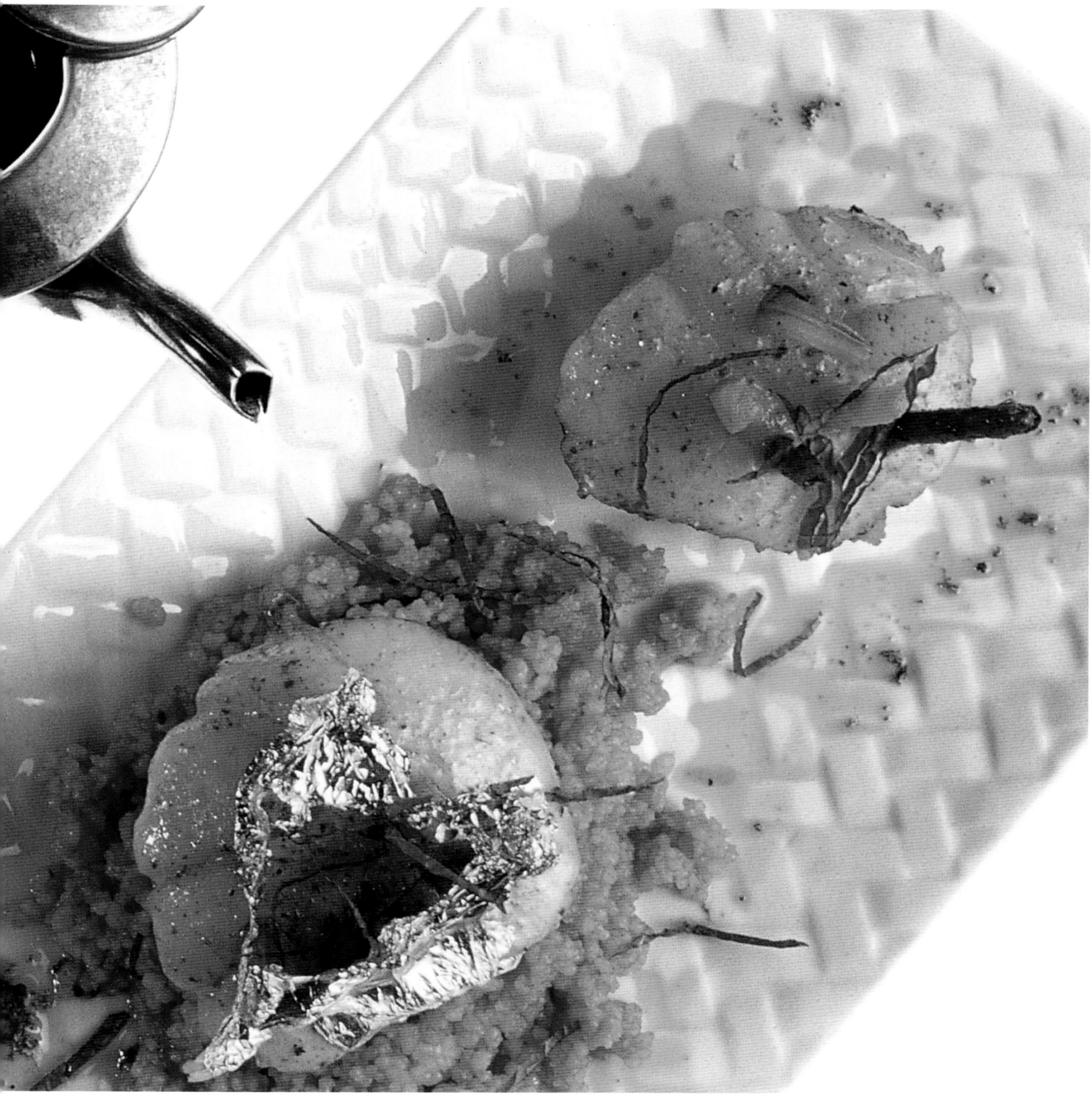

292 Potato Tasting
Mark Baker

292 Beluga Caviar Gâteau
Paul Ingenito

293 Ratatouille and Goat Cheese in Phyllo
Hubert Keller

293 House-Cured Prosciutto with Fava Beans and Polenta Crackers
Michael Chiarello

294 Cassolette of Crab
Gray Kunz

294 Cassolette of Risotto with Mushrooms
Gray Kunz

294 Cassolette of Shrimp and Scallop
Gray Kunz

295 Grilled Potato Bread with Seared Foie Gras
Mark Baker

295 Potato and Truffle Frittata
Mark Baker

296 Stuffed Tomatoes with Mussels
Pedro Larumbe

296 Stir-Fried Lobster Thai Stick
Norman Van Aken

297 Sashimi Tuna with Blood Orange Essence
Norman Van Aken

298 Stone Crab Cobbler with Key Lime
Allen Susser

299 New Age Steamed Buns
John Ash

300 Artichokes with Fava Beans
Yiorgos Hatzyiannakis

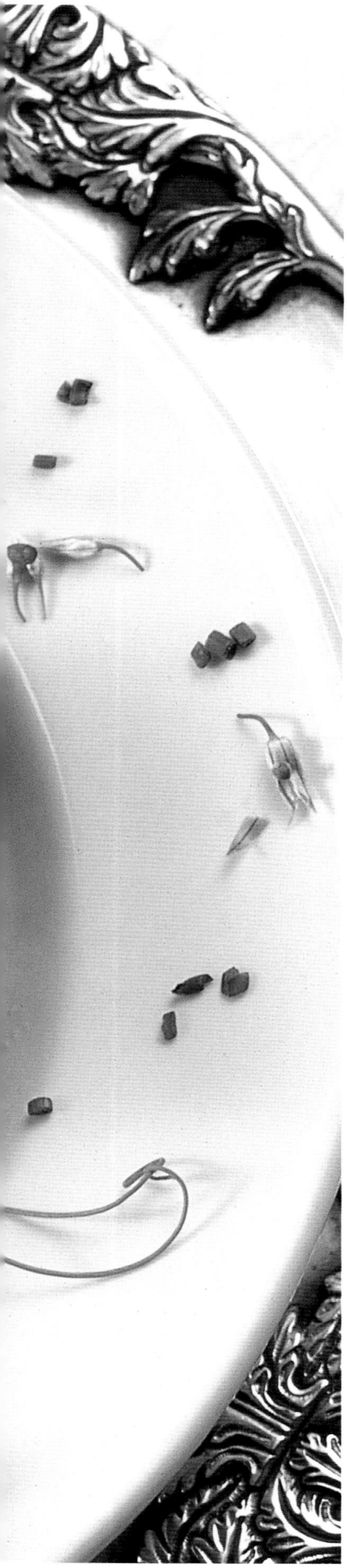

301 Modern Sashimi
Nobuyuki Matsushisa

301 Cod Taramasalata
Charles Bowman

301 Sashimi with Dressing
Nobuyuki Matsuhia

302 Individual Cheese and Tomato Pies
Yiorgos Hatzyiannakis

"It's good food and not fine words that keeps me alive."

Les Femmes savantes (1972)

"All is fish that cometh to net."

John Heywood

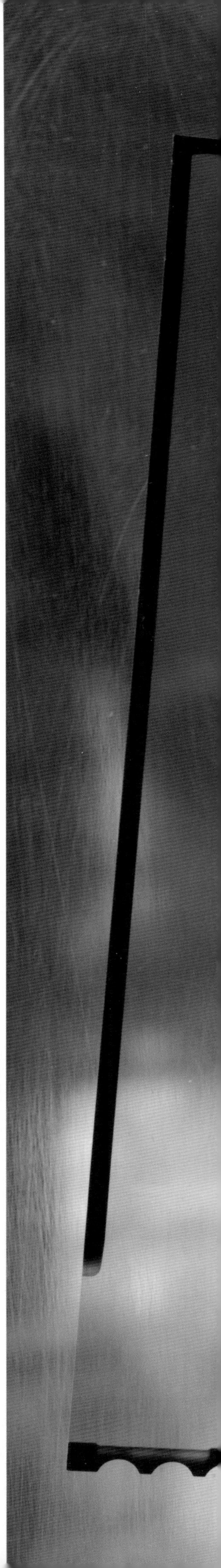

303 Baked Salmon
Christer Lingström

303 Steamed Seafood in Lotus Leaf
Cheung Kam Chuen

304 Scallops with Truffle and Yellow Pepper Oils
Jean-Georges Vongerichten

304 Steamed Abalone Wrapped in Melon
Cheung Kam Chuen

305 Shrimp with Carrot Cinnamon Oil
Jean-Georges Vongerichten

304 Seared Opakapaka with Lilikoi and Ginger Sauce
Roy Yamaguchi

306 Steamed Garoupa Rolls
Cheung Kam Chuen

306 Lobster with Cabbage and Corn
Daniel Boulud

307 Grilled Tuna with Eggplant Relish
Elizabeth Terry

308 John Dory Fillet in Parsley Crust
André Jaeger

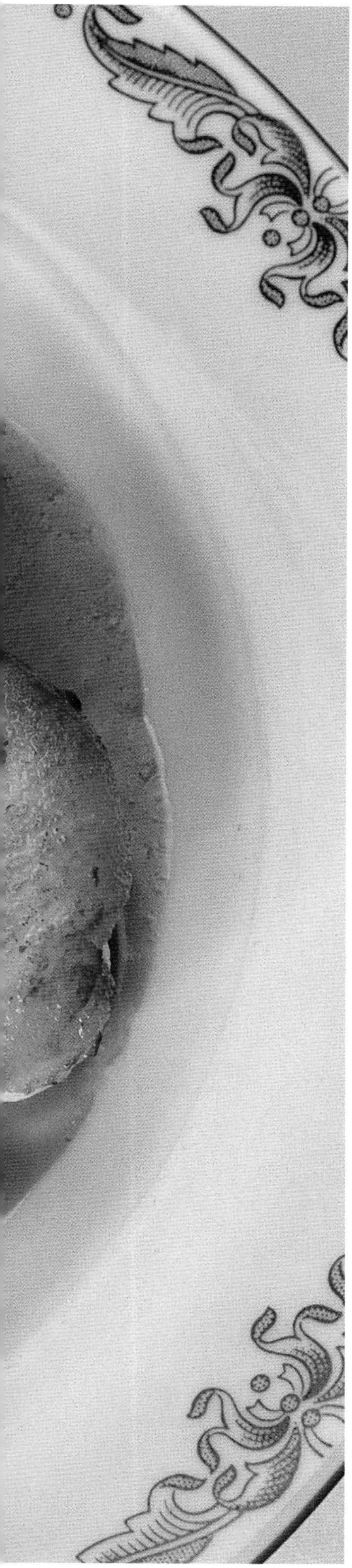

309 Poached Onaga with a Three Caviar Sauce
George Mavrothalassitis

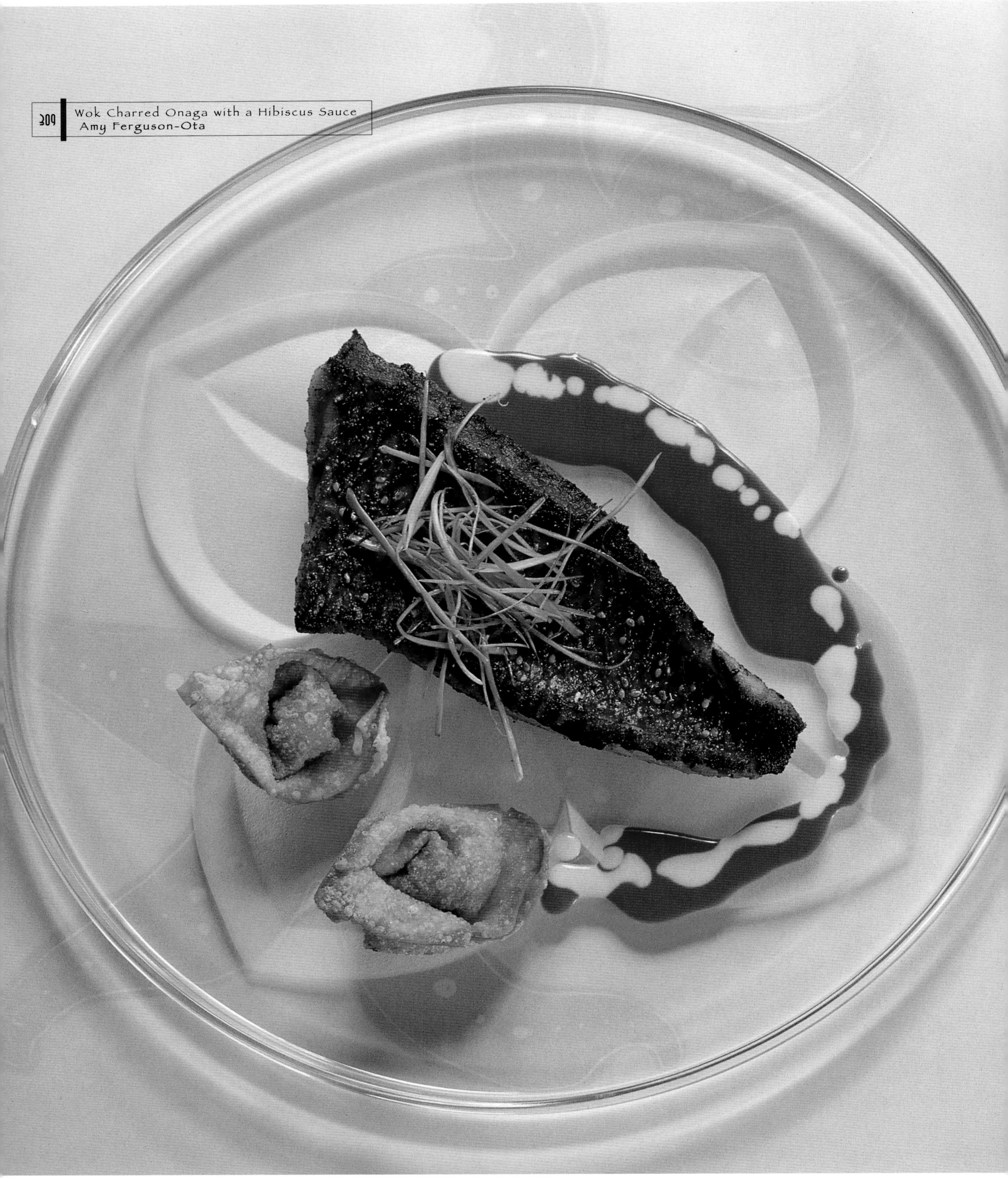

309 Wok Charred Onaga with a Hibiscus Sauce
Amy Ferguson-Ota

309 Bamboo Steamed Ehu with Oriental Vegetables
Amy Ferguson-Ota

310 Tuna with Asparagus and Curry Pasta
David Burke

310 Crayfish Cakes with Wild Rice Salsa
Jimmy Schmidt

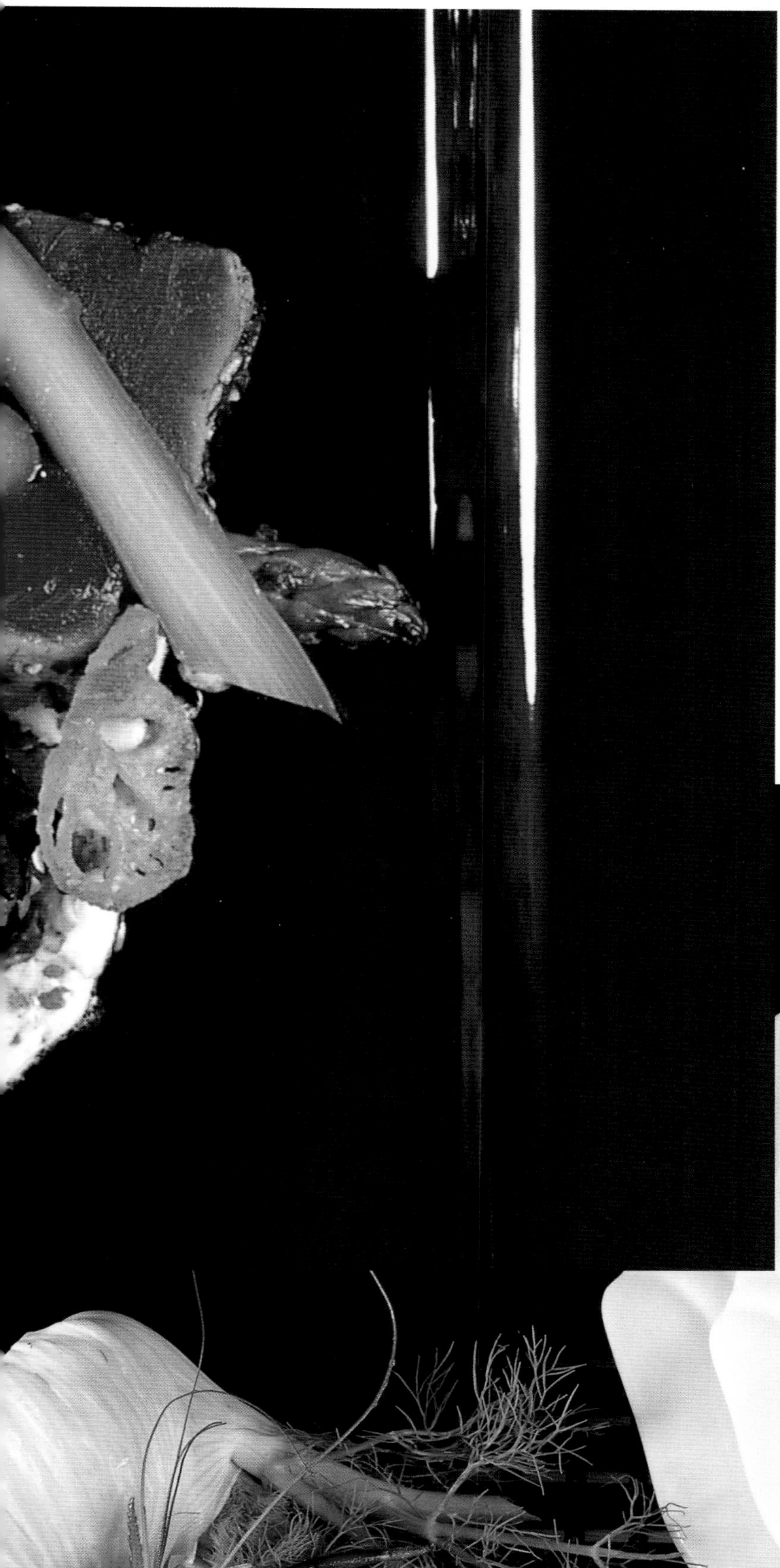

311 Seafood with Fava Beans in Fennel Broth
Francis Drillien

312 Roasted Salmon with Persillade
Alain Dutournier

312 Breaded Abalone with Green Herb Sauce
Martin Woesle

313 Triangle of Peppered Tuna
Michel Richard

313 Seared Tuna with Red Chili Vinaigrette
George Mahaffey

314 Mackerel Fillets with Celeriac Coulis
Antoine Westermann

314 Santa Barbara Shrimp
Mark Peel

315 Zander with Ginger Risotto
André Jaeger

315 Broiled Salmon in Horseradish Crust
Richard Riehm

315 Grilled Tuna with Corn Vinaigrette
Daniel Boulud

316 Roasted Sturgeon with Sauerkraut
Paul Haeberlin

316 Steamed Salmon with Artichokes
Brian Whitmer

317 Crusted Cod with Pepper Oil
Gilbert Le Coze

317 Matelote of Fish in Ravioli with Riesling
Antoine Westermann

318 Steamed Black Bass with Spinach
Gray Kunz

318 | Steamed Halibut with Flavored Oil
Gérard Pangaud

318 Brochette of Swordfish with Lentils
Mark Peel

319 Medallions of Tuna
George Morrone

320 Seafood Boudin with Caviar Sauce
Julian Serrano

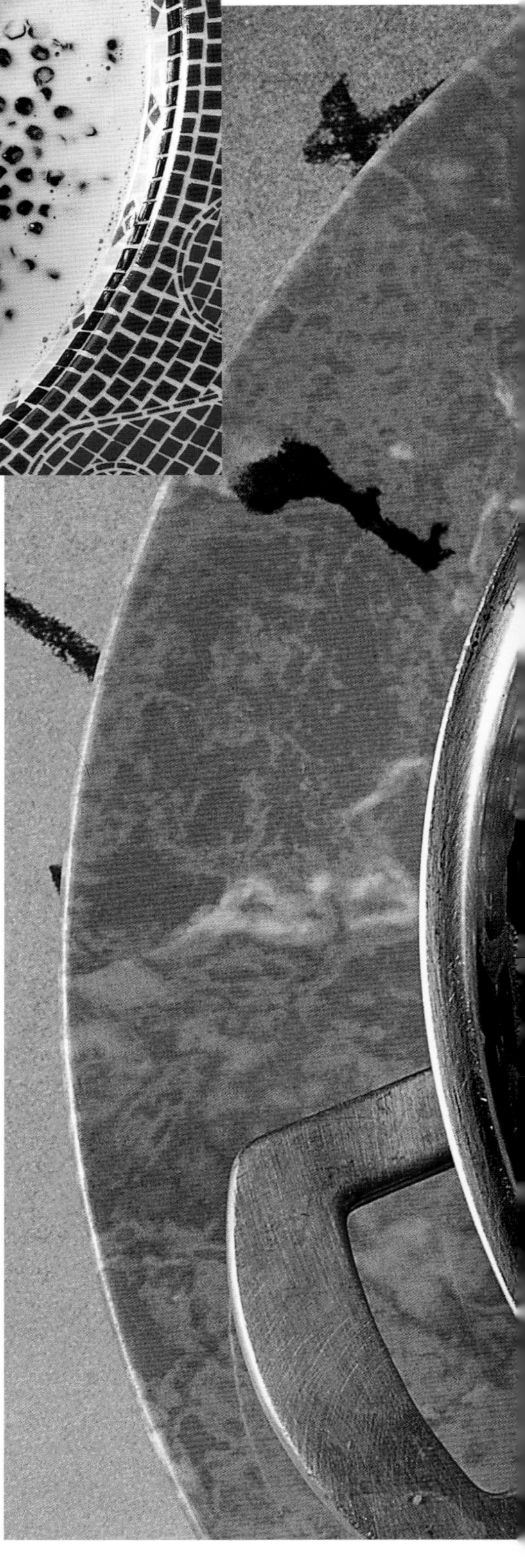

320 Littleneck Clams with Potatoes
Tomas Herranz

320 Red Snapper with Polenta
Gianni Cosetti

321 Sautéed Snapper in a Spicy Crust
Gérard Pangaud

321 Roasted Monkfish with Moroccan Barbeque Sauce
David Burke

322 Fried Spot Prawns in Arborio Rice Flour
Michael Chiarello

322 Fish Stew with Peppercorn Mayonnaise
Ken Hom

323 Maine Lobster with Foie Gras Soufflé
George Morrone

323 Duck Oysters on Chive Risotto
Michael Chiarello

324 Red Snapper with Champagne Sabayon
Jeremiah Tower

324 Curried Dumplings with Squid
David Burke

325 Pan-Roasted Pepper Salmon
Brian Whitmer

325 Fried Rock Cod
George Morrone

326 Lobster and Sweet Potato Stew
Mark Baker

374 Sautéed Daurade with Sweet and Sour Sauce Alain Ducasse

327 Cold-Smoked Swordfish with Gnocchetti
Michael Chiarello

328 Confit of Salmon
Gérard Pangaud

327 Barbecued Shrimp with Homemade Biscuits
Emeril Lagasse

328 Blini Royal
Paul Ingenito

329 Juniper Smoked Salmon with Trout Roe Sauce
Christier Larsson

329 Santa Barbara Shrimp with Spicy Sauce
Nobuyuki Matsuhisa

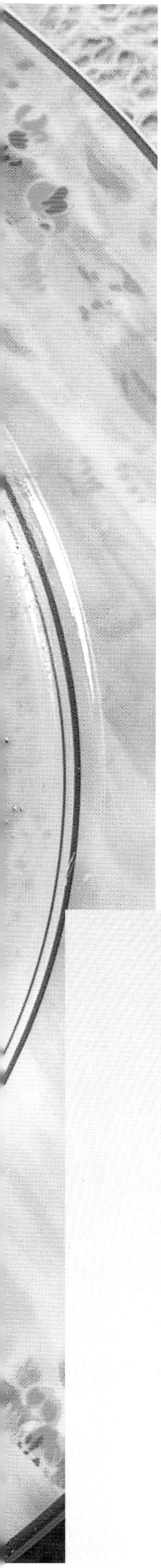

329 Charred Rare Tuna with Port Cream Sauce
Makoto Tanaka

330 Crispy Skin Salmon with Leek Compote
Christian Delouvrier

330 Steamed Salmon in Chinese Cabbage
Ken Hom

331 Tempura Tuna Sashimi with Sea Urchin Sauce
Makoto Tanaka

331 Florida Seafood with Citrus and Cumin
Allen Susser

332 Ocean Island Casserole
Ron Pickarski

333 Lobster and Shrimp with Thai Curries
Susur Lee

335 Loin of Salmon with Curry and Vanilla Oil
Jean-Georges Vongerichten

334 Sweetbread and Lobster Knödel
David Burke

335 Codfish with Garbanzo Beans
Tomas Herranz

"Poultry is for the cook what canvas is for the painter."

Anthelme Brillat-Savarin

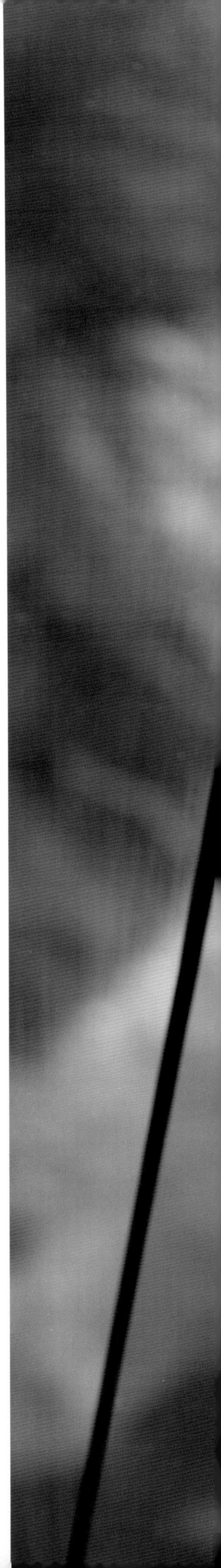

Kodak

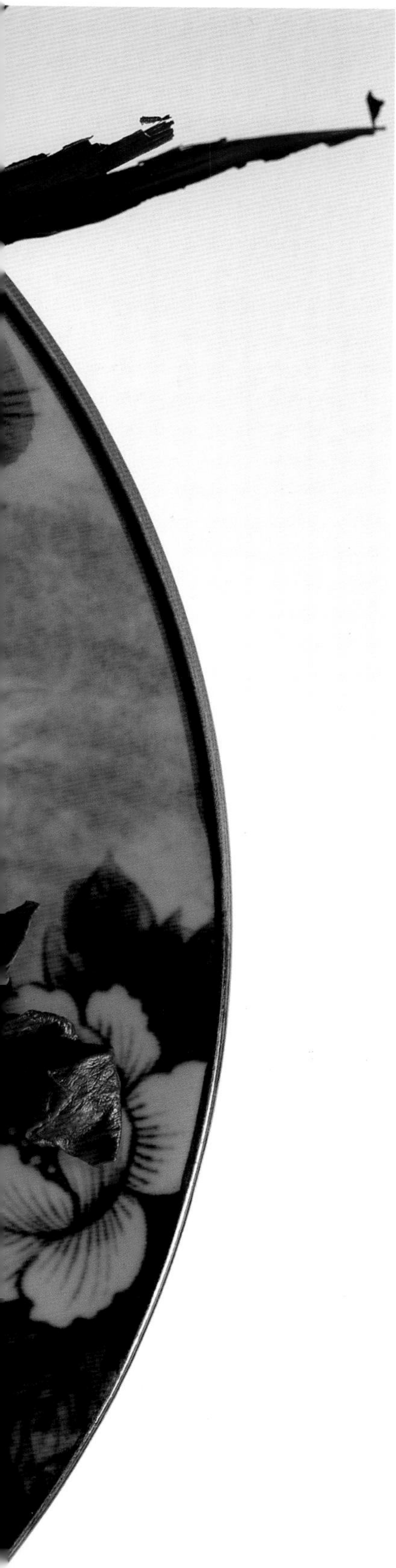

337 Roasted Chicken with Dried Fruits
Sim Siik

338 Peking-Style Duck with Cornmeal Waffles
Ken Hom

338 Barbequed Venison Pie
Emeril Lagasse

339 Smoked Grouse Breast
Sinclair Philip

341 Squab with Cabbage and Foie Gras
Michel Cousin

BLAM!
BLAM!

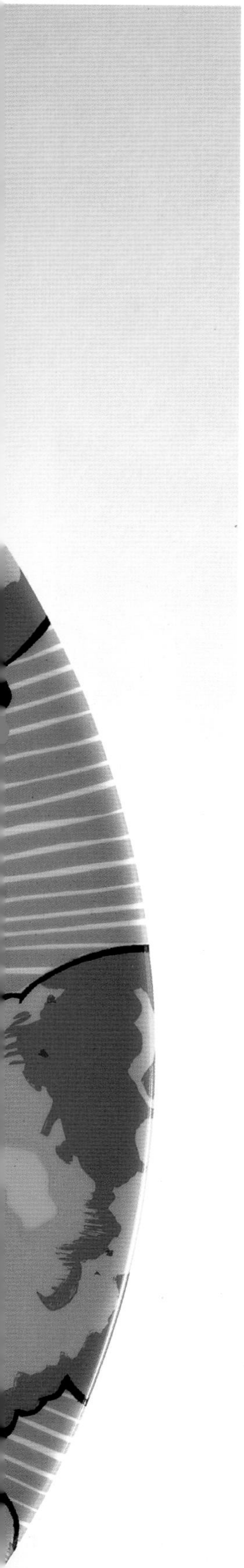

342 Wild Partridge with Vegetables and Foie Gras "en Vessie" with Cabbage
Jean-Louis Palladin

343 Chicken and Macaroni Gratin
Michel Rostang

342 Duck Sausage with Six-Bean Ragoût
Jeremiah Tower

343 Fillet of Moose with Cowberry Sauce
Sim Siik

344 Squab with Cèpes
Michel Richard

344 Boneless Roast Squab with Borlotti Bean Sauce
Paul Bartolotta

345 Barbecued Duck with Spaghetti Squash Latkes
Stephen Levine

345 Wild Pheasant "à la Ficelle" Roasted with Rosemary
Jean-Louis Palladin

346 Texas Antelope with Purple Sage
Christopher Hawver

346 | Squab with Star Anise Sauce
André Jaeger

347 Ragoût of Hare
Dennis Foy

347 Rabbit Loin with Potato and Bacon Hash
Joachim Splichal

348 Local Rabbit Braised in Pomerol
Patrick O'Connell

349 Venison with Caraway Potato Roll
Stephen Levine

349 Corn Risotto with Quail and Sage
Daniel Boulud

350 Barbecued Squab with Corn Salad
Stephen Levine

350 Shepherd's Pie with Olives
Gérard Pangaud

351 Open Ravioli with Squab and Mushrooms
Inaki Izaguirre

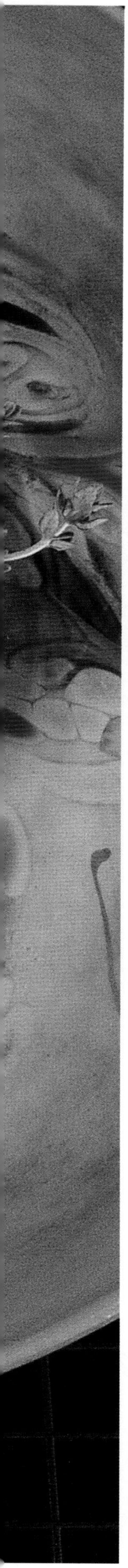

351 Braised Guinea Hen with Savoy Cabbage
Paul Bartolotta

"The nearer the bone, the sweeter the flesh."

Proverb

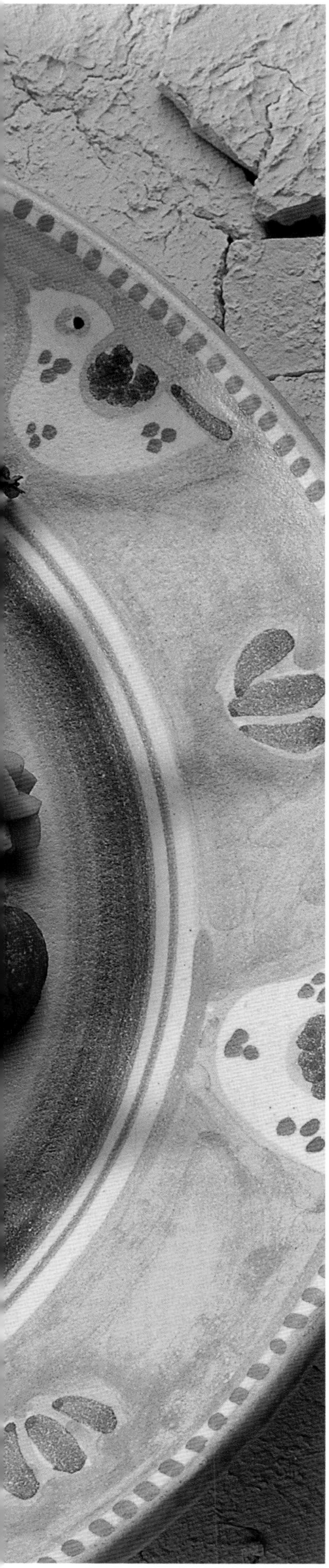

352 Cassoulet
Alain Dutournier

Ragoût of Lamb Brains and Sweetbreads
Jean-Louis Palladin

353 Lamb Chop with Eggplant Tart
Gray Kunz

355 Grilled Lamb Hearts with Onion Confit
Debra Ponzek

354 Confit of Lamb with Boulangère Garnish
Jean-Louis Palladin

354 Navarin of Lamb with Mint
Christopher Hawver

355 Black Sesame Cured Wild Boar Loin with Guava Sauce
Amy Ferguson-Ota

356 | Breaded Pigs' Feet with Celeriac Purée
Michel Rostang

356 | Fresh Cotechino Sausage
with Lentils and Puréed Potatoes
Paul Bartolotta

358 Potato Lasagne with Lamb Loin
Joachim Splichal

357 Roasted Loin of Lamb with Eggplant Chips
Jonathon Fox

358 Lamb Stuffed Potato with Goat Sour Cream and Pomegranate Oil
Jean-Georges Vongerichten

358 Grilled Lamb Onglets
Jean-Louis Palladin

359 Lamb Kidneys with Crispy Grits
Lydia Shire

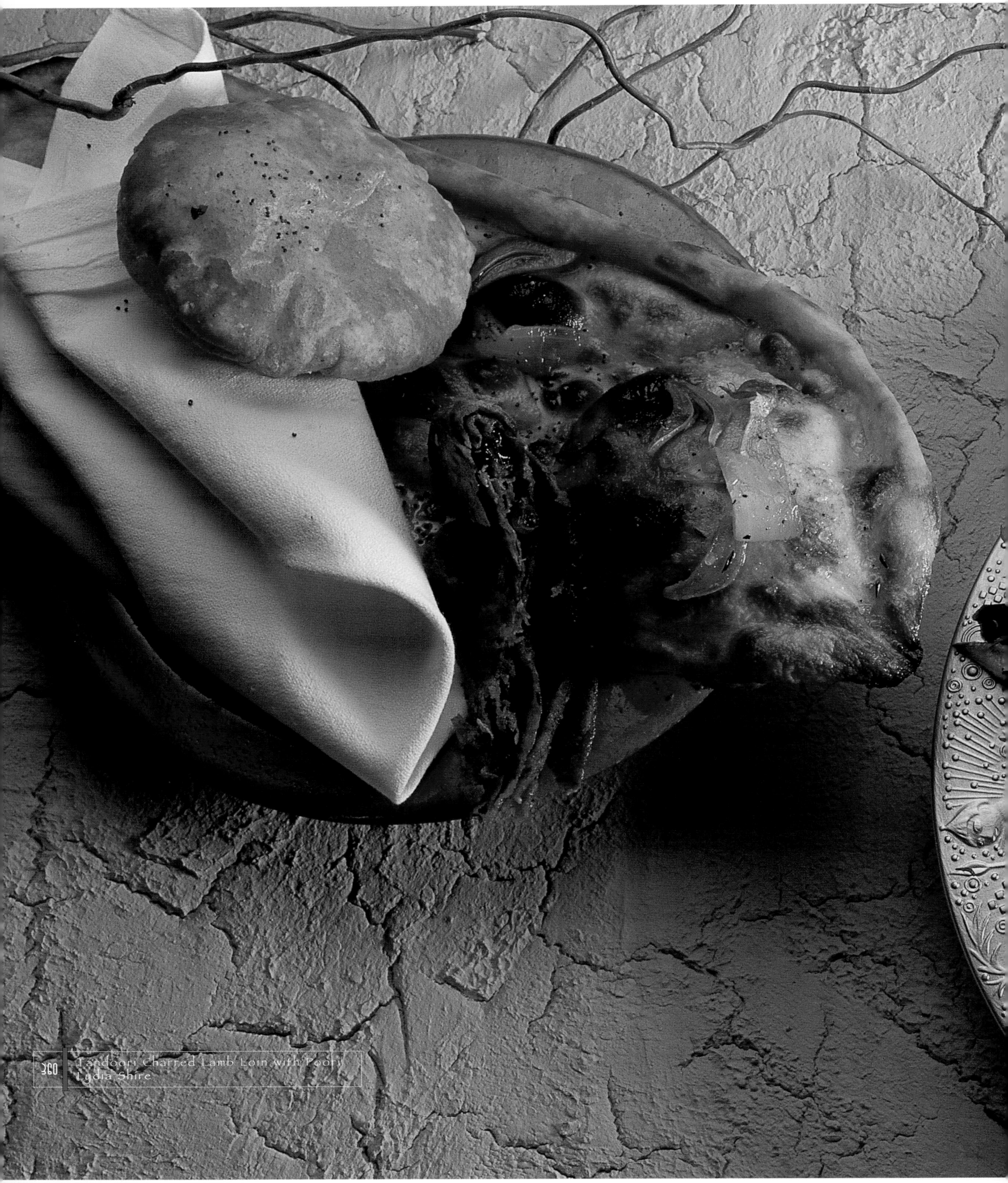

360 Tandoori Charred Lamb Loin with Poori
Lydia Shire

361 Roasted Rack of Lamb with Gremolata
Jan Birnbaum

362 Crispy Lamb with Potato and Basil Agnolotti
Lydia Shire

363 Dark Roasted Rack and Loin of Lamb
Lydia Shire

362 Mild Garlic Sausage with Lentils
Michel Rostang

364 Rack of Lamb with Grits
Jean-Louis Palladin

364 Braised Lamb Shanks
Jean-Louis Palladin

365 Barbecued Suckling Pig
Lam Kam Shing

366 Sweet and Spicy Lamb Ribs
Lydia Shire

367 Corn Breaded Pork Medallions, Black Bean Salad and Arugula Oil
Jean-Georges Vongerichten

366 Barbecued Pork
Lam Kam Shing

367 Lamb Pot Au Feu
Debra Ponzek

368 Lentils with Cured Pork
Francis Drillien

368 Lamb Tripe with Pancetta and Porcini
Jean-Louis Palladin

369 Lamb Loin with Ratatouille and Basil Oil
Debra Ponzek

370 Pork Tenderloin with Eggplant Terrine
Susur Lee

370 Lamb Kidneys with Risotto
Debra Ponzek

271 Rack of Lamb with White Bean Ravioli
Lydia Shire

"If I have done the hardest possible day's work, and then come to sit down in a corner and rat my supper comfortably-why, then I don't think I deserve any reward for my hard day's work-for am I not now at peace? Is not my supper good?"

Herman Melville

373 Braised Oxtail with Quinoa
Charlie Trotter

373 Tenderloin of Beef in a Potato Crust
Mark Baker

374 Grilled Beef Brisket with Gratin of Salsify
Gray Kunz

375 Spiced Beef Brisket in Bouillon
Gray Kunz

376 Roasted Veal Shank with Mint
Paul Bartolotta

376 | Calves' Brain Sandwich
David Burke

377 | Smoked Fillet of Veal with Black-eyed Pea Chili
Don Woods

377 Roasted Veal Loin with Vegetables
Alain Ducasse

378 Calves' Liver and Kidney Tartelette
David Burke

"I am not a vegetarian because I love animals, I am a vegetarian because I hate plants."

A. Whitney Brown

379 Kugelhopf with Escargots
Jean Joho

379 Chocolate Cherry Kugelhopf
Jean Joho

380 Smoked Salmon Kugelhopf
Jean Joho

380 Cinnamon Pecan Kugelhopf
Jean Joho

381 Vegetable Moussaka
Jonathon Fox

381 Stuffed Eggplants
Christoforos Veneris

382 Artichokes in Champagne Sauce
Jeremiah Tower

381 Rolled Soufflé with Spinach and Cheese
John Ash

383 Wild Mushrooms with Fennel Sauce
John Ash

384 Fresh Corn Tamales
David Walzog

383 Mushroom Tamales
David Walzog

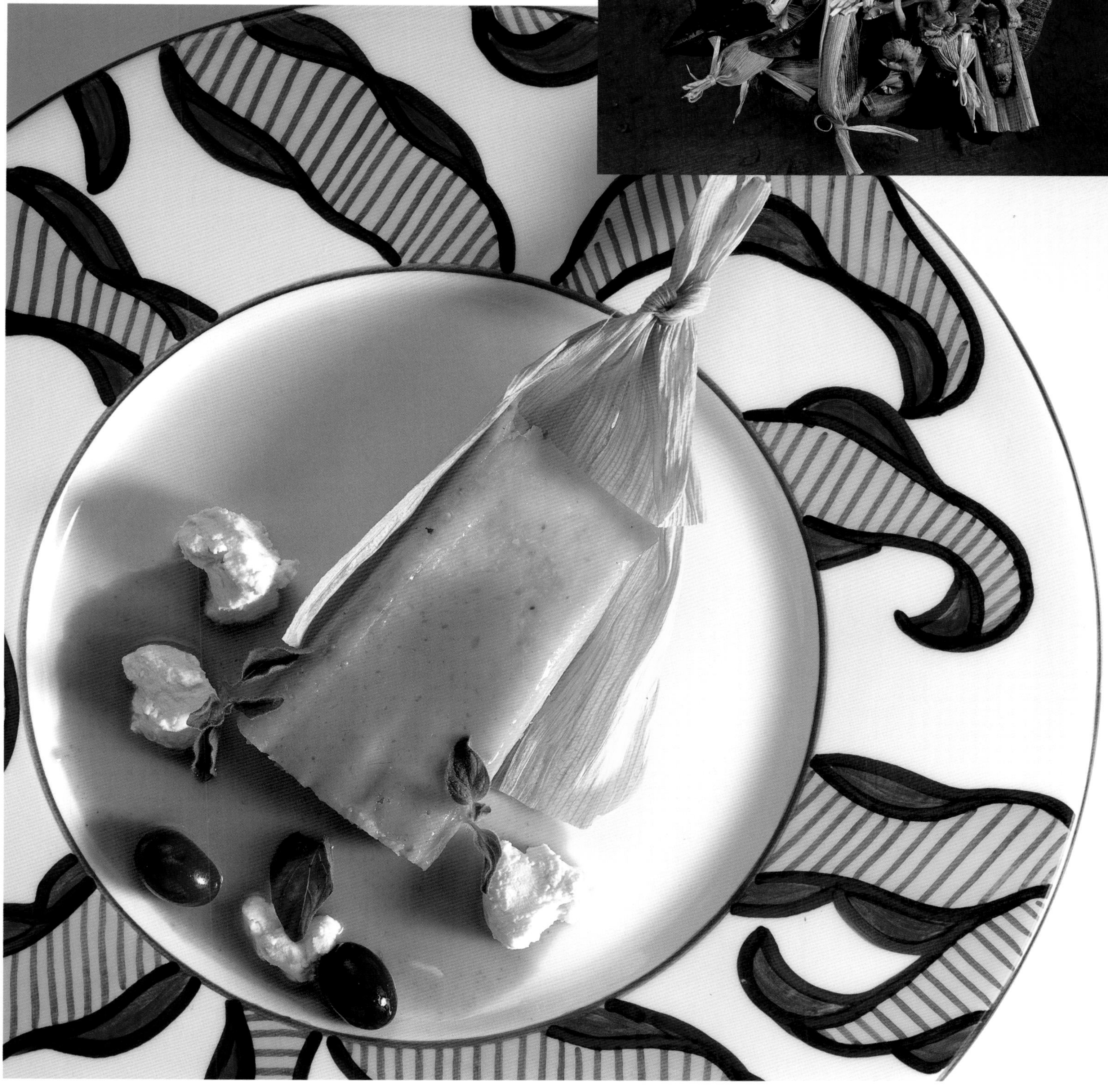

384 Greek Tamales
John Sedlar

384 Vegetarian Tamales
John Sedlar

385 Stuffed Artichoke Hearts with Pesto Broth
Hubert Keller

"Life is uncertain. Eat dessert first."

Ernestine Ulmer

38c | Tarragon and White Chocolate Terrine
Sinclair Philip

387 Gin Bavarian in Ginger Tulip
Chris Northmore

387 Peach Napoleon with Honey Pecan Ice Cream
Chris Northmore

388 Sabayon of Fruit au Gratin
Chris Northmore

389 Chocolate Napoleon with Mint Sauce
Chris Northmore

389 Chocolate Medley
Chris Northmore

391 Capuccino Bavarian with Carmel Sauce
Chris Northmore

392 Tiramisu with Espresso Sauce
Chris Northmore

393 Ginger Soufflé Glacé with Poached Apples
Richard Leach

394 Apple and Toasted Pistachio Terrine with Apple Strudel
Richard Leach

304 Caramelized Apple and Wheat Torte
Richard Leach

396 Apple Beignets with Pistachio Ice Cream
Bruno Tison

395 Mascarpone Sherbet with Wild Strawberries
Alain Ducasse

396 Chilled Golden Delicious Apple Mousse
Richard Leach

397 Caramel Flan
Roland Liccioni

398 Sweet Potato Sorbet
Joachim Splichal

398 Key Lime Tortilla with Tropical Fruit Salsa
Norman Van Aken

399 Filled Apple Crêpes
Inaki Izaguirre

399 Peche Haeberlin
Paul Haeberlin

399 Chestnut Fritters with Zabaglione
Gianni Cosetti

400 Warm Rhubarb Tart with Saffron Sauce
Gérard Pangaud

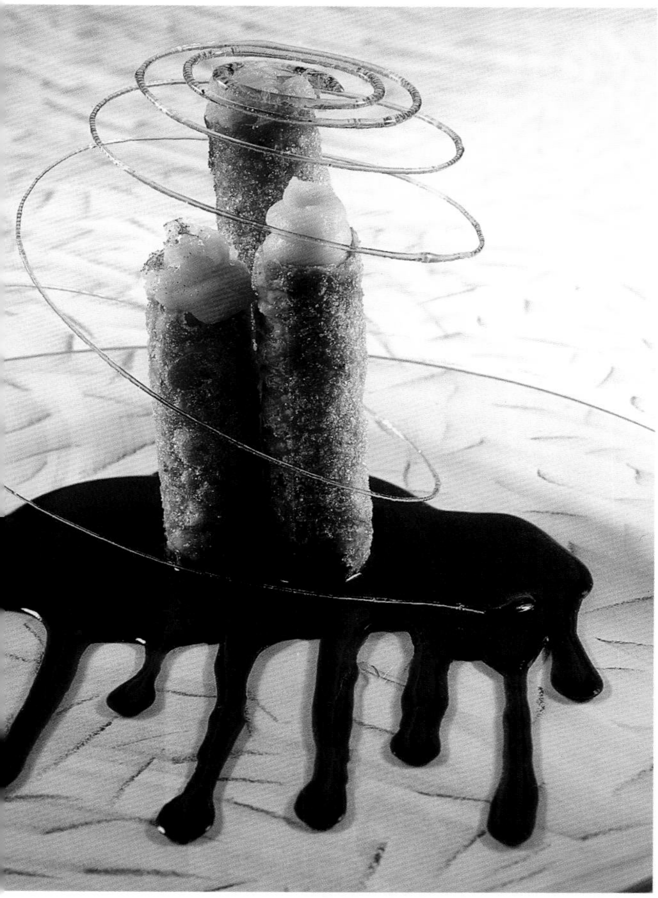

401 Fried Cannolis
Tomas Herranz

400 Chilled Apple Soupe with Apple Granité
Gray Kunz

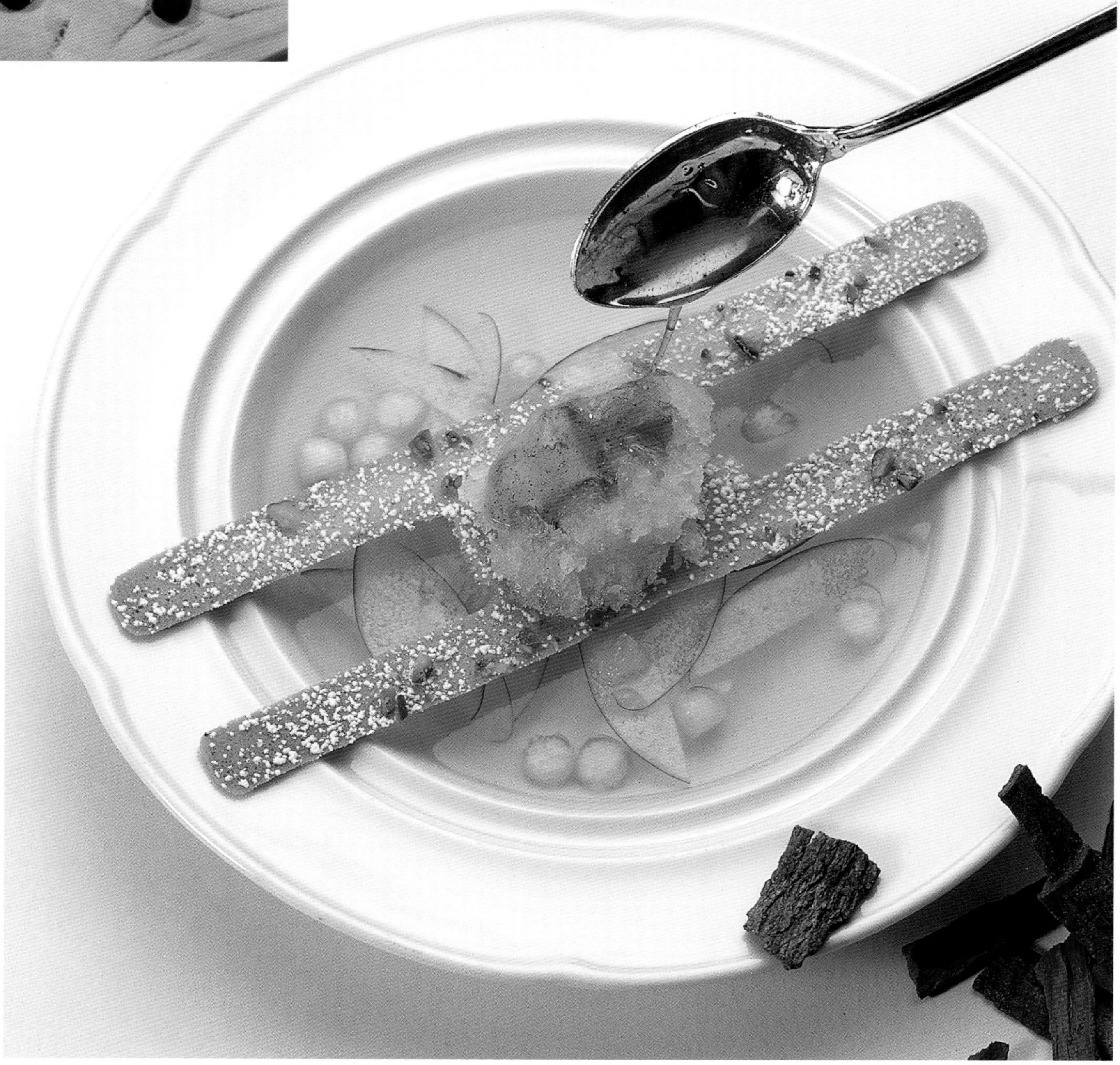

401 Spiced Peaches
Gérard Pangaud

402 Peach Dumplings
Peter Bührer

402 Cherry Strudel
Peter Bührer

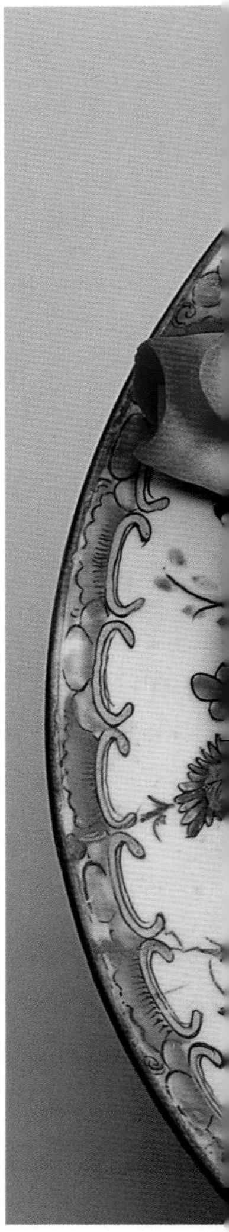

402 Mandarin Ice
with Fortune Cookies
Norman Van Aken

403 Apple Pudding with Caramel Sauce
Joan Winters

404 Lemon Verbena Sorbet
Jill Light

404 Brandy Snap with Glazed Citrus
Jill Light

405 Orange Blossom
Jill Light

411 Rice Pudding
Charles Bowman

406 Blood Orange Sherbet on Almond Gratinée
David Blom

406 Chocolate Mousse with Popcorn
Jacques Torres

407 Ginger and Plum Ice Cream with Lavender Bread Pudding
Dawn Rose

407 Mississippi Mud Pie
Dawn Rose

408 Buttermilk Ice Cream with Rosemary Biscuits
Dawn Rose

409 Frozen Tahitian Vanilla Soufflé
Dan Rundell

410 Frozen Pine Nut Nougat with Banana
Dan Rundell

410 Peking-Style Banana Fritters
Susur Lee

411 Sheep's Milk Ice Cream
Jean-Louis Palladin

412 Dried Cherry and Pistachio Baklava
Jonathon Fox

413 Dark Chocolate Tamales
Jody Denton

412 Upside-Down Corn Cakes
David Fye

414 Chocolate Tamales
John Sedlar

413 Petit Déjeuner
Jacques Torres

414 Trio of Sweet Tamales
Jody Denton

416 White Peach Soup with Berries
Alain Dutournier

415 Dessert Medley
George Morrone

"It's good food and not fine words that keeps me alive."

Les Femmes savantes

6 Yellow Melon Soup with Bamboo Piths

Serves 1

For the dish:
1 yellow melon, partially boiled
2 cups chicken stock
1 tablespoon yellow mushrooms
2 pieces bamboo piths or shoots
1 tablespoon sliced button mushrooms
2 teaspoons yunnan ham
Little night blossom

Cut yellow melon like a bowl. Add chicken stock to melon, along with yellow mushrooms, bamboo and button mushrooms. Place covered in a steamer and cook about 25 minutes.

To serve, garnish with ham and night blossom.

7 Cold Borscht

Serves 4

For the borscht:
3 large beets, peeled and julienned
1 tablespoon red vinegar
2 cups beet juice
½ cup superfine sugar
1½ cups beef consommé
Juice from ½ lemon
¼ cup red wine vinegar
Salt and pepper

For the garnish:
1 cup small squash and zucchini balls, blanched
½ cup carrot balls, blanched
½ cucumber, peeled and sliced
½ cup sour cream
1 bunch fresh dill sprigs
24 radishes, thinly sliced

To prepare the borscht, cook the beets until tender in a covered saucepan with 1 tablespoon red wine vinegar and enough water to cover. Remove from the heat and cool. Transfer the beets to a container with a cover. Add the extra beet juice and the superfine sugar. Stir until dissolved.
Cover and chill.

In the meantime, simmer the consommé for 2 minutes, remove from the heat and allow to cool to room temperature. Chill. Combine the chilled consommé with the beets and their juice, the lemon juice and the red wine vinegar. Season with salt and pepper. Chill for an additional hour or two.

To serve the borscht, arrange the julienne of beets in a nest around the middle of chilled serving bowls. Arrange the blanched vegetables around the beets. Drop a dollop of sour cream inside the beet nest. Place sprigs of dill between the thin slices of radish and arrange these sandwiches around the sour cream. Carefully fill the bowls with the cold borscht.

7 Mussel Soup with Saffron

Serves 4

For the mussels:
3¼ pounds mussels, cleaned
¾ cup water
1 cup white wine
1 bay leaf
5 whole white peppercorns
1 teaspoon thyme
1 teaspoon minced yellow onion

For the soup:
¼ teaspoon saffron
2¾ to 3 cups heavy cream
1 clove garlic, minced
Salt and freshly ground white pepper
Butter to taste
4 small potatoes, boiled and kept warm
2 tablespoons chopped parsley

For the garnish:
Italian parsley

For the mussels, bring water, wine, bay leaf, peppercorns, thyme and onion to a boil in saucepan. Add mussels. Place lid on pot and boil until mussels open. Remove all but 12 mussels from their shells. Set aside.

For the soup, strain mussel broth into pot and let boil, until reduced by half. Add saffron, cream and garlic. Let boil until reduced by half. Add salt, freshly ground white pepper and butter to taste. Strain soup.

To serve, slice warm, boiled potatoes and put them on a deep plate. Put shelled mussels on top. Heat up soup and add the chopped parsley. Pour soup over mussels and garnish with the shells of the mussels and a sprig of parsley.

Curried Pumpkin Soup with Shrimp Ravioli

Serves 4

For the ravioli:
½ pound shrimp, peeled and de-veined
4 tablespoons butter, softened
Coarsely ground salt and pepper to taste
20 3½-inch by 2-inch sheets semolina and black olive pasta
Egg wash
1 quart salted water

For the soup:
4 miniature pumpkins
Salt and pepper to taste
4 teaspoons butter
½ cup water
1 quart curry stock
½ cup butter

For the garnish:
20 medium shrimp, peeled and de-veined
Salt and pepper to taste
1 tablespoon ground sage
½ cup olive oil
1 green pepper, seeded and diced
¾ cup lima beans, blanched
1 bunch chives, chopped

For the ravioli, purée the shrimp in a food processor, gradually blend in the butter and season with salt and pepper. Pipe a small line of the filling along the length of each pasta sheet, seal the edges with egg, roll the ravioli and twist each end closed. The ravioli will look like saltwater taffy.

For the soup, scoop out each pumpkin, discarding the seeds and reserving the pulp for the soup. Season the insides of the pumpkins with salt and pepper, place 1 teaspoon of butter inside each shell and bake, with ½ cup water, in a covered baking pan at 350 degrees for about 50 minutes. Be careful not to overbake the pumpkins. They should be tender but firm enough to hold their shapes when filled. Bring the curry stock to a boil in a saucepan with the pumpkin pulp, season to taste and simmer for 20 minutes. Purée in a food processor and strain through a fine sieve. Return the purée to the saucepan and whisk in the butter.

To serve, cook the ravioli in boiling salted water for 2 to 3 minutes, until tender, and drain. Season the shrimp with salt, pepper and ground sage; sauté them in hot olive oil. Next sauté the green peppers and lima beans. Arrange the ravioli and the shrimp in the baked pumpkin shells and place the shells on warm soup plates. Ladle the soup around the pumpkins and garnish the dish with the peppers, limes and chives.

Sweet Corn Bisque with Lobster

Serves 12

For the bisque:
2 medium onions, diced
1 leek, cleaned and dice (white and green part)
Salt to taste
8 tablespoons butter
4 cups yellow corn kernels
4 cups double chicken consommé
2 cups heavy cream
Salt and white pepper to taste
1 to 2 tablespoons honey

For the garnish:
1 pound diced cooked lobster meat
4 tablespoons minced chives
1½ cups crème fraîche
Cracked black pepper

For the bisque, sweat onion, leek and salt in butter over low heat, covered, until soft. Add corn and sweat until it's moisture is released, about 10 to 15 minutes. Add consommé and cream and bring to a simmer. Remove from heat at once. Purée soup in blender and pass through a chinois. Taste and adjust seasoning with salt, white pepper and honey.

To serve and garnish, heat to steaming and ladle into bowls. Garnish with lobster, chives, crème fraîche and cracked pepper.

9 Borlotti Bean Soup

Serves 6

For the Minestra:

2 cups beans, soaked overnight
¼ cup diced carrot
¼ cup diced celery
1 clove garlic, minced
⅔ cup onion, minced
2 tablespoons chopped parsley
1 cup peeled and seeded tomatoes
4 tablespoons olive oil
Kernels from 6 ears of corn
½ cup diced, peeled potatoes
Salt and cracked black pepper
6 tablespoons grated parmigiana

For the minestra, cover the soaked beans with cold water and simmer for 1½ hours. Add in the carrots, celery, garlic, onions, the chopped parsley, tomatoes and 3 tablespoons of the olive oil; continue to simmer for another hour-the beans should be completely cooked, but firm. Add to this the corn, potatoes, salt and pepper; continue to simmer for another 30 minutes.

To serve, blend in the remaining olive oil, the fresh grated parmigiana cheese, and a pinch of cracked black pepper. Dish into warm soup plates.

10 Soup of Shrimp with Couscous

Serves 6

For the soup:

2 pounds fresh shrimp
2 quarts fish stock
2 tomatoes, chopped
1 clove garlic, peeled and chopped
Salt and cayenne pepper to taste

For the garnish:

1 red pepper
1 green pepper
1 small onion, peeled and chopped
4 tablespoons olive oil
1 cup cooked couscous
¼ cup raisins, soaked in water overnight
¼ cup toasted almond slivers
1 tablespoon freshly chopped cilantro
1 tablespoon freshly chopped mint
Pinch of saffron

For the soup, separate the shrimp tails from the bodies, peel and de-vein the tails, and set the tails aside. Place the shrimp bodies and peels in a pot, add the fish stock, chopped tomatoes and garlic, and simmer for 10 minutes. Strain the stock, season with salt and cayenne pepper.
Set aside and keep warm.

For the garnish, remove the seeds, stems and membranes from the red and green peppers and dice. Sauté the peppers and onion in the olive oil until tender, add the peeled shrimp tails and sauté for 3 to 4 minutes. Add the fish stock, bring to a boil, add the remaining ingredients and simmer for 5 minutes. Adjust the seasoning and serve.

12 Canadian Shellfish in a Pine Mushroom Broth

Serves 2

For the shellfish:
8 fresh mussels, preferably one of the wild, west coast varieties
8 manilla or littleneck clams
1 fresh sea cucumber*
2 3-ounce nasturtium tubers**
4 pine mushrooms***
2 red onions, peeled and sliced into ¼-inch slices
2 cloves garlic, peeled and thinly sliced
¼ cup Sauvignon Blanc
3 cups shellfish broth
1½ tablespoons brown rice miso
1 tablespoon white wine vinegar
6 kumomoto oysters, shucked, liquor reserved
8 pink swimming scallops
4 side-striped shrimp, heads attached, tails peeled and shells reserved

For the pine mushroom broth:
1 tablespoon safflower oil
Shrimp shells (reserved from above)
½ pound Grade 3 pine mushrooms
1 Spanish onion, peeled and coarsely chopped
1 clove garlic, peeled and washed
1 tablespoon tomato paste
½ cup dry vermouth
1 cup Sauvignon Blanc
Oyster liquor (reserved from above)

For the garnish:
Skin of 2 smoked steelhead trout
2 tablespoons maple syrup
2 tuberous nasturtium vines

To prepare the shellfish, remove the beard from the mussels. Scrub the mussels, clams and scallops under cold water to remove any sand. Soak the shellfish in cold, salted water (without any chlorine) for approximately 8 hours to remove any grit held inside the shells. Refrigerate for later use.

To prepare the sea cucumber, cut off both ends, approximately one inch from each end. Insert a knife lengthwise and slit it open. Lay the sea cucumber flat and remove the internal organs with your hands. All that should remain are the skin and the five beige-white strips of flesh attached to the skin. Placing your index finger under the middle of one of the beige-white muscular strips, lift it from the body. Then, slide your finger out towards the edges of the sea cucumber, until the strip is completely detached. The fresher the sea cucumber, the more easily the strip of muscle will come free. Remove all of the strips of muscle and discard the skin.

Scrub the nasturtium tubers and quarter them lengthwise into four equal pieces. Slice the pine mushrooms vertically into thirds.

To steam the shellfish, place a 2-quart saucepan over medium high heat. When the pot is hot, add the mussels, clams, garlic, red onion and wine. Bring to a boil and let boil for approximately one minute until the alcohol has evaporated. Add 2 cups of the shellfish broth, the miso and white wine vinegar. Cover and reduce the heat to medium-low.

Meanwhile, pour ½ cup of the shellfish broth into a small skillet and set over medium heat. Poach the oysters very briefly in this broth until the sides begin to curl. Turn the oysters and set aside. Keep warm.

After three or four minutes, check the pan with the steaming shellfish. As the mussels and clams begin to open, add the scallops, shrimp, sea cucumber, pine mushrooms and nasturtium tubers. Cover again and allow to steam together for two minutes.

When most of the bivalve shellfish are open, pour the steaming broth into a small saucepan. If the liquid is gritty or sandy, pass it through several layers of fine cheese cloth. Add the oyster poaching liquid. Bring the mixture to a rapid boil and reduce by ¼. Reserve for making the aromatic pine mushroom broth.

To prepare the aromatic pine mushroom broth, place the safflower oil, the reserved shrimp shells, pine mushrooms, Spanish onion and garlic in a 3-quart saucepan over medium heat. Sauté these ingredients together until the shrimp shells turn bright pink. Add the tomato paste and stir well until all of the ingredients are coated. Continue cooking for three or four minutes to brown the tomato paste.

Add the vermouth and wine to the pot and deglaze the pan. Scrape the tomato paste from the bottom of the pan with a wooden spoon. Allow the wine to come to a boil. Add three cups of the reduced shellfish poaching liquid and the reserved oyster liquor. Return the stock to a boil and reduce the heat. Simmer for 35 to 45 minutes. Skim off any surface residues as they form. Taste the broth for seasoning and adjust the miso and white wine vinegar to taste.

To prepare the trout skin, trim away the torn edges and scrape off any remaining flesh. Cut the skin lengthwise into eight uniform strips. Using a pastry brush, apply the the maple syrup evenly over both sides of the skin. Bake on a sheet pan in a 375 degree oven for 12 to 14 minutes until crisp. Cool.

To serve the dish, divide the shellfish among two soup plates. Pour the steaming broth over the shellfish and garnish with the trout skin, and tuberous nasturtium vine. Serve immediately.

* **Note:** Dried Asian varieties should not be used.
** **Note:** Nasturtium tubers (Tropaeolum tuberosum) are sometimes sold as anu or ysano in South American markets.
*** **Note:** Grade 1 pine mushrooms are the most prized. They are small and uniform in shape, with a compact head. Known as matsutake in Japanese markets.

11 Butternut Squash Soup

Serves 20

For the soup:
2 large butternut squash
2 tablespoons olive oil
1 strip bacon, diced
1 onion, peeled and diced
1 apple, peeled, cored and diced
¼ cup apple juice
3 quarts chicken stock
¾ cup heavy cream
2 teaspoons apple cider vinegar
Salt and pepper to taste
5 sprigs fresh thyme

To prepare the soup, cut the squash in half lengthwise, remove the seeds and toss the squash in olive oil. Place on a sheet pan, cut side down, and roast in a 350 degree oven until tender. Meanwhile, in a large, heavy stock pot, render the bacon until crisp. Add the onion and sauté until translucent. Add the apple and continue to sauté for five minutes. Add the apple juice and reduce until dry. Cut the roasted squash into large cubes and add to the soup. Cook for five to ten minutes. Add the stock and bring to a boil. Reduce the heat and simmer for 20 minutes. Purée the soup with an immersible, hand-held blender. Add the cream and bring the soup back up to a boil. Adjust the seasoning with salt and pepper. Add the sprigs of thyme and allow the soup to steep for 10 minutes. Remove the thyme and serve in warmed bowls.

13 Monterey Bay Salmon Soup

Serves 4

For the Salmon Broth:
4 pounds fresh salmon bones
1 large carrot, chopped
2 leeks, roughly chopped
1 medium onion, peeled and quartered
3 stalks celery, chopped
3 cloves garlic, peeled
5 white mushrooms
2 bay leaves, broken
1 tablespoon fennel seed, cracked
1 tablespoon coriander seed, cracked
1 tablespoon minced ginger
3 sprigs tarragon, chopped
Salt and pepper to taste

For the soup garnish:
1 large russet potato, peeled, diced and steamed
1 bunch watercress, stems removed
12 ounces salmon fillets, cut into ¼-inch dice and steamed.
1 ear sweet corn, shucked, steamed and kernels removed from the cob
1 large carrot, peeled and cut into long thin strips
1 red bell pepper, seeded and finely diced
1 bunch scallions, green part only, sliced on the bias
½ bunch dill, leaves only

To prepare the broth, wash the salmon bones in cold water. Place the bones in a large stock pot and add enough water to cover. Add the remaining ingredients. Bring the stock to a boil, skimming off any froth that rises to the top. Reduce the heat and simmer for two hours, skimming occasionally. Strain through a fine sieve. Adjust the seasoning.

To finish the soup, arrange the garnish in the soup bowls. Ladle in the steaming hot broth and serve immediately.

14 Ginger Broth with Crab Dim Sum

Serves 4

For the broth:
1 quart chicken consommé, prepared with garlic and ginger (see method)

For the hot pepper fool:
1 large red pepper, roasted, peeled, seeded and puréed
2 egg whites, whipped
1 dash toasted sesame oil
Tabasco sauce to taste

For the dumpling dough:
1 cup cornstarch
1 cup wheat starch
1 tablespoon peanut oil
1½ cups water
Salt to taste

For the dumpling filling:
½ cup cooked Dungeness crab meat
½ cup white fish mousse
1 tablespoon chopped chives
½ teaspoon chopped ginger
½ teaspoon chopped fresh cilantro

For the garnish:
Steamed crab meat
Chrysanthemum petals
Chopped scallions

For the broth, prepare a basic consommé of chicken, but instead of using any fresh herbs, roast garlic and ginger with the mirepoix. Clarify the consommé with egg whites to achieve a clear, perfumed broth.

For the hot pepper fool, whip together the puréed roasted red pepper, egg whites, sesame oil and Tabasco sauce. Adjust the seasoning.

To prepare the dumpling pastry, mix the cornstarch and wheat starch in a small bowl. Bring the water to a boil and add to the starches with the peanut oil and salt. Gently mix to form a soft dough. Set aside.

For the dumpling filling, mix all of the ingredients and adjust the seasoning. Divide the dumpling dough into 4 balls and roll them out into thin circles between 2 sheets of lightly-oiled plastic wrap. Remove the plastic wrap on top. Place a spoonful of the crab filling in the center of the pastry. Pinch the pastry together as shown. Steam the dumplings for 3 minutes.

To serve, gently heat the consommé without allowing it to come to a boil. Divide the broth among 4 bowls. Place one dumpling in each bowl and spoon the hot pepper fool into the soup. Garnish with crab meat, flower petals and chopped scallions.

15 Avgolemono Soup with Roasted Lobster

Serves 6

For the lobster:
1 1-pound live lobster
Virgin olive oil
1 clove garlic, peeled and minced

For the soup:
4 cups light chicken stock
2 cups light lobster stock
2 tablespoons extra virgin olive oil
2 tablespoons butter
½ cup all-purpose flour
Kosher salt to taste
¼ teaspoon white pepper
⅛ teaspoon cracked chili pepper
4 egg yolks
4 tablespoons extra-virgin olive oil

For the garnish:
1½ cups cooked trahana*
2 teaspoons lobster roe
Chopped chervil

To prepare the lobster, cut it in half lengthwise and set on a sheet pan. Coat the lobster with the olive oil and minced garlic. Roast at 425 degrees for approximately 15 minutes, or until cooked through. Cool. Remove the meat and slice. Set aside.

For the soup, combine the chicken and lobster stocks in a 2-quart saucepan and simmer over moderate heat for approximately 10 minutes. In a separate saucepan, heat the olive oil and butter. Add the flour and cook for about 2 minutes. Do not allow the flour to take on any color. Whisk this roux into the simmering stock. Add the salt, white pepper and chili pepper and cook for approximately 10 minutes, until the soup has thickened slightly and the taste of the flour has disappeared.

Whisk the egg yolks in a large stainless steel bowl set over simmering water until light and fluffy. Slowly whisk in the hot soup and the olive oil. Return the soup to a saucepan and bring to a boil. Remove from the heat. Gently heat the lobster meat. Ladle the soup into serving bowls. Spoon the trahana into the center of the bowls and garnish with the lobster meat and chopped chervil.

* **Note:** Trahana is a special Greek pasta made with sour milk and shaped into little pebbles. It can be made by hand or purchased in Greek and Middle Eastern specialty stores.

18 Warm Salad with Crisp Calves' Brain

Serves 4

For the Brains:
2 calves' brains
2 bay leaves
1 sprig thyme
Juice of ½ lemon
1 teaspoon salt
1 teaspoon black peppercorns
2 quarts water
1 cup cornmeal
1 tablespoon corn oil
2 tablespoons fresh tarragon leaves, chopped

For the salad:
1 head frisée, cleaned
2 cups mâche, cleaned
1 cup corn kernels, blanched
1 red pepper, peeped and diced
1 hard boiled egg, chopped
2 pieces cornichons, chopped
1 tablespoon capers
1 tablespoon fresh grated horseradish

For the dressing:
2 tablespoons èrès vinegar
5 tablespoons corn oil
1 tablespoon walnut oil
1 tablespoon fresh chervil, chopped
1 tablespoon chives, chopped
1 tablespoon parsley, chopped
Salt and pepper to taste

For the calves' brains, remove all the blood vessels and soak the brains in cold water overnight in the refrigerator. Rinse well and place in pot with 2 quarts of water, bay leaves, thyme, lemon juice, salt and peppercorns. Bring to a boil and simmer for 5 minutes. Remove from the heat and let cool in the liquid. Slice each brain into 3 to 4 slices, about ½ inch thick. Mix the cornmeal with the tarragon and dredge the brain slices in the mixture. Pat gently. Sauté the brain slices in a non-stick pan with corn oil until crisp and golden brown on both sides. Blot on paper towels and keep warm.

For the dressing, blend all ingredients in a mixing bowl and season with salt and pepper.

For the salad, toss the greens along with the corn kernels, chopped red peppers, egg, cornichons, capers and horseradish. Pour the dressing over all and mix well, reserving a small amount of dressing for garnish.

To serve, divide the greens onto the plates and top with crisp and still warm brain slices. Drizzle some of the dressing around perimeter of plates.

19 Warm Langoustine Salad

Serves 4

For the dressing:
⅔ cup olive oil
3 tablespoons truffle juice
2 tablespoons fresh lemon juice
Salt and fresh cracked pepper

For the salad:
1 cup snipped haricot vert, blanched
⅔ cup chopped peeled and seeded tomatoes
¼ cup fresh peas, blanched

8 small purple artichokes, blanched and quartered
¼ cup sliced fennel, blanched
⅓ cup small chanterelles, blanched
16 langoustines, shelled
4 tablespoons olive oil
Salt and fresh ground pepper

For the garnish:
Fresh chervil leaves

For the dressing, blend together the olive oil, truffle juice and the lemon juice; season and set aside.

For the salad, marinate all the blanched vegetables in the dressing for 10 minutes. Skewer the langoustines to keep them from curling; saute them quickly in the hot olive oil, drain them on a clean towel and remove the skewers. Season lightly.

To serve, divide the marinated vegetables between the 4 plates, draining the excess dressing. Arrange the cooked langoustines on top of the vegetables, with the tails pointing out from the centers, sectioning the dish in quarters. Drizzle a little of the dressing over the langoustines and garnish with the fresh chervil.

19 Warm Salad of Octopus, Shellfish, and White Beans

Serves 4

For white beans:
½ cup fresh shelled Val Nervia white beans
2 cups stock
1 bouquet of fresh herbs
Salt to taste

For the shellfish:
6 baby squid, cleaned
8 ounces octopus, sliced in thin rounds
36 small clams
26 ounce lobster tails
1 cup olive oil
1 cup white wine
6 tablespoons butter
1 tablespoon lemon juice
½ cup plum tomato concasse

For the salad:
3 tablespoons olive oil
2 teaspoons lemon juice
1 teaspoon sherry vinegar
Salt and pepper
1 cup mixed salad greens
(frisse, red oak, chicory)

For the garnish:
4 langoustines, broiled with olive oil
¼ cup chopped fresh parsley

For the beans, soak them overnight in lightly salted water. Drain and cook them for 1 to 1½ hours in the stock with the bouquet of herbs until they are tender, but firm. Reserve to the side.

For the shellfish, heat 2 tablespoons of the olive oil in a large skillet and sauté the squid, the octopus, the clams and lobster; deglaze with the wine and cook just to where the clams open. Remove the shellfish, reduce the liquid by half, and add in the remaining olive oil, the butter, lemon juice, tomato concasse and the white beans. As this simmers, de-shell the clams, reserving12 for garnish, slice the lobster tails into 4 medallions each and return all the shellfish to the pan.

To serve, make a dressing of the olive oil, lemon juice and vinegar; lightly toss with the greens and divide onto the center of each dish. Arrange the shellfish and beans over the salad with the warm broth and garnish the dish with the broiled langoustines and the chopped parsley.

20 Lobster and Crab Salad with Curry Vinaigrette

Serves 4

For the curry vinaigrette:
1 egg yolk
3 tablespoons sherry vinegar
Juice of 1 lemon
¾ cup curry oil
Salt and freshly ground
pepper to taste

For the lobster vinaigrette:
1 egg yolk
3 tablespoons sherry vinegar
Juice of 1 lemon
¾ cup lobster oil
Salt and freshly ground
pepper to taste

For the salad:
4 2-pound live lobsters
1 quart court-bouillon
½ pound lump crabmeat

For the garnish:
4 cups assorted greens
(endive, radicchio, Bibb)
8 asparagus spears
Sorrel leaves

For the curry vinaigrette, combine the egg yolk, vinegar and lemon juice; whisk in the curry oil until completely emulsified.
Season to taste and set aside.

For the lobster vinaigrette, combine the egg yolk, vinegar and lemon juice. Whisk in the lobster oil until completely emulsified and season to taste.

For the salad, skewer the lobsters through their tails to keep them from curling and plunge them, head first, into the boiling court-bouillon for 6 minutes. Remove the lobsters from the court-bouillon and shock them in an ice bath. Extract the meat from the shells and cut the lobster shells in half, crosswise, to use as a base for the salad. Place the crabmeat in a mixing bowl and mix it with some of the lobster vinaigrette. Cut the lobster tails into medallions and toss them lightly in the lobster vinaigrette.

To serve, pour the two sauces into a ring in the middle of each plate and place the cut lobster shells in the center. Spoon the crab salad around the inside of the sauce ring and arrange the lobster tail meat with the salad greens in the lobster shells. Garnish the dish with the lobster claws, asparagus spears and sorrel leaves.

21 Warm Salad of California Crayfish

Serves 2

For the crayfish stock:
16 Sacramento delta crayfish
1 teaspoon olive oil
1 cup mirepoix
1 bouquet of fresh herbs

For the crayfish:
1 cup Sacramento delta crayfish tails, cooked and peeled
4 tablespoons unsalted butter
1 teaspoon minced shallots
2 tablespoons dry white wine
½ teaspoon rice vinegar
½ teaspoon chopped tarragon
½ teaspoon chopped parsley
4 tablespoons crayfish stock
Salt and white pepper to taste

For the potatoes:
12 small chanterelles
1 tablespoon olive oil
12 asparagus tips, blanched
1 small plum tomato, peeled, halved and seeded
1 teaspoon minced shallot
1 teaspoon chopped tarragon
1 teaspoon parsley
1 tablespoon white wine
1 tablespoon chicken stock
Salt and white pepper

For the garnish:
1 teaspoon balsamic vinegar
1 tablespoon extra virgin olive oil
Salt and pepper
½ cup mixed greens
4 chives
1 teaspoon chopped fresh tarragon and parsley

For the crayfish stock, sautè the crayfish in a medium sautè pan in the olive oil with the mirepoix. Add in the water and the bouquet of herbs, and bring to a boil. Reduce the heat, skim the stock and simmer for 30 minutes. Strain the stock and reduce the liquid to 1 cup.

For the artichokes, cut each artichoke bottom into quarters. In a small sautè pan heat the oil and sautè the artichoke pieces for 30 seconds. Add in the minced garlic, the shallot, thyme, lemon juice and the white wine; season with salt and pepper and cook over a high heat until the liquid is evaporated. Moisten the artichokes with ¼ cup of the chicken stock and reduce again; add in the remaining stock and simmer until the artichokes are tender, but crisp. If necessary add a little water to keep the artichokes moist until fully cooked.

For the potatoes, peel and slice very thin. In a large non-stick, oiled sauté pan arrange overlapping slices of the potatoes to form 2 6-inch rings. Continue until the center of the rings are filled. Lightly season, and place the pan over medium heat, Cook until the potatoes are crisp and golden, turning once. Remove the potato rings from the pan and drain on a clean towel. Set aside and keep warm.

For the crayfish, gently sauté the crayfish tails in half the butter with the shallot for about 15 seconds, Add in the white wine, vinegar, the tarragon and the parsley; cook for another 15 seconds, and remove the tails. Add in the crayfish stock, reduce to thicken the sauce with the remaining butter. Set aside and keep warm.

For the vegetables, sauté the chanterelles in the olive oil for about 10 seconds; add in the asparagus and the tomato halves. Toss them lightly with the shallot, tarragon and the parsley. Deglaze with the white wine, add in the chicken stock, adjust the seasoning and continue to sauté until the liquid is nearly evaporated.

To serve, place the potato rings on warm plates and arrange the chanterelles, the asparagus, tomato halves, artichokes and crayfish in groups around the potato. Make a simple vinaigrette with the balsamic vinegar, olive oil, salt and pepper, Toss the greens with the vinaigrette and arrange the greens in the center of the dish, garnished with the chives. Drizzle the sauce over the crayfish and around the sauce over the crayfish and around the edge of the potato ring. Sprinkle with chopped herbs.

22 Tuna Niçoise

Serves 4

For the tuna:
16 ounce fresh tuna loin
Salt and pepper to taste
2 tablespoons olive oil

For the anchoyade:
1 garlic glove
1 ounce anchovies
4 drops lemon juice
1 tablespoon extra virgin olive oil

For the salad:
2 teaspoons lemon juice
3 tablespoons extra virgin olive oil
Salt and pepper to taste
4 small red potatoes, blanched, roasted and quartered
1 cup haricots verts, blanched
½ cup Niçoise olives
1 cup assorted greens

For the garnish:
4 tablespoons olive purée
1 tablespoon finely cut chives
2 hard-boiled eggs, chopped
4 thick slices olive bread
2 tablespoons anchoyade

23 Mixed Greens with Sweet Marjoram Vinaigrette

Serves 4

For the greens:
Chickweed
Miner's lettuce, with flowers
Ox-eye daisy greens
(Chrysanthemum leucantheum)
Wild sorrel (Rumex acetosella)
Batavia noir Grenobloise
Curly endive
Purple flowering kale
Lolla rossa
Tuberous nasturtium leaves
Red oak leaf
Tat soi

For the sprouts:
Borage leaf sprouts, picked at the cotyledonous stage of leaf growth
Popping corn sprouts
Fenugreek sprouts
Red radish sprouts
Sunflower sprouts, picked at the cotyledonous stage of leaf growth
Thyme seed sprouts, picked at a very early stage of growth

For the herbs:
Anise hyssop, stems removed
Garlic chives, chopped
Herb fennel greens
Sweet marjoram leaves

For the flowers:
Calendula flowers, petals only
Johnny Jump Up viola flowers, stems and tender leaves attached
Pineapple sage flowers, stems removed

For the vinaigrette:
1 egg yolk
2 medium yellow tomatoes
1/4 cup apple vinegar
1 cup sunflower oil
1 tablespoon finely chopped sweet marjoram

For the croutons:
1 whole grain baguette
3 tablespoons unsalted butter, melted

For the garnish:
Miniature yellow pear tomatoes

To prepare the salad, combine whichever greens, sprouts and herbs you have available, providing two ounces total per serving. Be sure that the flavors of the items you have chosen are well balanced and that no one flavor is overpowering. Wash in cold water, spin dry and allow to drain on a clean towel.

Collect the flowers as close to the time of serving as possible. If the flowers are clean, place them in a salad spinner to remove any insects. Be sure to handle them gently as they bruise easily. If the flowers are dusty, rinse in cold water and very gently pat the petals dry. Store the calendula petals in the refrigerator until ready to use.

WARNING: Do not use flowers from the florist or any flowers which have been sprayed with pesticides or other chemicals. Also, many flowers are poisonous and some poisonous flowers share common names that are similar or the same as flowers which are safe to consume.

To make the vinaigrette, combine the egg yolk, tomatoes and vinegar in a blender. Blend for two minutes at high speed. Lower the speed and slowly pour in the sunflower oil to form a smooth emulsion. Strain the mixture through a fine sieve into a shallow bowl. Whisk in the chopped marjoram.

To prepare the croutons, remove the ends of the baguette and cut the bread into 1/8-inch to 1/4-inch slices. Brush the bread on both sides with the melted butter. Set on a sheet pan and bake at 350 degrees for 15 minutes. Remove from the oven and cool. Store in a dry place.

Assemble the salad on pieces of flat slate or large white plates. Carefully position the greens and herbs on the slate, using the croutons to give height. Arrange some purple flowering kale and red oak leaf lettuce around the mound of greens. Place the miniature yellow pear tomatoes around the salad. Ladle the dressing around the plates and drizzle some over the greens. Garnish with the flowers and serve.

23 Salad of Lobster with Sweet Potato

Serves 4

For the salad:
2 1 1/4-pound live lobsters
1 head savoy cabbage, boiled
1 sweet potato, peeled and finely diced
1 carrot, peeled and diced
1 stalk celery, finely diced
1 leek, white only, peeled and finely diced
4 tablespoons butter
1 tablespoon Italian parsley, finely chopped
Salt and pepper to taste

For the sauce:
1 cup lobster stock
1/2 cup olive oil
1 tablespoon Italian parsley, finely chopped

For the garnish:
1/2 sweet potato, peeled and cut into long, thin strips
1 celery, peeled and cut into long, thin strips
1 parsnip, peeled and cut into long, thin strips
1/2 small beet, peeled and cut into long, thin strips
1 small carrot, peeled and cut into long, thin strip
Corn oil for deep frying

For the salad, blanch the lobsters in boiling salted water for 4 minutes. Shock in ice water to stop the cooking. Remove the meat and cut into large chunks. Julienne the inner leaves of the boiled cabbage and add to the lobster. Meanwhile, sauté the sweet potato, carrot, celery and leek in butter until tender. Add to the lobster and cabbage. Add the Italian parsley and season with salt and pepper.
Using circular cutters, cut disks out of the remaining cabbage leaves.

To construct the compressed salad, line the cutter on the bottom with one of these cabbage circles and fill with the lobster salad mixture. Top with a cabbage circle and set on plate. Remove the cutter.

For the sauce, heat the lobster stock and whisk in the olive oil to form a temporary emulsion. Add the parsley.

For the garnish, deep fry the vegetable strips in corn oil until golden brown. Drain on paper toweling.

To serve, drizzle the warm sauce over the salad and garnish with the fried vegetable strips.

24 Wild Mushroom Tamale Salad

Serves 6 to 8

For the masa:
2 cups masa harina
½ teaspoon salt
½ teaspoon sugar
½ cup water
¾ cup corn oil

For the beet masa:
1 cup masa harina
½ teaspoon salt
½ teaspoon sugar
½ cup beet juice
¾ cup vegetable oil

For the mushroom stuffing:
8 ounces assorted wild mushrooms, cleaned
2 tablespoons butter
3 cloves garlic, roasted and peeled
2 Arbol chilies, toasted and seeded
10 sage leaves, chopped
Salt and pepper to taste

For the vinaigrette:
⅓ cup balsamic vinegar
2 guajillo chilies, toasted
¼ cup olive oil
¼ cup peanut oil
Salt and pepper to taste

For the salad:
1 bunch red oak leaf lettuce, cleaned
1 bunch green oak leaf lettuce, cleaned
1 bunch frise, cleaned
1 bunch lola rossa, cleaned
4 fresh baby corn, in husks

For the garnish:
Roasted shallots
Assorted wild mushrooms
sautéed in olive oil

For the masa, combine all of the ingredients in a small bowl. Mix with a wooden spoon until blended. Beat with a whisk until light and fluffy. Cover with plastic wrap and set aside. Repeat this procedure with the beet masa.

To prepare the stuffing, sauté the wild mushrooms in butter. Add the roasted garlic, toasted chili and chopped sage. Season with salt and pepper. Cool. Dice this mixture very finely, forming a coarse paste. On lightly oiled sheets of parchment paper, spread out the two masas in a marbled pattern. Shape into small rectangles. Pipe a line of mushroom stuffing down the center of each rectangle. Roll up the parchment to form a log and twist the ends to seal. Steam for 12 minutes. To prepare the vinaigrette, whisk together the vinegar and the chilies. Whisk in the oils and season with salt and pepper.

To serve, peel the paper off the tamales and stack them like a log cabin on plates. Arrange the lettuce inside the log cabin and drizzle with the vinaigrette. Top with an ear of baby corn that still has the silk attached. Arrange the shallots and sautéed mushrooms around the plate and drizzle with the vinaigrette.

24 Rabbit Loin with Bulgur Salad

Serves 4

For the vinaigrette:
⅓ cup warm bacon fat
¼ cup soy sauce
2 tablespoons rice wine vinegar
1 tablespoon sesame oil

For the salad:
1 cup cooked bulgur
4 rabbit loins, trimmed
Grapeseed oil for sautéeing
Salt and pepper to taste
4 ounces mesclun
5 fresh shiitake mushrooms, thinly sliced

For the garnish:
1 yellow tomato, peeled, seeded and diced
1 red tomato, peeled, seeded, and diced
2 tablespoons chopped chives
1 cup haricots verts, trimmed and blanched
Preserved ginger, julienned

For the vinaigrette, whisk together all of the ingredients and keep warm until service.

For the salad, warm the bulgur. Sauté the rabbit loins in a small amount of grapeseed oil. Season with salt and pepper. Slice the sautéed rabbit loins on the bias. Using the same pan, wilt the greens and season with salt and pepper.

To serve, remove the wilted greens and arrange on plates. Quickly sauté the shiitake mushrooms in the same pan and strew them around the mound of wilted greens. Spoon some of the warm bulgur on and around the greens. Fan one loin of rabbit onto each plate. Dress with the warm soy-bacon vinaigrette. Garnish with the diced yellow and red tomatoes, chopped chives and haricots verts. Serve with preserved ginger.

25 Feisty Salad of Lambs' Tongue

Serves 6

For the tongues and brains:
3 whole lambs' brains
2 quarts court bouillon
2 lambs' tongues
Salt and pepper
Flour for dusting
4 ounces clarified butter

For the vinaigrette:
2 stalks lemon grass
2 fresh green chilies, stems removed and sliced
4 slices fresh ginger, peeled
½ cup Champagne vinegar
5 shallots, peeled and sliced
4 cloves garlic, peeled and finely chopped
2 scallions, sliced into rounds
¼ cup Italian parsley julienne
¼ cup fresh cilantro julienne
Zest and juice of 2 limes
¾ cup extra virgin olive oil
Salt and pepper to taste

For the herb purée:
6 cloves garlic, peeled and sliced
¾ cup extra virgin olive oil
1 cup parsley and cilantro leaves, tightly packed
2 scallions, sliced
1 green chili, stem removed
Zest and juice of 1 lime

For the salad:
Mixed greens, including peppercress, watercress, arugula and pea greens

For the garnish:
¼ cup very small capers
Fresh chervil
Peppered breadsticks

To prepare the brains, soak them in cold, acidulated water for about 1 hour. Remove the transparent membrane and soak again. Poach for 5 minutes in enough simmering court bouillon to cover. Remove from the heat and let cool in the court bouillon. Poach the lambs' tongues in gently simmering court bouillon for approximately 1 hour. Let cool in the poaching liquid.

To prepare the vinaigrette, very thinly slice the bottom 6 inches of each lemon grass stalk. Add the sliced chilies, ginger and vinegar. Simmer this mixture in a small saucepan for 5 minutes. Strain the vinegar and cool. To the flavored vinegar add the shallots, garlic, scallion, parsley, cilantro, lime zest and juice. Whisk in the olive oil. Add salt and pepper to taste.

For the herb purée, sauté the garlic in the olive oil until golden. Add the fresh herbs, scallions, chili, lime zest and juice and purée in a blender until smooth.

To assemble, slice the tongues lengthwise into very thin slices. Arrange 2 slices on each plate. Separate each brain into two sections. Season with salt and pepper and dust very lightly with flour. Sauté the brains in the clarified butter and arrange 1 piece on each plate. Toss the mixed greens with the lemon grass vinaigrette. Adjust the seasoning. Sprinkle the capers on the brains and tongue. Spoon the herb purée around the dish and garnish with fresh chervil. Serve with long, peppered breadsticks.

26 Lobster and Mango Salad with Lemon Grass

Serves 4

For the salad:
2 ripe mangoes
2 1½-pound live lobsters

For the dressing:
Juice of ½ lemon
1½ tablespoons thin homemade mayonnaise
3 to 4 tablespoons fresh lemon grass juice
½ teaspoon sugar
½ cup Thai basil leaves, gently packed
Salt to taste

For the carrot vinaigrette:
2 cups fresh carrot juice
Juice of 1 lemon
2 shallots, peeled and chopped
Sugar to taste
Salt and pepper to taste

For the garnish:
4 tablespoons thin
homemade mayonnaise
Thai basil
Chives

To prepare the salad, peel the mangoes and slice paper thin. Dice any slices which are unattractive or any flesh which has remained attached to the pit. Poach the lobster until the meat is just cooked through. Shock in ice water. Remove the tail meat and cut into bite-sized pieces. Carefully remove the meat from the claws in 1 piece to use as a garnish.

To prepare the lemon grass dressing, combine all of the ingredients in a blender and purée until smooth. For the carrot vinaigrette, combine all of the ingredients in a small saucepan. Set over medium heat and bring to a simmer. Reduce by half.

To serve, toss the lobster with the diced mango and enough lemon grass dressing to coat. Adjust the seasoning. Spoon the carrot vinaigrette on the plate and decorate with the mayonnaise as shown. Arrange the lobster on top of the sauce and arrange the thinly sliced mango around the lobster to form a small dome. Garnish with the meat from the lobster claws, fresh Thai basil and chives.

27 Tempura Salad

Serves 2

For the tempura batter:
2/3 cup unbleached white flour
2/3 cup arrowroot
2 teaspoons baking powder
1 tablespoon curry powder
1 1/2 teaspoons salt
1/2 teaspoon black pepper
1 cup water

For the nori roll:
1 tablespoon cider vinegar
1 1/2 cups shredded red cabbage
Additional cider vinegar
1/4 cup tamarin
2 cups hot water
1/2 cup dried arame*
3 sheets nori*
4 large carrots, peeled and julienned
2 bunches watercress
Flour for dredging
Oil for deep frying

For the maple vinaigrette:
1/2 cup balsamic vinegar
1/2 cup red wine
1/4 cup maple syrup
3 tablespoons Dijon mustard
1/4 teaspoon sea salt
1 clove garlic, minced
1 tablespoon lemon thyme
1/2 cup extra-virgin olive oil

For the garnish:
Assorted greens
Sliced tomatoes
Radish sprouts
Fiddlehead ferns, blanched
Pickled ginger

To prepare the tempura batter, combine all of the dry ingredients in a small bowl. Slowly add the water until the mixture has the consistency of a light batter. Set aside. This batter can be stored, covered in the refrigerator for future use.

For the nori roll, bring a large pot of salted water to boil. Add the tablespoon of cider vinegar. Drop the shredded cabbage into the boiling water and remove after 20 seconds. Shock the cabbage in ice water and drain. Rub the cabbage with some additional cider vinegar and press with a clean cloth to dry.

Mix the tamarin with the hot water and soak the arame in this mixture for 30 minutes. Drain and press dry with clean cloth. Lightly toast the nori sheets by holding them about 6 inches over a medium flame for 5 to 10 seconds on each side. Place a nori sheet on a flat work surface. Lay all of the vegetables in a row along the nori sheet. Roll up the vegetables tightly in the nori sheet, squeezing hard to eliminate as much liquid as possible. Roll a second sheet of nori around the roll. Wet the ends of the second sheet with water and seal the edges. Repeat with the third sheet of nori. Set aside until service.

To prepare the maple-mustard vinaigrette, whisk together the vinegar, red wine, maple syrup, mustard, salt, garlic and lemon thyme. Slowly beat in the olive oil to form an emulsion. Refrigerate until service.

Dredge the finished nori roll in flour to ensure the tempura batter does not fall off once it is fried. Heat the oil to 375 degrees. Dip the whole nori roll in the tempura batter and fry in the hot oil until golden brown. Remove and drain on paper towels.

To serve, toss the vegetable garnishes with the vinaigrette. Slice the nori roll and arrange on plates as shown.

***Note:** Arame and nori are both Japanese sea vegetables. Arame has a very mild flavor and is almost black in color. It is ready to eat after soaking in water for 30 minutes. It may also be cooked. Thin sheets of nori are called asakusa nori in Japanese. They should have a multi-hued red or green color (which shows that it has not been dyed).

27 Olive Bread Salad

Serves 6

For the salad:
½ pound olive bread
¼ cup garlic-flavored olive oil
3 heads frisée, cleaned
1 red pepper, seeded, grilled and cut into 1-inch strips
1 yellow pepper, seeded, grilled and cut into 1-inch strips
1 green pepper, seeded, grilled and cut into 1-inch strips
1 red onion, roasted, peeled and cut into 1-inch strips
24 small black olives

For the vinaigrette:
½ cup extra-virgin olive oil
3 tablespoons red wine vinegar
1 clove garlic, peeled and minced
½ teaspoon cracked black pepper
¼ teaspoon kosher salt

To prepare the salad, begin by toasting the bread. Brush the olive bread with the garlic-flavored olive oil and toast in a 300-degree oven until golden brown and crisp. Cool. Combine the bread with the remaining salad ingredients in a large bowl.

For the vinaigrette, combine all of the ingredients in a small bowl and mix well. Toss the salad with the vinaigrette until well coated. Arrange on plates and serve.

30 Lotus Seed Flowers

Serves 4

For the inner pastry:
9 ounces all-purpose flour, sifted
¾ teaspoon salt
¾ cup carrot juice
9 ounces unsalted butter, softened

For the outer pastry:
9 ounces all-purpose flour, sifted
¾ teaspoon salt
¾ cup spinach juice
9 ounces unsalted butter, softened

For the dish:
½ cup mashed lotus seeds
Vegetable oil for deep frying

For the inner pastry, in a medium bowl combine the flour and salt. Slowly add the carrot juice and mix until combined. Transfer to a lightly floured work surface and knead until smooth, about eight minutes. Cover with plastic wrap and set aside for 25 minutes. Unwrap the dough and roll out into an 8-inch square. Place the butter in the center and fold the dough over the butter. Place on a parchment-lined sheet pan and set aside in the refrigerator for 10 minutes. Transfer to a lightly floured work surface. Roll the dough to form a 24-inch rectangle. Fold the dough into thirds and turn by one-quarter. Roll the dough to form a 24-inch rectangle. Fold the dough into thirds, place on a parchment-lined sheet pan and set aside in the refrigerator for 15 minutes. Repeat the process four more times and set aside in the refrigerator to chill for 15 minutes. Form the dough onto 12 rounds, place on a parchment-lined sheet pan and set aside.

For the outer pastry, in a medium bowl combine the flour and salt. Slowly add the spinach juice and mix until combined. Transfer to a lightly floured work surface and knead until smooth, about eight minutes. Cover with plastic wrap and set aside for 25 minutes. Unwrap the dough and roll out into an eight-inch square. Place the butter in the center and fold the dough over the butter. Place on a parchment-lined sheet pan and set aside in the refrigerator for 10 minutes. Transfer to a lightly floured work surface. Roll the dough to form a 24-inch rectangle. Fold the dough into thirds and turn by one-quarter. Roll the dough to form a 24-inch rectangle. Fold the dough into thirds, place on a parchment-lined sheet pan and set aside in the refrigerator for 15 minutes. Repeat the process four more times and set aside in the refrigerator to chill for 15 minutes. Roll out the dough and cut out 12 4 by 4-inch squares. Place on a parchment-lined sheet pan and set aside.
To assemble the flowers, wrap the outer pastry around the inner pastry and with scissors, make incision in the outer pastry to make eight equal portions that resemble petals. Place onto a copper wire strainer and deep fry until the pastry becomes a peony in shape.

31 Pan-Fried Beef Cakes with Pine Nuts

Serves 3

For the beef cakes:
5½ ounces ground beef
Pinch preserved mandarin peels
Salt and pepper to taste
1 teaspoon cornstarch
1½ tablespoons pine nuts
1 cup bean sprouts
1 teaspoon vegetable oil

For the sauce:
½ cup chicken stock
2 teaspoons sugar
1 teaspoon wine vinegar
1 teaspoon mashed black beans
1 to 2 teaspoons cornstarch

For garnish:
Cilantro
Chopped green onions

For the beef cakes, mix beef with mandarin peel, salt, pepper and cornstarch. Pan fry 3 minutes, until cooked through. Deep-fry pine nuts until golden. Set aside. Saute bean sprouts in a little oil until hot.

For the sauce, combine chicken stock, sugar, vinegar, mashed beans and cornstarch. Stir until slightly thickened.

To serve, place bean sprouts on plate and top with beef cakes. Pour sauce over and garnish with pine nuts, cilantro and green onions.

31 Scallop Pockets

Makes 16 pockets:

For the pastry:
6.8 ounces wheat starch
1 teaspoon cornstarch
1 cup plus 2 tablespoons of boiling water
2 teaspoons carrot juice

For the filling:
3 scallops, diced
½ cup diced shrimp
2 tablespoons crabmeat
2 tablespoons shredded bamboo shoots
¼ teaspoon salt
1 teaspoon sugar
Pepper to taste
Sesame oil to taste
Minced carrot
1 piece leek

For pastry, sift wheat starch and cornstarch into mixing bowl. Pour in boiling water and carrot juice and stir rapidly. Knead into a soft dough. Set aside.

For the filling, combine the scallops, shrimp, crab meat, bamboo shoots, salt, sugar, pepper, sesame oil and cornstarch. Roll dough into a cylinder. Divide into small equal portions. Press into rounds with a pastry knife. Place filling into rounds and wrap them up. Add minced carrots to the top of the dumplings. Place the leek in hot water until soft. Divide leek into strips and tie up dumpling with a strip of leek. Place dumplings on rack in steamer. Steam over medium heat for 8 minutes. Serve with plum sauce.

32 Oysters with Shaved Sea Ice and Horseradish Oil

Serves 4

For the oysters and shaved sea ice:
16 shucked oysters
(reserve oyster liquor and oyster shells)
½ cup white wine

For the sauce:
½ cup heavy cream
8 oysters, diced
2 tablespoons freshly grated horseradish
Salt and pepper to taste

For the garnish:
8 chive sticks
4 tablespoons horseradish oil
2 tablespoons horseradish, julienned and deep-fried
8 rice crackers

For the shaved sea ice, combine the oyster liquor and white wine. Pour into a shallow pan and place pan in the freezer until mixture has frozen.

For the sauce, whip cream and add diced oysters and the grated horseradish. Mix well and season with salt and pepper.

To serve, shave oyster ice with a spoon and fill empty oyster shells with the granite. Place on plates. Put four spoonfuls of sauce onto the plate and top with two oysters. Decorate with chive sticks, a sprinkle of horseradish oil and top with deep-fried horseradish. Serve with rice crackers.

33 Five Warm Oysters

Serves 4

Oysters with Tomato Sauce
4 medium, ripe tomatoes, peeled and seeded
1 yellow onion, chopped
½ teaspoon dried thyme
1 bay leaf
1 tablespoon sugar
1 teaspoon tomato purée
Salt
Cayenne pepper
Freshly ground white pepper
1 tablespoon butter
4 oysters, shucked

For garnish:
Basil leaves

For the sauce, purée three tomatoes and the yellow onion. Pour along with thyme, bay leaf, sugar and tomato purée in a pot and boil until reduced by half. Add salt, cayenne pepper, and white pepper to taste. Add butter. Cook until thickened. Strain. Cut remaining tomato into triangles and place in sauce.

For the oysters, poach in their liquor until edges begin to curl. Place back in a warm half shell. Pour sauce over. Garnish with basil leaves.

Oysters with River Trout Roe and Chives
¾ cup beurre blanc
2 tablespoons river trout roe
2 tablespoons minced chives
4 oysters, shucked

For the sauce, heat the beurre blanc and add roe from the river trout along with chives.

For the oysters, poach in their liquor until edges curl. Pat dry and place back in warm half shell. Pour the warm sauce over the oyster.

Oysters au Gratin
6 tablespoons white wine sauce
(see mussel soup recipe and omit chives)
1 egg yolk
3 tablespoons heavy cream
4 oysters, shucked

For the sauce, heat sauce and add egg yolk and heavy cream.

For the oysters, poach in their liquor until edges curl. Pat dry and place back in warm half shell. Pour sauce over oyster and gratin under the broiler.

Oysters with Wine Sauce and Russian Caviar
6 tablespoons white wine sauce
(see mussel soup recipe and omit chives)
3 tablespoons heavy cream
4 teaspoons Russian caviar
4 oysters, shucked

For the sauce, warm sauce and add heavy cream. Poach oysters in their liquor until edges curl. Pat dry and place back in warm half shell. Pour sauce over and garnish with a small teaspoonful of Russian caviar.

Deep-Fried Oysters with Truffle Sauce
3 tablespoons white wine sauce
(see mussel soup recipe and omitchives)
½ truffle
2 tablespoons truffle juice
1 tablespoon butter
1 teaspoon raspberry vinegar
4 oysters, shucked
1 tablespoon grated parmesan cheese
1 tablespoon dry, sifted bread crumbs
Oil for deep-frying
Julienne truffle strips for garnish

For the sauce, heat wine sauce, pour into blender with truffle and truffle juice. Blend thoroughly until the sauce looks smooth. Pour the sauce into a pot, heat up and add butter. Add raspberry vinegar to taste.
Dredge oysters in cheese and breadcrumbs. Deep-fry until golden brown.

To serve, place sauce in empty half shells and place fried oysters on top. Garnish with truffle strips.

Place all oysters on serving plates lined with seaweed.

34 Triangle Dumplings

Makes 12 Dumplings
For the dough:
6.8 ounces wheat starch
Pinch cornstarch
¾ cup, or more, boiling water
2 teaspoons peanut oil

For the filling:
2 dried mushrooms, shredded
2 tablespoons shredded bamboo shoots
1 tablespoon peanut oil
2¾ ounces diced pork
1 tablespoon soy sauce
1 tablespoon hoison sauce
½ teaspoon salt
Pepper and white wine to taste
1⅓ ounces peeled, de-veined shrimp, diced

For the garnish:
3 tablespoons diced Yunnan or other ham
1 fried egg, diced
2 sprigs cilantro, diced

For the dough, sift wheat starch and cornstarch into a mixing bowl. Pour in boiling water and stir rapidly. Add peanut oil and knead until soft.

For the filling, combine mushrooms and bamboo shoots. Heat oil in wok and fry pork. Add soy sauce, hoison, salt, pepper and wine. Then add in mushrooms and bamboo shoots and shrimp. Place filling into mixing bowl and let cool.

Make dough into cylinder shape and cut into small equal portions. Press into rounds and place some filling on each round. Make into triangular shapes. Add ham, egg and cilantro to each dumpling. Place dumplings in steamer and steam on medium heat for 7 minutes.

35 Sweet Flour Dumplings with Sesame Seeds and Lotus Paste

Serves 24
For the dough:
2½ cups all-purpose flour
⅓ cup sugar
2½ tablespoons lard
1½ tablespoons baking soda
¾ tablespoon baking powder
1 egg
Water as needed
1 cup mashed lotus seed paste
½ cup white sesame seeds
Vegetable oil for deep-frying

For the dough, sift flour into bowl and make a hole. Add sugar, lard, baking soda, baking powder and egg. Add water as needed to make a dough and knead until smooth.

Cut dough into small portions. Place lotus paste in the center of each portion and use the palm of your hand to form a ball. Dredge in white sesame seeds. Deep-fry in hot oil until golden brown.

36 Warm Oysters with Rhubarb

Serves 1

For the oysters:
6 oysters
1 4-inch center of a rhubarb stalk
½ cup heavy cream
Salt and white pepper to taste

For the garnish:
Chervil leaves

For the oysters, shuck oysters and throw away the upper shell. Strain liquor into a small pot, cut loose the oyster from the lower shell, saving the lower shell.

Cut the rhubarb in ½-inch thick pieces, put them in the juice from the oyster, add the cream and let it boil until the rhubarb is soft and the cream has somewhat thickened. Put in the oysters for a short instant. Add salt and pepper to taste. Put each oyster in its shell and pour over the rest. Garnish with chervil leaves.

37 Veal Tongue Ravioli with Sea Urchin

Serves 6

For the vinaigrette:
4 tablespoons fresh ginger, peeled, sliced and blanched
½ cup red wine
¼ cup red wine vinegar
2 tablespoons sugar
½ cup olive oil
2 tablespoons sherry vinegar
1½ teaspoons soy sauce
1½ teaspoons coriander
½ teaspoon black pepper

For the garnish:
4 cups star anise
2 cups peppercorns
12 snow peas, sautéed
6 bay leaves, singed
Pickled ginger, julienned
6 potato chips infused with fresh herbs

For the ravioli:
1 sheet fresh semolina pasta dough
6 tablespoons chicken-tongue mousse

For the chicken-tongue mousse:
1 calf's tongue
1 cup kosher salt
2 bunches Italian parsley
1 bunch fresh thyme
6 shallots, chopped
2 garlic gloves
2 bay leaves
4 cups rendered duck fat
8 ounces chicken breast, puréed with 1 ounce ice
1 tablespoon chopped parsley
1 tablespoon chopped thyme
Salt and pepper to taste

For the sea urchin:
6 fresh urchins
1 cup tempura batter

For the chicken-tongue mousse, rub the tongue with salt. Combine the fresh herbs, the shallots, the garlic and bay leaves with the remaining salt and cure the tongue in this mixture for 4 to 5 days in a refrigerator. Rinse the excess salt and herb cure from the tongue and cook slowly in the rendered fat for 3 to 4 hours, until the tongue is very tender. Peel the outer skin from the cooked tongue and discard. Cool and slice lengthwise into thin strips. Dice the remaining tongue pieces and fold them into the chicken purée with parsley, thyme and salt and pepper. Roll the chicken mousse up in the tongue slices; making 12 to 15 rolls. Seal the rolls in plastic wrap and poach them for 5 minutes; chill the rolls and set them aside.

For the vinaigrette, steep the ginger in the red wine and reduce the wine to a syrup. Add in the vinegar and the sugar; reduce by ½ and reserve the liquid for the vinaigrette and the ginger for the garnish. Mix the olive oil, ginger syrup, sherry vinegar and the soy sauce together with the coriander and the black pepper.

For the ravioli, cut the pasta dough into 3 by 1½ inch rectangles; pipe 1½ teaspoons of the tongue mousse onto each piece, roll them up and pinch the ends tight like wrapped candy using a touch of water to seal the dough.
For the sea urchin, cut the bottom off the urchin with scissors to form an opening large enough from which to eat. Remove the roe and the gonad. Clean the shell thoroughly.

To serve, set a sea urchin shell in a small wood box filled with star anise and peppercorns. Cook the ravioli in salted boiling water and toss them lightly in the vinaigrette. Deep fry the sea urchin roe in the tempura batter, until it is crisp and golden brown. Place the fried roe and the ravioli in the urchin shells with some sautéed snow peas, 1 bay leaf and julienned, pickled ginger. Garnish the box with the herbed potato chip.

36 Asian Delicacies

Serves 3

For the salmon teriyaki:
1 4-ounce salmon fillet
2 tablespoons soy sauce
2 teaspoons sesame oil
Pinch of sugar

For the fish with bean sprouts:
3 3-ounce red snapper fillets
½ tablespoon minced ginger
½ tablespoon finely chopped cilantro
Salt and pepper to taste
1 cup julienned won ton wrappers
peanut oil for frying
½ cup of bean sprouts
1 tablespoon rice wine vinegar
3 tablespoons peanut oil
½ teaspoon grated ginger
Salt and pepper to taste

For the shrimp with rice noodles:
3 large shrimp
2 tablespoons peanut oil
½ tablespoon curry powder
1 teaspoon minced garlic
Salt and pepper to season
¼ cup of rice noodles
4 tips asparagus, blanched and cut julienne
1 tablespoon toasted pine nuts
1 tablespoon sesame oil
1 teaspoon rice wine vinegar

For the garnish:
¼ cup garden greens, julienned
3 vegetables flowers
15 cut chives
1 tablespoon sliced pickled ginger
3 large radicchio leaves
3 sprigs fresh dill
3 arugula leaves
Julienned red pepper
Julienned radish
Sprigs of Italian parsley
3 bouquets of wild flowers
chop sticks with holders
Chinese soup spoons filled with soy sauce

For the salmon, marinate the salmon fillet in 1 tablespoon of the soy sauce for 1 hour and sear it for a few seconds on a very hot grill. Make a dressing from the remaining soy sauce, sesame oil and sugar.
Set the dressing aside.

For the snapper, season the fillets with the ginger, cilantro, salt and the pepper. Coat the seasoned fillets in the julienned won ton wrappers and fry to a golden brown in hot peanut oil. Place the fried snapper on a paper towel and keep warm. Marinate the bean sprouts in the vinegar, oil, ginger, salt and pepper.

For the shrimp, marinate the shrimp in the oil, curry powder, the garlic, salt and the pepper for 15 minutes; grill the seasoned shrimp for 4 to 5 minutes, until done. Toss the cooked rice noodles with the asparagus and pine nuts in the sesame oil, vinegar, salt and the pepper.

To serve, cut the seared salmon into 3 slices, toss the greens in the sesame-soy dressing and arrange the greens in orchid dishes; laying the salmon on top, garnished with the vegetable flowers, the cut chives and sprinkled minced ginger. Divide the marinated sprouts between 3 bamboo steamers in the radicchio leaves; set the won ton crusted snapper fillets on top of the sprouts and garnish with the fresh dill and arugula. Place 1 grilled shrimp on top of the rice noodle salad in each lacquer dish; garnish the dish with the julienned red pepper, the julienned radish and the Italian parsley. Arrange the finished salmon, red snapper and the shrimp on lacquer trays with the wild flowers, chop sticks and the soy filled spoons.

38 Friuli Cheese Crisp

Makes 16 crisps

For the cheese crisps:
1 pound fresh Montasio cheese

For the dish, shred the cheese and divide into 1 ounce portions. Sprinkle each portion evenly into a non-stick skillet over a medium heat, allowing the cheese to melt quickly into a thin bubbly crisp. Be careful not to let the cheese brown, as it will be bitter. Cool the cheese crisps on parchment paper and fold while still slightly warm.

Herbed Cannelloni with Artichokes

Serves 6

For the filling:
1 cup baby spinach leaves
½ cup mesclun
(chicory, mâche and dandelion)
¼ cup bibb lettuce
¼ cup fresh chervil
¼ cup chopped endive
¼ cup purslane
1 tablespoon olive oil
1 garlic clove
1 egg yolk
¼ cup grated Parmesan
1 teaspoon olive oil
Salt, pepper and nutmeg to taste

For the pasta:
1¼ cups flour
3 whole eggs
3 tablespoons olive oil

For the cannelloni:
30 2½ by 1-inch pasta sheets
¼ cup freshly grated Parmesan
6 tablespoons butter
1 cup consommé
1 cup chicken stock
12 violet artichokes, cut into eighths*
1 tablespoon olive oil
2 cups baby spinach leaves
Salt and pepper to taste

For the filling, sweat the greens in a large sauté pan with the olive oil for 3 minutes; seasoning as you do by swirling the garlic clove around the pan on the end of a fork. Remove the cookie greens to cool on a sheet pan, press out the excess liquid and chop fine in a food processor. In a stainless bowl, mix together the finely chopped greens with the egg yolk, Parmesan cheese and olive oil. Adjust the seasoning and refrigerate until needed.

For the pasta, on a pastry board make a well in the middle of the flour, Add the eggs and salt into the center and slowly knead the flour into the eggs until all the flour is incorporated. Add the olive oil a drop at a time and continue to knead the dough until it is smooth and elastic. Let the dough rest for 2 hours covered with a cool damp cloth and roll out thin using a pasta machine into 30 2½ by 3-inch rectangles.

For the cannelloni, blanch the pasta sheets in boiling salted water and shock them in an ice bath. Pat the sheets dry with a clean towel, sprinkle with grated Parmesan, and leave covered until ready to fill. With a pastry bag, pipe about 2 tablespoons of filling onto the long edge of each pasta rectangle. Roll up and place each cannelloni onto a sheet pan, seam side down. Cover them with the butter, consemmé, stock and the remaining Parmesan.

To serve, heat the cannelloni in a 350 degree oven for 10 minutes; finish under a hot broiler for 5 minutes. In a hot pan, sauté the artichokes in the olive oil for 3 minutes, until tender; add in the spinach to lightly sauté and season. On each plate arrange a bed of the artichokes and the spinach. On top, place 5 cannelloni in and drizzle the dish with some of the warm stock and a light sprinkling of olive oil.

*__Note:__ Violet artichokes are a special, scarcely developed artichoke from Provence.

Shrimp Dumplings with Bamboo Shoots

Serves 8

For the dough:
4 ounces wheat starch
1 teaspoon cornstarch
½ cup boiling water
2 teaspoons lard or peanut oil

Filling:
5½ ounces peeled and de-veined shrimp
2 tablespoons minced pork fat
4 tablespoons shredded bamboo shoots
¾ teaspoon salt
¾ teaspoon sugar
½ teaspoon sesame oil
Pinch black pepper
1 teaspoon cornstarch
Vegetable oil

For garnish:
Chile oil
Soy sauce

For the dough, sift wheat starch and cornstarch into a mixing bowl. Pour boiling water into it and stir rapidly. Turn dough out onto a floured work surface and add lard or peanut oil. Knead into a soft dough by hand.

For the filling, cut shrimp into small dice. Set aside. Poach pork and bamboo shoots briefly, drain and combine with shrimp. Add salt, sugar, sesame oil, pepper and cornstarch. Pound this until firm and place in refrigerator for 30 minutes.

Cut dough into about 16 equal balls. Press into 3-inch rounds with a pastry knife or tortilla press. Place about a teaspoon of filling into each round and fold over into a half moon shape. Pinch to seal. Make five pleats at the edge, forming a bonnet-shaped dumpling.

Oil a steamer. Place enough water in a wok to come to the bottom of the steamer. Place dumplings in steamer, and steam over medium heat for 8 to 10 minutes.

To serve and garnish, add chile oil and soy sauce to the side.

40 Gnocchi with Crayfish and Rooster Crowns

Serves 4

For the crayfish:
36 live crayfish
2 cups court bouillon
2 tablespoons shellfish butter

For the Gnocchi:
⅔ cup ricotta cheese
1 egg yolk
3 tablespoons flour, as needed
Salt, pepper, nutmeg to taste
Clear stock for poaching
1 tablespoon melted butter
2 tablespoons grated parmesan

For the dish:
5 tablespoons butter
8 thin slices black truffle
4 fresh rooster crowns
8 fresh straw mushroom caps
½ cup quartered forest mushrooms (chanterelles, cèpes)
⅓ cup veal stock
1 tablespoon truffle juice
6 tablespoons crayfish juice
4 fresh rooster kidneys
3 ounces foie gras, diced
Salt and pepper to season
1 teaspoon lemon juice

For the garnish:
2 tablespoons fresh chervil leaves

For the crayfish, poach them quickly in the court bouillon and shock them in an ice bath. Reserve 4 whole crayfish with the tail shell peeled for the garnish; extract the tail meat from the remainder, and using a duck press, squeeze all the liquid from the crayfish bodies to be used as seasoning.

For the gnocchi, beat together the ricotta and the egg yolk; carefully knead into the cheese mixture enough of the flour to make a dough which is light and not too loose. It should be the consistency of cold mashed potatoes. Season with the salt, pepper and nutmeg. To cook, make small quenelles from the dough and poach them a few at a time in the stock. They will float when cooked. Remove the cooked gnocchi from the stock, toss them lightly in butter, coat in the parmesan cheese and set aside.

For the dish, simmer the truffles, rooster crowns, and mushrooms in the veal stock, truffle juice and crayfish juice for 5 to 6 minutes, allowing the butter to incorporate into the stock. Add in the kidneys and the foie grass and continue to simmer for another 2 or 3 minutes to cook the kidneys lightly.

To serve, scatter 8 gnocchi around each warm soup plate; quickly sauté the crayfish tails in the shellfish butter, placing them around the dish as well. Remove the truffles, rooster crowns, kidneys and the mushrooms from the saucepan and arrange them into the soup plate with the crowns and kidneys in the center. Season the liquid with a splash of fresh lemon juice, ladle the liquid into the bowls and garnish with the whole crayfish and fresh chervil leaves.

41 Oxtail Terrine with Herb Vinaigrette

Serves 16

For the terrine:
10 pounds beef oxtail
Course ground salt and pepper to taste
1 cup chopped celery
1 cup chopped carrots
1 cup chopped onions
1 head of garlic, halved
1½ cups chopped tomatoes
2 bay leaves
10 sprigs fresh thyme
2 quarts chicken stock
4 carrots, peeled and blanched
1 cup pearl onions, peeled and blanched

For the vinaigrette:
½ cup extra virgin olive oil
4 tablespoons minced shallots
½ cup finely cut chives
2 tablespoons chopped parsley
2 tablespoons white wine vinegar
2 tablespoons Dijon mustard
Salt and white pepper to taste

For the garnish:
32 baby green top carrots, peeled
16 baby green top turnips
32 baby leeks
64 small white potatoes, turned
2 cups chicken stock
16 crisp pastry triangles
2 tablespoons chopped parsley
2 tablespoons chopped chives
¼ cup frisée, blanched
2 tablespoons julienne smoked bacon, blanched

For the terrine, season the oxtail with the salt and pepper; place them in a roasting pan with the celery, carrots, onion, garlic, tomatoes, the bay leaves and the thyme; pour in the chicken stock, bring the stock to a boil over a high heat, cover tightly and braise in a 350 degree oven for 3 hours. Cool the oxtail to room temperature and carefully remove the meat from the bones, discarding the fat, while leaving the meat in one piece. Line a ceramic terrine with plastic wrap and lay the strips of oxtail meat, alternately with the carrots and the pearl onions, lengthwise in the mold as tightly as possible. Fold the plastic wrap over the top of the meat, press out any air pockets by pressing firmly with a weight, drain off any excess fat and chill overnight until firm.

For the vinaigrette, heat the olive oil and sweat the shallots, the chives and the parsley for 2 minutes; pour in the vinegar, simmer for 1 minute, whisk in the mustard and season. Set aside and keep warm.

To serve, unmold the terrine, remove the plastic wrap and cut into ½ inch thick slices; sprinkle lightly with course salt and warm in a 325 degree oven.

Steam the carrots, the turnips, baby leeks and potatoes in the chicken stock until tender. Spoon a pool of the warm vinaigrette to the center of each plate, lay a slice of the terrine off from the vinaigrette and arrange the steamed vegetables, with the potatoes set in the pastry triangles, to the top of the dish. Sprinkle the potatoes with the chopped parsley and chives and garnish the vegetables with the frisée and the julienne bacon.

41 Braised Snails with Mushrooms and Herbs

Serves 4

For the snails:
½ cup extra virgin olive oil
32 large snails
Salt to season
2 cloves garlic, minced
Pinch of crushed red pepper
½ cup each finely diced carrots, celery and onions
1 cup quartered finferli mushroom (chanterelles)
1 teaspoon finely chopped rosemary
1 teaspoon finely chopped sage
1 cup dry white wine
½ cup rich veal stock
1 tablespoon chopped parsley
4 tablespoons cold butter

For the garnish:
4 large bread croutons
Fresh Italian parsley leaves

For the snails, heat the olive oil in a skillet and sauté the snails over medium heat. Season with salt. Add the minced garlic, crushed red pepper, the diced carrots, celery and onions, and the quartered finferli mushrooms. Sauté them until golden. Add in the rosemary and sage. Deglaze the pan with the white wine, allowing the alcohol to evaporate. Pour in the veal stock, reducing it by half, and add in the chopped parsley. Finish the sauce by whisking in the butter, bit by bit.

To serve, place the croutons in the bottom of each soup plate; ladle the braised snails over the croutons, and garnish the dish with a leaf of fresh Italian parsley.

42 Pumpkin Gnocchi with Butter

Serves 4

For the gnocchi:
1 pound pumpkin
2 eggs
1½ cup flour
Pinch salt
4 sage leaves
2½ tablespoons butter

Peel the pumpkin, seed and chop. Steam or bake until tender, then pass it through a sieve. Allow it to cool. In a mixing bowl, combine the pumpkin purée, eggs, flour and salt. Mix thoroughly. If the resulting dough should be too soft, add a bit more flour. Using a spoon, form small quenelles of dough and drop them in salted boiling water. When the gnocchi float to the surface, skim them from the water with a slotted spoon. Then drop them in a pan of cold water. Stew the sage leaves in a pan with the butter. Dip the gnocchi a second time in salted boiling water, remove promptly and put them in the pan with the sage leaves and butter. Serve immediately.

43 Terrine of Pacific Fish with Saffron

Serves 10

For the terrine:
8 ounces pacific King salmon fillet
8 ounces California halibut fillet
8 ounces Ahi fillet
5 ounces Mahi Mahi fillet
2 Pacific lobster tails
1 leek, greens only, blanched
1 large parsnip, sliced in strips and blanched
2 ounces Beluga caviar

For the tomato dressing:
1 cup peeled and seeded tomatoes
1 tablespoon minced shallots
2 tablespoons sugar
2 tablespoons extra virgin olive oil
Salt to taste

For the garnish:
10 dill sprigs
10 parsley sprigs
10 edible flowers
60 tiny wild flowers

For the terrine, cut the salmon, halibut, Ahi and Mahi Mahi fillets into ¼ inch thick strips and slice the lobster tails into medallions. Lightly poach the cut fish in the white wine until rare and cool quickly. Line a wide low sided terrine first with the strips of leek and then with the strips of parsnip, leaving enough overlapping to cover the top of the terrine. Alternately layer the poached fish into the lined terrine, ending with a center row of the caviar topped with the Ahi. Slowly fill the terrine with the fish aspic, tamp out any air bubbles, and cover with the overlapped parsnip and leek. Chill overnight to completely set the aspic.

For the tomato dressing, place the tomatoes, shallots, sugar and olive oil in a blender and chop for 5 seconds; season with the salt to taste.

To serve, remove the terrine from the mold, cut it into 20 thin slices and place 2 slices, top to top, onto each plate. Garnish the terrine with the tomato dressing, dill and parsley sprigs and the flowers.

44 Marinated Langoustines with Caviar

Serves 6

For the cucumbers:
2 English cucumbers, thinly sliced

For the langoustines:
1¾ pounds langoustine tail meat
Salt and pepper
2 tablespoons Sherry vinegar
6 tablespoons extra virgin olive oil
1 tablespoon soy sauce
2 egg yolks
1 egg
6 ounces caviar
6 quail eggs

To arrange the cucumber crowns, use two concentric metal rings, one set inside the other. Place the rings on a serving plate and align the cucumber slices between them. Chill.

For the langoustines, cut the uncooked tail meat into fine strips. Add a dash of salt and pepper. Gently incorporate the vinegar, olive oil, soy sauce, egg yolks, whole egg, and caviar into the langoustine meat. Allow this mixture to marinate for 10 minutes.

Arrange the marinated langoustine mixture in the middle of the ring of cucumbers on the serving plates. Sprinkle with the salt and pepper. On top of each mound of langoustine place the yolk of 1 quail egg. Serve well chilled.

45 Sea Snails in a Potato Crust

Serves 4

For the sauce:
1 ounce diced bacon
1 tablespoon hazelnut oil
1 pound mushrooms, sliced
1 tablespoon chopped shallots
½ tablespoon chopped garlic
½ cup port wine
1 sprig fresh thyme
1 cup veal stock
1 cup chicken stock
1 ounce dried mushrooms, ground to a powder
Salt and pepper to taste
1 tablespoon heavy cream

For the snails:
2 tablespoons olive oil
1 tablespoon minced shallots
2 garlic cloves, minced
12 large sea snails, cooked
1 cup sliced shiitake mushrooms
½ cup mushroom sauce
Salt and pepper to taste
4 crisp potato cylinders

For the parsley glaze:
2 tablespoons water
1 cup fresh parsley leaves
1 egg yolk
Salt and pepper to taste

For the garnish:
12 snail shells
2 tablespoons fried julienne leeks
2 tablespoons julienne sushi kelp
4 tablespoons black caviar

For the sauce, sauté the bacon to render the fat and drain; add in the hazelnut oil and sauté the mushrooms until browned; add in shallots and the garlic, sauté for 2 minutes, deglaze with the port and add in the thyme; cook for 2 minutes more to burn off the alcohol, pour in the veal and chicken stocks, whisk in the powdered mushrooms and simmer for about 30 minutes to extract all the juices from the mushrooms and reduce the liquid to a light glaze. Strain the sauce through a fine sieve and season to taste. For the light colored sauce blend the heavy cream into 1 tablespoon of the mushroom sauce. Reserve both sauces and keep warm.

For the snails, heat the olive oil in a sauté pan and sauté the shallots and the garlic until translucent; sauté the mushrooms until tender and toss in the snails; pour in the mushroom sauce, simmer for 3 to 4 minutes and season.

For the parsley glaze, steep the parsley in the water for 2 minutes, until the parsley is bright green; purée in a blender. In a stainless steel bowl, whisk the hot parsley purée into the egg yolk and continue whisking over a double-boiler to thicken as you would when making a sabayon. Season with salt and pepper.

To serve, fill the potato baskets with the snail and mushroom ragoût, top them with the parsley sabayon and glaze under a broiler for 1 minute. Set the filled baskets to the top of each plate and arrange the snail shells off from the baskets, garnished with the julienne leeks and kelp. Swirl the sauces across the middle of the plates and finish with small mounds of the caviar.

45 Sea Urchin Medley with Shellfish Broth

Serves 4

For the broth:
10 langoustine shells
1 bouquet garni
3 cups mirepoix

For the medley:
1 pound cockles
½ pound periwinkles
1 pound clams
10 langoustines, tail meat only
12 oysters
12 urchin
1½ cups heavy cream
1 bunch dill, chopped
1 bunch chives, chopped
4 ounces caviar

For the garnish:
Seaweed, blanched
Sea salt
Butter
White bread, cut into 12 3-inch sticks

For the broth, combine the langoustine shells and claws, the bouquet garni, 2 quarts of water and the mirepoix in a large saucepan. Bring to a boil and allow to simmer for 3 hours. Strain through a chinois and reserve.

Cook the cockles, periwinkles and clams, and remove them from their shells. Cut the langoustine tails into thirds, across the width. Shuck the oysters. Gently open the urchin by tapping the bottom of the shell around the mouth area with the point of a knife. Remove the coral and set aside. Thoroughly clean the urchin shells.

Just before serving, slightly reduce the broth. Add the cream. Stir the shellfish, chopped herbs and caviar into the broth. Toast the bread sticks in butter.

Pour the shellfish broth into the cleaned urchin shells. Arrange the filled shells on plates that have been sprinkled with sea salt. Garnish the plates with the blanched seaweed and place one toasted bread stick in each shell.

4C Marinated Anchovies with Red Pepper Vinaigrette

Serves 4

For the marinated anchovies:
4 dozen fresh anchovies
Course ground salt
1 cup virgin olive oil
¼ cup sliced carrot
¼ cup sliced onion
¼ cup chopped celery
3 garlic cloves
2 bay leaves
1 small sprig of thyme
10 white peppercorns, cracked
¼ cup white wine vinegar

For the vinaigrette:
6 tablespoons extra virgin olive oil
1 tablespoon white wine vinegar
2 teaspoons lemon juice
Salt and fresh cracked pepper to taste

For the red pepper vinaigrette:
½ cup red pepper purée
¼ cup vinaigrette
Pinch of cayenne

For the timbales:
48 marinated anchovies
⅓ cup julienne carrot, blanched
⅓ cup julienne celery
⅓ cup julienne zucchini
⅓ cup julienne green beans, blanched
⅓ cup chopped cooked mushrooms
2 tablespoons vinaigrette

For the garnish:
4 tablespoons chopped fresh basil leaves
¼ cup julienne carrots, blanched
¼ cup julienne celery
¼ cup zucchini
4 sprigs fresh basil

To marinate the fresh anchovies, lay them out on a non-aluminum dish, sprinkle with salt and let them cure for 2 hours. In a saucepan, sauté the carrots, onions, celery and the garlic in 2 tablespoons of olive oil to soften the vegetables; pour in the remaining oil, along with the bay leaves, thyme and the peppercorns; simmer for 10 minutes and add in the vinegar. Rinse the anchovies of any excess salt, pour the warm marinade over the fish and marinate, covered in the refrigerator, for 24 hours.

For the vinaigrette, whisk together the olive oil with the vinegar and the lemon juice; season with the salt and pepper.

For the red pepper vinaigrette, blend the vinaigrette into the red pepper purée; adjust the seasoning.

For the timbales, line 4 soup cups with plastic wrap and arrange 12 of the marinated anchovies covering the inside of each cup. Toss the vegetables with the vinaigrette, allowing any excess to drain off, and fill the fish lined molds. Cover and refrigerate for 30 minutes.

To serve, unmold the timbales onto the center of each plate; pour the red pepper vinaigrette around the timbales so the bottom of the plates are completely covered and sprinkle the vinaigrette with the chopped basil. Garnish the dish with small mounds of the juilenned carrots, celery and zucchini; place 1 fresh basil sprig on top of each timbale.

4C Terrine of Foie Gras, Leeks, and Pears

Serves 14

For the terrine:
4 cups water
2 cup Sauternes
4 cups sugar
1 cinnamon stick
5 whole cloves
1 lemon, sliced
1 orange sliced
3 pears, peeled, halved, and cored
14 medium leeks, whites only, cut in 4 inch lengths
4 cups salted water
1½ sheets gelatin
1 pound goose liver, steamed and chilled (or prepared foie gras)

For the garnish:
1 cup vinaigrette
¼ cup tomato fondue
4 tablespoons finely snipped chives
14 cornichons, fanned
28 cocktail pearl onions
28 long cut chives
2 tablespoons fresh ground pepper

For the terrine, make a poaching liquid with the water, Sauternes, the sugar, cinnamon, cloves and the sliced lemon and orange; poach the halved pears, until they are soft, and refresh in an ice bath. Reserve 1 cup of the liquid for the aspic. Poach the leeks in the salted water until they are tender and refresh in an ice bath.

Dissolve the gelatin in the 1 cup of poaching liquid and keep warm. Line an oiled ceramic terrine with plastic wrap, leaving ample wrap overhanging to cover the mold. Cover the bottom of the mold with ⅓ cup of the aspic; arrange 3 rows of the leeks and brush them with the aspic. Cut the foie gras into ½ inch slices, make a layer in the terrine and brush with aspic. Arrange the pear halves with the flat side on the foie gras and brush them with aspic. Lay the remaining 4 rows of leeks into the terrine, cover them with aspic, fold over the excess plastic wrap and lay a 2 pound weight on top of the terrine. Let the weighted terrine stand overnight in the refrigerator.

To serve, carefully slice the terrine and place 1 slice in the middle of each plate. Rim the terrine with tiny pools of the vinaigrette-swirled with the tomato fondue and sprinkled with the snipped chives. Garnish the terrine with the fanned cornichons, the pearl onions and the long cut chives; sprinkle the dish with the fresh ground pepper.

47 Asparagus with Pickled Beets and Quail Eggs

Serves 6

For the beets and quail eggs:
¼ cup white wine
½ cup white wine vinegar
2 tablespoons sugar
1 cinnamon stick
2 whole cloves
1 bay leaf
2 beets, blanched and peeled
6 quail eggs, cooked and peeled

For the vinaigrette:
½ cup white wine vinegar
1 tablespoon Dijon mustard
1 cup salad oil
½ cup olive oil
1 teaspoon chopped capers
1 teaspoon chopped chives
1 teaspoon finely chopped parsley
Salt and pepper to taste

For the raspberry vinaigrette:
¾ pound fresh raspberries
¼ cup heavy cream, room temperature*
2 tablespoons raspberry vinegar
6 tablespoons olive oil
Salt and pepper to taste

For the asparagus:
36 asparagus spears
Salted water for steaming

For the garnish:
1 cup fried asparagus peels
18 small wild flowers
¼ cup whole and split pistachios
2 tablespoons capers
1 tablespoon chopped parsley
1 tablespoon fresh ground pepper

For the beets and quail eggs, combine the white wine and the vinegar in a saucepan with the sugar, cinnamon stick, the cloves and the bay leaf; bring to a boil and cook the beets until they are tender; allow the beets to cool to room temperature in their liquid, remove and reserve for the garnish. Place the quail eggs in the room temperature beet liquid and let them pickle overnight.

For the vinaigrette, combine the vinegar with the mustard in a stainless steel bowl and whisk in the salad oil and the olive oil; mix in the capers, the chives, the chopped parsley, and season to taste with salt and pepper.

For the raspberry vinaigrette, purée the raspberries in a food processor and strain through a fine sieve to remove all of the seeds. In a small mixing bowl, whisk together the purée and the heavy cream; slowly whisk in the vinegar with the oil and continue whisking until the mixture is thick and creamy. Season to taste with the salt and pepper.

For the asparagus, cut the ends and reserve for the asparagus peel garnish. Bring the salted water to a boil in a shallow pan and steam the asparagus, until tender, about 4 minutes. Immediately plunge the steamed asparagus into an ice bath to refresh; drain well and cover with the vinaigrette.

To serve, arrange 6 asparagus spears in the center of each plate, ribboned with the raspberry vinaigrette and topped with the fried asparagus peel. Garnish the plate with parisienne scoops of the pickled beets, the halved quail eggs, and the wild flowers. Scatter the plate with the pistachios, the capers, chopped parsley and the ground pepper.

***Note:** Using the cream at room temperature will keep it from curdling when combined with the vinegar.

48 Carpaccio of John Dory and Salmon

Serves 6

For the carpaccio:
1 1-pound salmon fillet
1 1-pound John Dory fillet
(porgy may be substituted)
6 tablespoons extra virgin olive oil
3 tablespoons balsamic vinegar
1 bunch sweet basil, picked
and finely shredded
3 ounces caviar
Salt and pepper

For the carpaccio, flatten the fillets of fish to a thickness of 1/16 inch between two lightly oiled sheets of plastic film. Chill the fish. Peel off the top sheet of plastic film and cut the fish into the desired shapes. Carefully arrange the fish on the serving plate. Salt and pepper the carpaccio. Brush the fish with the balsamic vinegar. Distribute the shredded basil over the salmon and the caviar over the John Dory. Serve well chilled.

49 Truffles in Potato Crust

Serves 4

For the truffles:
4 1-ounce truffles
4 medium-sized potatoes
3 egg yolks
Salt and pepper

To prepare the dish, carefully peel the truffles. Chop the peelings and reserve. Peel the potatoes. Boil two of the potatoes in water until tender, approximately 25 minutes. Purée these potatoes. Season with salt and pepper. Add the three egg yolks and the chopped peel of the truffles. Coat each truffle with a crust of this mixture.

Using a mandolin, cut the remaining two potatoes into julienne. Encase each truffle in a coat of the julienne potatoes. Gently deep-fry the potato-wrapped truffles in 350 degree oil for 10 minutes. Allow the truffles to drain, briefly, on paper towels. Serve with a truffle sauce.

49 Potato Risotto

Serves 4

For the potatoes:
1 teaspoon olive oil
1 tablespoon minced smoked bacon
2 tablespoons diced shallots
1 cup 1/8 inch diced potatoes
1/2 cup chicken stock, as needed
1/2 cup cream, reduced by 1/2
2 tablespoons butter
1 cup shredded savoy cabbage
1 tablespoon julienne truffle
1/2 teaspoon truffle juice
Salt and white pepper to taste

For the garnish:
4 crisp potato baskets
Savoy cabbage leaves, blanched
28 sliced truffle rounds
2 tablespoons cooked julienne bacon
1/3 cup savoy cabbage purée
1 tablespoon truffle oil

For the potatoes, heat the olive oil in a skillet and sauté the bacon for about 1 minute; add in the shallots and sauté for another 2 minutes; toss in the diced potatoes and add in the chicken stock a couple tablespoons at a time, allowing the stock to reduce before adding more, until the potatoes are nearly done, about 10 minutes; add in the reduced cream and simmer for 3 to 4 minutes to thicken. In another pan, sweat the shredded cabbage in the butter until tender; add in the julienne truffles, the truffle juice and sweat for 1 to 2 minutes more. Combine the potatoes with the cabbage, season and keep warm.

To serve, line the potato baskets with the blanched savoy cabbage leaves and carefully fill each basket with the warm potato mixture. Place the filled baskets to the top of each plate, swirl the cabbage purée and the truffle oil together across the center of the dish and garnish the baskets and the purée with slices of truffle and julienne bacon.

50 Spicy Tuna Tartare with Wild Rice Blini

Serves 4

For the blini:
½ small onion, minced
1 tablespoon peanut oil
2 tablespoons sesame oil
1 cup all-purpose flour, sifted
2 teaspoons baking powder, sifted
1 teaspoon salt
3 eggs
1 cup milk
1½ cups cooked wild rice

For the coulis:
1 English cucumber, peeled
½ cup yogurt
1 teaspoon minced red chili flakes
Juice of ½ lemon

For the sauce:
Soy sauce
Wasabi powder
Water

For the tartar:
6 ounces blue fin tuna, diced
Salt and pepper to taste
1 tablespoon sesame oil
2 teaspoons Asian chili sauce
1 tablespoon chopped chives
1 tablespoon sake

For the garnish:
Marinated seaweed

For the blini, sauté the onion in peanut oil. Cool. Combine the sautéed onion with the sesame oil, flour, baking powder, salt, eggs and milk. Add the wild rice. Ladle the batter onto a hot, lightly greased skillet. Cook until the edges are golden brown and flip. When the blini are cooked through, remove from the heat and keep warm.

For the cucumber coulis, combine all of the ingredients in a food processor or blender and purée until smooth.

For the soy-wasabi sauce, work a small amount of soy sauce with enough wasabi powder to form a smooth paste. Thin down the sauce with water until it has the same consistency as the cucumber coulis.

For the tartar, combine all of the ingredients and mix gently, being careful not to overwork the fish.

To serve, ladle the cucumber coulis onto the plates. Place a wild rice blini on each pool of coulis. Lay the marinated seaweed onto each blini and top with a large quenelle of tuna tartar. Drizzle the soy-wasabi sauce around the edges of the plate and serve.

51 Lemon Grass Crust Island Ahi with Ginger Rémoulade

Serves 4

For the fish:
1 tablespoon garlic minced
1 tablespoon chopped ginger
1 tablespoon chopped shallots
2 tablespoons chopped lemon grass
1 tablespoon soy sauce
3 tablespoons peanut oil
4 4-ounce ahi fillet steaks (tuna)
1 teaspoon shichimi togarashi
(Japanese seven spice powder)

For the ginger rémoulade:
2 tablespoons chopped celery, minced fine
2 tablespoons chopped onion
2 tablespoons chopped ginger, minced fine
1 tablespoon chopped capers
2 tablespoons parsley, chopped fine
1 cup mayonnaise
1 tablespoon ketchup
1 tablespoon caper juice

For the garnish:
4 tablespoons red caviar
4 tablespoons golden caviar
2 tablespoons pickled ginger
1 bunch radish sprouts
¼ teaspoon shichimi togarashi
1 teaspoon dark sesame seeds
1 teaspoon light sesame seeds

For the fish, mix together the minced garlic, ginger, shallots, and lemon grass with the soy sauce and the peanut oil. Season the ahi steaks with the shichimi and marinate them in the oil mixture for 1 hour.

For the rémoulade, fold the minced celery, onion, ginger, capers and parsley into the blended mayonnaise, ketchup and caper juice. Chill for 1 hour.

To serve, sear the ahi steaks in a hot sauté pan or wok until crusty and medium rare. Spoon a pool of the rémoulade to the top of each plate; slice the seared ahi steaks into 7 medallions and fan them out from the rémoulade. Garnish the tips of the ahi medallions alternating with a teaspoon of the red and the golden caviar; and the rémoulade with the pickled ginger and radish sprouts. Dust the plate with the shichimi and scatter the sesame seeds.

52

Chicken Sun-Dried Tomato Spring Rolls

Makes 35 to 40 spring rolls

For the spring rolls:
2 ounces bean thread noodles
½ pound boneless chicken breasts, cut into 3-inch strips
Salt and freshly ground pepper
2 teaspoons olive oil
1 tablespoon finely chopped fresh marjoram
2 tablespoons finely chopped fresh chives
2 tablespoons finely chopped sun-dried tomatoes
1 1-pound package Banh Trang rice-paper rounds
Peanut oil for frying

To prepare the spring rolls, soak the bean thread noodles in warm water for 15 minutes, or until they are soft. Drain the noodles in a colander and cut them into thirds. Squeeze out any excess moisture in a dish towel.

In a medium-size bowl, combine the chicken strips with the salt, pepper, olive oil, marjoram, chives and sun-dried tomatoes. Add the noodles, mix well, cover with plastic film and let the mixture sit in the refrigerator for about 1 hour.

When you are ready to make the spring rolls, fill a large bowl with warm water. Dip a rice paper round in the water and let it soften a few seconds. Remove and drain on a towel. Place 2 to 2½ tablespoons of the chicken mixture on the edge of the rice paper. Roll the edge over the mixture once, fold up both ends of the rice paper, and continue to roll to the end. The roll should be compact and tight, rather like a short, thick cigar about 3 inches long. Place it on a clean plate and continue the process until you have used up all the mixture.

Heat the peanut oil in a wok or deep-fryer to 350 degrees and deep-fry the spring rolls. They have a tendency to stick to one another at the beginning of frying, so do only a few at a time. Drain the spring rolls on paper towels and serve at once.

52

Couscous Stuffed Yellow Tomato with Tomato Essence

Serves 4

For the tomatoes:
¾ cup cooked couscous
4 ounces wild mushrooms, sautéed in olive oil
1 teaspoon assorted fresh herbs, chopped
Salt and pepper to taste
4 medium vine-ripened yellow tomatoes, tops removed and hollowed out

For the tomato essence:
1 large onion, peeled and chopped
1 head garlic, peeled and smashed
2 tablespoons olive oil
6 large tomatoes, diced
1 quart mushroom consommé
Salt and pepper to taste

For the garnish:
1 head Belgian endive, julienned and braised

For the stuffed tomatoes, warm the cooked couscous in the top of a double boiler and add the mushrooms and herbs. Season with salt and pepper. Stuff the hollow tomatoes with this couscous mixture. Replace the tops of the tomatoes and lightly rub each with a thin coating of olive oil. Roast at 375 degrees for 8 to 10 minutes, or until the tomato is just cooked through and the stuffing is very hot.

For the mushroom infused tomato essence, sweat the onion and garlic in olive oil. Add the diced tomatoes and stew for 6 minutes, stirring frequently. Add the mushroom consommé and simmer for 5 minutes. Blend using a hand-held mixer and pass mixture through a fine chinois. Season with salt and pepper.

To serve, warm the braised Belgian endive and place a few pieces on each plate. Place a cooked tomato in the center of each plate and drizzle the tomato essence around

53

Polenta and Scallop Terrine with Mustard Oil

Serves 6 to 8

For the terrine:
10 to 12 medium to large hand-harvested sea scallops
½ pound fresh spinach, cleaned and blanched
4 cups water
Salt
1 cup organic polenta
1 ear fresh corn, kernels removed
¼ cup sun-dried tomatoes, softened in water and diced

For the garnish:
Mixed greens
Beet juice
Herb coulis

Mustard oil
Coarse honey-mustard

For the terrine, sear the scallops on both sides and cook to medium rare. Remove from the heat and cool. Wrap each scallop in one leaf of blanched spinach, reserving remaining spinach for later use.

In the meantime, cook the polenta. Bring the water to a boil with the salt and slowly whisk in the polenta. Cook the polenta for 20 to 30 minutes until it attains a medium-stiff consistency. Just before the polenta is finished, add the corn kernels and the sun-dried tomatoes. Cool slightly.

Line a terrine with plastic wrap and line the plastic with remaining blanched spinach. Spoon in a layer of polenta. Arrange the spinach-wrapped scallops down the center of the terrine and spoon in the remaining polenta to fill the mold. Chill for 2 to 4 hours in the refrigerator.

To serve, cut a slice of the terrine and warm it slightly. Arrange the slice on the plate with the mixed greens. Drizzle the beet juice, herb coulis and mustard oil around the terrine.Serve with honey-mustard.

54 Tuna Carpaccio

Serves 4

For the sauce:
2 egg yolks
Juice of 2 lemons
Juice of 3 limes
2 tablespoons ginger juice
½ tablespoon grated lime zest
1 cup peanut oil
Salt and pepper to taste

For the carpaccio:
1 tablespoon olive oil
1½-ounce fresh tuna loin

For the garnish:
2 teaspoons chopped chervil
Chervil sprigs

For the sauce, whip the egg yolks with the lemon juice, lime juice, ginger juice and lime zest. Slowly whisk in the peanut oil until fully incorporated and slightly thickened. Season to taste with salt and pepper and set aside.

For the carpaccio, brush two layers of plastic wrap with the olive oil and gently pound the tuna between the pieces of plastic until paper thin. Cut the flattened tuna into 8-inch circles.

To serve, place one tuna circle on each plate and brush with the sauce. Garnish the dish with the chopped chervil and chervil sprigs.

55 Sea Scallops with Couscous

Serves 6

For the couscous:
1 cup tomato juice
¼ cup minced zucchini,
yellow squash and carrot
1 cup couscous
Salt to taste

For the scallops:
12 large sea scallops
24 1½-inch carrot sticks, blanched
24 1½-inch fennel sticks, blanched
1 cup haricot vert, blanched
½ cup curry oil
Salt, pepper and fennel to taste

For the garnish:
6 sheets gold leaf
2 tablespoons julienne basil

For the couscous, bring the tomato juice to a boil, add the minced vegetables and season with salt. Stir in the couscous, cover and remove from the stove. Allow the couscous to steam for 5 minutes.

For the scallops, remove the foot from each scallop and season with the salt, pepper and fennel. Spear the scallops with 2 sticks each of carrot, fennel and haricot vert so that the vegetables are sticking straight up. In a large skillet, heat the curry oil and quickly sear the scallops over a high heat, basting the vegetable-speared scallops with the hot oil. Finish cooking the scallops in a moderate oven for 3 to 4 minutes.

To serve, mound ¼ cup of the tomato couscous on one side of each plate. Place one of the scallops opposite the couscous and the second one on top of the couscous, garnished with the gold leaf. Sprinkle the dish with the julienne basil and hot curry oil.

56 Potato Tasting

Serves 6

For the potato-leek soup:
6 roasting potatoes, diced
1 bunch leeks, washed and finely julienned
½ cup whole butter
4 sprigs fresh thyme
2 quarts chicken stock
¾ cup crème fraîche
Salt and cracked pepper to taste
Parsley oil

For the mashed potatoes:
3 starchy potatoes
White truffle butter

For the potato-corn risotto:
3 shallots, peeled and minced
½ pound fingerling potatoes, diced
2 ears fresh corn, kernels removed
¾ cup chicken stock
¼ cup heavy cream, whipped
1 ounce Parmesan cheese, grated
Chopped chives
Salt and pepper to taste

For the goat cheese:
6 1-inch medallions fresh goat cheese
3 tablespoons flour
1 egg, beaten
2½ ounces potato flakes
Olive oil
Assorted greens

For the napoleon:
2 Idaho potatoes
1 each zucchini and squash
12 shiitake mushroom caps
Olive oil
1 clove garlic, peeled and minced
Assorted herbs, chopped
Salt and pepper to taste
1 large tomato, concasséd

For the soup, sweat potatoes and leeks in butter. Add the thyme and chicken stock and simmer for approximately 12 minutes. Finish with crème fraîche and simmer another 2 minutes. Remove from the heat and chill. Season before serving. Garnish with parsley oil.

For the mashed potatoes, prepare mashed potatoes as usual, but finish with the white truffle butter. Keep warm.

For the risotto, sweat the shallots, potatoes and corn together. Slowly add the chicken stock, one ounce at a time, simmering after each addition so that the liquid is absorbed by the potatoes. Continue until all of the chicken stock is used and the potatoes are tender. Fold in the whipped cream and Parmesan. Finish with chives and season with salt and pepper.

For the goat cheese, dredge the medallions in flour, pass through the beaten egg and coat in the potato flakes. Sauté the breaded cheese in olive oil until golden brown. Arrange with the assorted greens.

To prepare the napoleons, cut the potatoes, zucchini and squash into slices that are 2 inches by 4 inches by ½ inch thick. Brush the mushroom slices and caps with olive oil and coat with minced garlic and chopped herbs. Season with salt and pepper and grill until tender. Assemble the napoleons by alternating potato and vegetable layers. Square off the edges and top with tomato concassé. Using Japanese serving dishes, assemble each item on a tray.

58 Beluga Caviar Gâteau

Serves 4

For the sauce:
2 tablespoons champagne
¼ cup sour cream

For the blini:
1 pound buckwheat flower
9 ounces all-purpose flour
7 ounces sugar
6¾ cups milk
6 eggs, slightly beaten
4 ounces butter, melted
½ teaspoon dried yeast

For the gâteau:
12 blini
8 hard-boiled eggs
½ bunch chives, chopped
12 ounces Beluga caviar
8 long chives for garnish

To prepare the sauce, stir the champagne into the sour cream. If the sauce is too thick, add more champagne until the desired consistency is attained.

To prepare the batter for the blini, combine the buckwheat flour, all-purpose flour and sugar in a bowl. Set aside. In a saucepan, combine the milk, eggs, butter and yeast. Heat this mixture to 150 degrees, then remove the saucepan from the heat. Whisk together the dry ingredients and the heated liquid. Strain the batter through a chinois and refrigerate for 1 hour.

To make the blini, preheat a pancake griddle or large non-stick frying pan to 325 degrees. Lightly brush the surface with a small amount of melted butter. Deflate the batter with a spoon and pour about 3 tablespoons of batter onto the hot griddle to form a pancake approximately 4 inches in diameter. Cook the blini for 1 minute or until the top is bubbly and the bottom is golden. Flip the blini with a spatula and cook for an additional 30 seconds. Remove from the heat. Repeat until all of the batter is used. Keep warm.

To assemble the gâteau, cut the blini into disks that are 2½ inches in diameter. Separate the egg yolks from the whites and pass each through a sieve. Place a 2½-inch ring mold in the center of a plate. Lay one of the blini on the bottom of the ring.

Top the blini with a layer of egg yolk and chopped chives. Cover with a second blini and spread 3 ounces of caviar on top. Lay another blini on top of the caviar and cover with a layer of chopped chives and egg white. Top with a final blini. Remove the ring mold and garnish with the sour cream sauce, Beluga caviar and chives. Repeat 3 times and serve immediately.

59 Ratatouille and Goat Cheese in Phyllo

Serves 4

For the ratatouille:
¾ cup virgin olive oil
2 Japanese eggplant, cut into ¼-inch dice
Salt and pepper to taste
2 small zucchini, diced
2 small yellow squash, diced
1 red pepper, seeded and chopped
1 onion, peeled and diced
2 cloves garlic, peeled and finely chopped
2 medium tomatoes, peeled, seeded and diced
8 leaves fresh basil, chopped
3 sprigs fresh thyme, chopped
1 teaspoon black mustard seeds, soaked overnight in a mixture of ⅓ white wine,
⅔ water and a dash of vinegar
8 sheets phyllo dough
4 slices fresh goat cheese

For the garnish:
Assorted vegetables, blanched
Extra-virgin olive oil
Lemon juice
Tomato consommé
Soaked black mustard seeds (see above)

To prepare the ratatouille, heat 1 tablespoon of the virgin olive oil in a non-stick frying pan. Add the diced eggplant and sauté until soft. Season with salt and pepper and remove to a mixing bowl. Sauté the zucchini, yellow squash and red pepper, individually, in the same way. Combine the sautéed vegetables. Using the same frying pan and another tablespoon of virgin olive oil, sauté the diced onion until light golden in color. Add the chopped garlic and the diced tomatoes and season with salt and pepper. Lower the heat and keep simmering to evaporate the water. Add the sautéed vegetables to this mixture and gently toss over moderate heat for 5 minutes. Stir in the chopped basil, thyme and soaked mustard seeds. Adjust the seasoning and cool.

To form the phyllo bundles, lay 1 sheet of phyllo on the work surface and brush lightly with virgin olive oil. Cover the first sheet with a second and brush again with olive oil. Using a sharp knife, cut the phyllo into strips, 1 inch wide and about 10 inches long. Using a straight-sided round pastry cutter as a mold, lay 1 strip of phyllo over the cutter and press it down to line the mold. Lay a second strip of phyllo across the mold, slightly overlapping the first, and press it down as before. Repeat this procedure with a total of 8 or 9 strips until the pastry cutter is completely lined with phyllo and there is enough phyllo overhanging the mold to be able to envelope the filling.

Spoon the ratatouille into the center of the phyllo and gently pack it down with the back of a spoon. Set 1 slice of goat cheese on top. Enclose the ratatouille and goat cheese in the phyllo by folding the overhanging strips into the center of the mold, one at a time. Gently twist the pastry cutter and remove it. Place the ratatouille and phyllo package on a parchment-lined sheet pan. These bundles can be prepared and refrigerated up to 1 day in advance. Bake in a preheated 425-degree oven until the phyllo turns golden brown, about 6 to 8 minutes.

To serve, warm the blanched vegetables and dress with olive oil and lemon juice. Plate the ratatouille packages immediately from the oven. Drizzle the tomato consommé around the plate and garnish with the soaked mustard seeds.

59 House-Cured Prosciutto with Fava Beans and Polenta Crackers

Serves 4

For the salad:
½ cup of fava beans, blanched
½ small zucchini, diced and blanched
½ small yellow squash, diced and blanched
½ roasted red pepper, peeled and diced
½ small red onion, peeled and finely diced
⅓ cup new pressed olive oil
Juice of 1 lime
Salt and pepper

For the polenta cracker:
1 cup milk
1 teaspoon sugar
1 cup all-purpose flour
2 tablespoons polenta
⅕ cup water
1 tablespoon salt
1 tablespoon olive oil

For the prosciutto:
12 paper-thin slices prosciutto
Black pepper

To prepare the salad, combine the vegetables in a small bowl. Toss with the olive oil and lime juice. Season with salt and pepper.

For the cracker, whisk together the milk and sugar. Work in the flour and polenta to form a soft dough, adding water as needed. Finish with the salt and olive oil. Spread cookie pan and bake in a preheated 375 degree oven until crisp.

To present the dish, place a spoonful of vegetable salad in the center of each plate with some of the dressing running off the side. Cover the salad with the sliced prosciutto. Garnish each plate with a polenta cracker and freshly ground black pepper.

60 Cassolette of Crab

Serves 1

For the cassoulet:
1 egg yolk
1 ounce white wine
½ cup heavy cream, whipped
Salt and cayenne pepper to taste
4 ounces crabmeat, picked over

For the garnish:
Opal basil leaves, julienned
Lemon thyme sprigs
Pinch of saffron powder

For the cassoulet, whip the egg yolk with the white wine over a double boiler until frothy. Remove from heat, fold in the whipped heavy cream and season to taste with salt and cayenne pepper. Place the crabmeat into a casserole, top with the cream mixture and brown until a hot broiler.

To serve, garnish the cassoulet with the julienned basil leaves and lemon thyme sprigs and sprinkle with the saffron powder.

61 Cassolette of Risotto with Mushrooms

Serves 1

For the risotto:
¼ cup heavy cream
1 cup risotto, cooked two-thirds
1 tablespoon butter
1 tablespoon freshly grated Parmesan cheese
1 teaspoon chopped chives

For the garnish:
1 cup mousseron mushrooms, cleaned and stems removed
1 tablespoon butter
Salt to taste
Cracked black pepper
Chervil sprigs

For the risotto, bring the cream to a boil in a casserole, add the precooked rice and butter. Cover the casserole and simmer 5 to 6 minutes. When the rice is tender add the Parmesan cheese and chives and stir gently with a fork.

For the garnish, sauté the mushrooms in the butter until all the water has evaporated. Season to taste with salt.

To serve, top the risotto with the mushrooms and sprinkle with the cracked pepper. Garnish the casserole with chervil sprigs.

61 Cassolette of Shrimp and Scallop

Serves 1

For the sauce:
1 cup red wine
¼ cup gelatinous chicken stock
2 tablespoons butter
Salt to taste

For the shrimp and scallops:
4 large shrimp, peeled and de-veined
2 sea scallops
1 teaspoon curry powder
½ cup cornmeal
2 tablespoons butter
Salt to taste

For the garnish:
1 bunch watercress, washed
and stems removed
½ leek, white part only, julienned
1 tablespoon butter
Salt to taste

For the sauce, bring the wine to a boil and reduce by ⅔. Add the chicken stock, mix in the butter bit by bit and season to taste with salt. Set aside and keep warm.

For the seafood, season the shrimp with salt and curry powder and sauté them in a skillet with 1 tablespoon of butter to desired doneness. Set the shrimp aside and keep warm. Cut the scallops in half and season to taste with the salt and curry powder. Dredge the scallops in the cornmeal and sauté them with the remaining butter until they are crisp on the outside. Set aside and keep warm.

For the garnish, sauté the watercress and leeks in butter until they are tender. Season to taste with salt.

To serve, arrange the watercress and leek mixture in a casserole; top with the shrimp and scallops. Pour the sauce over the dish and serve.

G2 Grilled Potato Bread with Seared Foie Gras

Serves 4

For the potato bread:
2 ounces fresh yeast
½ cup warm water
2 cups mashed Idaho potatoes
2 medium onions, peeled,
diced and caramelized
2 tablespoons butter
2 tablespoons sugar
1 tablespoon salt
2 tablespoons black pepper
6½ cups flour
Egg wash

For the vinaigrette:
½ pint huckleberries
5 ounces rice wine vinegar
10 ounces grapeseed oil
Salt and pepper to taste

For the pecan oil:
½ cup shelled pecans, toasted
½ cup grapeseed oil
Zest of ½ an orange
1 teaspoon maple syrup

For the foie gras:
12 ounces fresh foie gras
Salt and cracked black
pepper to taste

For the garnish:
Olive oil
2 cups assorted greens
Fresh huckleberries

For the bread, soften the yeast in the warm water and allow to sit for 10 minutes. Combine the potatoes, yeast, caramelized onions, butter, sugar, salt and pepper with 2 cups of the flour. Blend well. Allow this dough to proof until double in volume. Punch down the dough and add the remaining 4½ cups of flour to make a smooth dough. Proof a second time until double in volume. Punch down again and shape into loaves scaled to 20 ounces. Proof in loaf pans until doubled. Brush with egg wash and bake at 375 degrees for 20 to 25 minutes until well browned. Remove from pans and cool.

For the huckleberry vinaigrette, bring the huckleberries to a boil with the rice wine vinegar. Cool and allow to sit for one hour. Whisk in the grapeseed oil and season with salt and pepper.

For the pecan oil, place all of the ingredients in a blender and blend until smooth.

To prepare the foie gras, slice the liver into 3-ounce medallions. Season the medallions with salt and cracked black pepper and sear on both sides in a hot pan, cooking the liver until just medium rare.

To serve, slice the potato bread ¾-inch thick. Dip the slices in olive oil and grill lightly on both sides. Place the grilled bread on plates and lay the seared foie gras on top. Arrange the salad greens on the plates and drizzle with the huckleberry vinaigrette and pecan oil. Garnish with the fresh huckleberries and serve warm.

G3 Potato and Truffle Frittata

Serves 4

For the vinaigrette:
⅓ cup aged sherry vinegar
⅓ cup truffle oil
⅓ cup virgin olive oil
2 shallots, peeled and chopped
Salt and black pepper to taste

For the frittata:
1 red onion, peeled and sliced
¼ cup olive oil
2 Idaho potatoes, baked,
peeled and sliced
6 eggs, beaten
2 black truffles, thinly sliced
Salt and pepper to taste

For the garnish:
4 slices pancetta, ⅛-inch thick
4 bouquets mixed greens
Long chives

For the vinaigrette, briskly whisk together all ingredients. Set aside.

For the frittata, sauté the red onion in olive oil in four individual, 3-inch, cast iron skillets. Add the sliced potatoes, beaten eggs and sliced truffles to each. Season with salt and pepper and mix quickly in the pan. Let the eggs brown slightly and flip the frittata to cook the other side. Reserve and keep warm.

To serve, grill the pancetta slices. Arrange the greens on plates. Lay the frittata in the center of the plates with the grilled pancetta. Drizzle the sherry vinaigrette around each plate and garnish with chives.

G3 Stuffed Tomatoes with Mussels

Serves 6

For the tomatoes:
6 ripe tomatoes, peeled
3 dozen mussels
2 tablespoons olive oil
2 shallots, peeled and chopped
1 cup white wine
1 tablespoon chopped parsley
Freshly ground black pepper
2 tablespoons mayonnaise
2 tablespoons mustard
1 tablespoon of the cooking liquid
1 tablespoon chopped parsley
2 medium potatoes, cooked and diced

For the sauce:
½ cup spinach leaves, washed and stems removed
½ cup watercress leaves
¼ cup parsley sprigs
¼ cup chervil sprigs
¼ cup tarragon sprigs
1 cup mayonnaise
Juice of 1 lemon

For the garnish:
1 carrot, peeled and julienned
3 tablespoons extra virgin olive oil
2 tablespoons salmon caviar
Parsley sprigs

For the tomatoes, cut ¼ inch off the bottom of each tomato. Remove all the seeds and most of the flesh. Set the hollowed-out tomatoes aside. Wash the mussels one by one and remove their beards with a sharp knife. In a heavy pot, heat the olive oil, add the shallots and sauté until golden brown. Add the cleaned mussels, white wine, parsley and black pepper. Cover the pot and cook until all the shells are open. Shake the pot well several times during cooking so that all the mussels cook equally. Do not overcook the mussels as they will become leathery and tough. Let the mussels cool in their own liquid. When cool enough to handle, remove the flesh from the shells and strain the liquid. Place the meat in the strained liquid and refrigerate. When the mussels have cooled completely, remove them from the liquid. Save the liquid. In a bowl, mix the mayonnaise, mustard, tablespoon of cooking liquid, and chopped parsley into a smooth sauce. Add the mussels and diced potatoes and mix well. Stuff each tomato with this mixture and refrigerate until ready to serve.

For the sauce, blanch the spinach, watercress and herbs for 30 seconds. Place these greens in a blender with the mayonnaise and lemon juice and blend until completely smooth.

To serve, pour pools of sauce onto chilled plates and top with the stuffed tomatoes. Arrange the julienned carrots next to the tomatoes and drizzle with the olive oil. Garnish each dish with the salmon caviar and parsley sprigs.

G4 Stir-Fried Lobster Thai Stick

Serves 4

For the vinaigrette:
1 cup chicken stock
½ cup rice wine vinegar
½ cup brown sugar
¼ cup soy sauce
¼ cup hoisin sauce
2 cloves garlic, peeled and minced
1 tablespoon minced fresh ginger
2 jalapeño peppers, seeded and minced
2 tablespoons roughly chopped cilantro
1 tablespoon nam plah fish sauce
1 tablespoon Thai Sriracha chili sauce
Juice of 1 lime

For the lobster thai stick:
2 Florida spiny lobster tails
½ cup virgin olive oil
1 tablespoon soy sauce
Juice of 1 orange
Juice of 1 lime
1 small bunch cilantro, roughly chopped
3 cloves garlic, peeled and sliced
Salt and pepper
Sesame oil
8 lumpia wrappers

For the stir-fry:
2 1-inch pieces of daikon, peeled, quartered and thinly sliced
1/4 cup shredded red cabbage
1/4 cup shredded cabbage
1/2 yellow pepper, seeded and finely julienned
1/2 orange pepper, seeded and finely julienned
1/2 red pepper, seeded and finely julienned
2 stalks bok choy, thinly sliced on the bias
6 ears baby corn, cleaned, cut in half lengthwise and sliced into thirds
1 fresh wood ear mushroom, finely sliced
1/2 cup somen noodles, cooked

For the ponzu sauce:
1/4 cup ponzu*
1/4 cup light soy sauce
Juice of 1 lemon
Juice of 2 oranges
2 tablespoons minced ginger
1 bunch scallions, chopped
2 tablespoons sesame oil
2 tablespoons mirin

For the peanut sauce:
1/2 cup dark brown sugar
1/3 cup sherry wine
2 tablespoons mirin
2 cloves garlic, peeled
2 jalapeño peppers, seeded
1/2 tablespoon Thai Sriracha chili sauce
1 1/2 cups peanuts, toasted
1/2 cup light soy sauce

To prepare the vinaigrette, combine the stock and vinegar in a saucepan and bring to a boil. Add the brown sugar, soy sauce and hoisin sauce, whisking vigorously.
Reduce the mixture by one-third to concentrate the flavors. Pour the vinaigrette into a clean container and chill. Once chilled, add all remaining ingredients.

To prepare the thai sticks, split the lobster tails lengthwise and remove the meat from the shell. Discard the shells. Combine the olive oil, soy sauce, citrus juices, cilantro and garlic. Place the lobster meat in this mixture and marinate, chilled, for two hours.

Meanwhile, prepare all of the vegetables for the stir-fry. After the two hours of marinating are up, remove the lobster tails from the marinade and set them aside on a plate. Heat a large sauté pan with sesame oil and sauté the lobster tails. Add one cup of the prepared stir-fry vegetables and sauté until the vegetables are tender, but retain a bit of a crunch. Remove the lobster meat and transfer the vegetables to a bowl to cool.

Cut the lobster into bite-sized pieces. Lift the vegetables out of the bowl and onto a cutting board. Combine the liquid that is left in the bowl with some of the vinaigrette in a saucepan and reduce to make an essence. Finely chop the cooked vegetables and combine them with the lobster meat. Add the reduced essence. Season with salt and pepper.

When this lobster filling has cooled to room temperature, lay one lumpia wrapper on the work surface. Lift up some of the filling with a fork, allowing any excess liquid to drain off, and spread about half an ounce of the filling across the bottom of the lumpia. Roll up the wrapper into a tight roll. Tuck in the sides as you roll and wet the top edge to seal. Repeat with the remaining filling and wrappers. Store the Thai sticks in an airtight container until ready to use.

To prepare the ponzu dipping sauce, combine all of the ingredients and set aside until service.

For the peanut sauce, combine the sugar, sherry, mirin, garlic, ginger and jalapeño in a food processor. Pulse until puréed. Add the peanuts and Sriracha. Drizzle in the soy sauce. Reserve until service.

Just before service, stir-fry the remaining vegetables in peanut oil. When they are just about cooked, add some of the vinaigrette and the cooked somen noodles. Deep fry the thai sticks until golden brown.
Serve with the ponzu and peanut dipping sauces.

*Note: A bitter orange juice product available in Asian markets.

33 Sashimi Tuna with Blood Orange Essence

Serves 4

For the blood orange essence:
1 cup blood orange juice, freshly squeezed and strained
1/2 cup canola or grapeseed oil

For the slaw:
2 chayotes, ends removed, sliced and brushed with olive oil
Salt and pepper to taste

For the dressing:
1 1/2 cups passion fruit juice, strained
2 tablespoons champagne vinegar
1/4 cup extra virgin olive oil
Salt and pepper to taste

4 fresh hearts of palm, cleaned and julienned
1 small red pepper, seeded and finely diced
1/2 poblano pepper, seeded and finely diced
1/2 red onion, peeled and finely diced
1 papaya, peeled, seeded and finely diced
3 scallions, peeled and minced

For the tuna:
4 2 1/2-ounce slices tuna
4 teaspoons virgin olive oil

For the garnish:
Fresh wasabi, cut into shapes
Lemon and lime sections, without membrane

To make the blood orange essence, reduce the juice in a saucepan over medium heat until only ¼ cup remains. Allow the juice to cool slightly. Pour the reduced juice into the bowl of an electric mixer and beat on a high speed. Slowly pour in the oil to make an emulsion. When all of the oil is incorporated, transfer the essence to a squirt bottle and set aside until service.

To prepare the slaw, season the chayote slices with salt and pepper, and grill. Set aside to cool. Slice into a fine julienne, leaving the skin attached.

To make the dressing for the slaw, combine the passion fruit juice and vinegar in a blender and whip on high. Slowly pour in the olive oil. Season with salt and pepper to taste and reserve.

Combine the grilled chayote, hearts of palm, red pepper, poblano pepper, red onion, papaya and scallions in a large mixing bowl. Add enough of the dressing to lightly coat. Season, cover and reserve.

On a firm, smooth cutting board just before service, lightly coat the raw tuna with olive oil and sandwich between two sheets of plastic film. Using a flat, heavy mallet or meat pounder, gently pound the tuna until thin and wide. Note that because the tuna already has a delicate texture, it does not have to be as thin as beef carpaccio.

To serve, transfer the pounded fish to chilled plates. Place a mound of the slaw on the plate and garnish with the lemon and lime sections. Lightly drizzle the blood orange essence over the fish, being sure not to get any on the slaw.

66 Curried Oysters with Apple Vinaigrette

Serves 5

For the vinaigrette:
2⅓ cups extra virgin olive oil
½ tablespoon sherry vinegar
½ tablespoon red wine vinegar
1 teaspoon soy sauce
4 drops Tabasco Sauce
1 pinch cayenne pepper
1 pinch ground coriander
½ apple, peeled, cored and finely diced
6 lime segments, diced
3 grapefruit segments, diced
4 orange segments, diced
½ teaspoon green peppercorns
1 tablespoon diced ginger
1 tablespoon chopped cilantro
Salt to taste

For the oysters:
25 belon oysters
2 tablespoons flour
2 tablespoons curry powder
2 tablespoons olive oil
2 cups assorted greens

For the garnish:
Seaweed, cleaned

For the vinaigrette, combine the olive oil, sherry vinegar, red wine vinegar, soy sauce, Tabasco, cayenne pepper, coriander and 2 tablespoons of hot water in a blender and mix well. Add the remaining ingredients, season to taste with salt and let the flavors infuse for 45 minutes.

For the oysters, shuck the oysters and remove the flesh from the shells. Mix the flour and curry powder and dredge the oysters through the curried flour. Heat the olive oil in a skillet and sauté the oysters for 10 seconds on each side.

To serve, arrange some greens on each shell, top with the warm oysters and drizzle with the vinaigrette. Place the oysters on a bed of seaweed and serve.

67 Stone Crab Cobbler with Key Lime

Serves 4

For the topping:
4 large stone crab claws
4 medium tomatillos
2 ears corn
1 tablespoon butter
2 large shallots, peeled and diced
1 large pepper, seeded and diced
4 sprigs fresh coriander, finely chopped
½ teaspoon ginger, minced
½ teaspoon curry powder
2 tablespoons rum
1 cup coconut milk
Salt to taste

For the cobbler:
1 cup flour
¼ teaspoon salt
1 teaspoon sugar
1½ teaspoons baking powder
1 tablespoon dried Key lime zest
8 tablespoons unsalted butter, diced and chilled
2 tablespoons coconut milk

For the cobbler, preheat the oven to 350 degrees. In the bowl of an electric mixer fitted with the paddle attachment, combine the flour, salt, sugar, baking powder and key lime zest and mix until combined. Add the butter and mix until the mixture resembles sand. Add the coconut milk and mix until just combined. Transfer to a medium bowl and set aside to rest for 1 hour.

Transfer the dough to a lightly floured work surface and roll to ¼-inch thickness. Using a 4-inch round cookie cutter, cut our four circles and transfer to 4 ramekins. Place on a parchment-lined sheet pan and place in the oven to bake until browned, about 5 minutes. Add the vegetable topping and bake for an additional 5 minutes. Remove from the heat and set aside keeping warm.

CQ New Age Steamed Buns

Yields 16 buns

For the basic bun dough:
½ tablespoon sugar
1 teaspoon flour
¼ cup warm water
½ tablespoon dry yeast
2 cups sifted all-purpose flour
1 teaspoon salt
½ cup warm milk
1 tablespoon olive oil

For the chipotle dough:
1 teaspoon minced chipotle peppers
2 tablespoons minced cilantro

For the lemon dough:
1 tablespoon lemon zest
1½ teaspoons finely ground black pepper
2 tablespoons minced parsley

For the black bean filling:
¾ cup cooked black beans
2 tablespoons minced red bell pepper
2 tablespoons minced yellow bell pepper
2 tablespoons minced green bell pepper
½ small red onion, minced
½ jalapeño pepper, seeded and minced
1 teaspoon minced cilantro
1 small clove garlic, minced
Juice of 1 lime
1 tablespoon raspberry vinegar
3 tablespoons olive oil

For the parsley pesto filling:
3 cups chopped parsley
2 cloves garlic, peeled and roughly chopped
1 cup grated Parmesan cheese
2 tablespoons wine vinegar
1½ teaspoons salt
1 teaspoon black pepper
¾ cup olive oil
1 cup sautéed and roughly diced shiitake mushrooms

For the yogurt-cucumber raita:
1 cup plain yogurt
1 small English cucumber, peeled, seeded and grated
1 teaspoon cumin seed, lightly toasted and crushed
¼ teaspoon cayenne pepper
Salt and finely ground black pepper to taste

For the mint-jalapeno chutney:
1 cup loosely packed mint leaves
Juice of 2 lemons
1 jalapeno pepper, seeded and chopped
1 green apple, peeled, seeded and diced
1 orange, peeled, seeded and diced
1 teaspoon salt

For the garnish:
Olive oil
White and black sesame seeds
Cracked black pepper
Chive flowers

For the buns, prepare two batches of the basic steamed bun dough. Dissolve the sugar and 1 teaspoon flour in the water. Add the yeast and whisk until foamy. Combine the flour and salt in the bowl of an electric mixer. Using the paddle attachment, add the milk, oil and yeast mixture and mix just until combined. For the chipotle dough, add the minced chipotle and cilantro.

For the lemon pepper dough, add the lemon zest, black pepper and parsley. Change to a dough hook and knead for 3 to 4 minutes, until the dough is firm. Turn out onto a board and continue kneading by hand until the dough is smooth and satiny. Place in an oiled bowl, cover and keep in a warm place until the dough has doubled in bulk, approximately 1 hour.

To prepare the black bean filling, combine all of the ingredients and refrigerate for at least one hour before using. Store any unused filling covered in the refrigerator for up to one week.

For the parsley pesto filling, combine the parsley, garlic, cheese and vinegar in a blender and purée. Scrape down the sides. With the machine running, add the oil in a thin stream. Adjust the seasoning with salt and pepper. Fold the mushrooms into the pesto.

To shape the buns, roll each dough with the palms of your hands into a cylinder about 2 inches in diameter. Cut each dough into 8 equal portions. Flatten each portion into a circle approximately 3½ inches in diameter.

Place a tablespoon of parsley filling in the lemon-pepper dough and black bean filling in the chipotle dough-in the center and pinch tightly to seal. Place the buns, seam side down, on an oiled, parchment-lined tray. Cover loosely with plastic and set aside at room temperature to rise for 30 minutes.

For the yogurt-cucumber raita, combine all of the ingredients and refrigerate for at least 2 hours before using. For the mint-jalapeno chutney, combine all of the ingredients in a blender and pulse until coarsely puréed, scraping down the sides as necessary.

Transfer buns to the oiled racks of a circular Asian steamer. Set the steamer over simmering water for 10 to 12 minutes. Remove the buns from the steamer and lightly brush with olive oil. Sprinkle the black bean buns with sesame seeds and the parsley pesto buns with cracked black pepper. Serve with the raita and chutney.

69 Artichokes with Fava Beans

Serves 4

For the artichokes:
1 lemon
8 young Cretan artichokes*, with stems
4 tablespoons extra-virgin olive oil
6 scallions, chopped
2 carrots, peeled and sliced
½ cup water
½ cup dry white wine
8 fresh fava bean pods,
  cut into 2-inch pieces
¼ bunch dill, chopped
Juice of ½ lemon
1 egg, separated
2 teaspoons cornstarch
Salt and freshly ground
black pepper to taste

To prepare the artichokes, trim the outer leaves away from the tender heart. Cut the stems to 2 inches and pare away the dark outer layer. Rub the artichokes with fresh lemon and set in acidulated water until ready to use. Heat the olive oil in a medium-sized saucepan. Add the scallions and sauté until tender. Add the carrots, artichoke hearts, water, wine, fava beans, dill, salt and pepper. Cover and let the artichokes steam for 15 to 20 minutes, until tender. Add the lemon juice and cook an additional 5 minutes. Adjust the seasoning with salt and pepper.

To finish the dish, whip together the egg white and cornstarch until light and frothy. Beat in the egg yolk. Slowly whisk the hot cooking liquid of the artichokes into this egg mixture. Pour the whole mixture back into the saucepan with the artichokes and cook for about 30 minutes over low heat until the sauce begins to thicken. Divide the artichokes among the plates, sprinkle with chopped dill and serve.

***Note:** Cretan artichokes are similar to Sardinian artichokes which are small with dangerous spikes on the leaves, long stems and a very tender choke which does not have to be removed. Sardinian-style artichokes are available in specialty produce stores or seasonally in Italian markets.

70 Risotto with Asparagus

Serves 6

For the risotto:
4 tablespoons butter
6 shallots, peeled and minced
1½ cups arborio rice
¾ cup sliced shiitake mushrooms
5 cloves garlic, roasted and peeled
½ cup dry white wine
5 to 6 cups vegetable stock
¼ cup freshly grated
  Parmesan or asiago cheese
Grated zest of 1 lemon
1 bunch young asparagus,
  thinly sliced on the diagonal
1 bunch chives, minced
Salt and freshly ground
  black pepper to taste

For the garnish:
Pea tendrils
Chive flowers
Shaved Parmesan cheese
Fresh asparagus juice

To prepare the risotto, melt 3 tablespoons of the butter in a medium saucepan and add the shallots. Cook over moderate heat until soft, not brown. Add the rice and shiitakes and cook evenly until the rice is translucent, about 3 minutes.

Add the garlic, wine and ½ cup of stock and cook, stirring constantly, until the liquid is absorbed. Continue adding stock and cooking in this manner until the rice is creamy but al dente, about 15 minutes.

When the rice is done, stir in the remaining 1 tablespoon of butter, cheese, lemon zest, asparagus and chives. Correct the seasoning. Serve in warm bowls garnished with pea tendrils, chive flowers, shaved Parmesan cheese and fresh asparagus juice.

71 Modern Sashimi

Serves 1

For the sashimi:
2 to 3 ounces sashimi-quality halibut
½ clove garlic, minced
Finely julienned fresh ginger
Finely julienned scallion
½ teaspoon sesame seeds

For the sauce:
3 tablespoons virgin olive oil
1 tablespoon toasted sesame seed oil
1 teaspoon soy sauce
1 teaspoon yuzu juice*

To prepare the sashimi, fillet the halibut and arrange it in a circle on the plate. Place the julienned ginger and julienned scallion on the fish and sprinkle on the sesame seeds. To prepare the sauce, heat the olive oil and sesame oil to 200 degrees Fahrenheit. Meanwhile, pour the soy sauce and yuzu juice on the fish. When the oil is ready, pour it over the fish. The hot oil will sear the fish. Serve immediately.

***Note:** Yuzu is a special Japanese lime. The juice is available in Japanese food stores.

72 Sashimi with Dressing

Serves 4

For the salad:
8 ounces sashimi-quality fish
(tuna, halibut, white fish)
Salt and pepper
4 ounces mesclun

For the dressing:
2 tablespoons soy sauce
2 tablespoons vegetable oil
2 tablespoons sesame oil
2 tablespoons rice wine vinegar
2 teaspoons water
1 small wedge Maui onion,
peeled and grated
¼ teaspoon freshly ground black pepper
¼ teaspoon sugar
¼ teaspoon salt
¼ teaspoon dry mustard

To prepare the fish, season the fillets with salt and pepper. If using tuna, quickly sear it on both sides and shock in ice water to stop the cooking. Slice the fish and set aside.

To prepare the dressing, combine all of the ingredients in a small bowl and mix well.

To serve, set the mixed greens on plates and arrange the fish on top. Drizzle the dressing over the greens and the fish.

72 Cod Taramasalata

Serves 6 to 8

For the taramasalata:
8 slices firm white bread
¼ small red onion, chopped
1 clove garlic, chopped
¼ cup tarama (cod roe)
Juice of ½ lemon
1 tablespoon white wine vinegar
¼ cup extra-virgin olive oil
¼ cup vegetable oil
¼ teaspoon sugar

For the garnish:
Salmon roe
Mixed greens
Toasts

Note: Taramasalata should be made a day ahead of serving.

To prepare the taramasalata, trim the crusts from the bread and spread the slices out on a tray to dry for about 24 hours.

In the bowl of a food processor, place the onion, garlic, tarama, lemon juice, and vinegar. Blend or process until smooth, scraping down the side of the container several times. With the processor running, gradually add a mixture of both oils through the feed tube. The oil must be added slowly enough so that it forms an emulsion.

Fill a large bowl with cool water. Drop the dried bread into the water, 1 slice at a time. When it is soaked, squeeze out as much water as possible and drop it into the processor feed tube. When all the bread has been added, add the sugar and process until smooth. Taste and add a little more vinegar and lemon juice, if necessary. The finished consistency should be something like softly whipped cream, just firm enough to mound slightly when dropped from a spoon.

Keep in mind that the dip will tighten up as it chills, so if it seems heavy at this point, gradually beat in a little water. Scrape into a serving bowl. Cover tightly and chill for several hours before serving. Garnish with the salmon roe, mixed greens and toasts.

73 Individual Cheese and Tomato Pies

Serves 4

For the pies:

1 sheet puff pastry
1 pint currant tomatoes*
½ pound chlorò,** grated
Dried oregano
Egg wash

To prepare the pies, mold the puff pastry into small tartlet shells. Fill with the tomatoes and grated cheese and sprinkle with oregano. Brush the pastry with egg wash and bake in a 425-degree oven until golden brown.

***Note:** Tomatoes grown on Santorini, like all produce from the island, are small and misshapen because of the stressed growing environment. As a result, the tomatoes are exceptionally sweet and flavorful. The closest substitute available in the United States are currant tomatoes, which are smaller than cherry tomatoes and much more flavorful.

****Note:** Chlorò is a slightly salty, semi-soft, fresh goat's milk cheese with a slightly acidic bite. Any semi-soft goat's milk cheese can be substituted.

78 Poached Sea Scallops with Thyme

Serves 4

For the ravioli:
1½ cups all-purpose flour
1 egg
1 egg yolk
1 dash olive oil and milk
4 tablespoons minced black olives
Egg wash

For the confit of tomatoes:
3 tomatoes, peeled, seeded and chopped
2 tablespoons olive oil
Salt and pepper

For the scallops:
2 tablespoons brunoise chopped leeks
2 tablespoons brunoise chopped zucchini
1 tablespoon butter
2 cups fish stock
48 sea scallops, cleaned
2 Italian parsley leaves, minced
2 basil leaves, minced
3 sprigs thyme, trimmed and minced
2 tablespoons brunoise chopped mushrooms
1 tablespoon capers
2 tablespoons butter
2 tablespoons lemon juice
Salt and pepper

For the ravioli, combine flour, egg, egg yolk and enough olive oil and milk so that mixture comes together into a ball. Knead on a floured surface until soft, yet workable. Let rest 30 minutes.

Roll out ravioli dough and cut into 24 squares. Place a teaspoon olive paste in the center of 12 squares and brush egg wash around edges. Top with remaining squares and press down to seal edges. Bring salted water to a simmer and cook until al dente. Drain and set aside.

For the tomato confit, cook tomatoes in olive oil until soft and liquid evaporates.

For the scallops, sweat brunoise of leeks and zucchini in butter until soft. Deglaze pan with fish stock. Add sea scallops and poach for a minute. Add herbs, mushrooms, capers, lemon juice and butter. Season with salt and pepper.

To serve, place scallop shells atop seaweed. Spoon on ravioli into each shell and top with scallop mixture. Garnish with tomato confit.

79 Baked Salmon

Serves 4

For the sauce:
3½ ounces morels
1 small onion, minced
1 teaspoon butter
3 ounces white wine
2 cups fish stock
1 cup heavy cream

For the salmon:
22 ounces salmon, cut from
the center of the salmon
1 teaspoon coarsely ground salt

For garnish:
½ teaspoon mustard seeds
Boiled, dill-sprinkled new potatoes
2 tomatoes
Finely julienned sorrel

For the sauce, parboil morels twice. Drain and chop finely. Sauté morels with onions in butter until tender. Pour in white wine, stir and let it cook in. Add stock and cream and let sauce cook until it has thickened to a nice consistency.

For the salmon, set the oven at 300 degrees. Clean the salmon pieces-5 to 6 ounces per person-of any bones. Place salmon on an ovenproof plate or pan and sprinkle them with salt. Put the salmon in the oven and let bake in its own juices exactly until fish changes in color from rose-red (Norwegian Fjord Salmon) to light-rose or from light-rose (Swedish Baltic Sea Salmon) to white-rose. The salmon is still elastic and bouncy when touched.

To serve, place on warm plates, sprinkle on the mustard seeds and serve immediately with the sauce surrounding the salmon. Garnish with tomatoes and sorrel.

80 Steamed Seafood in Lotus Leaf

Serves 6

For the dish:
6 pieces lotus leaf
6 sea scallops
6 crab claws
6 shrimp
6 lychees
6 dried mushrooms
6 green onions
6 Chinese chives
Julienne strips of Yunnan ham
Night blossoms
Salt and pepper to taste

For the bundles, poach lotus leaves in hot water for 1 minute. Meanwhile, season scallops, crab claws, shrimp, lychees, mushrooms and green onions with salt and pepper. Place items in lotus leaves. Tie into a bundle with Chinese chives. Steam 7 minutes. Untie bundles and garnish with ham and night blossoms.

81 Scallops with Truffle and Yellow Pepper Oils

Serves 4

For the scallops and beans:
1 pound fava beans
Salted water
24 scallops, cleaned
2 tablespoons olive oil
Salt and cayenne pepper

For the garnish:
4 tablespoons Yellow Pepper Oil
4 tablespoons Truffle Oil
1 yellow pepper

To make the truffle oil, place 2 fresh or canned chopped truffles and 4 tablespoons truffle juice in blender. Purée. Add 1 cup grapeseed oil and blend again until mixture is smooth and emulsified.

To make the yellow pepper oil, slowly reduce 2 cups pepper juice (from 8 to 9 large yellow bell peppers) to ½ cups, in a saucepan over medium-low heat. Strain through a fine mesh strainer and return to saucepan. Reduce until a syrup, no more than ¼ cup. Add 4 tablespoons olive oil and mix. Oil will be thick and sweet.

One day in advance, peel the yellow pepper and slice into very fine strips. Put on a tray in a warm area and allow to dry. Remove fava beans from pods and cut each bean in half. Cook in boiling salted water until tender. Remove and set aside in a warm place.

Heat the 2 tablespoons of oil in a pan until hot. Season the scallops with salt and cayenne pepper. Cook for approximately 1minute per side.

To serve, drizzle yellow pepper and truffle oils on plates. Top with the scallops, fava beans and dried yellow pepper.

81 Steamed Abalone Wrapped in Melon

Serves 4

For the dish:
1 fuzzy melon
Chicken stock to cover melon
8 pieces boneless roasted duck
8 pieces shredded abalone
8 mushrooms, sliced
3 tablespoons crab meat
Vegetable oil for sautéing
1 tablespoon crab roe

For the melon, cover with chicken stock and boil until soft. Drain and set aside to cool slightly.

Steam duck, abalone and mushrooms until just hot. Slice melon and place a portion of duck, abalone and mushrooms onto each melon slice and roll up.

Sauté crab and roe briefly in oil and pour atop abalone rolls to serve.

82 Seared Opakapaka with Lilikoi and Ginger Sauce

Serves 4

For the lobster:
8 lobster bodies
½ cup onion, chopped
¼ cup carrots, chopped
¼ cup celery, chopped
1 tablespoon peanut oil
2 tablespoons fresh parsley, chopped
2 cloves garlic
½ teaspoon fresh tarragon, chopped
1 medium tomato, peeled and seeded
4 tablespoons brandy
1 cup white wine
2 cups water

For the sauce:
1 cup white butter sauce
4 tablespoons lobster paste
3 tablespoons lilikoi juice
(passion fruit juice)
1 tablespoon ginger juice

For the fish:
4 7-ounce opakapaka fillets
4 tablespoons peanut oil
Salt and white pepper to taste
6 sea scallops, diced

For the garnish:
Sprigs of radish sprout leaves

For the lobster paste, brown the lobster shells, the onions, the carrots and the celery in a very hot heavy saucepan with the peanut oil. Add in the parsley, the garlic, tarragon and the tomato; continue to cook for 2 to 3 minutes and deglaze the pan with the brandy and the white wine. Add in the water and simmer the stock for another 40 minutes. Pulverize the vegetables and the shells; strain through a fine sieve and reduce the liquid to a runny paste.

For the sauces, mix ½ cup of the butter sauce with the lobster paste; ¼ cup with the lilikoi juice; and the remaining ¼ cup with the ginger juice.

For the fish, season the opakapaka fillets with peanut oil, and salt and pepper; sear the fillets in a very hot sauté pan or wok, until nicely browned and moist. Add in the seasoned scallops and lightly sauté. To serve, swirl the lobster sauce and the lilikoi sauce together onto the entire plate; set the opakapaka fillet in the middle of the swirled sauces, and scatter the diced scallops around the opakapaka. Swirl the ginger sauce lightly over the scallops and around the entire dish. Garnish each dish with the sprigs of radish sprout leaves.

02 Shrimp with Carrot Cinnamon Oil

Serves 4

For the shrimp:
24 shrimp
Salt and cayenne pepper
2 tablespoons olive oil
16 baby carrots, peeled, blanched and shocked in ice water to stop cooking

For the carrot baskets:
Shredded carrot
Vegetable oil for frying

For the garnish:
4 tablespoons carrot cinnamon oil

To make the cinnamon oil for the Carrot Cinnamon oil, place 3 tablespoons powdered cinnamon in bowl. Add 1 tablespoon water. Mix until a paste is formed. If paste is too dry, add a little more water. Place paste in a mason jar. Add 2 cups vegetable or grapeseed oil to paste. Cover jar. Shake vigorously.

Leave jar on a shelf in the kitchen for two days. Shake oil several times to increase taste. The dry spice will settle to the bottom. After 2 days, with a ladle, remove oil on top and filter just the oil through a coffee filter, or double thickness of cheesecloth. Don't filter solids. Store spiced oil in or out of the refrigerator for up to 1 month.

For the Carrot Cinnamon oil, place 2 cups of carrot juice (from 10 carrots) over medium-high heat and reduce by half. Strain through fine mesh strainer. Place back in saucepan over heat and reduce to a syrup, no more than ½ cup. Add ¼ cup cinnamon oil. Mix well. Add 3 drops of sherry wine vinegar to adjust flavor.

For the shrimp, season the shrimp with salt and cayenne pepper. Sauté the shrimp in olive oil until pink on each side. Keep warm.

For the carrot baskets, press shredded carrots into the inside of a strainer and fry in hot oil until crisp.

Reheat baby carrots.

To serve, arrange shrimp on plate. Fill carrot baskets with the carrots and pour carrot cinnamon oil around the plate.

03 Grouper with Black Beans

Serves 4

For the black beans:
1 pound black beans, rinsed and picked over
1 onion, peeled and stuck with 2 cloves
4 crushed garlic cloves
3 dried hot peppers
1 teaspoon coarse salt
½ teaspoon thyme
½ teaspoon marjoram
¼ teaspoon oregano
¼ teaspoon ground cumin
¼ cup olive oil
2 green onions, chopped

For the grouper:
2 tablespoons black peppercorns, coarsely ground
Small pinch saffron
2 tablespoons olive oil
Pinch coarse salt
½ tablespoon chopped Italian parsley
½ tablespoon chopped fresh thyme
Pinch cayenne pepper
1 small piece ginger, peeled and grated
2 tablespoons honey
4 8-ounce black or yellowfin grouper fillets

For the saffron butter sauce:
½ cup white wine
¼ cup sherry vinegar
2 shallots, minced
1 cup fish stock

1 bay leaf
1 dried hot pepper
2 tablespoons heavy cream
Small pinch saffron
Salt, pepper and lemon juice to taste

For the garnish:
Italian parsley leaves

For the beans, cover beans with 4 inches cold water in a large bowl and soak overnight. Drain. Transfer beans to a large cooking pot and cover with fresh cold water. Add onion, garlic, hot pepper, salt, thyme, marjoram, oregano and cumin. Simmer until tender, about 1 hour. Drain and toss with olive oil and green onions. Set aside.

While the beans are cooking, combine marinade ingredients. Purée in blender or food processor and rub into fish fillets. Let marinate, chilled, for 2 hours.

For the sauce, place wine, vinegar, shallots, stock, bay leaf and hot pepper in a non-aluminum pan over medium heat. Reduce to a glaze. Add cream and reduce slightly. Whisk in butter, bit by bit, adding more once the previous amount has been incorporated. Strain, add saffron, and season with salt, pepper and lemon juice to taste. Keep warm.

To cook grouper and serve, remove fish from marinade and grill or sear over a hot flame. Turn and cook until done, about 4 minutes per side. To serve, place sauce on plate and top with grouper. Garnish fish with black beans and parsley.

84 Steamed Garoupa Rolls

Serves 1 or 2
For the dish:
6 chives
2 pieces garoupa fillet
Salt and pepper to taste
Chinese wine
2 shiitake mushrooms
2 pieces Chinese celery
2 slices Yunnan ham
Lotus leaf

Boil chives until soft. Set aside.

Season garoupa with salt, pepper and Chinese wine. Lay fillet flat and place mushrooms, celery and ham on top. Roll up into two cigar shapes and tie with chives. Cut a round shape of lotus leaf and place into a bamboo steamer. Steam fish rolls for 5 minutes, then serve.

85 Lobster with Cabbage and Corn

Serves 4
For the vegetable sauce:
1 small head savoy cabbage
1 tablespoon butter
4 pearl onions, peeled and quartered
4 baby carrots, peeled and sliced
4 baby zucchini, sliced
3 ears corn, cooked and kerneled removed
1 teaspoon minced chives
Melted butter
2 cups black trumpet mushrooms, cleaned
½ tablespoon vegetable oil
4 tablespoons cold butter
2 tablespoons chopped chives
Salt and pepper to taste

For the roasted lobster:
4 1½-pound lobsters
2 tablespoons vegetable oil

For the lobster stock:
¼ cup sliced shallots
1 sprig thyme
¼ cup diced celery
1 clove garlic
1 tablespoon vegetable oil
1 cup white wine
2 cups water

For the garnish:
Chives
Lobster heads

For the roasted lobster, preheat oven to 450 degrees. Place live lobsters on the rack of a large roasting pan with oil. Roast for 7 minutes, turn over and cook another 5 minutes. Remove and let cool on the side. Crack lobsters open and remove all meat. Reserve the tails and claws. Dice the remainder of the lobster meat and set aside. Save cracked bodies for stock and heads for garnish. For the lobster stock, sweat shallots, thyme, celery and garlic in oil for 3 minutes. Crush lobster bodies and add to casserole. Toss well and add white wine. Let come to a boil for 5 minutes. Add the water and reduce stock down to ½ cup. Strain and reserve.

For the vegetables and sauce, blanch cabbage leaves in boiling water for a few seconds and drain well. Refresh in cold water. Reserve 34 nice leaves for the stuffing. Cut remaining cabbage into julienne strips and set aside. In a casserole with butter, sweat pearl onions, carrots and zucchini for 4 to 5 minutes over medium heat. Add the corn and diced lobster meat. Sweat 2 more minutes. Add minced chives. Spread lobster mixture onto the 4 cabbage leaves and shape into rounds. Brush cabbage rounds with melted butter and place in a warm place. Cut lobster tail meat into slices. Sauté mushrooms in oil in a hot pan for 3 minutes. Warm lobster stock with the julienned cabbage and reduce by half. Add the cold butter to make sauce, the lobster tail slices, claws and chopped chives. Stir well and season with salt and pepper to taste.

To serve, place stuffed cabbage rounds on warm plates. Place sauce, lobster and cabbage around it. Sprinkle plate with chives and scatter with sautéed mushrooms. Garnish with lobster heads.

85 Grilled Tuna with Eggplant Relish

Serves 6

For the tuna:
3 tablespoons olive oil
2 tablespoons sesame oil
1 teaspoon freshly ground white pepper
1 tablespoon soy sauce
6 6-ounce tuna steaks

For the celery cream:
1 bunch celery, washed and diced
½ potato, peeled and diced
½ cup white wine
2½ cups heavy cream
1 tablespoon fennel seed
½ teaspoon pepper
1 pound fresh spinach, washed and diced

For the eggplant:
1 medium eggplant
¼ cup olive oil
½ cup red onion, minced
1 tablespoon minced elephant garlic
¼ cup minced celery heart and leaves
¼ cup minced Italian parsley
2 tablespoons minced mint
2 tablespoons minced purple basil
⅓ cup extra virgin olive oil
1 pint yellow cherry tomatoes, chopped

For the garnish:
Fennel sprigs

For the tuna, combine oils, pepper and soy sauce. Brush mixture onto both sides of tuna steaks. Set aside in refrigerator to marinate for at least 30 minutes. Heat the grill.

For the celery cream, combine celery, potato, wine, cream, fennel seeds and pepper in saucepan. Simmer, uncovered, for 20 minutes. Add spinach and simmer another 3 minutes. Press mixture through a sieve. Reduce this if needed to about 1½ cups liquid. Discard remaining solids and set sauce aside.

For the eggplant, peel and dice eggplant very fine; it should make 2 cups. Warm olive oil in non-aluminum sauté pan. Add onion and wilt; add eggplant to same pan and wilt. Add garlic and celery to the hot eggplant and remove from the heat to cool. When cool, stir in herbs, oil and tomatoes. Set aside.

To finish, grill tuna steaks until medium, about 3 minutes per side. Spoon sauce onto 6 warm plates. Place tuna on plates and garnish with eggplant relish. Garnish with fennel sprigs.

86 Bouillabaisse of Hawaiian Fish

Serves 6

For the fish:
6 tails slipper lobster
1 whole 3 to 4 pound nohu (Hawaiian rock cod) fillet
1 whole 3 to 4 pound hapu'u (Hawaiian grouper) fillet
½ cup olive oil
1 teaspoon saffron powder

For the soup:
Bones and scraps from the fish
4 tablespoons olive oil
2 cups onion, diced
8 garlic cloves
4 tomatoes, peeled and seeded
1 bouquet of herbs, parsley, thyme and leek
2 teaspoons saffron powder
5 quarts water
Salt, pepper and cayenne pepper to taste

For the garnish:
6 tablespoons Aioli
6 seasoned croutons, from a baguette
18 turned potatoes
1 cup onion, fine julienne
1 tablespoon fresh parsley, minced

For the broth, sauté the fish bones and scraps in the olive oil over a high heat. Add in the chopped onions, the tomatoes, bouquet of herbs, the saffron powder, salt, pepper, cayenne pepper, the garlic cloves and the water. Bring this to a boil for 5 minutes and simmer for 1 hour. Pass this through a vegetable mill; strain it and set it aside.

For the fish, cut the hapu'u fillet into 6 3-ounce pieces with the skin on and the nohu fillet into 12 1½ ounce medallions, also with the skin on. Marinate the lobster tails and the fish fillets for 4 hours in the olive oil and the saffron.

For the bouillabaise, put the fish, the lobster and the potatoes in a saucepan over a high heat and pour the hot fish broth over the top. Bring to a boil for 5

minutes and let it continue to simmer for another 8 minutes more.
To serve, sauté the julienne onions in a little oil from the marinade. On each plate arrange the lobster tails, 1 fillet of the hapu'u, 2 medallions of the nohu, 3 turned potatoes, a tablespoon of aioli, 1 crouton, and a mound of the julienne onions in the center. Sprinkle the plates with the minced parsley and present the dish with the broth on the side.

97 John Dory Fillet in Parsley Crust

Serves 2

For the garnish:
1 kohlrabi, peeled and julienned
6 tablespoons butter
1 small eggplant
2 tablespoons olive oil
1 small head broccoli or
1 bunch fresh asparagus tips
½ cup cooked lentils
1 small tomato, peeled and diced
Thyme flowers
¼ cup black olives, pitted and halved

For the sauce:
1 cup fish stock
½ clove garlic
5 ounces butter, softened
¼ cup black olives, pitted
Fresh thyme
Salt and pepper

For the fish:
2 fillets of John Dory
4 tablespoons butter
Salt and pepper

For the garnish, braise the kohlrabi in a couple of tablespoons of butter until tender but al dente. Cut the eggplant in half, lengthwise, and coat with oil. Bake the eggplant in a 350 degree oven until the flesh has softened. Using a spoon, scoop the flesh out of the skin and cut into large dice. Cook the broccoli or the asparagus in boiling water until tender, but crisp. Sauté until lightly brown in butter. Sauté the lentils and eggplant in butter. Keep all the vegetables warm.

For the sauce, simmer the stock with the garlic. Using a blender or food processor, emulsify the stock with the butter and add enough of the black olives to flavor the sauce to your taste. At the last minute, add the fresh thyme to the sauce. Adjust the seasoning with salt and pepper.

For the fish, lightly brown the John Dory in a sauté pan with butter. Season with salt and pepper and keep warm.

To serve, place a portion of the diced eggplant and the sautéed lentils in the center of each plate. Top with a fillet of John Dory. Arrange the kohlrabi, the asparagus or broccoli around the fish. Pour the sauce around the fish and sprinkle with the diced tomato and flowers of fresh thyme.

98 Seared Anglerfish with Lobster Sauce

Serves 4

For the fish:
28 ounces anglerfish, cleaned
Salt and pepper
Vegetable oil or butter

For the garnish:
1 bunch parsley, stems removed
1 small onion, finely chopped
½ red bell pepper, peeled
and cut up in small cubes
2 tablespoons butter

For the sauce:
1½ cups good lobster sauce
2 tablespoons Calvados
½ cup heavy cream

For the seafood croquettes:
¾ cup chopped scallops
½ cup minced shrimp
½ cup chopped mussels
Salt and pepper
¾ cup thick bechamel sauce
or 2 egg yolks
1 cup fresh breadcrumbs
Oil for deep-frying

For the fish, cut fish in pieces that weigh about 3½ ounces each. Count two pieces per person. Heat fry pan thoroughly and add vegetable oil or butter. Season fish with salt and pepper. Sear fish on both sides in pan. Set aside and keep warm.

For the garnish, sauté parsley, chopped onion and bell pepper cubes in butter. For the sauce, bring lobster sauce to a boil and add calvados and the cream. For the croquettes, combine scallops, shrimp and and mussels. Season with salt and pepper. Bind with bechamel sauce or egg yolks into a batter. Chill. Roll batter into 8 balls and dredge in breadcrumbs. Deep fry in hot oil until golden brown.

To serve, arrange parsley mixture in two small mounds on each plate and top with a seafood croquette. Pour warm sauce onto plate and place fish in between croquettes.

89 Poached Onaga with a Three Caviar Sauce

Serves 4

For the dish:
4 fillets Onaga, skin on,
cut into 1 inch thick medallions
2 cups clam juice
½ lemon, juice only
½ cup butter
2 tablespoons Beluga caviar
2 tablespoons American golden caviar
2 tablespoons red lump caviar
2 tablespoons fresh chives, minced

For the chiffonnade:
1 bunch watercress, cut julienne
2 heads manoa lettuce, cut julienne
2 heads baby spinach, cut julienne
4 tablespoons butter
Salt and pepper to taste

For the dish, poach the medallions of onaga in the clam juice on a low heat for 10 minutes. Remove the fish, set it aside to keep warm and reduce the clam juice by half. Add in the lemon juice, whisk in the butter, and stir in the caviars and the chives.

To serve, sauté the greens in the butter and season them with salt and pepper. On individual plates, shingle 5 medallions of the onaga onto a bed of the chiffonnade of greens and then ladle the caviar sauce over the fish; letting some spill over onto the plates.

90 Wok Charred Onaga with a Hibiscus Sauce

Serves 6

For the fish:
1 tablespoon fennel seeds, crushed
2 teaspoons Oriental five spice powder
2 teaspoons fresh ginger. minced
Salt and pepper to taste
2 teaspoons white sesame seeds
2 tablespoons lemon juice
1 cup olive oil
6 7-ounce onaga fillets

For the sauces:
2 cups Tedeschi wine (Maui Blanc)
6 tablespoons shallots, sliced
16 hibiscus flowers
1 cup fish stock
1 cup heavy cream
2 cups butter
Salt and white pepper to taste
1 tablespoon lemon grass, minced

For the garnish:
½ cup lemon grass
12 fried won tons

For the fish, combine the spices and the sesame seeds with the lemon juice and the olive oil; marinate the onaga fillets for 1 hour.

For the hibiscus sauce, simmer 1 cup of the Tedeschi wine with 3 tablespoons of shallots and the hibiscus flowers until the wine is reduced by ⅓; add in half the fish stock and reduce again by ⅓; add in ½ cup cream and let it reduce by ⅓. Remove the flowers and purée them in a blender. Slowly whisk in 1 cup of the butter to the reduced wine and cream; pass the sauce through a fine sieve and blend in the puréed hibiscus flowers. Adjust the seasoning.

For the lemon grass sauce, simmer 1 cup of the Tedeschi wine with 3 tablespoons of shallots and the lemon grass until the wine is reduced by ⅓; add in the other half of the fish stock and reduce again by ⅓; add in ½ cup of cream and let it reduce by ⅓. Slowly whisk in the remaining 1 cup of butter to finish the sauce and pass it through a fine sieve. Adjust the seasoning.

To serve, char the onaga fillets in a very hot wok and place them, skin side up, in the center of each plate. Ladle the hibiscus sauce half the way around the fish from the bottom of the plate; then carefully drizzle the lemon grass sauce over the hibiscus sauce. Garnish the fish with the lemon grass, and set 2 fried won tons to the top of each onaga fillet.

91 Bamboo Steamed Ehu with Oriental Vegetables

Serves 6

For the fish:
6 7-ounce ehu fillets (red snapper)
Salt and pepper to taste
¼ cup fresh ginger, cut julienne
1 tablespoon fresh cilantro, chopped fine
½ cup dry sherry
3 cups salted water
4 red chili peppers
2 Chinese parsley roots

For the vegetables:
¾ cup carrots, cut julienne
¼ cup red bell pepper, cut julienne
¼ cup green bell pepper, cut julienne
½ cup zucchini, cut julienne
¼ cup scallions, cut julienne
¼ cup shiitake mushrooms, sliced
¼ cup snow peas, cut julienne

¾ cup asparagus tips
2 tablespoons sesame oil
Salt and pepper to taste
1 cup lemon grass consommé

For the garnish:
6 tablespoons dark sesame oil, warmed
6 sprigs cilantro
6 sprigs ogo (fresh seaweed)

For the fish, marinate the seasoned ehu fillets in the ginger, cilantro and dry sherry for 30 minutes. Bring the water, steeped with the chili peppers and the parsley roots, to a boil inside a wok. Place the bamboo steamer over the wok and steam the marinated ehu fillets for 6 to 8 minutes.

To serve, stir-fry the vegetables in two tablespoons of sesame oil in a hot wok; season the vegetables and add in the lemon grass consommé. Ladle 1 tablespoon of dark sesame oil onto each plate and place 1 fillet of ehu, skin side up, on the sesame oil. Spoon the stir-fried vegetables, with some of the lemon grass consommé, over the top of the steamed fish; letting the vegetables spill onto the plate, and the consommé run into the sesame oil. Garnish the dish with a cilantro sprig and an ogo sprig.

92 Crayfish Cakes with Wild Rice Salsa

Serves 4

For the cakes:
¼ pound scallops, feet removed
1 egg white
4 tablespoons unsalted butter
¼ teaspoon salt
¼ teaspoon freshly ground white pepper
1 tablespoon tomato paste
¼ cup heavy cream
1 pound cleaned crayfish tail meat
Breadcrumbs for dredging
4 to 6 tablespoons butter

For the salsa:
2 ears fresh corn
½ cup extra virgin olive oil
2 tomatoes, halved and seeded
3 tablespoons sherry vinegar
¾ cup cooked wild rice
Salt and freshly ground black pepper to taste

For the garnish:
1 cut scallion, green part only

For the crayfish cakes, purée the scallops in a food processor, add the egg white, continue to purée until smooth and keep chilled. Using a mixer, cream the 4 tablespoons of butter with the salt and white pepper; gradually add the chilled scallop purée, mixing until completely emulsified. Blend in the tomato paste, reduce the mixer to its slowest speed and gradually pour in the cream until it is just incorporated. Do not overwork the mousse or it will become grainy. Fold the crayfish tails into the scallop mousse, form into 8 cakes and thoroughly coat each cake with the breadcrumbs. Place the breaded crayfish cakes on a parchment-lined sheet pan and refrigerate, covered for at least 2 hours.

For the salsa, coat the ears of corn in olive oil and wrap each one in aluminum foil with the dull side out. Bake the corn on the lower rack of a 400 degree oven for 15 minutes. Remove the ears from the foil and lightly brown them under a hot broiler or in a hot skillet coated with olive oil. Cut the corn from the cobs, chill and set aside. Coat the seeded tomato halves with olive oil, place them in an ovenproof dish and bake for 10 to 15 minutes. Chill the tomatoes, peel away their skins, cut them into small pieces and reserve. In a small bowl combine the vinegar, salt and pepper, and whisk in ¼ cup of the olive oil. Add to this the corn, diced tomatoes and the cooked wild rice.

To serve, melt the remaining butter in a non-stick skillet over a medium-high heat. Bread the crayfish cakes again and sauté them on one side for about 3 minutes until completely done. Remove the cakes from the skillet and drain them on paper towels. Place 2 crayfish cakes in the center of each plate, spoon the salsa around the cakes and garnish with the cut scallion greens.

92 Tuna with Asparagus and Curry Pasta

Serves 4

For the curry oil:
2 cups olive oil
3 shallots, peeled and chopped
1 teaspoon toasted fennel seeds
1 teaspoon pink peppercorns
2 tablespoons curry powder
1 tablespoon coarsely ground salt

For the curry noodles:
3 cups bread flour
3 cups durum wheat flour
4 eggs
4 tablespoons strong curry stock
4 tablespoons curry oil
4 sheets nori (Japanese seaweed)
1 tablespoon soy sauce
Salt and freshly ground pepper to taste

For the sauce:
½ cup yogurt
¼ cup olive oil
1 tablespoon chopped cilantro
2 to 3 tablespoons water
Salt and pepper to taste

For the tuna:
4 5-ounce tuna loin steaks
12 asparagus spears, blanched
2 tablespoons curry oil
1 tablespoon coarsely ground salt
2 tablespoons coarsely ground pepper
1 tablespoon fennel seeds

For the garnish:
1 tomato, peeled, seeded and julienned
12 crisp lotus chips
8 1-inch pieces chives
1 teaspoon finely cut chives
1 teaspoon curry oil

For the curry oil, heat 2 tablespoons of the olive oil in a small saucepan; add the shallots, toasted fennel, peppercorns, curry powder and salt. Stir over low heat for 2 minutes, pour in the remaining oil and simmer slowly for 20 minutes. Remove the pan from the heat, allowing the oil to cool and the spices to settle. Strain and reserve.

For the noodles, sift together the flours and place the mixture on a dry pastry board, making a well in the middle. Lightly beat the eggs, pour them into the well and slowly incorporate the eggs into the flour, adding, alternately, the curry stock and oil until a smooth, elastic dough is formed. Allow the dough to rest, covered, for about 20 minutes and cut into linguine using a pasta machine. Cook the pasta in boiling salted water and drain completely, but do not rinse. Toss the cooked pasta lightly in curry oil and season to taste with salt and pepper. Lay the sheets of nori out on a dry pastry board, brush each one lightly with the soy sauce and roll the seasoned noodles in the nori to form tight cylinders. Reserve, covered, in the refrigerator.

For the sauce, place the yogurt in a stainless steel mixing bowl and whisk in the olive oil, cilantro and enough of the water to thin the yogurt to the desired consistency. Season with salt and pepper and reserve.

For the tuna, using a thin knife make three holes, two lengthwise and one crosswise, through the center of each steak. Slide one asparagus spear through each incision and coat each steak with curry oil and a mixture of the salt, pepper and fennel seeds.

To serve, sear the tuna steaks on a hot grill, turning them carefully to keep from damaging the asparagus. Spoon a pool of the sauce into the center of each plate. Slice the seared tuna, crosswise, splitting down the center of the asparagus, and place the tuna on the sauce. Slice the curry noodle rolls and arrange them around the tuna. Garnish the dish with the julienne tomato, crisp lotus chips, chives and drops of curry oil.

93 Seafood with Fava Beans in Fennel Broth

Serves 4

For the seafood:
¼ cup diced shallots
1 cup peeled, seeded and diced beefsteak tomatoes
2 tablespoons seeded and diced jalapeño pepper
4 small stalks fresh fennel
12 littleneck clams, cleaned
12 mussels, cleaned and beards removed
1 cup fish stock
8 fresh prawns
4 fresh baby squid, cleaned with bodies sliced into rings
4 tablespoons Pernod
1 cup butter
1 tablespoon chiffonade of fresh basil
1 tablespoon chiffonade of fresh mint
Salt to taste

For the beans:
1 cup dry fava beans, soaked or 2 pounds fresh fava bean pods, to yield 2 cups
1 onion, peeled and chopped
2 carrots, peeled and chopped
1 bouquet of herbs
1 quart salted water

For the beans, during the winter use fava beans from last harvest with blond skins. During the summer use fresh fava beans. For the dry fava beans, cook them with the onion, carrots and bouquet of herbs for 1½ to 2 hours, until tender. For the fresh fava beans, bring the water to a boil with the onion, carrots and bouquet of herbs and simmer for 30 minutes; blanch the fresh beans, chill them in an ice water bath, and remove the skins.

For the seafood in fennel broth, put the shallots, diced tomatoes, fava beans, jalapeño pepper, fennel stalks, the clams and mussels in a pot with the fish stock. Bring the stock to a boil and simmer until the clams and the mussels open. Add in the prawns, the squid, and the Pernod; continue to simmer for 3 to 4 minutes, until the squid and prawns are done. Finish with the butter, chiffonade of basil and mint. Adjust the seasoning as needed.

To serve, divide equally into four warm soup plates, garnishing the top of each dish with a fennel stalk and the prawns.

94 Roasted Salmon with Persillade

Serves 4

For the fish:
4 6 ounce salmon fillets
Salt and white pepper
2 tablespoons blanched minced garlic
2 tablespoons finely chopped Italian parsley
2 tablespoons fine toasted breadcrumbs
8 sheets brique, oriental spring roll pastry
4 tablespoons clarified butter

For the sauce:
6 tablespoons veal stock
2 tablespoons blanched minced garlic
½ tablespoon extra virgin olive oil
½ tablespoon lemon juice
Salt and white pepper

For the garnish:
¼ cup blanched fava beans
⅓ cup eggplant strips
⅓ cup peeled red pepper strips
½ cup zucchini strips
4 tablespoons extra virgin olive oil
2 baby artichokes, cooked and quartered
8 cloves roasted garlic
4 small tomatoes, blanched
and peeled, stems on
Salt to taste
¼ cup fried julienne brique pastry

For the fish, season the salmon fillets; in a mixing bowl combine the minced garlic, the parsley and the breadcrumbs; lightly brush the pastry sheets with the clarified butter, placing 2 sheets together so they overlap about 1 inch; sprinkle the buttered sheets with the "persillade" mixture, lay the salmon fillets onto the sheets and wrapping the dough around the fillets. Heat the remaining clarified butter in a skillet, lightly brown the wrapped fillets on each side and roast them in a 450 degree oven for approximately 5 minutes.

For the sauce, reduce the veal stock by ⅔ to a light glaze. In a small saucepan, sweat the minced garlic for 1 minute with the olive oil; add in the veal glaze, the lemon juice, and season; simmer for 1 to 2 minutes.

To serve, place the blanched fava beans, eggplant, zucchini and the red peppers in a sauté pan with the olive oil; bring the oil to a simmer, cover the pan and sweat the vegetables for 30 seconds; add in the artichoke quarters, the roasted garlic and the peeled tomatoes; cover for another 30 seconds and season lightly. Slice the ends from the salmon, slice each fillet into 3 pieces and place each trio, with the salmon facing up, out from the center to the right side of the plates. Arrange the vegetables off from the center of the dish where the three pieces of salmon meet, with the tomatoes set to the top; spoon small puddles of the garlic studded sauce around the plates and garnish the vegetables with the fried julienne brique pastry.

95 Breaded Abalone with Green Herb Sauce

Serves 6

For the sauce:
½ cup watercress leaves
½ cup spinach leaves
½ cup Italian parsley leaves
1 tablespoon lemon juice
1 cup crème fraiche
Salt and pepper to taste

For the abalone:
1½ pound abalone
Seasoned flour for dredging
2 egg whites, beaten
1 cup breadcrumbs
6 tablespoons butter

For the garnish:
18 small white potatoes,
peeled, scored and blanched
2 tablespoons olive oil
1 tablespoon shallots
Salt and pepper to taste
½ cup small spears red tomato flesh
¼ cup small spears yellow tomato flesh
3 tablespoons vinaigrette
Small sprigs of dill, parsley and oregano
6 small edible flowers

For the sauce, purée the watercress, spinach and parsley with the lemon juice in a blender; blend in the crème fraiche and season with the salt and pepper.

For the abalone, slice and pound the abalone between two sheets of plastic into 12¼ inch thick medallions. Dredge the medallions in the seasoned flour, dip in the egg whites and coat with the breadcrumbs.

To serve, sauté the potatoes with the shallots in the olive oil, and season. Quickly sauté the breaded abalone in the butter until golden brown-do not over cook or the abalone will be tough. Set 2 medallions of the sautéed abalone to the edge of each plate on a pool of the herb sauce. Arrange the tomato spears into flowers and set them in the center of the plates; drizzle the flowers with the vinaigrette. Place the sautéed potatoes off from the tomatoes and garnish the dish with the herbs and the small flowers.

95 Triangle of Peppered Tuna

Serves 4

For the lentils:
½ pound green lentils, soaked
2 cups chicken stock
1 tablespoon olive oil
¼ cup julienne smoked bacon
½ cup finely diced carrots
½ cup finely diced onions
2 tablespoons minced shallots
2 tablespoons balsamic vinegar
1 tablespoon finely cut chives
2 tablespoons butter
Salt and pepper to taste
2 cups mashed potatoes, flavored with garlic

For the tuna:
2 pounds tuna loin, cut square
Seasoned flour for dredging
1 egg, beaten
4 tablespoons cracked black pepper
Oil for frying

For the garnish:
½ cup parsley sprigs

For the lentils, bring the chicken stock to a boil, add in the lentils and simmer for 25 to 30 minutes, until they are cooked, but still firm. Drain and reserve 1 cup of the cooked lentils for the pyramids. In a skillet, sauté the bacon in the olive oil; add in the carrots, onions, and the shallots and sauté until the carrots are tender; add in the cooked lentils, deglaze with the vinegar, and add in the chives and the butter; season with the salt and pepper.

For the tuna, slice the loin diagonally into 2 triangles; dredge in the seasoned flour, dip in the beaten egg and completely coat with the cracked black pepper. Deep fry the pepper coated tuna for 20 seconds and finish cooking in a 400 degree oven for 2 minutes- the tuna should be served rare.

To serve, mix the reserved cup of lentils with the garlic flavored mashed potatoes and form into pyramids in the middle of each plate. Slice the rare peppered tuna into 12 triangles and place 3 per plate against each side of the pyramids. Ladle the vegetable studded lentils around the pyramids and garnish the dish with the fresh parsley.

96 Seared Tuna with Red Chili Vinaigrette

Serves 2

For the fish:
½ cup chopped lemon grass
1 tablespoon chopped cilantro
1 tablespoon chopped garlic
1 teaspoon white pepper
1 tuna loin, cut in a triangular shape, 4 inches in length, to have a remaining weight of 8 ounces
4 tablespoons peanut oil
Salt and pepper to taste
1 tablespoon wasabi powder
2 tablespoons cold water
4 tablespoons toasted sesame seeds
4 tablespoons black sesame seeds

For the noodles:
1 tablespoon diced ginger
¼ cup water
¼ cup sugar
2 tablespoons grenadine
½ tablespoon rice vinegar
2 garlic cloves, peeled, blanched and sliced thin
¼ cup peanut oil
½ cup cooked soba noodles
1 tablespoon diamond cut red peppers
1 tablespoon bias cut scallion greens

For the vinaigrette:
1 tablespoon sweet rice vinegar
½ teaspoon chopped garlic
½ teaspoon red chili flakes
1 tablespoon peanut oil
1 teaspoon sesame oil
Salt to taste

For the garnish:
1 medium sized seedless cucumber, peeled and sliced thin
2 small sprigs cilantro
Salt

For the fish, combine the lemon, cilantro, garlic and the pepper. Rub this seasoning mix all over the tuna and marinate for 8 hours in the refrigerator. Whip the tuna clean of all the seasoning, and heat the peanut oil until it is smoking hot in a sauté pan. Season the fish with salt and pepper and sear for 5 seconds on each side; remove from the pan and allow the seared fish to cool. Make a paste with the wasabi powder and the cold water. Brush the seared tuna with the paste, cut in half and grill half in the toasted sesame seeds and half in the black sesame seeds. Do not roll the diagonal cut sides in the seeds. Keep refrigerated until service.

For the vinaigrette, combine the vinegar, the garlic and the red chili flakes in a mixing bowl; whisk in the peanut oil, sesame oil and season to taste. Blend well and set aside at room temperature.

For the noodles, poach the ginger in the water, sugar, grenadine and the vinegar for 15 minutes, drain, cool and reserve. In a small pan, heat the peanut oil to 350 degrees and fry the blanched garlic until golden brown. Toss the cooked soba noodles lightly in a little vinaigrette with the poached ginger, fried garlic, the diamond cut peppers and the scallions.

To serve, lightly salt the sliced cucumber and fan them into a ring around the entire plate. Dish the soba noodles onto the cucumber ring, scattering a few of the pepper diamonds around the edge of the cucumbers. Cut each piece of tuna into 2 slices and place 1 slice of the toasted sesame loin and 1 slice of the black sesame loin overlapping on the middle of the dish. Sprinkle some red chili vinaigrette over the cucumbers and garnish each plate with a cilantro sprig.

97 Mackerel Fillets with Celery Coulis

Serves 4

For the mackerel:
3 leeks, cleaned
Salt and pepper
6 tablespoons peanut oil
4 tablespoons vinegar
1½ pounds mackerel fillets
1 ounce caviar
½ cup crème fraîche
2 tablespoons fish stock
3 tablespoons celery purée
Juice of 1 lemon

To begin, boil the leeks in salted water until tender. Chill and dice into small pieces. Arrange the diced leek into circles in the center of the serving plates. Season with salt and pepper. Drizzle the peanut oil and vinegar over the cooked leeks. Set aside.

Pan fry the mackerel fillets, skin side down, until very crispy. Meanwhile, prepare the caviar cream by combining the caviar, crème fraîche, fish stock, celery purée and lemon juice. Season with salt and pepper. Arrange the mackerel on top of the leeks and sprinkle with salt. Pour the caviar cream around the plate and serve.

97 Santa Barbara Shrimp

Serves 4

For the shrimp:
36 fresh Santa Barbara shrimp
Salt and white pepper to taste
4 tablespoons unsalted butter

For the sauce:
16 garlic cloves, blanched and sliced
½ cup unsalted butter
2 tablespoons lemon juice
2 tablespoons finely chopped chervil
Salt and white pepper to taste

For the garnish:
1½ ounces red caviar
¼ cup fresh chervil sprigs

For the shrimp, remove the heads and the feet. Split the shrimp and thoroughly clean them under cold running water. Season, brush them with butter, and grill for 3 to 4 minutes.

For the sauce, lightly sauté the blanched garlic in 2 tablespoons of the butter; pour in the lemon juice and simmer for 1 minute. Add in the chopped chervil and whisk in the remaining butter over a low heat so the butter does not separate. Season to taste.

To serve, arrange the grilled shrimp in a crown, with the tails in the center, on each plate. Sprinkle the shrimp with the red caviar. Spoon on the sauce and garnish the dish with the chervil sprigs.

98 Lobster Ragoût

Serves 2

For the ragoût:
6 tablespoons butter
2 teaspoons minced shallots
6 tablespoons dry vermouth
Pinch of saffron
6 baby carrots, blanched
4 baby turnips, blanched
6 potatoes, scooped into small rounds and cooked
4 ears baby corn, blanched
12 English peas
6 asparagus spears
3 1½-pound lobsters, blanched and shelled
Salt and white pepper to taste

For the ragoût, melt 2 tablespoons of the butter in a saucepan and sweat the shallots. Add the dry vermouth and the saffron and reduce the vermouth until ⅓ remains. Add in the fish stock with all of the vegetables and reduce the liquid to ⅔. Add in the lobster meat, letting it simmer slowly for 3 to 4 minutes, and finish with the remaining butter, the salt and the pepper.

To serve, arrange the ragoût into 2 warm soup plates, with three whole claws standing around the rim of each dish intermittent with the carrots, tulips and potatoes; and 1 tail standing out from the center with the baby corn, peas and asparagus spears.

99 Zander with Ginger Risotto

Serves 2

For the risotto:
4 tablespoons sake
2 teaspoons finely grated ginger
2 cups basmati rice, cooked
4 tablespoons butter
½ cup toasted pine nuts
Chicken broth as needed
Salt, pepper and sugar to taste
1 tablespoon chopped chives

For the fish:
2 7-ounce zander fillets*
2 teaspoons Oriental five spice powder
Salt and pepper to taste
2 tablespoons oil

For the garnish:
2 tablespoons plum sauce
2 sprigs fresh sage leaves
2 leaves Italian parsley
1 lychee, cut in half

For the risotto, bring the sake and the ginger to a boil. Add the cooked rice with the butter and the pine nuts, stirring constantly. Add the chicken broth as needed, until the rice is hot and moist. Season to taste with the salt, pepper and sugar. Toss lightly with the chives, set the risotto aside and keep warm.

For the fish, make several cuts on the skin side and coat the fillets with the Oriental five spice, salt and pepper. Heat the oil in a skillet and sauté the fish quickly for a crisp golden crust.

To serve, mount the risotto just to the center of the plate, laying the crisped fillet, skin side up, across the risotto. Spoon a small pool of plum sauce to the head of the fish and garnish each dish with the fresh herbs and a lychee half.

*__Note:__ A member of the perch family, this fish is commonly found in the lakes and rivers of Central Europe. The zander is related to the North American Walleye.

100 Broiled Salmon in Horseradish Crust

Serves 8

For the salmon:
3 cups white breadcrumbs
⅔ cup lightly salted butter, softened
8 5-ounce salmon fillets
8 tablespoons freshly grated horseradish
Salt and white pepper to taste
Butter for greasing a sheet pan

For the vodka broth:
½ cup orange juice
½ cup vodka
Juice of 1 lemon
1 tablespoon caraway seeds
2 tablespoons olive oil
½ cup fresh chopped dill
4 tablespoons salmon caviar

Preheat the oven or broiler to its highest setting.

For the salmon, combine the breadcrumbs, butter and horseradish and work the ingredients into a smooth paste. Season this mixture with white pepper. Salt and pepper the salmon fillets and spread them evenly with the horseradish crust mixture. Place the encrusted fillets onto a buttered sheet pan and refrigerate.

For the broth, combine the orange juice, vodka, lemon juice, caraway seeds and olive oil in a non-reactive saucepan. Place the salmon fillets under the broiler crust side up. Do not flip the fillets while cooking. Meanwhile, gently heat the broth without boiling it. When the salmon crust is golden brown, add the fresh dill and salmon caviar to the broth. Pour the broth onto the plates and place a salmon fillet on each.

101 Grilled Tuna with Corn Vinaigrette

Serves 4

For the corn vinaigrette:
3 ears corn
2½ tablespoons corn oil
1½ tablespoons sherry vinegar
2 pinches nutmeg
Salt and pepper to taste

For the peppers and fennel:
2 large red bell peppers
1 to 2 bulbs fennel, cleaned
1 to 2 heads curly chicory
2 tablespoons minced chives

For the tuna:
2 8-ounce tuna steaks
1 tablespoon corn oil
Salt and pepper to taste

For the garnish:
Fennel sprigs

For the corn vinaigrette, shuck corn and boil ears in salted water for 5 minutes. Remove from water, let cool slightly and scrape off kernels with sharp knife. Purée kernels in blender and add oil, vinegar, nutmeg, salt and pepper to taste.

For the vegetables, split, clean and broil peppers until skins are charred. Wash off skin under running water, dry in a towel and set aside. Slice fennel bulbs finely. Mix with chicory and chives. Add 2 tablespoons vinaigrette and toss well.

For the tuna, brush fish with oil and season with salt and pepper. Grill or broil until rare.

To serve, place broiled red peppers on bottom of plates. Arrange fennel and chicory salad on top. Slice and divide tuna between plates. Decorate with fennel sprigs and drizzle corn vinaigrette around plate.

102 Steamed Salmon with Artichokes

Serves 6

For the artichokes:
4 cups water
¾ cup lemon juice
1 cup white wine
30 baby artichokes
1 lemon
2 bay leaves
1 onion, peeled and sliced
18 baby carrots, peeled
½ pound butter, cubed and chilled
12 yellow cherry tomatoes, halved
12 cherry tomatoes, halved
1 bunch chervil, chopped
1 bunch dill, chopped
1 bunch chives, chopped
Salt and pepper to taste

For the salmon:
6 6-ounce salmon fillets,
cut thinly on the bias
Salt and pepper

To prepare the artichokes, combine the water, lemon juice and white wine in a stock pot. Trim the outer leaves of the artichokes to reveal the tender, lime-colored inner leaves. Cut away the prickly tops and trim the dark outer surface of the bottoms. Rub each artichoke with the cut side of half a lemon and set in the pot with the white wine and lemon juice mixture. Add the bay leaves, onion and baby carrots to the pot and cover with a napkin. Set over high heat and bring to a boil, cooking 4 to 8 minutes until the artichokes are tender, but firm. Transfer the entire mixture to another container and cool in the refrigerator. When cool, remove the baby artichokes and carrots, cut each in half and return them to the broth.

For service, season the salmon fillets with salt and pepper and steam until medium rare. Bring the artichoke mixture to a boil. Add the cubed butter, halved tomatoes and herbs. Season with salt and pepper to taste. Spoon this mixture onto serving plates and lay the steamed salmon in the center of the plate. Drizzle with some more of the broth and serve.

102 Roasted Sturgeon with Sauerkraut

Serves 4

For the sturgeon:
12 new potatoes
1 2-pound fresh sturgeon fillet
Salt and pepper
Flour for dredging
5 ounces sweet butter
2 cups uncooked sauerkraut, drained
1 cup white wine sauce,
slightly thickened

For the garnish:
Fresh chives and chervil
2 ounces sevruga caviar
1 tomato, peeled, seeded and diced

To prepare the dish, boil the potatoes in salted water for approximately 15 minutes or until they are tender. Peel. Meanwhile, salt and pepper the sturgeon fillet and dredge in flour. Brown the fillet in butter just until colored, about 1 minute on each side. Carefully wrap the sturgeon fillet in a sheet of aluminum foil and allow to sit for 10 minutes. In a tablespoon of butter, sweat the sauerkraut for 5 minutes until it is warm and tender.

Finish the white wine sauce by adding a couple of tablespoons of butter. Lightly brown the potatoes in butter.

At the top of the serving plates, mound the warm sauerkraut. Decorate with a dab of caviar. Place the potatoes around the sauerkraut. Pour the finished sauce onto the base of the plate. Slice the sturgeon fillet and place around the sauerkraut. Decorate with the caviar, chives, diced tomatoes and chervil.

103 Crusted Cod with Pepper Oil

Serves 4

For the pepper oil:
1 cup extra virgin olive oil
2 red peppers, seeded and chopped
1 jalapeño pepper, seeded and chopped
3 garlic cloves
2 sprigs fresh thyme

For the fish:
4 6-ounce cod fillets
Salt and pepper
1 small zucchini, julienned
¼ eggplant, julienned
1 red pepper, seeded and julienned
1 small onion, peeled and sliced
½ teaspoon chopped thyme

For the garnish:
4 tablespoons balsamic vinegar
Flowering thyme sprigs

For the pepper oil, sauté the peppers in a lightly oiled skillet over high heat until the peppers are dark. Add the remaining oil, garlic and thyme. Simmer slowly for 30 minutes, strain, discard the solids and save the oil.

For the fish, season the fillets with salt and pepper and sauté them in the pepper oil for 3 to 4 minutes. The cod fillets should be crusty but still moist. Remove the fillets from the skillet and keep warm. Sauté the zucchini, eggplant and red pepper in a small amount of the oil with the sliced onion and thyme, until all the vegetables are tender. Season to taste with salt and pepper.

To serve, arrange the cod fillets with the sautéed vegetables as shown. Drizzle the fillets and vegetables with some of the pepper oil and balsamic vinegar and garnish with the thyme sprigs.

104 Matelote of Fish in Ravioli with Riesling

Serves 4

For the ravioli:
7 ounces flour
2 eggs
Olive oil
Salt
Stock

For the filling:
¼ pound mushrooms
1 leek
1 lemon wedge
1 onion, peeled and chopped
1 tablespoon vinegar
Salt and pepper

For the sauce:
Fish heads and bones
3 cups mirepoix

For the matelote:
1 shallot, peeled and chopped
Olive oil
¾ pound pike fillets
¾ pound sandre fillets (pike-perch, pickerel or perch may be substituted)
¾ pound eel fillets
Salt and pepper
1 cup dry Riesling
2 cups fish stock
¾ cup heavy cream
3 tablespoons butter

For the ravioli, mix the flour and eggs with a drop of olive oil and a pinch of salt. Work the mixture into a smooth dough and allow to rest. Using a rolling pin or a pasta machine, roll the dough out as thin as possible. It should be transparent. Cut the dough into rectangles 4 inches by 6 inches. Plunge the pasta into boiling water for several seconds and then chill in ice water. Drain.

For the filling, julienne the mushrooms, reserving the stems for the sauce. Blanch the mushrooms in boiling water with the lemon wedge. Season with salt and pepper and reserve. Finely julienne the leeks and boil until tender. Season with salt and pepper and reserve. Sauté the onion in butter and add a dash of vinegar. Reserve.

For the sauce, make a stock using the fish bones and mirepoix. Pass through a chinois. There should be at least 2 cups of finished stock. Season with salt and pepper.

For the matelote, sweat the shallot in olive oil. Add the fish fillets and season with salt and pepper. Add the Riesling and the stock. Reduce the cooking liquid by two-thirds and add the cream and butter. Mix well and reserve.

To finish the dish, place a large rectangle of pasta that has been parboiled in chicken stock on to a buttered plate. Spread on the julienne of mushroom and leek. Place the fish on top of the vegetables and the onion on top of the fish. Cover with a spoonful of sauce and top with another rectangle of pasta. Seal the ravioli and reheat briefly in a hot oven. Serve immediately.

105 Steamed Black Bass with Spinach

Serves 4

For the sauce:
1 shallot, peeled and chopped
1 tablespoon butter
2 red bell peppers, seeds, membranes removed and chopped
2 kaffir lime leaves
1 cup vegetable stock
3 ounces unsalted butter
Salt and pepper to taste

For the fish:
4 6-ounce black bass fillets
2 tablespoons butter, melted
1 shallot, peeled and chopped
1 tablespoon chopped parsley
1 clove garlic, blanched and julienned
1 tablespoon finely diced lemon rind
1 tablespoon finely diced orange rind
2 tablespoons chopped chives

For the garnish:
1 pound spinach, cleaned and stems removed
1 tablespoon butter
Salt and pepper to taste

For the sauce, sauté the shallots in 1 tablespoon of butter until they become translucent. Add the bell peppers, vegetable stock, lime leaves and simmer until the peppers are tender. Remove and set aside the lime leaves for later use. Purée the peppers in a blender until smooth. Pour the pepper purée back into a saucepan and add the butter bit by bit. Chop the lime leaves and add to the sauce. Salt and pepper to taste and keep warm. For the fish, place the bass fillets in a shallow pan, brush the fillets with butter and sprinkle with the chopped shallots. Cover the pan and steam the fillets. For the garnish, blanch the spinach leaves in salted water for 1 minute. Pour the spinach leaves into a colander and drain well. Toss the spinach leaves with the butter and season to taste with salt and pepper.

To serve, ladle a pool of sauce into preheated plates. Divide the spinach and form into beds. Top with the steamed bass fillets and sprinkle with the chopped parsley, julienned garlic, diced lemon and orange rind, and chopped chives.

106 Steamed Halibut with Flavored Oil

Serves 4

For the oil:
¼ cup virgin olive oil
½ teaspoon coriander
½ teaspoon fennel seeds
¼ teaspoon cumin
¼ teaspoon ground ginger
½ teaspoon paprika
Pinch of ground clove

For the vegetables:
2 carrots, peeled and sliced
1 fennel bulb, sliced
1 tablespoon olive oil
Salt and pepper to taste

For the sauce:
3 ripe tomatoes
Flavored olive oil
Juice of 1 lime
1 bunch chives, chopped
Salt and pepper to taste

For the fish:
4 7-to 8-ounce halibut fillets

For the garnish:
Fennel sprigs

For the oil, mix the olive oil with all the spices. Pour the oil mixture into a bottle and shake vigorously. Keep the oil at room temperature for 24 hours, allowing the flavors to infuse.

For the vegetables, blanch the carrots and fennel in slightly salted water until they become tender. Drain the vegetables, add the olive oil, salt and pepper, and toss. Keep the vegetables warm.

For the sauce, peel, seed and dice the tomatoes. Heat the flavored oil and add the diced tomatoes, lime juice and chives. Season with salt and pepper.

To serve, cook the fillets in a steamer to desired doneness. Place the fillets on preheated plates, top with the sauce and serve with the vegetables. Garnish with fennel sprigs.

107 Brochette of Swordfish with Lentils

Serves 4

For the fennel-onion salad:
1 cup thinly sliced fennel bulb
½ cup thinly sliced red onion
Coarse ground salt and white pepper to taste
1 teaspoon champagne vinegar
1 teaspoon lemon juice
2 tablespoons extra virgin olive oil

For the lentils:
1½ quarts chicken stock
1 cup green lentils, soaked
Salt and pepper to taste
2 bay leaves
¼ cup finely diced carrots
¼ cup finely diced onions

¼ cup finely diced celery
3 garlic cloves, minced
4 tablespoons virgin olive oil
½ cup balsamic vinegar
1 teaspoon chopped rosemary
1 teaspoon chopped thyme

For the brochettes:
1½ pounds swordfish
Salt and white pepper to taste
¼ cup virgin olive oil
4 long rosemary spears
16 fresh bay leaves
(or dried leaves soaked in water)

For the garnish:
1 tablespoon chopped parsley
4 sprigs fresh parsley

For the lentils, bring 1 quart of the chicken stock to a boil. Add the soaked lentils, salt, pepper and the bay leaves. Simmer for 30 minutes and drain. In a heavy saucepan, sweat the carrots, onions, celery and the garlic in the olive oil until the vegetables are soft. Stir in the cooked lentils, pour in the balsamic vinegar and simmer until the vinegar is reduced to a light syrup stirring as you do to keep the lentils from scorching. Add in enough of the stock to cover the lentils, and season with the rosemary, the thyme, salt and pepper. Continue to simmer for about 15 minutes, until the lentils are tender, but still firm.

For the salad, combine the sliced fennel and red onions in a mixing bowl. Season with the salt and white pepper. Pour in the vinegar, the lemon juice and the olive oil; toss together and let the salad stand at room temperature until service.

For the brochettes, cut the swordfish into 16 1½-ounce cubes, season the cubes with salt and pepper and toss them lightly in the olive oil. Skewer the seasoned swordfish onto the rosemary spears, 4 pieces of fish per brochette, alternating with the fresh bay leaves.

To serve, grill the brochettes over a hot flame, for about 4 minutes, turning them to mark each piece of the fish. Keep the tops of the rosemary spears away from the flame. or wrap the ends in foil, to keep the tops green. Arrange the fennel salad on each plate, align with the grilled brochettes. Spoon on the lentils, partially covering the brochettes. Sprinkle chopped parsley over the lentils and garnish the fennel salad with the parsley sprigs.

107 Medallions of Tuna

Serves 1

For the red wine sauce:
2 shallots, peeled and sliced
2 tablespoons mushroom stems and trimmings
1 tablespoon butter
½ cup Cabernet Sauvignon
¼ cup red wine vinegar
1 cup veal semi-glace
1 sprig fresh thyme

For the potato cakes:
2 large Kennebee potatoes
2 shallots
Salt and pepper
Clarified butter

For the mushrooms:
1 clove garlic, peeled and chopped
1 shallot, peeled and minced
4 sprigs fresh thyme
¼ cup olive oil
2 tablespoons white wine vinegar
1 large portobello mushroom

For the tuna:
2 ounces fresh spinach
Salt, pepper and oil
2 3-ounce medallions Ahi tuna
2 1-ounce slices foie grass

To prepare the red wine sauce, sweat the shallots and mushroom trimmings in the butter. Pour in the red wine and the vinegar and reduce by ⅓. Add the semi-glace and the thyme. Reduce by half. Strain.

For the potato cakes, peel and shred the potatoes and the shallots. Season with salt and pepper. With your hands, squeeze as much liquid out of the potatoes as possible. Fluff the mixture with a fork to break up the clumps. Heat the clarified butter in a 6-inch sauté pan. Mound the potato mixture in the hot pan and press and shape it, pulling in the sides, to make a compact disk. Brown the cake on both sides and finish in a preheated 400 degree oven for 10 to 15 minutes. Cut the potato cake into wedges to match the size and shape of the tuna.

For the mushrooms, combine the garlic, shallot, thyme, olive oil and vinegar to make a marinade. Remove the stem of the mushroom and cut the cap into ½ inch strips. Brush the strips with the marinade and grill until tender. Dice the grilled strips.

To finish the dish, warm the diced mushrooms in the red wine sauce. Heat the potato wedges in the oven. Gently sweat the spinach and season with salt and pepper. Drain the spinach and keep warm in a dish towel. Season the tuna with salt, pepper and oil. Grill until rare. While the tuna is grilling, heat a sauté pan for the foie gras. Sear the foie gras slices on one side, turn them over and remove the pan from the heat.

For the assembly, place two potato wedges on a plate and arrange the spinach on top. Place the grilled tuna medallions on the spinach and the foie gras on top of the tuna. Add the fat from the foie gras pan to the red wine sauce and spoon the sauce and mushrooms over the dish.

108 Seafood Boudin with Caviar Sauce

Serves 6

For the boudin:
1 pound scallops
1 live 1-pound lobster
1 pound white shrimp, peeled and de-veined
1 carrot, peeled
Olive oil
4 shallots, peeled and diced
1 bunch thyme, chopped
½ bunch chives, chopped
Salt and white pepper
Natural sausage casing, cleaned and soaked

For the sauce:
1 pound small mussels
1 pound clams
1 cup white wine
4 sprigs parsley
1 bay leaf
2 shallots
1 sprig thyme
½ cup heavy cream
5 ounces butter
Juice of ½ lemon
3 ounces osetra caviar

To prepare the boudin, clean the scallops, shrimp and lobster and cut them into thumbnail-size pieces. Set aside in a large aluminum bowl. Finely chop the carrot in a food processor. Sauté the chopped carrot in olive oil. Add the shallots, thyme, chives, salt and white pepper and sauté until tender. Cool. Combine this mixture with the seafood.

Using a sausage stuffer or a pastry bag with a large round nib, stuff the casings with this seafood filling. Tie off the boudin at 5-inch intervals. Cook the boudin in simmering water for 4 minutes. Remove from the water and discard the string.

For the sauce, clean the mussels and wash the clams of any sand. Put the mussels and clams in a large pan with the white wine and 1 cup of water. Add the parsley, bay leaf, shallots and thyme. Cover the pan and cook over high heat for 4 minutes. The mussels and the clams may be used for another preparation. Pass the cooking liquid through a fine chinois lined with cheesecloth. Place this strained liquid in a small saucepan and add the cream. Reduce for 1 minute. Whisk in the butter and the lemon juice. Just before serving, add the caviar to the warm sauce. To serve, ladle the sauce onto the bottom of each plate. Top with a whole link of the seafood boudin.

109 Littleneck Clams with Potatoes

Serves 6

For the potatoes:
3 medium potatoes
1 cup flour
3 eggs
3 tablespoons milk
1 clove garlic, peeled and chopped
2 tablespoons chopped parsley
1 cup olive oil

For the clams and sauce:
3 shallots, peeled and chopped
2 cloves garlic, peeled and chopped
2 tablespoons olive oil
6 dozen littleneck clams, washed
6 cups vegetable stock
1 tablespoon chopped parsley

For the potatoes, peel the potatoes and slice into ⅛ inch thick pieces. Dredge the potato slices through the flour, shake off the excess flour and set aside. In a bowl, mix the eggs, milk, garlic and parsley into a smooth batter. Heat the olive oil in a flat skillet, dip the potatoes in the egg batter and sauté the slices in the olive oil until they are soft on the inside and crisp on the outside. Remove the potatoes from the skillet and blot on paper towels. Keep the potatoes warm.

For the sauce, in a deep pan sauté the shallots and garlic in the olive oil until they become translucent. Add the cleaned clams, the vegetable stock and chopped parsley, cover and bring to a boil. Simmer until all the clams have opened. Discard any clams that have not opened during the cooking process. Remove the clams from the sauce and keep warm. Reduce the sauce by half and season to taste with salt and pepper.

To serve, return the clams to the sauce, add the potatoes, bring to a boil and serve.

110 Red Snapper with Polenta

Serves 6

For the polenta:
6 cups of water
½ teaspoon salt
2 cups coarse-grained cornmeal
Butter for sautéing

For the snapper:
6 8-ounce snapper fillets
Salt and pepper to taste
3 tablespoons butter
1 cup dry white wine
1cup carrot sticks, blanched
1 cup celery sticks, blanched
1 cup zucchini sticks, blanched

For the polenta, bring the water to a boil in a heavy pot. Add the salt and turn the heat down to medium low so that the water is just simmering. Add the cornmeal in a very thin stream, stirring constantly with a long wooden spoon. Continue stirring for 20 minutes after all the cornmeal has been added. The polenta is done when it tears away from the sides of the pot. When done, pour the polenta onto a cookie sheet and allow to cool. When cool, cut the polenta into desired shapes with a cookie cutter.

For the snapper, preheat the oven to 325 degrees. Season the fillets with salt and pepper. Melt the butter in a sauté pan, and sauté the fillets for 2 minutes on each side. Place the pan in the oven and bake the fish for 6 to 8 minutes, depending on the thickness of the fillets. When done cooking, remove the fish and keep warm. Deglaze the pan with the wine, add the vegetables and simmer until reduced by half. Season to taste with salt and pepper.

To serve, sauté the polenta shapes on both sides in the butter until golden brown. Place the vegetables in the center of the plate, top with the fish and nap with the cooking liquid.

Sautéed Snapper in a Spicy Crust

Serves 4

For the carrots:
½ cup olive oil
2 cloves garlic, chopped
2 oranges
1½ pounds carrots, peeled
1 tablespoon cumin
Salt to taste

For the snapper:
1 tablespoon coriander seeds
1 tablespoon cumin
1 tablespoon fennel seeds
3 cloves
8 black peppercorns
Pinch of nutmeg
4 7- to 8-ounce red snapper fillets
2 tablespoons olive oil
½ cup fish stock
2 tablespoons chopped chervil
1 tablespoon chopped chives
Salt to taste

For the garnish:
Orange peels
Chervil

For the carrots, heat the olive oil in a deep pan, add the chopped garlic and sauté briefly. Remove the rind from 1 orange and cut into a fine julienne. Extract the juice from both oranges. Add the peeled carrots, orange rind, orange juice, cumin and salt to the sautéed garlic and mix well. Cover the pot, bring to a boil and place in a 250 degree oven. Cook for 45 minutes or until the carrots are tender.

For the snapper, put all the dry spices into a blender cup and pulverize them. Evenly cover the fish fillets with the spice mixture. Heat the olive oil in a pan, add the red snapper fillets and sauté the fish on both sides. Finish cooking the fish in an oven to desired doneness. Remove the fillets from the pan, deglaze the pan with fish stock and reduce the sauce by half. Add the chopped chervil and chives and season to taste with salt.

To serve, place pools of the sauce on preheated plates, top with the snapper fillets and garnish with the orange peels and chervil. Arrange the carrots next to the snapper fillets.

Roasted Monkfish with Moroccan Barbeque Sauce

Serves 4

For the sauce:
2½ cups honey
1 cup rice wine vinegar
½ cup soy sauce
1 cup ketchup
Juice of 2 lemons
2 cinnamon sticks
5 star anise
3 cloves garlic, peeled and chopped
1 teaspoon red pepper flakes
1 teaspoon ground cardamom
1 tablespoon coriander seeds
1 tablespoon green peppercorns
1¼ tablespoons dried lavender
1¼ tablespoons chopped fresh ginger
1 teaspoon whole cloves
1 teaspoon ground mace
½ cup chopped cilantro

For the fish:
4 6-ounce monkfish fillets (tail section)
Salt and pepper to taste
2 tablespoons olive oil
2 tablespoons fennel seeds
2 tablespoons pink peppercorns

For the garnish:
4 lattice-cut potatoes, cooked
Cilantro

For the sauce, combine all the ingredients, whisk together and place over medium heat. Bring to a boil, reduce the heat and simmer until reduced by ⅔, whisking occasionaly. Remove from the heat and set aside.

For the fish, season the fillets with salt and pepper. Heat the olive oil in a skillet and brown the fillets evenly on all sides. Drain the oil from the skillet, brush the fillets with the sauce and sprinkle with the fennel seeds and peppercorns. Finish cooking the monkfish in a moderate oven for 3 to 4 minutes. To serve, arrange the monkfish and Moroccan barbeque sauce on plates and garnish with the lattice-cut potatoes and cilantro.

112 Fish Stew with Peppercorn Mayonnaise

Serves 6

For the fish:
2 pounds firm white fish (sea bass, cod and monkfish, for example)
2 teaspoons salt
2 tablespoons finely chopped coriander
1 spring onion, finely chopped
1 tablespoon fresh ginger juice
3 tablespoons olive oil
1 teaspoon sesame oil
Freshly ground black pepper

For the mayonnaise:
8 fresh jalapeño peppers
2 egg yolks
2 small cloves garlic, peeled and finely chopped
1 teaspoon Chinese seasoned salt
Salt and freshly ground white pepper
2 tablespoons orange juice
½ cup olive oil
½ cup peanut oil

For the stew:
2 quarts fish stock
2 thick slices fresh ginger
3 cups tomato concassé
8 ounces snow peas, ends trimmed
4 fresh kumquats, coarsely chopped

To prepare the stew, cut the fish fillets into 1 inch by 2 inch pieces. Combine the salt, coriander, spring onion, ginger juice, olive oil, sesame oil and black pepper in a medium-sized bowl. Add the cubed fish and allow to marinate for 30 minutes.

For the mayonnaise, roast the hot peppers over a gas burner until the skin is charred on all sides. Place the peppers in a plastic bag and close tightly. Allow the peppers to steam for 15 minutes. Cut the peppers in half lengthwise. Peel the skin and remove the seeds. Finely chop and set aside.

Combine the peppers, egg yolks, garlic, seasoned salt, salt, pepper and orange juice in a mortar or food processor. Process until the ingredients form a thick paste. Add the olive oil and then the peanut oil in a slow steady stream, whisking until the oils are fully incorporated. The final result should not be as thick as most mayonnaise. Set aside.

To finish the stew, bring the fish stock to a simmer in a medium-sized pot. Add the ginger slices and simmer the stock for 15 minutes. Remove the ginger with a slotted spoon and discard. Add the marinated fish and simmer for 5 minutes. Add the tomato concassé, snow peas and kumquats and simmer for 5 minutes more. Serve with the mayonnaise.

112 Fried Spot Prawns in Arborio Rice Flour

Serves 4

For the vinegar:
1 tablespoon Dijon mustard
½ cup champagne vinegar
1 tablespoon mustard seeds, toasted
1 small shallot, peeled and minced
Black pepper

For the prawns:
20 spot prawns, peeled with head and tail attached
Buttermilk
1 cup Arborio rice flour
2 tablespoons polenta
Salt and pepper
Peanut oil for frying

To prepare the vinegar, purée the Dijon mustard and champagne vinegar in a blender until smooth. Remove from the blender and add the mustard seeds and shallot. Season with black pepper to taste. Reserve.

For the prawns, soak them in buttermilk. Combine the rice flour and polenta and season with salt and pepper. Dredge the soaked prawns in the rice flour mixture and deep-fry in peanut oil at 375 degrees until crispy and golden brown. Arrange the fried prawns on plates and drizzle with the vinegar.

113 Maine Lobster with Foie Gras Soufflé

Serves 4

For the foie gras butter:
5 ounces fresh foie gras
4 ounces butter, softened

For the Riesling sauce:
2 bottles off-dry Riesling
10 shallots, peeled and chopped
20 white peppercorns
1 cup white grape juice
9 ounces foie gras butter
30 fried grapes
Salt and pepper

For the braised cabbage:
½ medium white onion, peeled and sliced
4 strips bacon, diced
2 ounces unsalted butter
2 heads cabbage, julienned
2 cups chicken stock
Salt and pepper

For the soufflé of foie gras:
1 tablespoon unsalted butter
1 tablespoon flour
4 eggs, separated
¼ cup truffle juice
2 ounces fresh foie gras
Pinch of salt
Pinch of cream of tartar
4 ounces foie gras, diced

For the lobster:
3 gallons water
4 2½-pound lobsters
2 cups lobster stock

For the garnish:
8 small slices foie gras
Chopped chives

To make the foie gras butter, pass the fresh liver through a fine sieve to make a purée. Combine the puréed liver with the softened butter. Chill.

To prepare the Riesling sauce, pour the wine into a saucepan and add the shallots and peppercorns. Bring to a boil and reduce to 1 cup. Add the white grape juice. Finish by mounting with the foie gras butter. Add the fried grapes. Season with salt and pepper.

For the cabbage, sweat the onions and bacon with the butter in a small covered saucepan. Add the cabbage and chicken stock. Season with salt and pepper. Cover the saucepan and simmer until the cabbage is tender, about 20 minutes.

For the soufflé, preheat the oven to 500 degrees. Butter and flour 4 4-ounce ramekins and set them in the freezer. Beat together the egg yolks and the truffle juice in the top of a double boiler placed over, not touching, boiling water. Whisk until light and fluffy. Let cool to room temperature.

Pass the 2 ounces of foie gras through a fine sieve to purée. Mix the purée into the egg mixture. Beat the egg whites with a pinch of salt and a pinch of cream of tartar until stiff. Gently fold the whites into the foie gras mixture. Pour the soufflé into the ramekins, filling them halfway. Divide the diced foie gras among the ramekins and top with the remaining soufflé mixture. Place the soufflés in a deep baking dish and make a water bath, filling the baking dish with hot water until it reaches halfway up the sides of the ramekins. Bake for 15 minutes.

To prepare the lobsters, bring the water to a rolling boil. Plunge the live lobsters into the boiling water and cook for 8 minutes. Remove the lobsters and shock in ice water. Remove the meat from the tails and claws and place them on a half sheet pan. Pour the lobster stock over the meat and cook for an additional 5 minutes in a preheated 400 degree oven.

To finish the dish, saute the slices of foie gras in a very hot pan until browned on both sides. Divide the braised cabbage among four serving plates. Position one souffle, taken directly from the oven on top of each cabbage portion. Lay the lobster meat on and around the cabbage and position the foie gras slices in the lobster claws. Spoon the Riesling sauce over the lobster and garnish with the fried grapes. Sprinkle with chopped chives. Serve immediately.

114 Duck Oysters on Chive Risotto

Serves 4

For the risotto:
1 onion, peeled and minced
1 large clove garlic, peeled and minced
Olive oil
1 cup Arborio rice
Salt and pepper
2 tablespoons white wine
2 cups white duck stock, boiling
8 ounces foie gras, diced
½ cup robiola cheese
½ cup grated Parmesan cheese
2 tablespoons butter
2 bunches chives, finely chopped
Salt and pepper

For the duck oysters:
8 duck testicles
All-purpose flour
Egg wash
Seasoned breadcrumbs
Olive oil

To prepare the rice, sweat the minced onion and garlic in the olive oil. Add the rice and stir until well coated with the oil. Season with salt and pepper. Add the wine and cook on medium heat until dry. Add the hot duck stock one ladle at a time, stirring until the stock is absorbed after each addition. Add the diced foie gras and continue cooking for 2 minutes. Fold in the robiola, the Parmesan and the butter. Add the chives and adjust the seasonings if necessary.

For the oysters, bread the duck testicles with the flour, egg wash and seasoned breadcrumbs. Pan fry the breaded oysters in olive oil until golden brown. Slice each testicle in half. Keep warm.

To assemble the dish, spoon the rice into 4 bowls and place 4 halves of duck oysters on top of each portion. Serve hot.

115 Red Snapper with Champagne Sabayon

Serves 4

For the hash:
½ pound sea scallops, cleaned
Court-bouillon
¼ cup fish and shellfish stock
½ pound unsalted butter, cubed and chilled
Salt and pepper
Assorted seashells

For the sabayon:
¼ cup fish and shellfish stock
4 egg yolks
½ bottle brut champagne
¼ cup heavy cream, whipped

For the snapper:
4 6-ounce fillets red snapper
Salt and pepper
Court-bouillon

For the hash, cook the scallops in the court-bouillon. Remove from the liquid and chop very finely by hand. Bring the fish stock to a boil and reduce by half. Whisk in the butter to make a sauce. Add the chopped scallops to the sauce and heat through. Season with salt and pepper and keep warm.

To make the sabayon, whisk the fish stock into the yolks. Add the champagne and continue beating in a double boiler until thick and ribboned. Keep warm.

To prepare the fish, season the snapper fillets and poach in the court-bouillon.

To serve, fold the whipped cream into the warm sabayon. Arrange the fish on plates and cover with the sabayon. Place the scallop hash in seashells around the fillets.

115 Curried Dumplings with Squid

Serves 4

For the dumplings:
4 potatoes, peeled
1 quart salted water
1 cup durum wheat flour
¼ cup curry powder
½ cup grated Parmesan cheese
1 egg
Salt and pepper to taste
1 quart curry stock

For the squid:
2 tablespoons olive oil
1 shallot, peeled and chopped
8 small squid, cleaned with bodies sliced into rings
1 small zucchini, finely diced
Salt and pepper to taste

For the garnish:
2 tablespoons fresh tomato paste
Cilantro leaves

For the dumplings, cook the potatoes in boiling salted water until tender. Pass them through a food mill (do not use a processor or the dumplings will be gummy) and fold in the flour, curry powder, grated cheese and egg. Season to taste and cool to room temperature. Form the cooled dough into large dumplings, pinched at the top, and cook them for 4 to 5 minutes in the curry stock. Place the cooked dumplings into serving bowls, keep them warm and reduce the stock quickly over high heat.

For the squid, sauté the shallots in the olive oil just long enough to soften them. Add the squid and zucchini, and sauté for an additional 2 to 3 minutes. Season to taste.

To serve, divide the squid and zucchini mixture among the 4 bowls containing the dumplings. Top the dumplings with the tomato paste and pour ¼ cup of the reduced curry broth into each bowl. Garnish the dish with the cilantro and serve

116 Pan-Roasted Pepper Salmon

Serves 2

For the salmon:
2 5-ounce salmon fillets, bones removed
1 tablespoon black peppercorns, cracked
Salt

For the lentils:
1 ounce morels, washed and cut in half
1 clove garlic, peeled and minced
1 large shallot, peeled and finely chopped
2 tablespoons olive oil
1 ounce pancetta, cut into ¼-inch dice, rendered until crisp
3 ounces French lentils, steamed until tender
1 cup chicken stock
1 sprig rosemary, mince
2 tablespoon chopped Italian parsley
2 tablespoons butter, softened
⅓ cup balsamic vinegar
Salt and pepper to taste

For the garnish:
1 small russet potato, peeled, cut into ¼-inch dice and blanched
1 teaspoon chopped Italian parsley
1 head frisée, core removed and cleaned

To prepare the salmon, rub the fillets with the cracked black pepper. Set aside.

For the lentils, sauté the morels with the garlic and shallots in the olive oil. Add the pancetta, lentils and stock. Bring to a boil. Add the rosemary, butter, parsley and balsamic vinegar. Adjust the seasoning with salt and pepper. Add more vinegar, if necessary.

For the garnish, deep fry the blanched potato until golden parsley.

For service, lightly salt the salmon fillets and sear in a hot skillet until medium-rare. Place a small mound of frisée in the middle of plates and lay the salmon on top. Spoon the lentils around the salmon and garnish with the fried potatoes. Serve.

117 Fried Rock Cod

Serves 2

For the champagne and honey sauce:
2 tablespoons honey
3 tablespoons champagne vinegar
3 cups brown chicken stock
Salt and pepper

For the cod:
1 whole rock cod, gutted, trimmed and scored
Salt and pepper
2 tablespoons cornstarch
½ cup peanut oil

For the final assembly:
½ cup champagne and honey sauce
Cucumber pickles
Pickled onions
Pickled pineapple
2 scallions, grilled

To prepare the sauce, caramelize the honey in a saucepan. Deglaze the pan with champagne vinegar. Bring the vinegar to a boil. Add the chicken stock and reduce until the sauce has thickened and the flavors are very concentrated. Adjust the seasoning with salt and pepper and correct the sweet and sour balance with more honey or more vinegar if necessary.

For the cod, season the fish with salt and pepper and dredge in the cornstarch. Heat the peanut oil in a large sauté pan. Fry the fish until crispy and brown on both sides. Remove from the pan and pat dry.

To serve, heat the champagne and honey sauce. Place the fish on a serving platter and pour the hot sauce over the top. Garnish with the pickled vegetables and grilled scallions.

119 Lobster and Sweet Potato Stew

Serves 8

For the stew:
4 live Maine lobsters
Court bouillon
¼ pound bacon, diced
½ red onion, peeled and diced
2 sweet potatoes, peeled and diced
2 bunches fresh rosemary, stems removed
2 yellow tomatoes, peeled, seeded and diced
2 plum tomatoes, peeled, seeded and diced
¼ cup dry white wine
¼ cup brandy

For the lobster cream:
16 shallots, peeled and chopped
2 pounds lobster shells
½ bunch celery, diced
Zest from 2 lemons
½ bunch tarragon, roughly chopped
1 cup dry vermouth
1 cup brandy
2 quarts heavy cream
Salt and pepper to taste

To prepare the stew, blanch the lobsters in the court bouillon for 2 minutes. Cool. Carefully remove the lobster meat from the shells, saving the shells to make the lobster cream. Cut the meat into large chunks.

Sweat the bacon and onions until translucent. Add the sweet potatoes and cook until tender. Add the lobster meat and rosemary and sauté for approximately 2 minutes. Add the tomatoes. Deglaze the pan with the white wine and brandy. Reduce the liquid by half.

For the lobster cream, sauté the shallots with the lobster shells and celery until the vegetables are tender. Add the lemon zest and tarragon. Deglaze the pan with the vermouth and brandy. Add the cream and reduce by half. Pass the liquid through a china cap, then purée in a blender. Pass through fine cheesecloth and keep warm.

Just before service, add 1 quart of lobster cream to the lobster stew. Simmer approximately 2 minutes. Season with salt and pepper and serve piping hot.

120 Striped Bass with Port Wine Sauce

Serves 4

For the sauce:
1 cup Ruby Port
½ cup sherry vinegar
4 ounces unsalted butter
Salt and pepper to taste

For the fish:
4 6-ounce striped bass fillets
4 tablespoons Chinese five-spice powder
Salt and pepper to taste
4 tablespoons oil

For the mushrooms:
1 tablespoon peanut oil
4 whole cèpes, trimmed
1 shallot, peeled and chopped
2 sprigs parsley
3 sprigs thyme
Salt and pepper to taste

For the garnish:
Chives

For the sauce, reduce the Port and the vinegar to a syrup in a heavy saucepan. Whisk in the butter, season to taste with the salt and pepper. Set aside and keep warm.

For the fish, season each fillet with the Chinese five-spice powder, salt and pepper. Sauté in hot oil until crusty on the outside but still moist on the inside. Remove from the skillet and keep warm.

For the mushrooms, heat the oil in a skillet and sauté the cèpes for 2 to 3 minutes until they are crisp on the outside. Add the chopped shallot, parsley and thyme. Continue sautéing until the chopped shallot becomes translucent. Season to taste with salt and pepper.

To serve, cover the surface of each plate with the Port sauce. Arrange the crusted striped bass fillets in the center of each plate and garnish with the cèpes and chives.

121 Cold-Smoked Swordfish with Gnocchetti

Serves 4

For the fish:
4 6-ounce cold-smoked swordfish steaks
Pepper to taste
Olive oil

For the tomato vinaigrette:
6 cherry tomatoes, split
½ cup yellow pear tomatoes, split
1 clove garlic, peeled and minced
1 shallot, peeled and minced
½ cup basil oil
Juice of 1 lemon
1 teaspoon chopped fresh basil
1 teaspoon chopped fresh tarragon
1 teaspoon chopped Italian parsley
Salt and pepper

For the pasta:
1 cup dried gnocchetti
Olive oil

For the garnish:
Basil oil
Fried basil leaves

For the fish, season the swordfish steaks with the pepper. Pan roast the steaks in olive oil to desired doneness.

To prepare the vinaigrette, combine the tomatoes, garlic and shallot in a bowl. Add the basil oil and lemon juice. Toss. Add the chopped herbs and adjust the seasoning with salt and pepper.

Boil the gnocchetti in salted water until cooked al dente. Strain and toss with olive oil to coat.

For the final assembly, combine the cooked pasta with the tomato vinaigrette and gently heat in a sauté pan. Place this warm pasta salad in the center of each plate. Top with a swordfish steak and garnish with basil oil and fried basil leaves.

122 Barbecued Shrimp with Homemade Biscuits

Serves 4

For the biscuits:
½ pound unsifted all-purpose flour
1 tablespoon baking powder
1 teaspoon salt
3 ounces shortening
6½ ounces milk

For the shrimp:
24 large shrimp, peeled to the tail and de-veined
1 tablespoon creole seasoning (recipe shown below)
1 tablespoon cracked black pepper
2 tablespoons olive oil
1 cup heavy cream
4 ounces barbecue base
4 tablespoons sweet butter

For the creole seasoning:
(Yields approximately ½ cup)
2½ tablespoons paprika
2 tablespoons salt
2 tablespoons garlic powder
1 tablespoon black pepper
1 tablespoon onion powder
1 tablespoon cayenne pepper
1 tablespoon dried leaf oregano
1 tablespoon dried leaf thyme

For the barbecue base:
(Yields approximately 1 quart)
10 lemons, peeled and cut in half
2 ounces ground black pepper
4 ounces cracked black pepper
4 ounces creole seasoning
1 quart Worcestershire sauce
1 quart shrimp stock
2 ounces minced garlic

For the barbecue sauce, combine all of the ingredients in a large saucepan. Reduce by half over a low flame until thick. Cool

For the creole seasoning, combine all the ingredients and blend well. Store in an airtight container until needed.

To prepare the biscuits, mix together the flour, baking powder and salt. Cut in the shortening until the mixture resembles coarse crumbs. Add the milk and mix until a soft dough forms. Turn out onto a lightly floured work surface and knead 15 to 20 times. Pat out until ½-inch thick. Cut with a 1-inch biscuit cutter. Bake on an uncreased sheet pan at 425 degrees for 12 to 15 minutes, until risen and golden brown.

To prepare the shrimp, season the shrimp with the creole seasoning and black pepper. Heat the olive oil in a skillet and sauté the shrimp until pink. Add the heavy cream and barbecue base. Reduce the liquid by ¼ and mount with the butter. Serve with the biscuits.

122 Confit of Salmon

Serves 4

For the confit:
2 cups olive oil
4 6-ounce salmon fillets

For the dressing:
½ carrot, peeled and finely diced
¼ celery root, peeled and finely diced
⅔ cup extra virgin olive oil
2 tablespoons balsamic vinegar
1 shallot, peeled and finely chopped
½ avocado, peeled and finely chopped
2 tablespoons chopped dill
Salt to taste

For the garnish:
4 new potatoes
4 purple potatoes
Rock salt and freshly cracked pepper to taste
Dill sprigs

For the confit, heat the oil to 125 degrees. Remove from heat and place the salmon fillets into the oil for 30 minutes.

For the dressing, blanch the carrot and celery root for 1 minute, drain and let cool. Combine the remaining ingredients, season to taste with salt and finally add the diced carrot and celery.

For the garnish, cook the potatoes in lightly salted water until tender, remove from heat and let cool. Peel the cooked potatoes and slice into ¼-inch-thick pieces. Arrange on plates along with the salmon and serve with the dressing. Sprinkle the salmon with rock salt and cracked black pepper. Garnish the dish with dill sprigs.

123 Blini Royal

Serves 3

For the blini:
1 pound buckwheat flour
9 ounces all-purpose flour
7 ounces sugar
6¾ cups milk
6 eggs, slightly beaten
4 ounces butter, melted
½ teaspoon dried yeast

For the eggs:
2 tablespoons sweet butter
6 eggs, slightly beaten
6 tablespoons heavy cream
Salt and pepper to taste

To prepare the batter for the blini, combine the buckwheat flour, all-purpose flour and sugar in a bowl. Set aside. In a saucepan, combine the milk, eggs, butter and yeast. Heat this mixture to 150 degrees, then remove the saucepan from the heat. Whisk together the dry ingredients and the heated liquid. Strain the batter through a chinois and refrigerate for 1 hour.

To make the blini, preheat a pancake griddle or large non-stick frying pan to 325 degrees. Lightly brush the surface with a small amount of melted butter. Deflate the batter with a spoon and pour about 3 tablespoons of batter onto the hot griddle to form a pancake approximately 4 inches in diameter. Cook the blini for 1 minute or until the top is bubbly and the bottom is golden. Flip the blini with a spatula and cook for an additional 30 seconds. Remove from the heat. Repeat until all of the batter is used. Keep warm.

For the eggs, heat the butter in a stainless steel sauté pan. Add the eggs. Whisk the eggs while cooking over moderate heat. Add the heavy cream and season with salt and pepper. Continue whisking and cooking until the eggs form very small, moist curds. Cover with buttered wax paper and set aside. Keep warm.

To assemble the dish, create a lattice border around the plates using the blanched chives. With a ring mold 3 inches in diameter, cut the blini into disks. There should be a total of 12 disks.

Use the ring mold to build the blini royal. Place the ring (you may require 2 to give enough height) in the center of the plate and lay down one of the blini as a base. Place the equivalent of one egg's worth of the cooked egg mixture on top of the blini and spread evenly with the back of a spoon. Place another blini on top of the egg and spread it with a layer of the smoked salmon julienne. Place another blini on top of the salmon and spread a second layer of egg. Top the royal with a fourth blini and lift off the ring(s). Garnish with a dollop of sour cream and a spoon of salmon caviar. Serve immediately.

124 Juniper Smoked Salmon with Trout Roe Sauce

Serves 4
For the salmon:
Coarse sea salt
4 6-ounce salmon fillets, skin attached
Freshly ground white pepper
1 bunch juniper bush

For the sauce:
1 cup crème fraîche
1 bunch dill
2 ounce trout roe
Lemon juice
Salt and pepper to taste

To prepare the salmon, pour an even layer of sea salt on the bottom of a sheet pan. Lay the salmon fillets skin side down on the salt and cover completely with more salt. Allow the salmon to sit for four hours. Remove the salmon from the salt and rinse under cold water. Season the fillets with white pepper and let dry. Place the juniper in the bottom of a smoke box and lay the salmon fillets on the rack above. Cover the smoke box and set it on top of a hot flat-top range. Allow the fish to smoke for 3 to 4 minutes at 400 degrees.

For the four sauce, combine all of the ingredients in a small bowl. Serve the salmon warm with the sauce on the side.

126 Santa Barbara Shrimp with Spicy Sauce

Serves 4
For the shrimp:
8 Santa Barbara shrimp, under 10-count
2 tablespoons plus
1 teaspoon extra-virgin olive oil
3 tablespoons Japanese sake
2 tablespoons soy sauce
½ clove garlic, minced
Juice of ½ lemon
1 teaspoon yuzu juice*
Pinch cayenne pepper

For the garnish:
½ beet, cut into threads
Sprouts

To prepare the shrimp, butterfly the shrimp lengthwise, on the backside, and de-vein. Rinse thoroughly and pat dry. Grill the shrimp until just opaque at the thickest part, about 2 minutes. In a small saucepan, heat the olive oil, sake, soy sauce and garlic until boiling. Remove from the heat and add the lemon juice, yuzu juice and cayenne pepper. Arrange the shrimp on plates and drizzle with the sauce. Top with the beet garnish and fresh sprouts.

*Note: Yuzu is a special Japanese lime. The juice is available in Japanese food stores.

127 Charred Rare Tuna with Port Cream Sauce

Serves 2
For the tuna:
6 ounce tuna fillet
Sesame oil
Pink peppercorns
Fresh ginger, minced
Scallions, chopped

For the sauce:
2 tablespoons pink peppercorns
1 scallion, chopped
¼ cup port wine
2 tablespoons red wine
2 tablespoons soy sauce
1 tablespoon honey
¼ cup heavy cream
1 teaspoon butter
Salt to taste

For the garnish:
¼ bulb fennel, shaved
1 piece bok choy, steamed
Pink peppercorns

To prepare the tuna, marinate it with the sesame oil, pink peppercorns, ginger and scallions for at least 1 hour.

For the sauce, combine the pink peppercorns, scallion, port and red wine in a small saucepan. Bring to a boil and reduce for 1 minute. Add the soy sauce and honey and reduce until thick. Add the cream. Strain the sauce through a fine chinois into another saucepan. Finish with the butter and adjust the seasoning with salt.

Grill the tuna over hot coals for 30 seconds on each side. Slice. Toss the shaved fennel with some of the sauce and place in the center of the plate. Lay the sliced tuna on top of the fennel and ladle the sauce around. Garnish with the steamed bok choy and sprinkle pink peppercorns around the plate.

127 Crispy Skin Salmon with Leek Compote

Serves 1

For the leek compote:
4 tablespoons unsalted butter
3 leeks, white part only, washed and julienned
¼ cup créme fraîche

For the sauce:
2½ cups verjus
½ cup veal stock
4 tablespoons unsalted butter
1 pinch chopped dill
Salt and pepper to taste

For the tomatoes:
2 tablespoons coriander seeds, crushed
3 cloves garlic, peeled and minced
1 pinch coarse salt
2 plum tomatoes, peeled, halved and seeded
½ cup olive oil

For the salmon:
1 7-ounce fillet salmon, boneless with skin attached
2 tablespoons soy sauce
1 teaspoon Chinese five-spice powder
Freshly ground black pepper

To prepare the leeks, melt the butter in a skillet. Add the leeks and sweat until translucent. Drain any excess butter and/or liquid. Deglaze the pan with the créme fraîche and continue cooking until the leeks are tender. Set aside. To prepare the sauce, reduce the verjus to almost dry in a small saucepan. Add the veal stock and reduce by half again. The resulting sauce should be the consistency of a light glace. Mount with the butter and add the fresh dill. Adjust the seasoning with salt and pepper. Set aside.

For the tomatoes, toast the coriander, garlic and coarse salt in a skillet. Add the tomato halves and the olive oil and toss. Cover the skillet with aluminum foil and transfer to a 350 degree oven.

To prepare the salmon, rub the fillet with the soy sauce and season with the Chinese five-spice powder and black pepper. Heat a sauté pan until very hot. Lay the salmon in the hot pan, skin down. Cook on the skin side until almost done. Turn the fillet and continue cooking. Remove the skin and any dark colored patches on the salmon. On a flat-top or in another hot pan, crisp the skin. Finish the salmon in the oven.

For service, ladle the sauce onto a serving plate. Using a ring mold, shape the leeks in the center of the plate. Position the salmon fillet on the leeks and garnish with the roasted tomatoes and crispy salmon skin.

128 Steamed Salmon in Chinese Cabbage

Serves 4

For the salmon:
4 6-ounce salmon fillets
4 large Chinese cabbage leaves, blanched
Sea salt to taste
1 teaspoon roasted ground Szechuan peppercorns

For the sauce:
2 small shallots, peeled and finely chopped
1 tablespoon chopped ginger
2 tablespoons rice wine
6 tablespoons fish stock
1 tablespoon lemon juice
1 tablespoon orange juice
2 tablespoons cold butter, cut in small pieces
Salt and freshly ground white pepper to taste
2 teaspoons finely chopped fresh coriander
2 teaspoons finely chopped fresh chives
1 teaspoon finely chopped spring onion
1 tablespoon finely chopped red pepper

For the salmon, place each fillet on one end of a cabbage leaf. Sprinkle with the sea salt and Szechuan peppercorns. Roll up each leaf, folding in the sides as you go. Steam the wrapped fillets on a plate over simmering water for 8 minutes.

In a saucepan, combine the shallots, ginger and rice wine and cook over high heat until all the wine has evaporated. Add the fish stock, lemon juice and orange juice. Add the juices that have accumulated from the steamed fish. Reduce the liquid by half until it lightly coats the back of a spoon. Whisk in the butter a few pieces at a time. Salt and pepper the sauce to taste. Add the fresh coriander, chives, spring onion and pepper. Cook for 30 seconds. Spoon the sauce over each cabbage-wrapped fillet of salmon.

129 Tempura Tuna Sashimi with Sea Urchin Sauce

Serves 4

For the tuna:
1 pound very fresh ahi tuna fillet
4 sheets nori
4 thin asparagus spears, peeled and blanched

For the sea urchin sauce:
1 tablespoon unsalted butter
1 large shallot, peeled and minced
1 cup dry champagne or white wine
3 ounces fresh sea urchin roe, about 12 pieces
1 cup heavy cream
½ teaspoon wasabi powder mixed with just enough cold water to make a thick paste
½ teaspoon chili flakes
½ teaspoon soy sauce
Salt and freshly ground white pepper to taste

For the tempura batter:
2 eggs
½ cup milk
2 tablespoons sake
1 tablespoon ground ginger
1 scallion, minced
½ cup all-purpose flour
Shichimi togarashi*
Peanut oil for frying

For the garnish:
Red and green shiso leaves
Fine julienne of carrot

To prepare the tuna, use a very sharp knife to cut the fillet into 12 thin strips about 2 inches wide by 7 inches long. Lay the nori, shiny side up, on a flat surface. Arrange 3 slices of tuna on each piece of nori, overlapping the strips, to cover about half of the seaweed. Make the tuna layer thicker at the top. Lay 1 asparagus spear across the center of the tuna and roll the seaweed and tuna very tightly around the asparagus (the asparagus will be in the center of the finished roll). Moisten the remaining half of the seaweed to seal. Refrigerate until needed.

To prepare the sauce, melt the butter in a medium-sized saucepan. Sauté the shallot over medium heat in the butter for 2 minutes. Pour in the champagne, bring to a boil and reduce until only ¼ cup remains. Add the cream and reduce by half. Transfer to a blender, add the sea urchin roe, wasabi, chili flakes and soy sauce and blend until well mixed. Season with salt and pepper to taste and set aside.

To prepare the tempura batter, whisk together the eggs, milk, sake, ginger and scallion. Slowly whisk in the flour until the batter is slightly thick. Flavor with the shichimi togarashi to taste and set aside.

Heat 3 inches of peanut oil in a wok until a drop of batter dropped into the oil sizzles and floats to the surface. Cut each tuna roll in half and dip into the batter, coating thoroughly. Carefully place the batter-dipped roll in the hot oil and fry until golden brown, about 30 seconds. Do not overcook; the fish should be raw.

To serve, spoon the sea urchin sauce in the center of the plate. Slice each roll and arrange around the dish. Garnish with the carrot julienne and shiso leaves.

*__Note:__ Shichimi togarashi is sometimes referred to as Japanese seven-spice seasoning or seven-spice pepper and is composed of szechuan peppercorns, sesame seed, mustard seed, pepper, poppy (or hemp) seed, flakes of nori and powdered tangerine peel. It is available in Japanese specialty stores and should be purchased in small quantities, because it loses its aroma quickly.

130 Florida Seafood with Citrus and Cumin

Serves 6

For the seafood:
½ pound conch meat
6 fresh water prawns
8 ounces tuna loin
6 calamari
12 mussels
Juice of 2 limes
1 small jalapeño pepper, seeded and finely chopped
2 sprigs fresh cilantro, chopped
2 tablespoons olive oil
1 sprig thyme, finely chopped
Freshly ground black pepper
Sea salt
1 sprig rosemary, chopped
1 clove garlic, peeled and finely chopped
1 medium shallot, peeled and diced
½ cup white wine

For the hearts of palm:
2 medium blood oranges
3 medium tangerines
1 large grapefruit
4 small hearts of palm
2 teaspoons black pepper, freshly ground
1 medium jalepeño pepper, seeded and diced
1 large anaheim pepper, seeded and diced
2 tablespoons cumin seed
1 medium red pepper
4 sprigs cilantro, chopped
½ teaspoon ginger, minced
Sea salt
1 teaspoon cider vinegar
1 teaspoon virgin olive oil

Prepare each of the different types of seafood separately. Grill the conch, prawns, tuna and calamari. Slice each and chill. Steam the mussels. Combine the remaining ingredients to make a dressing. Once the seafood is chilled, toss each one separately with dressing.

To prepare the hearts of palm, peel and segment the blood oranges, tangerines and grapefruit. Remove the seed and place the sections in a stainless steel bowl. Finely slice the hearts of palm and add to the citrus segments. Add some freshly ground black pepper and set aside to marinate for one hour.

Combine the jalapeño and anaheim peppers. In a dry pan over medium heat, toast 1 tablespoon cumin seed until slightly browned. Remove from the heat and allow to cool. Add the remaining cumin, red pepper and remaining ingredients to the marinated palm hearts. Chill.

To serve, arrange the seafood on serving plates and garnish with the hearts of palm.

131 Ocean Island Casserole

Serves 4 to 6

For the tofu mixture:
1½ pounds firm tofu
1 tablespoon oil
3 tablespoons arrowroot
1 teaspoon salt
¼ teaspoon white pepper
1 teaspoon agar powder*
1 teaspoon dried marjoram
1 teaspoon dried thyme
2 cloves garlic, peeled and minced
½ teaspoon black pepper
¼ cup chopped wakame**

For the cima mixture:
½ cup finely chopped onions
2 tablespoons olive oil
1 cup whole wheat breadcrumbs
¼ pound seitan, ground
(see recipe on following page)
¼ pound textured soy grits
¼ pound firm tofu, crumbled by hand
2 teaspoons dried marjoram
2 teaspoons dried thyme
2 teaspoons sea salt
1½ cups water
1 cup chopped fresh spinach
½ red bell pepper, roasted,
peeled, seeded and finely diced
½ cup shelled pistachio nuts
1 cup green peas
1 tablespoon agar powder
½ cup gluten flour
2 tablespoons liquid lecithin

For the lobster mushrooms:
12 ounces fresh lobster mushrooms
3 cups water
½ cup white wine
½ teaspoon sea salt
½ teaspoon vegetable soup base

For the renaissance sauce:
1 tablespoon olive oil
½ medium onion, peeled and diced
¼ cup fresh fennel, diced
2 cloves garlic, peeled and minced
2 tablespoons chopped fresh basil
1 teaspoon fresh oregano
1 teaspoon fresh thyme
1 teaspoon fresh marjoram
8 saffron threads
1 red bell pepper, roasted,
peeled, seeded and chopped
1 yellow bell pepper, roasted, peeled,
seeded and chopped
½ cup red pepper juice
½ teaspoon sea salt
8 ripe tomatoes, peeled and crushed

For the garnish:
Miniature beets, blanched
Broccoli florets, blanched
Brussels sprouts, blanched
Pearl onions, blanched
Daikon, cut into a net
Carrot threads

For the seitan:
Yields 1 pound, cooked
6 cups stone-ground whole
wheat bread flour or high-gluten
unbleached white flour
3 cups water
½ cup tamarin
12 slices fresh ginger
1 3-inch piece kombu

Seitan is a meat substitute made from wheat protein. The following recipe comes from Friendly Foods by Ron Pickarski.

To prepare the seitan, mix the flour and water by hand or in a machine to make a medium-stiff but not sticky dough. More water may be necessary to form the dough. Knead the dough by hand on a breadboard or tabletop, until it has the consistency of an earlobe, or by machine until the dough forms a ball that follows the path of the hook around the bowl Knead for 10 to 12 minutes by hand, 6 to 8 minutes by machine. Allow the dough to rest in a bowl of cold water for about 10 minutes. While the dough is resting, prepare the stock. In a large pot, bring to boil 3 quarts of water. Add the tamarin, ginger and kombu and cook for 15 minutes. Remove from the heat and set aside to cool. This stock must be cold before it is used.
The dough must be kneaded under water to remove the starch. Begin with a large bowl filled with warm water. Knead the dough, immersed in the widower, until the water turns milky. Drain off the water and refill the bowl with fresh water. Repeat this procedure through 8 changes of water. The dough will feel firmer and more elastic and the water will no longer become cloudy. Be sure to work toward the center of the dough so that it does not break into pieces. For the last few changes of water, use cold water to tighten the dough. To make sure the dough is kneaded enough, lift it out of the water and squeeze it. The liquid oozing out should be clear, hot, and milky.
To shape the seitan, lightly oil a 1-pound loaf pan. Place the rinsed seitan in the pan and let rest until the dough relaxes. After it has rested for 10 minutes, it will be much more flexible. The seitan is cooked in 2 steps. Bring 3 quarts of unsalted water to a boil. Boil the seitan for 30 to 45 minutes, or until it floats to the surface. Drain the seitan and cut it into usable pieces (steaks, cutlets or medallions). Return the seitan to the cold tamarin stock. Bring the stock to a boil, lower the temperature and simmer the seitan for 1½ to 2 hours (45 minutes for smaller cut pieces). To store the seitan, keep it refrigerated, immersed in the tamarin stock.

To prepare the tofu filling, wash the tofu and pat it dry. Cut it into small pieces and place in a blender with all of the remaining ingredients. Blend until smooth.

For the cima mixture, sauté the onion in the olive oil until translucent. Remove from the heat. Add the breadcrumbs, seitan, soy grits, tofu, seasoning and water to the onions. Mix well. Add the spinach, roasted pepper, pistachios and green peas. In a small bowl, mix the agar powder with the gluten flour. Warm the liquid lecithin and add it to the onion mixture. Stir well. You will have twice as much of this mixture as you need for this recipe. You can use the cima mixture as a meat substitute in other recipes. Shape the cima mixture into a square log. Spread the tofu mixture evenly on a piece of plastic wrap about 28 inches long by 12 inches wide. Gently place the cima log on the tofu mixture and wrap with the tofu-coated plastic. Smooth out the tofu mixture seam around the cima log. Steam the log for about 30 minutes. Remove from the heat, cool for 10 minutes and remove the plastic wrap. Meanwhile, poach the lobster mushrooms. Place all of the ingredients in a 2-quart saucepan and bring to a boil. Simmer for 10 minutes. Remove the mushrooms and slice.

For the renaissance sauce, heat the oil in a large sauté pan. Sauté the onion, fennel, garlic and herbs over medium heat until tender, about 5 to 8 minutes. Add the roasted peppers, pepper juice, sea salt and tomatoes and bring to a simmer. Cook for an additional 10 minutes. Remove from the heat, transfer to a blender and blend until smooth.

To serve, slice the cima loaf into thin slices and arrange with the vegetable garnishes, warm poached lobster mushrooms and hot renaissance sauce.

***Note:** Agar, also known as kanten, is used as a thickener or vegetarian substitute for gelatin. It is derived from the algae agar-agar and is available in powder flakes and bars. If using flakes or bars, the agar must be cooked for about 10 minutes in an oil-free liquid to dissolve.
** Wakame is a Japanese sea vegetable that is available fresh or dried. If using dried, soak for 30 minutes in warm water.

131 Lobster and Shrimp with Thai Curries

Serves 4

For the green curry:
1 teaspoon minced fresh galanga root
2 shallots, peeled and minced
1 clove garlic, peeled and minced
1 teaspoon minced Kaffir lime zest
3 teaspoons minced fresh lemon gras
2 to 3 small fresh green Asian chilies, seeded
½ cup coconut milk
Thai fish sauce (nam plah) to taste

For the red curry:
1 teaspoon minced fresh galanga root
2 shallots, peeled and minced
1 clove garlic, peeled and minced
1 teaspoon minced Kaffir lime zest
3 teaspoons minced fresh lemon gras
2 to 3 small fresh red Asian chilies, seeded
½ cup coconut milk
Thai fish sauce (nam plah) to taste

For the red rice noodle cake:
4 ounces rice threads
2 red peppers, roasted,
peeled, seeded and puréed
Salt and pepper to taste
Peanut oil for frying

For the seafood:
2 small lobsters, steamed until medium-rare
8 shrimp, shelled, de-veined and steamed until medium-rare

For the garnish:
6 ounces black trumpet mushrooms, cleaned
2 tablespoons peanut oil
Salt and pepper to taste
Fresh herbs

To prepare the green curry, combine the galanga, shallots, garlic, lime zest, lemon gras and green chilies in a blender and blend to form a smooth paste. Repeat the process for the red chili paste, using the red chilies instead of the green chilies. Stir each chili paste into ½ cup of coconut milk and simmer in a small saucepan over a low flame for 20 minutes. Adjust the seasoning with fish sauce.

For the rice noodle cake, drop the rice threads into salted boiling water and when they are soft, about 45 seconds, remove them. Drain. Stir in the red pepper paste until the noodles are evenly coated. Adjust the seasoning. Shape the noodles into cakes using round cutters. Heat the peanut oil in a large skillet and fry the noodle cakes until crisp and golden brown on both sides.

Meanwhile, reheat the lobster in the green curry sauce and the shrimp in the red curry sauce. Be careful not to overcook the meat. Sauté the black trumpet mushrooms in peanut oil until tender. Season with salt and pepper.

To serve, spoon the 2 sauces onto the bottom of the plate. Lay the lobster and shrimp on top of the sauce and top with the rice noodle cake. Garnish with the black trumpet mushrooms and fresh herbs.

133 Sweetbread and Lobster Knödel

Serves 6

For the lobster oil:
6 lobster bodies from 1½ pound lobsters, crushed
2 cups olive oil
1 leek, chopped
4 tablespoons fresh tomato paste
8 peppercorns
Salt to taste

For the watercrest oil:
1 cup olive oil
2 bunches watercress, blanched, shocked and puréed
Salt and pepper to taste

For the sweetbread and lobster knödel:
12 ounces sweetbreads, blanched and cubed
6 tablespoons lobster oil
3 ounces sweetbreads, raw
1 egg
4 tablespoons heavy cream
6 lobster tails, sliced into 1 ounce pieces
2 ounces lobster roe, steamed and strained
¼ cup leeks, blanched and julienned
¼ cup carrots, blanched and julienned
¼ cup celery, blanched and julienned
¼ cup baby spinach leaves
Salt and pepper to taste

For the garnish:
2 tablespoons lobster oil
2 tablespoons watercress oil
12 lobster claws, shelled and sautéed
6 sprigs watercress

For the lobster oil, in a heavy saucepan braise the crushed lobster bodies in a few tablespoons of hot olive oil for 15 minutes. Add in the leek, celery, the fresh tomato paste, the peppercorns and the remaining olive oil; add salt to taste. Simmer slowly for 20 minutes until the liquid has evaporated from the oil. Let the oil stand overnight and strain.

For the watercress oil, blend the olive oil together with the watercress purée in a food processor. Adjust the seasoning.

For the knödel, sauté the cubed sweetbreads in 4 tablespoons of the hot lobster oil and set aside to cool. Purée the raw sweetbreads in a food processor together with the egg until the mixture is smooth. Blend in remaining 2 tablespoons of lobster oil and the cream. In a stainless mixing bowl fold the diced sweetbreads, the lobster meat, lobster roe and the vegetables into the sweetbread mousse and adjust the seasoning with salt and pepper. To form the knödel, brush the insides of 2½ sphere molds (or 3 ounce ladles) with lobster oil, fill each mold with the mousse, and tightly wrap 2 molds together with plastic wrap. Poach the knödel in 180 degree water for 15 minutes.

To serve, carefully unmold the knödel and set one in the middle of each plate with the lobster and watercress oils. Finish each dish with the lobster claws and fresh sprigs of watercress.

132 Loin of Salmon with Curry and Vanilla Oil

Serves 4

For the salmon:
4 sheets rice paper
4 loins salmon, cut from the fillet,
6 ounces each
12 cilantro leaves
4 tablespoons olive oil
Salt and pepper

For potato windows:
2 Idaho potatoes
Melted butter
Salt

For the garnish:
¼ vanilla bean
4 tablespoons curry oil
Assorted herbs

To prepare the curry oil, place 3 tablespoons powdered spice in bowl. Add 1 tablespoon water. Mix until a paste is formed. If paste is too dry, add a little more water. Place paste in a mason jar. Add 2 cups vegetable or grapeseed oil to paste. Cover jar. Shake vigorously. Leave jar on a shelf in the kitchen for 2 days. Shake oil several times to increase taste. The dry spice will settle to the bottom. After 2 days, with a ladle, remove oil on top and filter just the oil through a coffee filter or double thickness of cheesecloth. Don't filter solids. Store spiced oil in or out of the refrigerator for up to 1 month.

For the salmon, take the four sheets of rice paper and lay them side by side on a counter on top of a towel. Dampen them with water and cover with another damp towel to prevent them from drying. When they are completely soft, place one loin of salmon on each piece of rice paper. Put three cilantro leaves on top of each loin. Roll the rice paper around the loin to enclose. Set aside.

For the potato windows, peel the potatoes and slice very thin. Cut into thin long strips and in a bowl, add a little melted butter and coat well. Arrange on a non-stick sheet tray, four across and four down to form a window. Make four in all. Cook in a 400-degree oven until the bottoms start to brown. Turn over and cook on the other side until lightly brown and crispy. Remove from the oven and drain on a paper towel. Salt lightly.

To flavor curry oil, cut vanilla bean open lengthwise and scrape the inside seeds into the curry oil. Mix and set aside.

Heat olive oil in a non-stick pan until smoking hot. Season the salmon rolls with salt and pepper and add to the pan. Cook on both sides until brown and crispy. Finish in the oven at 325 degrees until desired doneness.

To serve, slice the salmon roll into three equal pieces. Place on a plate and pour the curry vanilla oil around the plate. Decorate with the window potato and the herbs.

133 Codfish with Garbanzo Beans

Serves 4

For the codfish rolls:
1 dozen red beet leaves,
washed and stems removed
12 2-ounce codfish strips
2 tablespoons butter
2 shallots, finely chopped
½ cup dry white wine
Salt and pepper to taste

For the sauce:
1 cup fish stock
1 shallot, peeled and chopped
1 clove garlic, peeled and chopped
¼ cup heavy cream
4 ounces butter
½ teaspoon paprika
Pinch of saffron
Salt and cayenne pepper to taste

For the garnish:
1 beet, cooked and peeled
½ cup flour
2 eggs, beaten with a fork
1 cup breadcrumbs
1 cup garbanzo beans
1 teaspoon chopped parsley
1 hard-boiled egg, chopped

For the codfish rolls, blanch the beet leaves in salted water for 2 to 3 minutes. Plunge the leaves in ice water to stop the cooking process. Remove the leaves from the ice water and pat dry. Wrap each piece of codfish in a leaf and arrange in a buttered shallow braising pan. Add the chopped shallots and white wine, season with salt and pepper, and cover. Place the covered braising pan in a 350 degree preheated oven, cook for 6 to 8 minutes and cool. Remove the pieces from the pan and keep warm. Reduce the liquid by half, strain and save for later use.

For the sauce, combine the reduced liquid from the codfish rolls and the fish stock in a pot. Add the chopped shallot and garlic and bring to a boil. Simmer for 10 minutes, add the heavy cream and simmer for an additional 10 minutes. Slowly add the butter bit by bit and stir well. Strain the sauce, add the paprika, saffron, salt and pepper, and simmer for 5 minutes. Remove the sauce from the heat.

For the garnish, cut the beet into ¼ inch by ¼ inch sticks. Dredge the sticks first through the flour, then the beaten eggs and finally through the breadcrumbs. Fry the breaded beet sticks in hot oil until golden brown.

To serve, arrange the codfish pieces on preheated plates, cover them with sauce and garnish with the fried beet sticks, garbanzo beans, chopped parsley and chopped egg.

158 Duck Cassoulet

Serves 10

For the confit:
10 duck legs
1 cup duck gizzards
Salt to season
4½ pounds duck fat

For the duck sausage:
¼ pound duck meat
2 ounces lean pork butt
1 ounce duck fat
2 ounces pork fat
1½ teaspoons sugar
Kosher salt and freshly ground pepper to taste
1½ teaspoons finely chopped sage
1½ teaspoons finely chopped thyme
1½ teaspoons finely chopped fresh marjoram
1 tablespoon finely chopped fresh parsley
¾ teaspoon chili powder
1½ teaspoons minced garlic
1½ teaspoons minced shallots
¾ teaspoon dried red chili flakes
1½ teaspoons gin
1½ teaspoons brandy
¾ tablespoon triple sec
Sausage casings

For the brine:
1½ quarts water
¼ pound kosher salt
1/8 pound brown sugar
½ tablespoons chopped garlic
1/8 cup lemon juice
½ onion, diced

For the cassoulet:
1 pound pancetta, diced
1½ cups diced onions
2 cups great white Northern beans, soaked
5 cups fresh plum tomatoes, peeled
5 cloves garlic, crushed
2 bay leaves
4 tablespoons brown sugar
1 tablespoon chopped fresh thyme
Salt and pepper to taste
2 cups duck stock, as needed
10 2-ounce reserved duck sausages
Reserved duck leg confit
Reserved duck gizzard confit

For the duck confit, place the duck legs in a medium bowl and season with coarse salt ¼ ounce per pound and place in the refrigerator for 24 hours, allowing the salt to penetrate into the flesh. Cook in a large copper cauldron with the duck fat for 2 hours. The fat should simmer but not boil. Remove from the heat, and while the fat is still hot, strain it into a stoneware pot and place the legs in the fat, being certain that they are completely covered. Cool and then cover the pot. Remove the duck legs and gizzards from the fat. Slice the gizzards and set aside.

For the sausage, coarsely chop and mix together the duck, pork, fats, sugar, salt and the pepper. Grind this mixture through the large blade of a meat grinder, then add the herbs and spiced. Mix in the liquids and refrigerate, covered, with plastic wrap, overnight.

For the brine, mix all of the ingredients together and allow it to sit for a few hours. Pipe the sausage mixture into casings with the sausage horn of a mixer, or use a pastry bag without a tip. Twist into sausage links, soak in the brine for several hours, then wipe dry and smoke the sausages in a hot smoker for 10 minutes on each side.

For the cassoulet, sauté the pancetta and the onions until the onions are transparent; add in the soaked beans, the plum tomatoes, garlic, bay leaves, brown sugar, and the thyme. Season with the salt and pepper, cook slowly until the beans are tender-adding duck stock as needed to keep the desired consistency. Place the cooked beans with the duck sausage, the legs and the gizzard confit in a moderate oven and bake for about 15 minutes.

To serve, divide the baked beans, studded with the gizzards, into each dish; place a leg in the center of the beans, skin side up; cut each sausage into two pieces and place the halves adjacent to the dusk leg near the edge of the dish. Garnish the sausage and the duck leg with sprigs of fresh thyme.

136 Banzai Tamales

Yields 6 tamales

For the masa:
1½ cups water
¼ cup corn oil
2 cups masa harina
½ teaspoon baking powder
Salt and pepper to taste

For the filling:
1 Chinese barbecued duck

For the sauce:
½ cup plum wine*
2 tablespoons sugar
1 cup tamarind pods*, cleaned, soaked and passed through a sieve to remove the seeds
½ cup concentrated duck stock
Salt and pepper to taste

For the garnish:
6 corn husks
3 miniature bok choy, blanched and cut in half
6 shiitake mushrooms, sautéed with garlic in butter
1 package daikon sprouts, cleaned
Black sesame seeds
Fried rice noodles

To prepare the masa, bring the water and oil to a boil in a medium-sized saucepan. Sift the masa harina through your fingers into the boiling water and whisk until smooth. Add the baking powder, salt and pepper and continue stirring until the masa has become shiny and it pulls away from the sides of the pot. Cool.

For the filling, remove the duck meat from the bone. Trim away any fat and dice the meat. Set aside.

To form the tamales, spread the masa on the corn husks. Place the duck in the center and roll and tie.

To prepare the sauce, reduce the plum wine by half in a small saucepan. Add the sugar and tamarind pulp and boil for another minute. Add the concentrated duck stock and season with salt and pepper to taste.

To serve, steam the tamales for 10 to 15 minutes, until the masa is firm. Unwrap and plate with the remaining corn husks. Spoon the sauce over the tamale. Garnish with the blanched bok choy, sautéed shiitakes, daikon sprouts, black sesame seeds and fried rice noodles.

***Note:** These ingredients can be purchased in most Asian specialty shops.

137 Roasted Chicken with Dried Fruits

Serves 4

For the chicken:
9 ounces dried mixed fruit
1 twig of spruce
2 chickens, 1½ pounds each
1 tablespoon dried crushed juniper berries
1 teaspoon dried tarragon
2 teaspoons salt
2 tablespoons butter

For the sauce:
1 cup pan juices
1 tablespoon flour
⅓ cup heavy cream
Salt and pepper

For the garnish:
Steamed broccoli flowerettes

For the chicken, let the dried fruit soak in water to cover for 2 hours and cut the twig of spruce into small pieces. Boil the spruce and the fruit for 1½ hours in water. Strain it and keep the liquid. Rub the chicken with the spices and fill them with the spruce and fruits.

In butter, brown chickens in a frying pan. Place them in a roasting pan and roast at 425 degrees for 1 hour. Baste chickens occasionally with the liquid.

For the sauce, strain pan juices and boil until a cup remains. Thicken pan juices with flour and cream that you have whisked together over medium heat. Let mixture cook until thickened and season with salt and pepper.

To serve, slice chicken and serve with sauce and broccoli.

138 Peking-Style Duck with Cornmeal Waffles

Serves 4

For the duck:
1 4-pound duck
Salt and pepper
1 cup orange juice
1 quart water
3 tablespoons dark soy sauce
2 tablespoons honey
1 cup water

For the sauce:
¼ cup grated orange zest
1 cup chicken stock
1 tablespoon rice wine
Salt and pepper
½ teaspoon chopped ginger
1 tablespoon Grand Marnier
2 tablespoons cold butter, cut into small pieces

For the waffles:
3 cups water
1 cup yellow cornmeal
2 egg whites
¼ pound butter, melted
2 teaspoons sesame oil
1 egg yolk
½ cup rice flour
1 teaspoon baking powder
¾ cup milk
1 scallion, finely chopped
2 teaspoons chopped ginger

To prepare the duck, season it with salt and pepper and pour the orange juice into the body cavity. Close both ends of the duck with skewers and secure with string wrapped lengthwise around the skewers.

In a medium-sized pot, combine the quart of water, dark soy sauce and honey. Bring to a boil. Turn off the heat and baste the duck several times with the hot liquid. Allow the duck to dry either in a cool drafty place for 5 hours or in front of a fan for 2 hours. When the duck is properly dried, the skin will feel like parchment paper.

Preheat the oven to 500 degrees. Place the duck on a rack inside a roasting pan. Pour the cup of water into the pan. Roast the duck for 20 minutes, then turn down the heat to 400 degrees and cook for 40 minutes. Raise the temperature to 500 degrees again and roast for 10 minutes more.

Remove the duck from the oven and release the juice inside the duck into a saucepan. Add to the juice the orange zest, chicken stock, rice wine, salt, pepper, ginger and liqueur. Bring the sauce to a boil and reduce by half. Whisk in the butter and remove from the heat.

To prepare the waffles, bring the water to a boil in a small saucepan and add the cornmeal and some salt. Cook for 5 minutes. Cool. Beat the egg whites until stiff. Set aside. In a food processor or a large bowl, combine the remaining waffle ingredients. Be careful not to overmix. Incorporate the cooked cornmeal and then gently fold in the egg whites. Grease both sides of a hot waffle iron with melted butter or peanut oil. Pour the batter into the bottom half, close the top and cook until browned. Repeat until all the batter is used. Keep the waffles warm in the oven until ready to serve.

To serve, carve the warm duck and arrange the pieces on a serving platter. Spoon the sauce over the duck and garnish with the waffles.

139 Barbecued Venison Pie

Serves 4

For the pie:
1 pound venison leg meat, cut into small dices
5 tablespoons creole seasoning
1 potato, peeled and dice
1 rutabaga, peeled and diced
1 turnip, peeled and diced
2 carrots, peeled and diced
Olive oil for sautéing
1 cup all-purpose flour
½ cup olive oil
1 onion, peeled and diced
3 cloves garlic, peeled and minced
1 cup beef stock
1 cup barbecue sauce
8 6-inch rounds puff pastry
1 egg, beaten
Barbecue sauce
Salt, pepper, Tabasco and Worcestershire sauce to taste

For the Creole seasoning mix:
Yields approximately ½ cup
2½ tablespoons paprika
2 tablespoons salt
2 tablespoons garlic powder
1 tablespoon black pepper
1 tablespoon onion powder
1 tablespoon cayenne pepper
1 tablespoon dried leaf oregano
1 tablespoon dried leaf thyme

For the creole seasoning mix, combine all of the ingredients and blend well. Store in an airtight container until needed.

For the barbecue sauce:
Yields approximately 2 cups
½ cup barbecue base (see recipe on next page)
1 cup smoked tomato sauce (see recipe on next page)
4 ounces unsalted butter

Combine the barbecue base with the smoked tomato sauce in a small saucepan and heat. Mount with the unsalted butter. Cool.

For the barbecue base:
Yields approximately 1 quart
10 lemons, peeled and cut in half
2 ounces ground black pepper
4 ounces cracked black pepper
4 ounces Creole seasoning
(see recipe on previous page)
1 quart Worcestershire sauce
1 quart shrimp stock
2 ounces minced garlic

Combine all of the ingredients in a large saucepan. Reduce by half over a low flame until thick. Cool.

For the smoked tomato sauce:
Yields approximately 2 quarts
30 roma tomatoes, split lengthwise
2 celery stalks, chopped
2 carrots, peeled
3 onions, peeled
1½ quarts chicken stock
2 tablespoons creole seasoning
(see recipe on previous page)
3 bay leaves
4 cloves garlic, peeled and chopped

To prepare the sauce, begin by smoking the tomatoes, celery, carrots and onion for 15 to 20 minutes at very low heat. Place the remaining ingredients in a large stock pot and add the smoked vegetables. Bring to a simmer and lower the heat. Continue cooking for 15 to 20 minutes. Purée in a blender and strain well. Cool.

For the pie, preheat the oven to 450 degrees. In a small bowl combine the venison and two tablespoons of the Creole seasoning. Toss to combine and set aside. In a medium sauté pan, heat two tablespoons of the olive oil over medium heat. Add the potato, rutabaga, turnip, and carrots and sauté until tender, about 10 minutes. Remove from the heat, season and set aside to cool. Set aside ¼ cup of the vegetables for garnish. In a small a bowl combine the flour with the remaining Creole mix and toss to combine. Add the venison and toss to coat. In a large sauté pan heat the remaining oil over medium heat. Add the venison and sear on all sides. Add the onion and garlic and sauté until translucent. Add the beef stock and the barbecue sauce and simmer for five minutes. Remove from the heat and set aside to cool. Lay out four of puff pastry rounds on a parchment-lined sheet pan and spoon some of the venison and root vegetable mixture in the center of each round. Cover with the remaining rounds, press the edges together to seal and brush with the egg. Place in the oven to bake until golden brown, about 10 minutes. Remove from the heat and set aside keeping warm.

To serve, place a pie in the center of the plate and slice. Drizzle some barbecue sauce and vegetables around the dish.

140 Smoked Grouse Breast

Serves 4

For the syrup:
2 tablespoons finely chopped
licorice fern root*
2 tablespoons
Gewürztraminer ice wine
¾ cup water

For the grouse:
2 12-ounce wild grouse
breasts, bone in, skin removed
3 cups dried alder cones

For the camas bulbs:
12 camas bulbs (Camassia quamash,
C. Cusickii or C. Leichtlinii can be used),
cleaned and rinsed in cold water

For the salad and juniper berry sauce:
1 cup water
1½ cups Pinot Blanc
3½ cups salad berries
1½ tablespoons maple syrup
7 black peppercorns
8 dried juniper berries, finely chopped
⅓ cup water
1½ teaspoons balsamic vinegar

For the wild rose hip oil:
20 fresh nootka rose hips, ends trimmed
⅓ cup corn oil
1 tablespoon white wine vinegar
1 tablespoon boiling water
4 calendula flower petals

For the beebalm oven cakes:
¼ cup all-purpose flour
2 eggs
¼ cup whole milk
2 scratches fresh nutmeg
2 turns freshly ground white pepper
1 pinch salt
1 tablespoon finely chopped beebalm
4 teaspoons unsalted butter

For the nodding onions:
16 nodding onions (Allium cernuum),
washed and roots removed
Canola oil

For the wild burdock:
2 cups water
2 tablespoons apple cider vinegar
1 8-inch long wild burdock root
(Arctium minus Bernh) from
a yearling plant, cleaned

To prepare the licorice fern root glaze, place all of the ingredients into a small, non-reactive saucepan. Gently simmer for 20 minutes, being careful not to let the mixture come to a rolling boil or the resulting syrup will be astringent. Remove the syrup from the heat and transfer to a sealable glass jar. Let rest at room temperature for at least 12 hours. After the mixture has steeped, pass it through a fine chinois into a small sauce pan. Reduce the liquid until the mixture has the consistency of liquid honey.

For the grouse breast, heat the alder cones in a sauté pan use over high heat until they begin to smolder. Lightly brush the breasts with the licorice fern root glaze and set on top of the smoldering alder cones. Cover the pan tightly and smoke for approximately 3 hours. Remove the breasts from the bone when they are cooked through, but not dried. Keep warm. To cook the camas bulbs, gently steam them for two hours until cooked through and slightly tan in color. Set aside.

To prepare the salad and juniper berry sauce, pour the water and wine into the base of a perforated double boiler. Place the salad berries in the top section of the double boiler. Cover and gently steam for two hours. Next, gently press the berries with a rubber spatula to extract any remaining juice. Discard the berries and retain the syrup collected in the base of the double boiler. Add the remaining ingredients to the syrup. Bring this mixture up to a boil and immediately remove from the heat. Set aside for 10 minutes to allow the flavors to infuse. Strain this mixture through a fine chinois and return the syrup to medium heat. Reduce for an additional five minutes, until the sauce takes on the consistency of a light glaze.

To prepare the wild pink nootka rose hip oil, place all of the ingredients in a blender and blend until smooth. Set aside until service.

To prepare the beebalm oven cakes, combine the flour, eggs, milk, nutmeg, white pepper and salt to make a batter. Strain through a china cap. Add the beebalm. Place one teaspoon of butter into four, non-stick, 4-ounce timbale molds. Place the molds in the oven for approximately two minutes until the butter is hot. Pour 1½ ounces of the batter into each mold and return the timbales to the oven immediately. Bake for approximately 15 minutes, or until the cakes are firm.

To prepare the nodding onions, heat a skillet with enough canola oil to cover the bottom. When the oil is very hot, add the onions and let them cook until the green portion starts to crisp or become rigid. Be careful not to burn them. Remove from the pan and place on a paper towel until the rest of the dish is finished.

For the wild burdock root, bring the water and vinegar to a boil. Add the burdock root and cook until tender. Dice.

To present the dish, place the beebalm cake in the center of the plate. Wrap the onions around the base of the cake and fill the hollow of the cake with the camas bulbs and wild burdock root. Slice the grouse breasts thinly against the grain. Fan out the slices in front of the cake. Drizzle the rose hip oil and berry sauce around the plate and serve.

***Note:** No other fern root can be substituted. Sweet cicely root will produce a syrup with a nice flavor.

141 Duck Oysters and Chive Risotto

Serves 4

For the risotto:
1 onion, peeled and minced
1 large clove garlic, peeled and minced
Olive oil
1 cup Arborio rice
Salt and pepper
2 tablespoons white wine
2 cups white duck stock, boiling
8 ounces foie gras, diced
½ cup robiola cheese
½ cup grated Parmesan cheese
2 tablespoons butter
2 bunches chives, finely chopped
Salt and pepper

For the duck oysters:
8 duck testicles
All-purpose flour
Egg wash
Seasoned breadcrumbs
Olive oil

To prepare the rice, sweat the minced onion and garlic in the olive oil. Add the rice and stir until well coated with the oil. Season with salt and pepper. Add the wine and cook on medium heat until dry. Add the hot duck stock one ladle at a time, stirring until the stock is absorbed after each addition. Add the diced foie gras and continue cooking for 2 minutes. Fold in the robiola, the Parmesan and the butter. Add the chives and adjust the seasonings if necessary.

For the oysters, bread the duck testicles with the flour, egg wash and seasoned breadcrumbs. Pan fry the breaded oysters in olive oil until golden brown. Slice each testicle in half. Keep warm.

To assemble the dish, spoon the rice into 4 bowls and place 4 halves of duck oysters on top of each portion. Serve hot.

141 Squab with Cabbage and Foie Gras

Serves 4

For the stock:
4 1½ pound squabs
1 tablespoon vegetable oil
1 cup chopped onion
½ cup chopped carrot
1 garlic clove, crushed
Salt and fresh cracked white pepper
2 quarts water
1 bouquet of fresh herbs

For the dish:
1 tablespoon oil
4 boneless squab breasts, split
Salt and fresh cracked white pepper
4 cups lightly blanched shredded green cabbage
1 cup squab stock
7 ounces foie gras, diced

For the garnish:
¼ cup chiffonade Swiss chard

For the stock, cut the breasts from each squab, remove the bone, the skin and reserve for the dish. Cut the legs, thighs and wings from the squab and chop the carcass into pieces. Coat the bottom of a large saucepan with the oil, heat the pan to where the oil just starts to smoke and brown the squab completely; add in the chopped onion, the carrot and the garlic, continuing to brown and stirring from time to time to allow for even cooking. Season the squab and the vegetables lightly, pour in the water, add in the bouquet of herbs and simmer for one hour. Strain the stock and reduce it to 1 cup.

For the dish, heat the oil in a large skillet; season the squab breasts and quickly sauté them, until rare, in the hot oil, lightly browning each side. Remove them from the pan to rest. Add the shredded cabbage to the skillet and let it braise for about 5 minutes; deglaze with half of the stock to moisten the cabbage, lightly season, and add in the diced foie gras around the edge of the skillet to warm.

To serve, mound the braised cabbage in the middle of each plate; slice the rare squab breasts into 4 thin slices each and lay 8 slices crowning the cabbage; toss the swiss chard into the skillet to warm just a bit; scatter the warmed foie gras around the edge of the cabbage; garnish the dish with the chard and drizzle the breasts with more of the stock, letting the stock run down onto the plate around the cabbage.

142 Chicken Tamales

Yields 6 tamales

For the masa:
1½ cups water
¼ cup corn oil
2 cups masa harina
½ teaspoon baking powder
Salt and pepper to taste

For the tomatillo chili sauce:
8 tomatillos, husks removed
2 jalapeño chilies, seeded and chopped
1 bunch cilantro, leaves only
¼ cup chicken stock
Salt and pepper to taste

For the filling:
2 cups shredded, poached chicken breast meat
2 potatoes, boiled and diced
⅓ cup tomatillo chili sauce (from above)

For the wrapping:
6 corn husks, soaked
Corn husk strips for tying

For the garnish:
6 Corn husks
Red pepper brunoise
Cooked corn

To prepare the masa, bring the water and oil to a boil in a medium-sized saucepan. Sift the masa harina through your fingers into the boiling water and whisk until smooth. Add the baking powder, salt and pepper and continue stirring until the masa has become shiny and it pulls away from the sides of the pot. Cool.

To prepare the tomatillo chili sauce, combine all of the ingredients in a blender and purée until smooth.

For the filling, combine the chicken with the diced potatoes. Toss with the chili sauce.

To form the tamales, spread the masa on the reconstituted corn husks. Place some of the chicken filling in the center and roll and tie them. Steam for 10 to 12 minutes, until the husks pull easily away from the filling.

To serve, unwrap the steamed tamales. Set on serving plates with corn husks. Garnish with the pepper brunoise and cooked corn.

143 Wild Partridge with Vegetables and Foie Gras "en Vessie" with Cabbage

Serves 2

For the partridge:
3 ounces fresh foie gras, cut into ¾-inch squares
1 10-ounce wild partridge, cleaned
2 cloves garlic, peeled
5 fresh sage leaves
Sea salt
Freshly ground black pepper
1 tablespoon duck fat
1 cup consommé or stock
3 large outer leaves of savoy cabbage, blanched
1 cleaned pork bladder, soaked in cold water for 2 hours
2 carrots, turned and blanched
½ turnip, turned and blanched
12 pearl onions, peeled and blanched
2 stalks celery, turned and blanched
6 baby leeks, trimmed and cut into thirds
2 branches of fresh sage
2 gallons consommé or stock for poaching the stuffed bladder

For the garnish:
2 sprigs of fresh sage

For the partridge, heat a non-stick skillet for 3 minutes over high heat. Season the foie gras cubes well with salt and pepper and place in the hot pan. Sauté until well browned on all sides. Remove and drain on a cotton towel.

Season the partridge well, inside and out, with salt and pepper. Carefully place the garlic cloves, sage leaves and foie gras inside the partridge. Using butcher's string, tie the bird securely. Heat the duck fat in a non-stick skillet for 3 minutes. Place the partridge, breast side down, in the hot pan and brown well on all sides. Remove and set aside.

Degrease the pan, and while still over high heat, add one cup of consommé. Bring to a boil and reduce by half. Set aside.

Remove the center core from the blanched cabbage and lay out the leaves flat, overlapping them a bit to form a 10-inch square. Place the partridge in the center and bring the sides up around it to form a wrapped bundle.

To stuff the bladder, drain it well and pat dry with paper towels. Ensure that there are no holes other than the open end. Cut the opening wide enough to place the cabbage-wrapped partridge inside. Place the blanched vegetables around the partridge along with the sage branches. Pour the consommé from the pan inside the bladder. Now, as if blowing up a balloon, blow up the bladder with all of the ingredients inside. Inflate it until it is very firm. Tie securely with butcher's string.

In a five-gallon stockpot, bring the two gallons of consommé to a simmer over medium-high heat. Carefully place the bladder inside, so it floats on top of the consommé. Gently cook the partridge "en vessie" for 45 minutes, ladling hot consommé over the top every 15 minutes or so.

Serve the partridge to guests "en vessie" on a base of hot consommé. Carefully open the top of the bladder with a sharp knife. Remove the partridge and cut in half. Remove the foie gras and place in the center of each plate. Remove the breast meat from the bone and slice it into medallions. Carefully place the breast meat along with the trimmed leg and thigh across the foie gras. Arrange the vegetables around the partridge and spoon the juices over the top. Garnish with a sprig of fresh sage.

144 Duck Sausage with Six-Bean Ragoût

Serves 6

For the sausage:
12 ounces duck leg meat, chopped
8 ounces foie gras, cubed
6 ounces veal shank meat, ground
1 squab breast, julienned
14 ounces pork back fat
½ bottle champagne
Seasonings, such as thyme, bay leaves and rosemary
Salt and pepper to taste
6 duck neck skins
Duck stock for poaching

For the bean ragoût:
Duck stock
5 varieties of dried beans, soaked
Bouquet garni
24 pods fava beans, shucked
½ cup rendered duck fat
Salt and pepper

To prepare the sausage, mix the meats, champagne and seasonings together by hand. Stuff the mixture into the duck neck skins. Securely tie the ends.

For the bean ragoût, cook the soaked beans in the duck stock with the bouquet garni until tender but firm. Add the cleaned fava beans and continue cooking an additional 10 minutes. Drain the beans. Add the duck fat and some stock to keep them moist. Season with salt and pepper and keep warm.

Poach the sausages in the duck stock at a low temperature for 30 minutes. Remove the sausages from the liquid and allow to rest in a warm place for 15 minutes before slicing.

To serve, arrange the sausage slices on plates over portions of the bean ragoût.

144 Chicken and Macaroni Gratin

Serves 8

For the chicken:
4 tablespoons virgin olive oil
2 2 pound fowl, cut in 8 pieces
Salt and fresh cracked pepper
1 cup aged white wine vinegar
2 cups seeded tomatoes
2 garlic cloves, crushed

For the macaroni:
4 cups milk
2 cups heavy cream
2 teaspoons salt
1 pound macaroni
½ cup grated swiss cheese
Fresh cracked black pepper

For the garnish:
2 tablespoons chopped parsley

For the chicken, heat the olive oil in a large skillet, season the chicken, and brown each piece thoroughly on all sides; remove the browned chicken from the pan, pour out the juices and reserve; deglaze the pan with the vinegar and reduce the vinegar to ¼ cup. Add in the chicken, the tomatoes and the garlic; simmer for 20 to 25 minutes. When the chicken is fully cooked, remove once again, de-bone and cut into small pieces. Add the reserved juices to the tomatoes and reduce until the liquid is nearly evaporated; add in the cooked chicken and keep warm.

For the macaroni, bring the milk and the cream to a boil, season, and add in the macaroni, stirring until the milk returns to a full boil. Turn off the heat and stir every 5 minutes- the pasta will cook by itself- allowing the pasta to stand until it is room temperature.

To serve, mix the cooked pasta with the tomatoes and the chicken.divide into lightly oiled oven-proof dishes, cover with the grated cheese and black pepper; bake in a 300 degree oven for 15 minutes. Sprinkle with chopped parsley.

145 Fillet of Moose with Cowberry Sauce

Serves 4

For the mousse:
22 ounces mousse filet

For the sauce:
Butter
1 carrot, chopped
1 onion, chopped
Parsley sprigs
3 cups water
¾ cup red wine
White peppercorns
1 bay leaf
1 teaspoon soy sauce
3 ounces cowberries
Salt and pepper
3 ounces heavy cream
Fresh cowberries

For the timbales:
4 potatoes
1 small piece of leek
1 carrot
1 parsnip
1 small piece of turnip
Butter
Salt and pepper to taste

For the garnish:
Thin green beans, steamed

For the mousse, trim filet and set aside. For the sauce, brown trimmings in butter with the carrot and onion. Add parsley sprigs. Pour mixture into a saucepan. Add water, red wine and white peppercorns. Add bay leaf, soy sauce and cowberries. Cook over medium heat until reduced by half. Skim foam as the sauce cooks. Strain sauce. Set aside and keep warm.

Brown the filet in a fry pan. Season with salt and pepper. Place the filet in a 400-degree oven approximately 10 minutes. Turn filet after 5 minutes. Let meat rest for 15 minutes in a foil packet. Open the packet carefully and pour the pan-gravy into the pan of sauce. Add cream and let boil for a few minutes. Season with salt and pepper. Add a handful of fresh cowberries to the sauce.

For the timbales, peel vegetables and cut into small slices. Rinse the leek and cut in small pieces. Parboil the vegetables in lightly salted water to cover. Strain the vegetables and dry them out. In a fry pan, add butter and sauté slightly. Add salt and pepper to taste. Pack vegetables in small timbales and place them in the 400-degree oven approximately 5 minutes.

To serve, turn out timbales and carve meat. Serve them with the sauce and thin green beans for garnish.

146 Squab with Cèpes

Serves 4

For the sauce:
1 teaspoon olive oil
½ cup sliced carrots
1 cup sliced onions
6 garlic cloves, sliced
2 cups Côtes-du-Rhone wine
1 cup rich squab stock,
Salt and black pepper to taste

For the squab:
4 fresh squabs, wings and legs removed
Salt and pepper to taste
1 tablespoon olive oil
1 cup pearl onions, peeled
1 cup cèpes, quartered

For the garnish:
½ cup fava beans, blanched
¼ cup mashed potatoes
48 crisp round potato "tuiles"
4 cooked black trumpet mushrooms

For the sauce, in a skillet, lightly caramelize the carrots, the onions and the garlic in the olive oil; deglaze with the wine and reduce by ½; add in the stock, reduce to a light glaze and season to taste.

For the squabs, season them with the salt and the pepper; sauté quickly in the olive oil and roast in a 350 degree oven for about 20 minutes until they are pink inside and the skin is crisp. Remove the roasted squabs from the pan, slowly glaze the pearl onions in the drippings, adding in a little of the sauce, and sauté the cèpes; add in the remaining sauce and simmer for 2 minutes.

To serve, split the squab breasts open and fill them with a few glazed onions, mushrooms and warm fava beans; spoon the remaining mushrooms and pearl onions, scattered with the remaining fava beans, around the plate with a generous amount of the sauce; place the filled roasted squabs in the center of the mushrooms.

To garnish, scoop a ball of the mashed potatoes and fan the crisp potato tuiles around by sticking them into the mashed potatoes; set to the top rim of each dish and top with the black trumpet mushrooms.

147 Boneless Roast Squab with Borlotti Bean Sauce

Serves 4

For the bean sauce:
2 cups of olive oil
1 piece fat from prosciutto
1 cup coarsely chopped onions
¼ cup chopped celery
4 cloves garlic, chopped
1 bunch Italian parsley
1 bunch fresh rosemary
1 bunch fresh sage
2 ripe tomatoes, seeded and chopped
Sea salt to taste
1½ cups borlotti beans, soaked
4 cups chicken stock
6 tablespoons olive oil
3 cloves garlic, finely chopped
1 tablespoon chopped fresh parsley
1 tablespoon chopped fresh rosemary
1 tablespoon chopped fresh sage

For the squabs:
4 squabs, cleaned, boned and quartered
Salt and pepper to season
½ cup olive oil

For the garnish:
1 cup Brussels sprouts' leaves, blanched
2 tablespoons olive oil
4 sprigs fresh rosemary

For the sauce, heat the olive oil and prosciutto fat in a large pot. Add the onions, celery, garlic, the fresh herbs and the tomatoes; simmer at a medium heat for 15 minutes. Salt to taste and add in the borlotti beans, covering completely with the cold chicken stock. Bring the seasoned stock to a boil and cook the beans for 2 hours, skimming them every ½ hour. When the beans are cooked, discard the prosciutto and set aside ½ cup of the beans. Blend the remainder of the beans with the stock and pass the sauce through a fine sieve (the sauce can be thinned with the chicken stock, if it is too thick). To finish the sauce, heat the 6 tablespoons of olive oil in a saucepan and sauté the chopped garlic, parsley, rosemary and sage, being careful not to brown the garlic or the herbs. Pour in the puréed bean sauce, add the whole beans, adjust the seasoning, and keep warm.

For the squabs, place the seasoned squab pieces into a casserole with the olive oil. Roast the squabs at 425 degrees for 10 minutes, until nicely browned on all sides.

To serve, lightly sauté the Brussels sprout leaves' in olive oil, fill each dish with the bean sauce and sprinkle the sautéed Brussels sprouts' leaves on top. Arrange the quartered squab in the center of the sauce and garnish with a sprig of fresh rosemary.

147 Barbecued Duck with Spaghetti Squash Latkes

Serves 4

For the barbecue sauce:
1 cup soy sauce
½ cup ketchup
1 Scotch bonnet pepper, seeded and finely chopped
1 large Spanish onion, peeled and finely chopped
1 teaspoon ground allspice
½ teaspoon ground cloves
1 tablespoon chopped fresh thyme
1 clove garlic, peeled and chopped
1 teaspoon ground black pepper
1 teaspoon ground white pepper

For the duck:
2 4-pound Peking ducks, cleaned and trussed

For the latkes:
3 large Idaho potatoes, peeled and grated
1 spaghetti squash, cooked, seeded and shredded
2 eggs
1 teaspoon baking powder
½ cup all purpose flour
½ small onion, peeled and grated
4 tablespoons unsalted butter
Salt and pepper to taste

For the sauce:
4 red bell peppers, seeded and diced
¼ cup peanut oil
Salt and pepper to taste

For the garnish:
Sprigs of cilantro

To prepare the barbecue sauce, combine all ingredients in a small bowl. Set aside.

To prepare the duck, poach the ducks in heavily salted boiling water for 12 minutes. Oven-roast the birds at 450 degrees for 15 minutes. Reduce the oven temperature to 350 degrees, brush the ducks with the barbecue sauce and continue roasting for another 20 minutes. When the duck is cooked to medium rare, remove from the oven and let stand for 10 minutes. Meanwhile, combine all of the ingredients for the latkes. Drop the mixture by heaping tablespoons onto a buttered griddle. There should be 16 latkes.

To prepare the sauce, run the red peppers through a juicer. Discard the pulp. In a small saucepan reduce the juice by two-thirds. Place the reduced juice in a blender and gradually drizzle in the peanut oil until emulsified. Season to taste with salt and pepper.

To assemble the dish, carve the duck off the bone. Serve with four latkes and a ladle of red pepper sauce. Garnish with sprigs of fresh cilantro.

148 Wild Pheasant "à la Ficelle" Roasted with Rosemary

Serves 4

For the pheasant:
1 pheasant, cleaned
1 head garlic, left whole
1 stale roll
2 sprigs fresh rosemary
Sea salt
Freshly ground black pepper

For the confit of peppers:
1 tablespoon extra virgin olive oil
1 red bell pepper, skin removed and julienned
1 yellow bell pepper, skin removed and julienned

For the ragoût of vegetables:
2 tablespoons extra virgin olive oil
1 shallot, peeled and chopped
1 clove garlic, peeled and chopped
1 medium onion, peeled and chopped
1 2-ounce piece prosciutto, preferably with skin
1 medium zucchini, cut into small dice
1 medium yellow squash, cut into small dice
½ eggplant, cut into small dice
1 large tomato, peeled, seeded and diced
2 tablespoons chopped green olives
2 tablespoons chopped fresh basil
½ cup consommé or stock
½ cup tomato juice

For the celery root purée:
1 large celery root
1 lemon
1 cup heavy cream
4 tablespoons butter, softened
Freshly ground nutmeg
Sea salt
Freshly ground pepper
4 sprigs fresh basil

For the pheasant, cut the wing joint from the bird and discard it. Clean the pheasant well and season inside and out with salt and pepper. Stuff the inside with the garlic, bread and rosemary.

Truss the bird and roast either for 45 minutes on a rotisserie over hot coals or in a 475 degree oven for 25 minutes. If using a rotisserie, be sure to use a drip pan to collect the juices as the bird cooks.

For the ragoût of vegetables, confit the red and yellow peppers. Heat the olive oil in a non-stick saute pan over medium to high heat for 3 minutes. Add the peppers and cook over low heat, stirring often, for 1 hour. Reserve.

In another non-stick sauté pan, heat the 2 tablespoons of olive oil over medium high heat for 3 minutes. Add the shallot, onion, garlic and thyme. Cook for 3 minutes, without browning. Add the prosciutto, zucchini, yellow squash, eggplant and tomato. Sauté for 5 minutes. Add the confit of peppers, green olives, basil, tomato juice and consommé. Turn the heat to medium low and cook gently for 30 minutes.

For the celery root mousseline, peel the celery root. Halve the lemon and rub the outside of the celery root to prevent discoloration. Chop the celery root into large pieces and place in a pan of salted water. Add the two lemon halves and bring to a boil. Cook until tender.

When cooked, pass the celery root through a tamis or fine sieve into a bowl. Stir in the cream and the butter; add the nutmeg, salt and pepper to taste. Reheat the mousseline in a bain-marie just before serving.

To serve the dish, place the hot celery root purée into a pastry bag fitted with a large star tip. Slice the breast off the pheasant and cut into medallions. Remove the legs and cut at the first joint into two pieces. Place a spoonful of the vegetables on the lower half of the plate. Place 3 medallions of pheasant and a piece of leg meat over the vegetables. Pipe the celery root purée onto the plate, just above the pheasant. Garnish with fresh basil and serve.

150 Texas Antelope with Purple Sage

Serves 2

For the antelope:
1 pound trimmed loin of antelope or venison
Salt and white pepper
Vegetable oil or clarified butter

For the sauce:
1½ teaspoons minced shallots
8 leaves purple sage, minced
1 cup rich game stock
8 fresh morels, sliced into quarters
¼ cup chopped roasted hazelnuts
3 tablespoons hazelnut oil
Salt and pepper

For the garnish:
4 leaves purple sage
4 whole morels, sauteed in butter or oil
Pink peppercorns

For the antelope, season with salt and white pepper. Sear on all sides in hot oil or clarified butter. Place in 375-degree oven and roast for 10 to 12 minutes, or until medium-rare. Remove and set aside.

For the sauce, degrease roasting pan. Place it atop heat and sauté shallots until just browned. Add half the minced sage, the game stock, quartered morels and hazelnuts. Bring to a boil, reduce slightly and turn off heat. Whisk in hazelnut oil and remaining minced sage. Adjust seasoning with salt and pepper.
Set aside and keep warm.

To serve, slice antelope and arrange in circle on plate. Garnish with whole morels and sage leaves. Whisk sauce and spoon around meat on plate. Scatter pink peppercorns in middle.

***Note:** If you must use dried morels, reconstitute in water and save water. Reduce it and add 1 tablespoon to sauce for added flavor.

151 Squab with Star Anise Sauce

Serves 4

For the sauce:
1 tablespoon grapeseed oil
Bones from 4 squabs
½ cup mirepoix
½ cup red wine
1 cup veal stock
1 teaspoon star anise
Salt and pepper to taste
1 tablespoon butter

For the vegetable roulades:
4 savoy cabbage leaves, blanched
1 cup assorted julienned vegetables, blanched
1 tablespoon butter, melted
Salt and pepper to taste

For the squabs:
4 squabs, breasts and legs
Salt and pepper to season
2 tablespoons butter

For the garnish:
½ cup small savoy cabbage leaves
4 cremini mushroom caps
Sprigs of fresh tarragon and chervil
1 tablespoon rock salt
1 teaspoon ground white pepper

For the sauce, heat the oil in a heavy skillet and thoroughly brown the squab bones; add in the mirepoix, continuing to brown until nicely caramelized. Deglaze the pan with the red wine, allowing the alcohol to evaporate; pour in the veal stock, with the star anise and let it simmer until reduced to a light glaze. Strain through a fine sieve, season with the salt and pepper, and finish with the butter.

For the roulades, lay out the cabbage leaves and divide the julienned vegetables, alternating the colors to form a mosaic pattern, between the 4 leaves. Roll each filled leaf up into a small pouch, place them on a baking sheet, drizzle the roulades with melted butter season and heat in a moderate oven until warm.

For the squabs, season the meat with salt and pepper, and sauté quickly in the butter, remove the breasts when they are pink and juicy, allowing the legs to cook a little longer.

To serve, make a small pool of the sauce at the bottom of each plate and arrange the sautéed squab onto the sauce. Cut each vegetable roulade in half and stand the halves up just to the top of the squab. Garnish the dish with the small savoy leaves, the mushrooms, fresh herbs and sprinkled rock salt and ground white pepper.

152 Ragoût of Hare

Serves 4

For the Ragoût:
1 saddle of hare, boned and trimmed
2 cups dry red wine
1 cup mirepoix
1 bouquet garni
1 teaspoon juniper berries
Salt and pepper to taste
2 tablespoons olive oil
2 strips bacon, cut into ¼-inch pieces
1 cup game stock
1 sprig thyme
1 spring rosemary
2 springs tarragon
1 tablespoon butter

For the garnish:
½ cup baby carrots, peeled and blanched
1 leek, white part only, cut in half and blanched
½ cup white turnips, peeled and blanched
6 pieces new potatoes, peeled and blanched
½ cup pearl onions, peeled and blanched
2 tablespoons butter
Salt and pepper to taste
Chervil sprigs

For the ragoût, cut the meat into 1½-ounce medallions and marinate in the wine. Add the mirepoix, bouquet garni and juniper berries. Refrigerate for six hours. Remove the meat from the marinade, and pat the meat dry. Save the marinade for later use. Season the meat with salt and pepper and sauté in a hot sauté pan with the olive oil. Remove the meat from the pan, set aside and keep warm. Discard the excess grease from the pan, add the bacon and sauté until crisp. Deglaze the pan with ½ cup of the marinade, reduce by half, add the game stock, the thyme, rosemary, and tarragon, and reduce again by half. Strain the sauce, add the butter, season to taste with salt and pepper and set aside.

To finish the ragoût, sauté the carrots, leek and turnips in butter until they have taken on some color, and add the potatoes, pearl onions, the meat and the sauce. Simmer for 2 to 3 minutes, season with salt and pepper to taste, and arrange on plates. Garnish with sprigs of chervil.

153 Rabbit Loin with Potato and Bacon Hash

Serves 4

For the hash:
2 ounces apple-smoked bacon, finely diced
½ clove garlic, peeled and minced
2 Idaho potatoes, peeled and finely diced
2 shallots, peeled and finely chopped
Salt and pepper to taste
1 tablespoon Italian parsley, finely chopped

For the rabbit loins:
4 rabbit loins
Salt and pepper to taste
Butter for sautéing

For the sauce:
4 rabbit kidneys
½ cup rabbit stock
4 tablespoons butter, chilled

For the hash, sauté the bacon with the garlic, potatoes and shallots until tender and the bacon has begun to turn golden brown. Season with salt and pepper and add the parsley.

For the rabbit loins, season the loins with salt and pepper and sauté in butter until medium rare. Remove the loins from the pan and set aside. Using the same pan, sauté the rabbit kidneys for the sauce. Finely chop the kidneys and 1 of the sautéed loins. Bring the stock to a boil and whisk in the butter. Add the chopped kidneys and loins.

To serve, place the hash on plates. Slice the loins very thinly on the bias and lay the slices on top of the hash. Drizzle the sauce over and serve.

Local Rabbit Braised in Pomerol

Serves 4

For the polenta:
3 cups stock
1 cup corn meal
1 cup chopped wild mushrooms
1 head of garlic
4 tablespoons olive oil
2 tablespoons chopped sage leaves
Salt and pepper to taste

For the rabbit stock:
2 rabbits, boned with hind legs, loins and livers reserved
½ cup chopped onion
¼ cup chopped leek, white part only
¼ cup chopped carrot
½ cup mushroom pieces
2 garlic cloves
1 bay leaf
¼ cup tomato concassé
½ cup Pomerol
1½ quarts chicken stock

For the rabbit:
4 strips thick cut bacon
4 rabbit hind legs
Salt and pepper to taste
½ cup chopped onion
¼ cup chopped leek, white part only
¼ cup chopped carrot
½ cup chopped mushroom pieces
2 garlic cloves
1 bay leaf
¼ cup tomato concassé
¼ cup chopped parsley stems
½ cup Pomerol
1 quart rabbit stock
1 cup dried currants, soaked in red wine
4 boneless rabbit loins
4 rabbit livers
16 pearl onions, blanched and peeled
2 tablespoons olive oil
1 cup small shiitake mushrooms
2 tablespoons chopped parsley
2 sprigs thyme
¼ cup brandy
2 tablespoons cold butter

For the polenta, break the garlic into cloves, coat them with the 2 tablespoons of the olive oil and roast them in a 325 degree oven until they are soft, about 15 minutes. Remove the cloves from their skins and mash, reserving the oil. Bring the stock to a boil, whisk in the cornmeal, being careful to avoid the formation of lumps. Stir in the mushrooms and the garlic; cook over a medium heat for 20 minutes, stirring constantly, and season with the sage, the reserved olive oil and the salt and pepper. Cook for an additional 10 minutes and spread onto a plastic wrap-lined sheet pan to a thickness of ½ inch. Cover, chill until firm and cut into triangles.

For the stock, roast the rabbit bones in a hot oven until evenly browned. Add in the chopped onions, leeks, carrots, mushroom pieces, the garlic cloves, bay leaf and the tomato concassé; continue roasting until the mirepoix is lightly caramelized and deglaze the pan with the Pomerol wine. Remove the roasted bones and mirepoix from the roasting pan and place into a stock pot with the chicken stock; simmer for 3 to 4 hours, allowing the stock to reduce by no more than ⅓; season and strain.

For the rabbit, render the bacon in a braising pan; remove the bacon, season the legs with salt and pepper, and brown them in the bacon fat; remove the legs and keep warm. Brown the chopped onions, leeks, carrots, mushroom pieces and the garlic; add to this the bay leaf, the tomato concassé and the parsley stems; deglaze with the wine, allowing the alcohol to evaporate and add in the rabbit stock and ½ cup of the currants. Return the legs to the pan, cover them with the strips of bacon and braise for ½ hour in a 275 degree oven. Remove the legs and the bacon from the pan, strain the liquid and reserve. Skewer the rabbit livers with pieces of the bacon and the blanched pearl onions and season the loins with salt and pepper. In a skillet, heat the olive oil and brown the loins and the skewered livers with the remaining pearl onions and the shiitake mushrooms; drain off the olive oil and add in the remaining currants with their liquid to deglaze the pan. Add in the braised legs, the remaining bacon and the braising stock; bring this to a simmer and place, covered, in a 375 degree oven for 4 to 5 minutes.

To serve, remove the pan from the oven and place over a medium high heat; remove the pieces of rabbit and the skewers. Add in the chopped parsley, the thyme and the brandy and quickly reduce the liquid to a light glaze; remove the thyme, whisk in the cold butter to finish the sauce and season to taste with salt and pepper. In another skillet brown the polenta in olive oil and drain the excess oil on a clean towel. Ladle a pool of the mushroom, onion and currant studded sauce onto each plate, slice the loins and arrange the slices on the sauce with the braised legs, the skewered livers and the polenta.

154 Venison with Caraway Potato Roll

Serves 4

For the venison:
1 8-rib rack of venison
1 1-pound venison loin, cleaned
4 tablespoons coarse sea salt
1 cup balsamic vinegar
3 cloves garlic, peeled and chopped
4 tablespoons paprika
2 tablespoons celery seed
1 cup coarsely ground coriander seed
¼ cup coarsely ground white
and black pepper

For the potato roll:
3 Yukon Gold potatoes, peeled,
boiled and mashed
1 leek, diced and sweated in butter
¼ cup chopped chives
2 teaspoons caraway seeds, toasted
Salt and pepper to taste
4 8 by 8-inch spring roll wrappers
Egg wash
Peanut oil for frying
1 egg

For the vinaigrette:
2 tablespoons whole grain mustard
⅓ cup champagne vinegar
1 tablespoon anchovy paste
1 cup olive oil
½ cup mustard oil

For the mustard oil:
(Yields 2 cups)
3 tablespoons mustard powder
1 tablespoon water
2 cups grapeseed oil

To prepare the oil, place the mustard powder in a small bowl, add the water and mix to form a paste. If the paste is too dry, add a few more drops of water. Transfer the mustard paste to a mason jar. Add the oil and cover the jar. Shake vigorously. Leave the jar at room temperature for two days, shaking the jar often to infuse the flavors into the oil. After two days, remove the oil with a ladle and filter it through a coffee filter Store the spice oil in the refrigerator or at room temperature for up to 1 month.

For the venison, place the rack and loin in a shallow pan. Combine the sea salt, vinegar and chopped garlic in a separate bowl. Spread this mixture evenly over the meat. Combine the remaining seasonings and rub into the meat. Let marinate for 1 hour. Cold-smoke the venison for 1 hour to impart a faint smokey flavor Spit-roast both the rack and the loin until medium rare. Alternately, the meat can be roasted in a 400 degree oven.

For the potato roll, preheat the oil to 360 degrees. Combine the mashed potatoes, egg, leeks, chives, caraway, salt and pepper. To assemble the roll, place three ounces of potato stufing in the center.Brush the corners with the egg wash. Fold three corners toward the center, forming an envelope. Roll t up toward the remaining point and seal tightly and fry until golden brown. Drain on a paper towel.

To prepare the vinaigrette, combine the mustard, vinegar, and anchovy paste in a medium bowl. Add the olive oil and mustard oil, but do not emulsify. The vinaigrette should appear broken and set aside.

To present the dish, thinly slice the venison loin and cut the rack into chops. Arrange the venison, greens and potoat rolls on plates Drizzle with the mustard oil vinaigrette and ganish with herbs.

155 Corn Risotto with Quail and Sage

Serves 4

For the corn:
4 ears yellow corn, shucked

For the quail:
4 partially boned quail
1 tablespoon corn oil
Salt and pepper to taste
1 shallot, sliced
6 cloves garlic, unpeeled
½ sprig sage
½ cup chicken stock

For the chanterelles:
½ tablespoon corn oil
8 ounces chanterelles
Salt and pepper to taste
½ tablespoon butter

For the risotto:
3½ cups chicken stock, or more as needed
2 green onions, minced
½ tablespoon corn oil
1 cup arborio rice
¼ cup dry white wine
2½ tablespoons butter
2 tablespoons grated Parmesan cheese
3 leaves sage, chopped
Salt and pepper to taste

For the garnish:
Sage leaves

For the quail eggs:
Corn oil for brushing the pan
4 quail eggs

For the corn, boil ears in salted water for five minutes. Drain, cool and remove kernels. Keep ¼ cup kernels aside and purée the rest in a blender. Set aside.

For the quail, preheat the oven to 400 degrees with roasting pan in the oven. Rub corn oil on quail, season with salt and pepper and roast breast-side up for two minutes. Add shallots, garlic, and sage to pan. Turn quail over on the backbone and roast for 8 to 10 minutes more. Remove quail from the pan. When cool enough to handle, remove breasts and the legs from the bone. Set meat aside and place bones back in roasting pan.Return to the oven for 15 to 20 minutes. Remove garlic cloves and set aside with quail meat. Pour chicken stock over bones, let simmer until liquid reduced to ¼ cup. Strain and reserve jus.

For the chanterelles, heat sauté pan with corn oil over high heat. Add chanterelles and salt and pepper to taste. Toss until cooked and lightly colored, about 5 minutes. Finish tossing with butter and set aside.

For the risotto, warm chicken stock. In casserole dish, sweat onions in oil over medium heat. Add rice and toss well. Cook rice lightly, but do not color. Add wine. Mix well and cook until wine evaporates. Slowly add chicken stock to cover rice, stirring. Add more stock, a little at a time, while rice is cooking. Simmer 15 to 17 minutes, making sure rice stays moist. Just before serving, add butter, Parmesan, corn purée, reserved corn kernels, chopped sage and salt and pepper.

For the quail eggs, brush a non-stick pan with oil. Heat over medium heat and cook quail eggs sunny-side up. Reheat quail, chanterelles and garlic in oven.

To serve, spoon risotto onto plates. Slice breast of quail and place it in the middle of the plate. Place quail legs, garlic and chanterelles around it. Place quail eggs in the center. Pour warm jus around plate, and garnish with sage leaves.

156 Barbecued Squab with Corn Salad

Serves 4

For the squab:
¼ cup orange juice
¼ cup sugar
¼ cup red wine vinegar
1 tablespoon tomato paste
2 tablespoons soy sauce
2 tablespoons Thai nam plah fish sauce
6 whole star anise
1 large clove garlic, peeled and chopped
1 tablespoon chopped ginger
4 squabs, quartered

For the carrot-anise sauce:
4 cups carrot juice
6 whole star anise
¼ cup peanut oil
Salt and pepper to taste

For the salad:
2 tablespoons olive oil
2 ears corn, shucked and kernels removed
1 cup chanterelles, cleaned and sliced
1 shallot, peeled and chopped
1 teaspoon basil purée
Salt and pepper to taste

For the garnish:
Fried julienne of carrot
Star anise
Chopped chives

To marinate the squab, combine the orange juice, sugar, vinegar, tomato paste, soy sauce, nam plah, anise, garlic and ginger in a small bowl to make a marinade. Place the squab in a shallow pan and evenly coat with the marinade. Allow to stand for six hours.

Meanwhile, prepare the carrot-anise sauce. Combine the carrot juice and star anise in a non-reactive saucepan. Over a low flame, reduce to a quarter cup, whisking constantly. Strain out the star anise and transfer concentrated juice to a blender. While blending on high speed, slowly add the peanut oil to make an emulsion. Season with salt and pepper to taste. Set aside.

To prepare the corn and chanterelle salad, set a sauté pan over high heat. Add the olive oil, corn kernels, chanterelles, shallot, basil purée, salt and pepper. Cook for five minutes. Keep warm.

To finish the dish, roast the squab over a charcoal or wood fired grill, basting with the remaining barbecue sauce until cooked. Arrange the squab on serving plates with the corn and chanterelle salad. Dress liberally with the carrot-anise sauce and garnish with the fried julienne of carrot, star anise and chopped chives.

157 Shepherd's Pie with Olives

Serves 2

For the duck confit:
4 duck legs
Salt to season
4½ pounds duck fat

For the pies:
2 Idaho potatoes
½ cup heavy cream
1 tablespoon olive oil
Salt and pepper to taste
Reserved duck leg confit
1 cup niçoise olives, pitted
2 tablespoons breadcrumbs
1 tablespoon olive oil

For the sauce:
1 cup duck stock
½ cup niçoise olives, pitted
2 ounces virgin olive oil

For the garnish:
Snipped chives

For the duck confit, place the duck legs in a medium bowl and season with coarse salt, ¼ ounce per pound, and place in the refrigerator for 24 hours, allowing the salt to penetrate into the flesh. Cook in a large copper cauldron with the duck fat for 2 hours. The fat should simmer but not boil. Remove from the heat, and while the fat is still hot, strain it into a stoneware pot and place the legs in the fat, being certain that they are completely covered. Cool and then cover the pot.

For the pies, peel and quarter the potatoes and cook in salted water until they become completely soft. Pour the potatoes into a colander, spread the potatoes on a sheet pan and let cool to room temperature. When the potatoes have cooled off, squeeze them through a potato ricer. Heat the cream with the olive oil, add the potatoes, salt and pepper, and mix well. Do not overmix the potatoes. Slowly heat the duck legs, remove from the fat and pick the meat from the bones. Place 4 4-inch ring molds on a sheet pan, line the perimeters of the molds with the olives, and divide the duck meat among the molds. Top each mold with mashed potatoes, sprinkle with breadcrumbs and drizzle with olive oil. Place the tray in a preheated oven at 375 degrees. Bake for 15 minutes.

For the sauce, bring the stock to a boil, simmer and reduce by half. Add the olives and olive oil and purée in a blender until completely smooth.

To serve, pour pools of sauce on preheated plates, place pies on top and remove the ring molds. Garnish each pie with the snipped chives.

157 Open Ravioli with Squab and Mushrooms

Serves 4

For the filling:
4 young squabs
2 tablespoons olive oil
4 shallots, peeled and chopped
2 cups assorted mushrooms, stems cup off the base
1 cup dry fino sherry
1 cup dark chicken stock
Salt and pepper to taste
1/8 cup fresh sage leaves

For the glaçage:
1 cup hollandaise sauce
1 cup heavy cream, whipped

For the ravioli:
8 2½ inch by 5 inch pasta squares, cooked
4 tablespoons foie gras
1 tablespoon chopped chives

For the garnish:
Cherry tomatoes
Julienned truffles
Mint leaves

For the filling, cut each squab into 8 pieces. Heat the olive oil in a large skillet, add the shallots and sauté until translucent. Add the squab pieces and cook until they begin to color. Move the squab pieces to a platter. Place the mushrooms in the pan and cook until all the water has evaporated. Deglaze the pan with the sherry and reduce the sauce by half. Put the squab pieces back in the pan, pour in the chicken stock and add the salt, pepper, and sage leaves. Cover the pan and simmer until the meat is completely tender. Remove the squab pieces, pick the meat off the bones and return the meat to the sauce. Keep the filling warm.

For the glaçage, mix the hollandaise and the whipped cream.

For the ravioli, place 1 sheet of the pasta on each plate, divide the filling among 4 sheets, ladle some glacage over the filling, add the foie gras and chopped chives, and top with the remaining pasta sheets. Place the plates under a hot salamander and broil until the sauce begins to bubble and turns golden brown. Garnish the dish with cherry tomatoes, julienned truffles and mint leaves.

159 Braised Guinea Hen with Savoy Cabbage

Serves 4

For the guinea hen:
1 3-pound guinea hen
Salt and pepper to season
3 tablespoons butter
½ cup extra virgin olive oil
5 cloves garlic, peeled
1 sprig fresh rosemary
1½ cups sliced porcini mushrooms
2 cups coarsely chopped savoy cabbage
4 cups chicken stock
Salt and freshly ground white pepper to taste

For the garnish:
4 small sprigs rosemary

For the dish, season the hen with salt and pepper and truss. Place the trussed bird in a baking dish with the butter and 2 tablespoons of the olive oil. Bake at 300 degrees for one hour, turning frequently. In a copper or stainless steel saucepan heat the remaining olive oil with the garlic and rosemary, but do not allow the garlic to brown; cool and discard both the garlic and the rosemary after the flavor is infused into the oil. Place the mushrooms in the same saucepan with the oil and sauté over a high flame for about 2 minutes. Add in the chopped cabbage and the chicken stock and simmer for about 30 minutes. Season to taste with the salt and pepper. When the guinea hen is done, remove it from the oven and skim off the fat. Add the sautéed cabbage and the porcini mushrooms to the hen; cover and bake at 300 degrees for about 10 minutes.

162 Crépinettes with Chestnuts

Serves 10

For the mirepoix:
5 carrots, peeled and diced
5 onions, peeled and diced
5 leeks, washed and diced
8 stalks celery, diced

For the crépinettes:
15 lamb tongues, cleaned
15 lamb cheeks, trimmed
15 lamb kidneys, cleaned
15 lamb livers, cleaned
2½ quarts consommé
1 bunch thyme, stems removed
1 bay leaf
Caul fat, soaked
1 cup rendered duck fat
Salt and pepper to taste

For the chestnuts:
10 pounds fresh chestnuts
2 cups heavy cream
½ pound unsalted butter

For the sauce:
5 shallots, peeled and sliced
1 cup vermouth
2 cups consommé
2 cups heavy cream
Salt and pepper to taste

For the mirepoix, combine all of the diced vegetables. Set aside until needed.

To prepare the crépinettes, simmer the tongues and cheeks in the consommé with ½ of the mirepoix mixture, the thyme and bay leaf for 3 hours. Remove the meats and dice finely. Strain the cooking liquid and reduce to a glace.

Roast the kidneys on top of the remaining mirepoix in a hot oven until cooked through. Cool and dice finely. Dice the liver and sauté in some of the duck fat. Combine the tongues, cheeks, kidneys, liver and the glace. Shape into 4-ounce balls, season with salt and pepper and wrap in caul fat.

To prepare the chestnuts, blanch and peel all of the chestnuts. Set 30 whole chestnuts aside for the garnish and purée the rest. Divide the purée in half. Scald the heavy cream and mix into one half of the chestnut purée. Pass through a fine chinois and reserve. Set the remaining purée aside to make the sauce.

To prepare the sauce, sweat the shallots and vermouth with the remaining chestnut purée and consommé. Simmer for 20 minutes. Add the cream, purée the whole mixture and pass through a fine chinois. Cook the reserved whole chestnuts in boiling water with ¼ pound of the butter until tender. Drain and sauté the chestnuts in the remaining butter until golden brown.

Just before service, place the crépinettes on a sheet pan and baste with the remaining duck fat. Roast the crépinettes until golden brown. Place one crépinette in the middle of each serving plate. Garnish with the whole chestnuts and the chestnut purée. Ladle the sauce around the plate and serve.

163 Cassoulet

Serves 6

For the cassoulet:
2 cups dry small white beans, soaked
1 dry cured ham bone
1 pound lean cubed lamb shoulder
5 ounces fresh pork fatback, cut in strips
1 cup finely diced carrots
1 cup finely diced onions
3 garlic cloves, crushed
5 ounces dry cured ham, diced
⅔ cup white wine
2 quarts water
1 bouquet of fresh herbs
1 clove
Pinch of nutmeg
8 freshly cracked peppercorns
3 duck legs, confits
1 duck breast, confits
1 pound fresh pork sausage
6 goose gizzard, confits
1 cup, diced, peeled and seeded tomatoes
Salt to taste

For the cassoulet, scald the soaked beans for 10 minutes in boiling water; drain and shock in cold water- this will allow the beans to cook without splitting. Cook the ham bone in the 2 quarts water for 30 minutes to flavor the water; reserve the bone to be used again. Heat a large casserole or high-sided heavy skillet and brown the lamb; add in the pork fat and continue to braise the lamb for another 5 minutes. Toss in with the lamb, the carrots, onions, garlic and the ham-allowing the juices to lightly caramelize. Remove the strips of fat, deglaze with the white wine and add in the ham flavored water. Season with the bouquet of herbs, the clove, nutmeg and cracked peppercorns. Add in the ham bone, the blanched beans, and simmer for 1 hour-skimming from time to time.

While the beans are cooking, place the duck confits, with a little of the fat on a sheet pan and bake at 350 degrees, for 20 minutes- basting the confits with the hot fat every 5 minutes. After 10 minutes add in the pork sausages to roast, and then the goose gizzards. When the confits are crisp, cut the legs in half and the breast into 6 pieces. After the first hour of cooking, add the confits, the sausage and the gizzards and the diced tomatoes to the beans; adjust the seasoning, add more water if necessary to keep the beans covered and continue cooking for another 30 minutes, until the beans are done.

To serve, divide the beans, with equal portions of the lamb, ham, sausage, duck breasts, the duck legs and the gizzards into serving crocks. Bake each portion in a 350 degree oven for 8 to 10 minutes and set with an underliner on individual plates.

164 Ragoût of Lamb Brains and Sweetbreads

Serves 10

For the trofie pasta:
3 pounds all-purpose flour
5 ounces truffle flour
Pinch of salt
19 ounces hot water, by weight
½ teaspoon truffle oil

For the ragoût:
3 lamb brains, cleaned
1 quart consommé
2 carrots, peeled and chopped
2 onions, peeled and chopped
8 stalks celery, chopped
2 leeks, cleaned and chopped
1 bunch thyme
5 pounds lamb sweetbreads, cleaned
1 pound lobster mushrooms, julienned
2 cloves garlic, peeled
2 tablespoons olive oil
2 black truffles, julienned
1 can truffle juice
Salt and pepper to taste

To prepare the trofie, mix the flours in an electric mixer fitted with a dough-hook for 30 seconds until blended. Add the salt, water and truffle oil and knead in the mixer for 20 minutes. If the dough is sticky, add more all-purpose flour.

To form the noodles, flatten a small piece of dough under the palm of your hand while drawing your palm towards you along the work surface. Reverse the motion of your palm and roll the dough up along the full length of your extended pinky, flicking the noodle off the tip of your finger to give it a crooked shape. Toss in flour and continue shaping the remainder of the dough. Boil the trofie for 8 to 10 minutes, just until al dente, in salted water. Drain, rinse and set aside.

For the ragoût, simmer the brains in the consommé for 12 minutes. Let cool in the liquid. Combine the carrots, onions, celery, leeks and thyme on the bottom of a roasting pan. Lay the sweetbreads on top of the vegetables and roast in a hot oven for 12 minutes. Cool and dice. Sauté the sweetbreads, lobster mushrooms and garlic in the olive oil. Add the truffle, truffle juice and the consommé used to cook the brains. Add the trofie. Season with salt and pepper. Slice the cooked brains on the bias, ¼-inch thick.

To serve, place the sweetbread and trofie ragoût on the bottom of a large soup plate. Arrange the slices of brain around the dish and sauce with more consommé if needed.

165 Lamb Chop with Eggplant Tart

Serves 4

For the eggplant tarts:
3 eggplants
½ cup olive oil
4 cloves garlic, peeled and chopped
3 tomatoes, peeled and diced
2 bay leaves
1 onion, peeled and sliced
½ teaspoon curry powder
1 tablespoon vinegar
1 tablespoon chopped parsley
1 tablespoon chopped chives
1 tablespoon chopped basil
Salt and pepper to taste

For the sauce:
1 cup carrot juice
1 teaspoon finely diced fresh ginger
2 tablespoons butter
Salt and cayenne pepper to taste

For the lamb chops:
4 6-ounce lamb chops
Salt to taste
2 tablespoons olive oil
¼ teaspoon brown mustard seeds
½ teaspoon coriander seeds
¼ teaspoon cumin
¼ teaspoon curry powder
¼ cup breadcrumbs
¼ cup toasted pine nuts, chopped
1 tablespoon chopped mint

For the garnish:
1 tablespoon chopped chives
Thyme sprigs

For the eggplant tarts, cut 2 of the eggplants in half, brush the halves with olive oil and roast in a 350 degree oven until the flesh is tender. Remove the eggplant from the oven, scoop out the flesh and purée in a blender until smooth. Press the purée through a fine sieve and set aside. Cut the remaining eggplant lengthwise into thin slices and sauté in a large skillet with a generous amount of olive oil until golden brown on both sides. Remove the slices from the pan and set aside. In the same skillet, sauté the garlic until golden brown. Add the diced tomatoes and bay leaves and simmer until the tomatoes start falling apart. In a second skillet, sauté the sliced onion in olive oil over high heat until dark brown. Add the curry powder, cook for 1 minute and deglaze the pan with vinegar.

In a bowl, mix the eggplant purée with the sautéed tomatoes and onions. Add the chopped herbs and season to taste with salt and pepper. Line 4 5-inch ring molds with the sautéed eggplant slices, fill the molds ¾ full with the seasoned eggplant purée and heat in a 250 degree oven for 15 minutes. For the sauce, reduce the carrot juice by half, add the chopped ginger and simmer for 4 to 5 minutes. Strain the carrot juice, add the butter bit by bit, season to taste with salt and pepper, and keep warm.

For the lamb chops, sprinkle the chops with the salt and sauté in the olive oil to desired doneness. Remove the chops from the skillet, mix all remaining ingredients and top each chop with a generous amount of this mixture. Brown the chops under a hot broiler until the topping becomes golden brown.

To serve, remove the rings from the eggplant tarts, center the tarts on preheated plates, and top each tart with a lamb chop. Drizzle the sauce around the eggplant tart and garnish with chopped chives and thyme sprigs.

ICG Confit of Lamb Boulangère Garnish

Serves 14

For the lamb:
1 pound coarse sea salt
1 bunch thyme, stems removed
1 bunch rosemary, stems removed and chopped
¼ cup whole black peppercorns
2 lamb shoulders, boned, rolled and tied
2 quarts rendered duck fat

For the boulangère garnish:
10 small celeriac, peeled
5 russet potatoes, peeled
5 yellow onions, peeled and finely julienned
1 quart consommé
Salt and pepper to taste
1 cup grated Parmesan cheese
1 cup breadcrumbs

For the thyme sauce:
2 carrots, peeled and chopped
1 onion, peeled and chopped
1 leek, cleaned and chopped
3 stalks celery, chopped
4 tablespoons unsalted butter
2 bunches thyme
2 quarts consommé
1 cup brown veal stock
Salt and pepper to taste

To prepare the lamb shoulders, combine the sea salt, thyme, rosemary and black peppercorns. Cover the lamb with this mixture and let marinate for 5 hours. Rinse. Completely cover the lamb with the duck fat and simmer for approximately 3 hours, until the outside is golden brown and the meat is very tender.

For the boulangère garnish, use a mandolin to slice the celeriac and potatoes very thinly. Set the slices in cold water. Simmer the julienned onions in the consommé until tender. Butter a shallow, half-hotel pan. Beginning with the onions, alternate layers of the onions and consommé, potatoes and celeriac, seasoning with salt and pepper after every third layer. Top with the grated Parmesan cheese and breadcrumbs. Bake covered in a 325 degree oven for 45 minutes. Finish baking uncovered for 15 minutes until golden brown.

To prepare the thyme sauce, sweat the carrots, onion, leek and celery in the butter. Add the thyme and the consommé. Cook for 30 minutes and add the brown veal stock. Purée. Pass through a chinois. Reduce to a sauce consistency. Adjust the seasoning with salt and pepper.

To serve, cut the boulangère garnish into rounds. Ladle the sauce on the bottom of the plates. Slice the lamb and serve with the garnish.

ICG Navarin of Lamb with Mint

Serves 2

For the lamb:
1 loin of lamb, bones and trimmed
1 tablespoon clarified butter
½ cup rich, dark, reduced lamb stock
½ cup heavy cream
1 cup cleaned and blanched fresh fava beans
½ bunch fresh mint, minced
Salt and pepper to taste

For the garnish:
4 mint leaves
¼ cup diced tomato

For the lamb, cut tenderloin into 1-inch cubes. Season with salt and white pepper. Heat clarified butter in heavy casserole until almost smoking. Add lamb cubes and sear on all sides, but leave centers rare. Remove lamb to a warm place. Deglaze pan with lamb stock and add heavy cream. Reduce slightly, until thickened. Add fava beans, minced mint leaves and lamb. Cook until just coated with sauce. Adjust seasoning.To serve spoon lamb mixture into bowls and top with mint leaves and diced tomato.

166 Grilled Lamb Hearts with Onion Confit

Serves 4

For the rosemary oil:
2 sprigs fresh rosemary
½ cup olive oil

For the lamb hearts:
4 lamb hearts
Milk
Olive oil
Fresh thyme
Fresh rosemary
Cracked black peppercorns
4 cloves garlic, minced

For the onion confit:
2 Vidalia onions, thinly sliced
2 tablespoons olive oil
Salt and pepper to taste

For the garnish:
1 russet potato, boiled, peeled and diced
1 sweet potato, boiled, peeled and diced
2 tablespoons olive oil
Salt and pepper to taste
1 bunch mustard greens
1 tablespoon butter

For the rosemary oil, heat the rosemary in the olive oil. Cool to room temperature, cover and refrigerate for 1 day. To prepare the lamb hearts, place the hearts in a small bowl, cover with milk and let soak for 6 hours. Rinse and clean the hearts of any membranes and fat. Toss the hearts with the olive oil, fresh herbs, pepper and garlic and let marinate overnight. On the day of service, caramelize the Vidalia onions in the olive oil until golden brown. Season with salt and pepper. Remove the hearts from the marinade. Season with salt and pepper and grill until medium-rare. Set aside to rest.

To prepare the garnish, sauté the boiled diced potatoes in the olive oil until golden brown. Season and keep warm. Wilt the mustard greens in the butter and season with salt and pepper. To serve, arrange the onion confit in the center of the serving plates. Place the wilted mustard greens on top of the onions. Slice the grilled hearts thinly on the bias and arrange on top of the greens. Garnish with the diced potatoes and rosemary oil.

168 Black Sesame Cured Wild Boar Loin with Guava Sauce

Serves 8

For the wild boar:
½ cup sugar
¼ cup kosher salt
⅓ cup shallots, minced
2 tablespoons garlic, minced
2 tablespoons fresh thyme
2 tablespoons fresh cilantro
2 tablespoons lemon grass, chopped
2 tablespoons ginger
1 3-pound center cut wild boar loin
4 tablespoons sesame oil
1 cup black sesame seeds

For the sauce:
1 guava, peeled and seeded
1 tablespoon shallots, minced
1 teaspoon fresh ginger root, grated
¼ teaspoon garlic, minced
1 tablespoon fresh lime juice
1 tablespoon rice vinegar
1tablespoon sugar
¼ cup salad oil
1 teaspoon fresh lemon thyme leaves
Salt to taste

For the garnish:
Sprigs of sunflower sprouts

For the boar, mix together the sugar and the salt with the minced shallots, minced garlic, the fresh herbs and the ginger root. Coat the boar loin with the sesame oil and rub it thoroughly with the spice-herb mixture. Completely coat the seasoned loin with black sesame seeds; pressing them into the meat so they will stick. Wrap the loin in plastic wrap and let it cure over night. Smoke the wild boar loin over mango wood until it is medium in doneness.

For the sauce, purée the guava with the shallots, the garlic, and the ginger root. Blend them together with the lime juice, the rice vinegar and the sugar. Slowly mix in the oil, adjust the seasoning and sprinkle in the lemon thyme.

To serve, slice the smoked boar into medallions, ladle a pool of the guava sauce in the middle of the plates and arrange 3 medallions fanned out from the center. Garnish the dish with a sprig of sunflower sprouts.

169 Breaded Pigs' Feet with Celeriac Purée

Serves 6

For the pigs' feet:
6 pigs' feet
2 quarts clear white stock:
veal, chicken or pork
1 cup mirepoix
1 bouquet of herbs: thyme, bay leaf, parsley
3 ounces thick smoked bacon, diced
2 garlic cloves
2 tablespoons parsley
Salt and fresh cracked pepper
3 tablespoons Dijon mustard
3 ounces caulfat
1 egg, beaten
1 cup soft white breadcrumbs
4 tablespoons butter

For the celeriac purée:
2 cups diced celeriac
1 cup milk
1/4 cup chopped leek, white part only
1 bay leaf
1 small sprig of thyme
1 tablespoon butter
1/2 cup cream, as needed
Salt and white pepper taste

For the sauce:
1 tablespoon finely diced bayonne ham
1 1/2 cups sliced red onions
1/4 cup dry white wine
1/2 cup red wine
1/2 teaspoon chopped thyme
1/2 teaspoon chopped parsley
Salt and fresh cracked pepper

For the garnish:
6 leaves Italian parsley

For the pigs' feet, singe off any hairs from the pigs' feet over an open flame and rinse them thoroughly. Place the rinsed pigs' feet in a stock pot with the cold stock, the mirepoix and the bouquet of herbs; bring to a boil, skim, reduce the heat and simmer for 3 hours. When the pigs' feet are fully cooked, cool just enough to where they can be handled and remove the bones - this will be very difficult if the feet are cold.

In a sauté pan, cook the bacon - but do not brown - and drain off the excess grease. Sauté the garlic until softened, add in the parsley and cook for another minute. Cool and chop fine. Form the boned pigs' feet into the shape of a sausage, fill each one with a little of the bacon mixture, season and wrap them with the caulfat; smear the stuffed pigs' feet with the mustard, coat them with breadcrumbs, dip them in the beaten egg and roll them again in the crumbs. Chill to help the breading adhere.

For the celeriac purée, steam the celeriac in the milk with the leek, bay leaf and the thyme for about 20 minutes, until the celeriac is soft; remove the herbs, puree in a blender, whip in the butter and as much cream as is necessary- the purée should be the consistency of mashed potatoes- season with salt and pepper.

For the sauce, in a medium sauté pan over medium heat, sauté the ham for three minutes, or until the fat has rendered. Add the onions and sauté until caramelized. Deglaze with the white and red wine. Add the veal stock and simmer, loosely covered, for 30 minutes, until the onions are fully cooked and the liquid is reduced to a light glaze. Add the thyme and parsley. Remove from the heat, season and set aside, keep warm.

To serve, place the breaded pigs' feet on a sheet pan, drizzled with butter and bake in a 400 degree oven for 15 to 20 minutes, until the breading is crisp and the filling hot. Form the celeriac purée into 4 quenelles for each serving and set them fanned out to the top of each plate; ladle the onion sauce around the bottom of the plates and place the breaded pigs' feet onto the sauce. Garnish with the fresh parsley leaves.

169 Fresh Cotechino Sausage with Lentils and Puréed Potatoes

Serves 10

For the sausage:
1 pound pork shoulder
1/4 pound lean pork loin
1 pound neck or jowl meat
1 pound pork fatback
6 tablespoons salt
1 teaspoon saltpeter
1 tablespoon fresh cracked black pepper
1/4 teaspoon ground cloves
1/4 teaspoon ground cinnamon
1/4 teaspoon ground nutmeg
Natural beef casting, rinsed clean
Olive oil for brushing

For the lentils:
1/4 cup finely diced carrots
1/2 cup finely diced onions
1/2 cup finely diced celery
2 tablespoons extra virgin olive oil
4 tablespoons chopped chives
4 tablespoons chopped parsley
2 cups soaked lentils
2 cups beef or pork broth
Salt to taste

For the potato purée:
2 1/2 cooked and peeled potatoes
1/2 extra virgin olive oil
2 tablespoons hot water
Salt and white pepper to taste

For the garnish:
Fresh sprigs Italian parsley

For the sausage, cut the pork shoulder, loin, jowl meat and fatback into strips small enough to be pushed through the meat grinder; keeping the fatback separate and warm enough to absorb the seasonings. Mix together the salt, saltpeter, the black pepper, ground cloves, cinnamon and the nutmeg and toss with the meat and fatback. Grind the seasoned meat and the fatback once through the large blade of a meat grinder; cover and refrigerate overnight. The following day unravel a few feet of the beef casing; soak in lukewarm water for 30 minutes and rinse thoroughly from the faucet, checking as you go for any holes in the casing. Drain the excess liquid from the ground meat, and mix the meat thoroughly with the fatback. Using a sausage stuffer, fill the casing with the sausage farce; being careful to not allow any pockets of air, or to fill the skin too tightly. Tie both ends of the casing and secure the whole sausage with butcher's twine to hold the shape during the cooking. If you wish, leave the sausage to rest overnight so that the flavors might mellow. Blanch the sausage for 3 or 4 minute in simmering water to allow it to stiffen. Brush it with the olive oil and cook it slowly in a 325 degree oven, turning often so it browns evenly.

For the lentils, sauté the diced carrots, onions and celery in the olive oil until tender, but not brown. Add in the soaked lentils, the chopped parsley and the chives, cover with the hot broth, season with the salt, and simmer for about 30 minutes, until the lentils are cooked and the broth has been absorbed.

For the potatoes, pass them through a food mill into a saucepan. With a spoon, whip in half of the olive oil. Using a whip, add in the 2 tablespoons of hot water and then the remaining olive oil. Season the purée with salt and pepper.

To serve, slice the sausage into 1 ounce medallions; cover half of each dish with the cooked lentils and fan out 5 slices of the sausage on top. Make 2 quenelles of the potato purée for each dish and set them in the middle of the plate, just to the top of the lentils. Garnish each dish with a fresh sprig of parsley.

170 Roasted Loin of Lamb with Eggplant Chips

Serves 6

For the lamb:

1 boneless lamb loin, one side only
6 cloves garlic, peeled and minced
2 sprigs fresh rosemary, chopped
2 sprigs fresh thyme, chopped
2 sprigs fresh oregano, chopped
1 tablespoon cracked black pepper
½ cup extra-virgin olive oil
Kosher salt

For the garnish:

2 small eggplants, cut into ¼-inch slices
1 red onion, peeled and cut into 1-inch slices
2 vine-ripened tomatoes, diced
2 tablespoons extra-virgin olive oil
2 tablespoons balsamic vinegar
3 sprigs fresh mint, chopped
½ teaspoon dried oregano
Cracked black pepper to taste

For the eggplant chips:

2 eggplant, cut into very thin slices
Flour for dusting
Olive oil for frying
Salt and pepper to taste

For the sauce:

1½ cups lamb demi-glace
Salt and pepper to taste
For the herbed mayonnaise:
1 bunch fresh parsley, stems removed and cleaned
1 bunch fresh mint, stems removed and cleaned
2 egg yolks
Juice of ½ lemon
1 tablespoon coarse-grained mustard
1½ cups virgin olive oil
Salt and pepper to taste

To prepare the lamb, trim the loin of any excess fat. Season with the garlic, rosemary, thyme, oregano, black pepper and olive oil. Tie with butcher's twine and let marinate for 24 hours. Once marinated, set the lamb on a spit. Season with kosher salt and roast until medium-rare.

To prepare the garnish, grill the eggplant and red onion slices on high heat until tender. Dice. Mix the eggplant, red onion, tomato, olive oil, vinegar, mint, oregano and cracked black pepper. Adjust the seasoning.

For the eggplant chips, lightly sprinkle the thin eggplant slices with salt. Let sit 15 minutes. Lightly dredge the eggplant in flour and pan-fry in olive oil until golden brown and crisp. Blot dry with a paper towel and season with more salt and pepper to taste.

To prepare the sauce, reduce the demi-glace until thick. Adjust the seasoning with salt and pepper.

For the mayonnaise, purée the fresh herbs in a food processor. Add the egg yolks, lemon juice and mustard. While the machine is running, drizzle in the olive oil to form an emulsion. Season with salt and pepper.

To serve, ladle the sauce on the bottom of the plate. Using a squeeze bottle, pipe the herbed mayonnaise around the plate. Slice the roasted lamb. Garnish with the grilled vegetable salad and eggplant chips.

170 Potato Lasagne with Lamb Loin

Serves 4

For the lasagne:
2 large Idaho potatoes, peeled, sliced lengthwise and cut into rectangles
¼ cup clarified butter
1 pound lamb loin
Salt and pepper to taste
Butter for sautéeing
2 bunches spinach, washed
16 pearl onions, peeled and roasted
1 truffle, thinly sliced

For the sauce:
1 cup lamb stock
4 tablespoons butter, chilled

For the lasagne, coat the potato slices with clarified butter and bake on a sheet pan in a 200 degree oven for 5 minutes or until al dente.

Meanwhile, season the lamb loin with salt and pepper and sauté in butter to medium-rare. Let the cooked loin rest for 8 minutes, then slice thinly.

Arrange the baked potato rectangles with the sliced lamb, making three layers, ending with potato.

Sauté the spinach in butter. Add the pearl onions and season with salt and pepper. Garnish the lasagne with this mixture and the sliced truffle.

For the sauce, heat the lamb stock to a boil and whisk in the chilled butter. Pour the sauce over the lasagne and serve piping hot.

171 Lamb Stuffed Potato with Goat Sour Cream and Pomegranate Oil

Serves 4

For the potatoes:
4 Idaho potatoes
Vegetable oil for frying
1 cup warm milk
2 tablespoons hazelnut oil
Salt and pepper to taste

For the lamb:
2 racks of lamb
Salt and pepper
Vegetable oil

For the goat sour cream:
1 cup goat yogurt
¼ cup diced cucumber
1 teaspoon cumin seed
1 tablespoon mint, cut into fine strips

For the garnish:
¼ cup pomegranate oil
Mint leaves

For the pomegranate oil, chop 2 pomegranates and put through a juicer to obtain juice. Place juice in a saucepan over medium heat and reduce to a syrup. Add ¼ cup of grapeseed oil and mix well.

For the potatoes, bake potatoes in a 450-degree oven for 45 minutes or until tender. Slice in half lengthwise and scoop potato pulp from the skin, being careful not to rip skins. Fry the potato skins until crispy and set aside. Purée the inside of the potatoes and add the milk and hazelnut oil. Season with salt and pepper.

For the lamb, heat the oil in a pan until smoking hot. Season the lamb with salt and pepper and cook in the pan until brown on one side. Turn over and finish the lamb in a 500-degree oven until desired doneness.

Fill half of the potato skins with the puréed potatoes. Slice the lamb and place chops on top of the filled potato halves. Place the remaining potato skins alongside of the chops.

For the goat sour cream, combine all ingredients and keep refrigerated until ready to use.

To serve, place goat sour cream and pomegranate oil around potato on plate. Garnish with mint leaves.

172 Grilled Lamb Onglets

Serves 4

For the lamb:
8 lamb onglets*
15 shallots, peeled and thinly sliced
1 bunch sage, roughly chopped
1 cup olive oil
Salt and pepper to taste

For the potatoes:
4 russet potatoes, peeled, not washed
1 cup rendered duck fat
Salt and pepper to taste
1 bunch parsley, picked and chopped

To prepare the tenders, clean them of any fat and sinew. Macerate the tenders in the shallots, sage, olive oil, salt and pepper for several hours.

To prepare the potatoes, cut 2 of the 4 potatoes into small dice. Slice the remaining 2 potatoes using a spiral slicer. Lay the spirals flat on the work surface and line them up to form a raft-like structure. Wrap a cylinder with plastic wrap and roll the potato raft around the cylinder to form a tube. Deep fry the potato tube until golden brown. Remove the cylinder and return to the fryer to cook the inside.

Grill the marinated tenders until medium-rare. Transfer to serving plates. Sauté the shallots used to macerate the tenders until translucent. Place the sautéed shallots over the grilled tenders. Sauté the diced potatoes in the duck fat until golden brown. Season with salt and pepper. At the last minute, toss with the chopped parsley. Fill the potato ring with the potatoes and serve with the tenders.

****Note:** The onglet is a French cut known as a "hanging tender" in England. It is cut from the diaphragm muscle and hung for many days to tenderize.*

173 Lamb Kidneys with Crispy Grits

Serves 6

For the kidneys:
8 shallots, peeled and chopped
5 cloves garlic, peeled and chopped
½ cup olive oil
½ bunch thyme
½ cup pomegranate juice
3 tablespoons cracked black pepper
12 baby lamb kidneys, butterflied, white nerves removed
8 scallions, cut into 2-inch pieces

For the grits:
½ Spanish onion, peeled and chopped
2 shallots, peeled and minced
6 tablespoons butter
2 cups chicken stock
2 cups water
1 cup hominy grits
¼ cup heavy cream
¼ cup grated Parmesan cheese
Clarified butter for frying
Salt and pepper to taste

For the bacon:
½ pound double-smoked slab bacon, sliced ½-inch thick
1 tablespoon maple sugar

For the sauce:
2 cups roasted lamb jus
½ cup kidney marinade, from above
Salt and pepper to taste

For the garnish:
Fried Italian parsley
Butter
Fresh herbs

To prepare the marinade for the kidneys, sauté the shallots and garlic in the olive oil. Add the thyme, pomegranate juice and black pepper. Let the kidneys marinate in this mixture for 30 minutes. Once marinated, skewer the kidneys on bamboo skewers, alternating with pieces of scallion. There should be two kidneys per skewer. Set aside.

For the grits, in a large saucepan, sauté the onions and shallots in the butter until translucent. Add the chicken stock and water and bring to a boil. Sprinkle in the grits, whisking to prevent the formation of lumps. Lower the heat and continue cooking for approximately 45 minutes, stirring occasionally. When cooked, the grits should have the consistency of polenta. Remove from the heat. Stir in the heavy cream, Parmesan cheese, salt and pepper. Pour into a generously greased half-sheet pan and cool. Cut the grits into shapes and sprinkle with some dry grits. Set aside.

To prepare the bacon, sprinkle the slices with maple sugar. Set aside until service.

For the sauce, combine the lamb jus and marinade in a saucepan and reduce until the consistency of a light sauce.

Just before service, sauté the grits cut-outs in clarified butter until golden brown on both sides. Grill the kidney skewers, charring moderately on one side. The kidneys should be pink. Grill the bacon, being careful not to overcook it. It should be tender, but not crispy. Arrange the grits on plates. Lean one of the kidney skewers over the grits. Spoon the sauce around the kidneys. Sprinkle the plate with fried Italian parsley and dab the grits with butter. Garnish with herbs.

190 Lamb Loin with Ratatouille and Basil Oil

Serves 4

For the ratatouille:
2 onions, peeled and diced
1 red pepper, seeded and diced
1 yellow pepper, seeded and diced
1 cup olive oil
1 clove garlic, peeled and minced
Salt and pepper
Cayenne pepper
½ eggplant, finely diced
2 zucchini, finely diced
2 yellow squash, finely diced
15 tomatoes, peeled, seeded and chopped
1½ tablespoons tomato paste
2 bay leaves
Fresh thyme and parsley stems

For the basil oil:
4 ounces basil, blanched
3 cups vegetable oil

For the sauce:
1 small onion, peeled and diced
1 carrot, peeled and diced
1 cup mushroom stems, chopped
1 stalk celery, chopped
2 tablespoons olive oil
1 bay leaf
Fresh thyme
Whole black peppercorns
Parsley stems
6 cups lamb stock
1 head garlic, split in half

For the lamb:
2 boneless lamb loins
Salt and pepper
Olive oil

For the garnish:
Fried basil leaves

To prepare the ratatouille, sauté the onions and peppers in ½ cup of the olive oil for approximately 5 minutes, until the onions are translucent. Add the garlic and cook for an additional minute. Season with salt, pepper and cayenne. Drain off any excess oil. In the remaining olive oil, sauté the eggplant, zucchini and yellow squash for 4 to 5 minutes. Season with salt and pepper and drain.

In a medium-sized, oven-proof pot, combine all of the cooked vegetables, tomato paste and herbs. Bring to a boil. Cover with a sheet of buttered parchment and a lid and set in a 225 degree oven for 1½ to 2 hours. Adjust the seasoning.

For the basil oil, combine the basil and vegetable oil in a blender and process until smooth. Strain through a fine chinois and store in a covered glass jar.

To prepare the sauce, sauté the onion, carrot, mushroom stems and celery in the olive oil until tender. Add the herbs and spices. Pour in the lamb stock and add the garlic. Reduce until the sauce is thick enough to lightly coat the back of a spoon. Pass through a fine chinois and adjust the seasoning.

Just before service, season the lamb loins with salt and pepper. Heat some olive oil in a heavy skillet. Sear the lamb on all sides and cook until medium-rare. Using a metal ring, spoon the ratatouille in the center of each serving plate. Slice the lamb on the bias and arrange on top of the ratatouille. Drizzle the sauce and basil oil around the plates and garnish with the fried basil leaves.

174 Tandoori Charred Lamb Loin with Poori

Serves 6

For the lamb:
1 tablespoon chopped ginger
3 cloves garlic, chopped
3 tablespoons olive oil
2 24-ounce lamb loins, trimmed
2 dried red chilies, crushed
1 tablespoon ground turmeric
½ teaspoon cumin seed, toasted and crushed
1 teaspoon coriander seed, toasted and crushed
1 teaspoon mustard seed, toasted and crushed
1 teaspoon fenugreek seed, toasted and crushed
½ teaspoon black peppercorns, crushed
2 tablespoons honey
4 sprigs cilantro, chopped
4 scallions, chopped
1 red onion, peeled and quartered

For the sauce:
2 cups lamb jus
1 tablespoon lamb marinade
2 tablespoons butter
Lime juice

For the poori:
½ cup milk
½ cup water
1 cup all-purpose flour
¾ cups whole wheat flour
2 teaspoons salt

2 tablespoons ghee or clarified butter
Peanut oil for deep frying
Poppy seeds
Coarse salt

For the cucumber salad:
1 English cucumber
¾ cup yoghurt
4 scallions, peeled and chopped
½ small red onion, peeled and finely chopped
¼ teaspoon ground cumin
½ teaspoon salt
Juice from ½ lime
Salt and pepper to taste

To marinate the lamb, sauté the ginger and garlic in the olive oil. Cut each loin into 3 8-ounce portions and place in a medium-sized bowl. Add the sautéed ginger and garlic and the remaining ingredients. Let marinate for at least 3 hours or overnight.

To prepare the sauce, combine the lamb jus with the marinade, removing as little oil from the marinade as possible. Reduce until the consistency of a light sauce, adjusting the spices with more marinade as necessary. Finish with 2 tablespoons of butter and a squirt of lime juice.

To prepare the poori, heat the milk and water in a small saucepan to 140 degrees Fahrenheit. Mix the flours and salt on a clean work surface. Add the ghee to the flour and crumble until the mixture resembles coarse meal. Make a well in the center and add the warmed liquid. Using a fork, work the mixture to form a soft dough. Knead until smooth and elastic. Let rest for 1 hour. Divide the dough into 16 balls. Roll each ball out into a 4-inch circle. Set aside.

Just before service, prepare the cucumber salad. Cut the English cucumber in half, lengthwise, and slice thinly on an extreme bias to form slices that are 3 inches long. Toss the sliced cucumber with the remaining ingredients and adjust the seasoning. If using a tandoor oven, skewer the marinated lamb and secure the lamb on the skewers with the quartered red onion. Otherwise, the lamb should be cooked over a very hot wood or charcoal fire. Char the lamb until the outside is dark brown and caramelized. Be sure the meat remains rare. Remove the lamb from the heat and let rest.

Fry the poori in 360 degree peanut oil until brown, basting the poori with hot oil to ensure even cooking. Remove from the oil and sprinkle with poppy seeds and coarse salt.

To serve, slice the lamb and plate. Ladle the sauce over the lamb. Serve with the cucumber salad, grilled onion and poori.

176 Roasted Rack of Lamb with Gremolata

Serves 6

For the potatoes:
2 pounds russet or Finnish potatoes, peeled and quartered
1 quart boiling water
2 teaspoons salt
¼ cup melted butter
½ teaspoon freshly ground white pepper
½ cup heavy cream, warmed
½ cup crème fraîche

For the lamb:
1 full rack of lamb, split, chine and feather bones removed
Salt and pepper to taste
3 large porcini mushrooms, cleaned and sliced
1 shallot, peeled and minced
1 clove garlic, peeled and minced
1 cup red wine
1½ cups veal glace

For the gremolata:
Zest of 2 lemons
2 cloves garlic, peeled and minced
¼ cup chopped fresh parsley

To prepare the mashed potatoes, cook the potatoes in boiling salted water for 20 to 30 minutes until they begin to fall apart. Drain and lay out on a sheet pan. Set the sheet pan in a 350 degree oven for 5 to 10 minutes to remove any excess moisture. Mash the potatoes and stir in the remaining ingredients. Adjust the seasoning.

Season the lamb racks and sear until brown. Finish in the oven, roasting until medium rare. Remove the racks from their roasting pan and set the pan over medium heat. Add the porcini, shallot and garlic to the pan and sauté until soft. Deglaze the pan with the red wine and add the veal glace. Reduce slightly.

For the gremolata, combine all of the ingredients. Set aside until service.

To serve, slice the racks into 3-bone sections and serve with the mashed potatoes, sautéed mushrooms and jus. Sprinkle the gremolata over the lamb.

177 Crispy Lamb with Potato and Basil Agnolotti

Serves 6

For the lamb:
2 1-pound lamb shanks, trimmed and scored
Salt and pepper
¼ cup olive oil
1 cup mirepoix
½ bottle white wine
4 cherry tomatoes
2 cups chicken stock
½ cup clarified butter
1 tablespoon cumin seed, toasted and crushed
1 tablespoon fennel seed, toasted and crushed
2 tablespoons Italian parsley julienne
Salt and pepper

For the pesto:
1 cup extra virgin olive oil
6 cloves garlic, peeled
2 cups fresh basil leaves, washed
¼ cup pine nuts
Salt and pepper to taste
½ cup freshly grated Parmesan cheese

For the pasta dough:
1¼ cups all-purpose flour
1¼ cups potato starch
2 to 3 potatoes, baked, cooled, peeled and passed through a ricer
2 tablespoons crème fraîche
4 tablespoons butter, melted
2 egg yolks
Salt to taste

For the agnolotti filling:
2 potatoes, boiled until tender
¼ cup pesto, from above
Salt and pepper to taste
Light egg wash

For the garnish:
Crème fraîche
Cracked black pepper
Grated Parmesan cheese
Fried basil leaves

To prepare the lamb, season the shanks with salt and pepper. In a deep sauté pan, brown the shanks in the olive oil. Add the mirepoix, white wine and cherry tomatoes. Pour in enough chicken stock to cover the shanks half way. Cover and simmer slowly until the meat is very tender. Skim the braising liquid as it simmers because this will be used later for the broth. When cooked, remove the shanks and let cool. Shred the meat off the bone with the tines of a fork. Strain the braising liquid. Skim off any fat and return about ¼ cup of the cooked mirepoix to the broth. Set aside

To prepare the pesto, combine the olive oil, garlic, basil and pine nuts in a blender and purée until smooth. Transfer to a bowl and stir in the salt, pepper and grated Parmesan cheese.

For the pasta dough, sift together the flour and potato starch. Add the riced potatoes. Make a well in the center of this mixture and add the crème fraîche, melted butter, egg yolks and salt. Knead to form a smooth dough. Cover and set aside.

For the filling, mix the potatoes with the pesto and adjust the seasoning with salt and pepper.

To shape the agnolotti, roll out the dough into long strips, approximately ⅛-inch thick and 4 inches wide. Place teaspoonfuls of the potato filling along one side of the pasta strips, spaced 2 inches apart. Brush the dough with a very light egg wash and fold it over to cover the filling. Using a scalloped pastry cutter, cut the dough into semicircles. Boil the agnolotti in salted water for approximately 4 minutes. The dough will be very soft and delicate. Drain.

To finish the lamb, heat the clarified butter in a large skillet. Add about 6 tablespoons of the shredded lamb, scattering it over the bottom of the pan. Sprinkle in the cumin, fennel seeds, parsley, salt and pepper. Cook the meat until it is crispy on one side, moist on the other.

To serve, ladle 4 ounces of the hot lamb broth into each soup plate. Place 2 agnolotti in each bowl and top each agnolotti with a teaspoon of crème fraîche. Sprinkle with black pepper and Parmesan cheese. Top with the crispy lamb and spoon dabs of the pesto around the bowl. Garnish with fried basil leaves.

178 Mild Garlic Sausage with Lentils

Serves 8

For the sausage:
½ pound pork fatback, cubed
¾ pound lean pork loin, cubed
Salt and fresh cracked black pepper to taste
Pinch of nutmeg
Pinch of mace
2 cloves blanched garlic
Fresh hog casings

For the lentils:
2 cups lentils, soaked
2 tablespoons butter
½ cup diced onions
¼ cup carrots
1 garlic clove, minced
2 quarts stock, pork, chicken or veal
Salt and pepper to taste

For the tomato vinaigrette:
1 tablespoon shallot vinegar
½ teaspoon tomato paste
1 garlic clove, crushed
¼ cup extra virgin olive oil
Salt and cracked pepper to taste

For the garnish:
2 tablespoons diced, peeled and seeded tomatoes
1 tablespoon chopped parsley
8 leaves Italian parsley

For the sausage, cut the pork into strips small enough to be pushed through the meat grinder. Add the salt, pepper, nutmeg, mace and garlic. Put the mixture through the large blade of a meat grinder; cover and refrigerate overnight. The following day, unravel a few feet of the lamb casing; soak in lukewarm water for 30 minutes and rinse thoroughly under the faucet, checking as you go for any holes in the casing.

Drain the excess liquid from the ground meat and mix the meat thoroughly with the fatback. Using a sausage stuffer, fill the casing with the sausage mixture; being careful to not allow any pockets of air, or to fill the casing too tightly. Tie both ends of the casing and secure the whole sausage with butcher's twine to hold the shape during the cooking process. Cook the sausage in simmering water for 35 to 40 minutes.

For the lentils, sauté the onions, carrots and the garlic in the butter until the onions are translucent. Stir in the lentils, cover with the stock, and simmer for 45 minutes. Adjust the seasoning, drain and keep warm.

For the vinaigrette, mix together the vinegar, tomato paste and the garlic. Whisk in the olive oil, season and set aside at room temperature. Strain before service.

To serve, using a 4 inch ring, mold each portion of the lentils onto the center of each plate; cover the top of the lentils with sausage slices. Pour the tomato vinaigrette around the lentils and garnish the vinaigrette with diced tomatoes, alternating with chopped parsley. Finish the dish with parsley leaves.

179 Dark Roasted Rack and Loin of Lamb

Serves 6

For the lamb:
6 shallots, peeled and chopped
6 cloves garlic, peeled and chopped
½ cup olive oil
1 large, boneless loin of lamb, trimmed
2 lamb racks, 8 chops each, trimmed and frenched
1 8-ounce bottle Syrian pomegranate juice
2 tablespoons chopped fresh thyme
2 tablespoons chopped fresh rosemary
3 tablespoons black peppercorns, cracked
Rind and juice of 2 lemons

For the braised endive:
3 Belgian endive
2 tablespoons sugar
Juice of 1 lemon
Pinch of salt
½ cup butter

For the endive cream sauce:
1 cup heavy cream
1 Belgian endive, thinly sliced crosswise
Salt and pepper to taste
Lemon juice
2 tablespoons finely chopped Italian parsley

For the lamb jus:
2 cups roasted lamb jus
¾ cup lamb marinade
2 tablespoons butter
Salt and pepper to taste

For the endive salad:
1 Belgian endive, julienned
Salt to taste
Freshly ground black pepper
Lemon juice
1 tablespoon virgin olive oil

For the gremolata:
¼ cup finely julienned Italian parsley
Zest of 1 lemon, finely chopped
2 cloves garlic, peeled and finely chopped

To marinate the lamb, sauté the shallots and garlic in the olive oil until translucent. Place the loin and racks of lamb in a large dish. Add the sautéed shallots and garlic, the pomegranate juice, thyme, rosemary, peppercorns, lemon rind and juice. Marinate for 2 to 3 hours. Once it has marinated, grill or broil the lamb until charred, being careful to keep the meat rare. Chill the loin and reserve the racks at room temperature until service.

For the braised endive, set the endive in a small saucepan and cover with water. Add the sugar, lemon juice and salt. Simmer slowly until tender. Remove from the braising liquid and cool on a rack. Cut each endive in half lengthwise and set aside.

To prepare the endive cream sauce, reduce the heavy cream in a small saucepan with the sliced endive. When the cream has the consistency of a thin sauce, season with salt, pepper and lemon juice. Just before service, add the parsley.
For the jus, combine the roasted lamb jus and the marinade in a small

saucepan. Try to remove as little of the olive oil from the marinade as possible. Reduce this mixture until it has the consistency of a light sauce. Mount with the butter and adjust the seasoning with salt and pepper.

Just before service, combine all of the ingredients for the endive salad. In a separate bowl, combine the ingredients for the gremolata.

To serve, roast the racks of lamb at 400 degrees until medium-rare. Remove from the oven and let rest. Meanwhile, slice the chilled lamb loin on an electric slicer lengthwise into very thin strips. Overlap 2 to 3 slices of the loin on each plate. Set the plates in a 300 degree oven until the lamb loin is barely warm.

Sauté the braised endive in the remaining butter until deep golden brown. Season with salt and pepper. Place 1 endive half askew on each portion of lamb loin. Cut the roasted racks into 12 chops and arrange 2 chops on each plate as shown. Ladle a small amount of the hot endive cream sauce on each chop. Arrange a mound of endive salad on each plate and ladle the hot lamb jus over the loin. Sprinkle with the gremolata and serve.

179 Rack of Lamb with Grits

Serves 4

For the grits:
2 quarts consommé
Fresh thyme
Cumin seed
Cardamom pods
Curry powder
1 clove garlic, peeled
Ground turmeric
Saffron threads
½ pound grits

For the lamb:
4 racks milk-fed lamb, trimmed
Salt and pepper
½ cup olive oil

To prepare the grits, begin by making a spice essence. Combine the consommé with the assorted spices in a large sauce pan and reduce by ⅓ over a low flame. Strain. Transfer 1 quart of this essence to another saucepan and bring to a boil. Add the grits and simmer for 40 minutes over a low flame. Reserve the remaining essence.

For the lamb, season the racks with salt and pepper and coat with the olive oil. Roast in a hot oven for 6 minutes on each side. Remove from the oven and let rest 10 minutes. Reheat the remaining spice essence.

To serve, spoon the grits into a large soup bowl. Cut the lamb into chops and arrange around the grits. Pour in the essence and serve.

180 Braised Lamb Shanks

Serves 2

For the fruit:
4 ounces dried figs
4 ounces dried cherries
4 ounces dried apricots
4 ounces dried cranberries
4 ounces dried blueberries

For the shanks:
6 lamb shanks, trimmed, scored and frenched
Salt and pepper to taste
3 shallots, peeled and diced
1 onion, peeled and diced
4 cloves garlic, peeled and diced
1 carrot, peeled and diced
1 leek, washed and diced
1 turnip, peeled and diced
1 tomato, peeled, seeded and diced
2 ounces tomato paste
½ cup white wine
2 sprigs thyme, stems removed
1 bay leaf
1 quart consommé

The day before service, soak the dried fruits in water to rehydrate.

On the day of service, season the lamb shanks with salt and pepper. Sear the shanks in a very hot dutch oven until golden brown on all sides. Remove the shanks. Add the vegetables and sweat until tender. Add the tomato paste. Deglaze the pan with the white wine. Add the thyme and bay leaf. Return the shanks to the pan. Add enough consommé to completely cover the shanks. Cover the roasting pan and set in a 300 degree oven for 2 hours.

When the meat is well cooked and pulls away from the bone, carefully remove the shanks. Strain the braising liquid through a fine chinois. Drain the dried fruits and add to the braising liquid. Reduce to the consistency of a thin sauce.

To serve, place the lamb shanks in the center of the plate, bones standing upright. Arrange the fruits around the shanks and ladle the sauce over top.

181 Barbecued Suckling Pig

Serves 10 to 12

For the suckling pig:
1 15- to 16-pound suckling pig, hair removed, skin on
1 tablespoon salt
¼ cup hoi sin sauce
2 cloves garlic, minced
10 slices fresh ginger, peeled
¼ cup dark soy sauce
3 tablespoons rice wine vinegar
3 tablespoons toasted sesame oil
½ teaspoon freshly ground black pepper
½ teaspoon Chinese five-spice powder
Small pinch red food coloring powder
¼ cup honey

For the garnish:
Chinese pancakes
Assorted steamed vegetables

To prepare the pig, begin one day in advance. Thoroughly clean the pig, rinsing with boiling water. Pat dry with a clean towel. Combine the remaining ingredients except for the honey in a small saucepan and simmer for two minutes until slightly reduced. Rub the marinade all over the surface of the pig. Hang to dry for about 10 hours, until the skin starts to feel like paper.

Set the pig on a spit over an open charcoal pit and roast until very well done, basting frequently with honey. The skin on a suckling pig should be wafer-like and melt in the mouth.

Serve pieces of the pig cut into rectangles on Chinese pancakes.

182 Rack of Lamb with White Bean Gratin

Serves 8

For the rack:
2 double racks of lamb, split, trimmed and frenched
Olive oil
Fresh rosemary
Fresh thyme
1 bay leaf
8 shallots, peeled and sliced
8 cloves garlic, peeled and sliced

For the bean gratin:
1 pound dried white beans, soaked overnight and cooked until tender
8 cloves garlic, roasted and peeled
3 tablespoons extra virgin olive oil
7 tablespoons heavy cream
Salt and pepper
5 tablespoons grated Parmesan cheese

For the sauce:
1½ cups lamb jus
10 leaves opal basil, julienned
1 cup cooked flageolets or fava beans
8 sun-dried tomatoes, julienned
Salt and pepper

For the garnish:
2 small zucchini, thinly sliced into rounds
Olive oil
Salt and pepper
Fresh herbs

The day before service, marinate the racks of lamb in the olive oil, fresh herbs, shallots and garlic. Cover and set in the refrigerator overnight.

To prepare the bean gratin, purée the beans, roasted garlic, olive oil and heavy cream in a food processor until smooth. Season the purée with salt and pepper. Spoon the bean purée into a 3-inch ring mold set on a sheet pan. Remove the ring and repeat to form 8 gratins. Generously sprinkle the tops of the gratins with the grated Parmesan cheese and set in the refrigerator until service.

For the sauce, combine all of the ingredients in a small saucepan and simmer for 10 minutes. Adjust the seasoning with salt and pepper. Keep warm.

To prepare the garnish, boil the zucchini slices in salted water until tender. Drain and shock in ice water. Reserve.

To serve, remove the racks of lamb from the marinade. Season with salt and pepper. Roast the racks in a very hot oven until medium-rare, about 10 minutes. Remove from the oven and let rest. Meanwhile, set the white bean gratins in a preheated 400 degree oven for 5 minutes. Finish by glazing under the broiler until the cheese is golden brown. Reheat the zucchini rounds in a little olive oil in a small saucepan. Season with salt and pepper. Arrange the zucchini slices in the shape of a circle on the serving plates. Place the hot bean gratins on top. Slice the racks into chops and lay 3 on each serving plate. Spoon the sauce over the lamb and garnish with the fresh herbs.

183 Sweet and Spicy Lamb Ribs

Serves 4

For the ribs:
4 to 5 pounds lamb ribs
3 dried poblano chilies, stems removed
1 teaspoon red chili flakes
1 tablespoon cumin seed, toasted
1 tablespoon black peppercorns
4 tablespoons salt
4 tablespoons sugar
Olive oil
Additional salt and pepper

For the barbecue sauce:
8 cloves garlic, peeled and sliced
1 jalapeño pepper, seeded and diced
2 chipotle peppers, diced
1 Spanish onion, peeled and chopped
¼ cup olive oil
¼ cup brown sugar
¼ cup red wine vinegar
1 cup lamb stock
8 ripe plum tomatoes, diced
1 teaspoon red pepper flakes
¼ cup chopped cilantro
Salt and pepper to taste

For the chips:
2 russet potatoes, peeled
1 large beet, peeled
Clarified butter
Flour for dredging
Peanut oil for frying
Cider vinegar

To prepare the ribs, remove the skin from the backside of the lamb ribs using a kitchen towel to reinforce your grasp. In a blender, grind the chili flakes, cumin seed and pepper. Add the salt and sugar. Sprinkle the ribs on the meaty side with this spice mixture. Set in a smoker and smoke for approximately 45 minutes over fruit wood chips. Once the ribs have taken on the flavor of the wood, remove them from the smoker, wrap in aluminum foil and roast slowly in a 275 degree oven until tender, approximately 1½ hours.

In the meantime, prepare the barbecue sauce. Sweat the garlic, peppers and onions in the olive oil until tender. Add the brown sugar, vinegar and lamb stock. Simmer for 15 minutes. Add the plum tomatoes, red pepper flakes and cilantro. Season to taste. Cook for 10 more minutes.

When the ribs are tender, remove the foil and baste with the barbecue sauce. Set aside.

To prepare the chips, slice the potatoes and beet into very thin sheets using a Japanese mandolin. Cut the potatoes on an acute angle. Dip the potato slices in clarified butter and set on a sheet pan. Roast in a hot oven until crisp. Slice the beet slices in 7-inch strips. Lightly dredge these strips in flour and deep fry in 360 degree peanut oil until brightly colored and crisp.

To serve, drizzle the roasted ribs with olive oil and season with salt and pepper. Char the ribs on a hot grill until brown. Cut the ribs between the bones. Arrange in a white paper bag. Serve with additional barbecue sauce. Arrange the potato and beet chips on the plate. Sprinkle the chips with vinegar and serve.

184 Barbecued Pork

Serves 8

For the pork:
1½ pounds boneless pork belly or loin, trimmed
1 teaspoon salt
1 scallion, finely chopped
1 knob fresh ginger, peeled and minced
2 cloves garlic, peeled and minced
¼ cup Chinese rice wine
¼ cup light soy sauce
¼ cup sugar
¼ teaspoon white pepper
1 pinch red food coloring powder
2 tablespoons honey

If using pork belly, score the rind with a sharp knife. Cut the meat into strips, one inch in width. Rub the salt into the meat. Combine the remaining ingredients except for the honey. Rub this mixture into the meat and let marinate for at least 30 minutes.

Place the pork on a spit over a charcoal fire or hang in a standing barbecue pit and cook until the skin is crisp and golden and the meat is well done, approximately 30 minutes. While cooking, baste with the honey. Cut into thin slices and serve with Chinese vegetables.

184 Corn Breaded Pork Medallions, Black Bean Salad and Arugula Oil

Serves 4

For the pork:
8 2-ounce pork medallions, 1/4 inch thick
2 tablespoons prepared mustard
1/2 cup cornmeal
1 tablespoon butter

For the black bean salad:
1 cup dried black beans
5 cups water
1 tablespoon chopped onion
1 teaspoon minced garlic
1/2 teaspoon minced hot pepper
3 tablespoons hazelnut oil
3 tablespoons sherry wine vinegar
1 tablespoon chopped cilantro

For the garnish:
4 tablespoons arugula oil
1 tablespoon balsamic vinegar
1 bunch arugula leaves
4 slices of corn bread

For the arugula oil, blanch basil or arugula, including stems, in boiling water for 30 seconds. Drain and dry well. Chop herbs finely by hand or in a small food processor. Mix 1 cup herbs to 2 cups vegetable oil (grapeseed or corn oil) in a jar or in a bowl. Mix well. Oil is ready. Store in closed jar in the refrigerator for up to 1 week.

For the pork, trim the medallions of all fat. Brush with mustard on both sides and dredge them in the cornmeal. Set aside.

Soak the black beans in cold water for 2 hours. Cook them approximately 35 minutes. Remove from water and set aside. Sweat the onion, garlic, and hot pepper in hazelnut oil. Deglaze with sherry vinegar. Add to the beans along with chopped cilantro and keep at room temperature until ready to use.

To serve, sauté the pork medallions in butter until lightly brown and crispy on both sides. Sprinkle a few drops of balsamic vinegar and arugula oil around the plate. Garnish with the bean salad, arugula leaves and toasted corn bread.

185 Lamb Pot Au Feu

Serves 6 to 8

For the stock:
Bones from a shoulder of lamb
2 gallons cold water
3 tablespoons coarse salt
1 tablespoon white peppercorns
1 leek, diced
2 stalks celery, diced
2 heads garlic, cut in half
1 onion, peeled and diced
1 turnip, peeled and diced
1/4 head Savoy cabbage, diced
2 bay leaves
Fresh thyme
Fresh parsley

For the pot au feu:
1 lamb shoulder, boned
Salt and pepper
Garlic
2 lamb breasts, each cut into 3 pieces
2 lamb shanks
4 lamb tongues, soaked overnight in water
2 large turnips, peeled and tournéed
3 carrots, peeled and tournéed
3 parsnips, peeled and tournéed
1 head Savoy cabbage, quartered and tied
3 leeks, white part only, cleaned and tied
3 potatoes, peeled and tournéed
8 lamb sweetbreads, soaked overnight in water

For the condiments:
Dijon mustard
Coarse salt
Cracked black peppercorns
Chopped cornichons
Horseradish

The day before service, prepare the stock. Place the bones in a large stock pot and cover with the cold water. Bring to a boil and skim off any foam that rises to the surface. Boil rapidly for 2 to 3 minutes to remove any impurities and to ensure a clear stock. Add the remaining ingredients and simmer for 3 hours. Pass the stock through a chinois and cool.

While the stock is simmering, prepare the boneless lamb shoulder. Trim any fat from the shoulder. Season with salt and pepper and rub with garlic. Roll and tie the shoulder. Season the outside of the roll with salt and pepper. Refrigerate the stock and the shoulder for 1 day.

On the day of service, skim any fat that has coagulated on the top of the stock. Add the rolled shoulder, lamb breast and shanks to the cold stock. Bring to a boil and skim. Simmer the meat for 1 3/4 hours. Add the tongue and continue cooking for 25 minutes. Add the vegetables and cook for 10 minutes. Add the sweetbreads and simmer for another 10 minutes. Adjust the seasoning with salt and pepper.

To serve, arrange the meats in a serving bowl or on a platter. Place the vegetables around the meat and pour the broth over the meats and vegetables. Serve the condiments on a side plate.

186 Lentils with Cured Pork

Serves 5

For the lentils and cured pork:
3 cured pork hocks
1 onion spiked with 3 cloves
2 whole peeled carrots
1 bouquet of herbs
1 pound cured pork shoulder
3 cups green lentils, soaked
9 ounces cured pork belly or slab bacon
2 onions spiked with 2 cloves each
9 ounces garlic sausage
2 whole peeled carrots
1 whole garlic head, cut in half
1 bouquet of herbs
2 tablespoons grated fresh ginger
1 cup heavy cream

For the garnish:
2 tablespoons chopped parsley

For the lentils and cured pork, cook the pork hocks in cold water with the clove-spiked onion, the carrots and bouquet of herbs for 1 hour; adding in the pork shoulder after 15 minutes when the water has begun to boil. Put the lentils in another pan with 1 pint of cold water, the slab bacon and the 2 clove-spiked onions; Bring the lentils to a boil and simmer for 10 minutes. Remove and drain the pork hocks and shoulder from the other pot with the lentils; add in the garlic sausage, the remaining carrots, garlic, herb bouquet and ginger. Pour in enough water to just cover the lentils and meats; continue to simmer for 30 minutes, until the lentils are tender, but firm.

To serve, remove the onion, garlic, herb bouquet, the carrots and meats from the cooked lentils. Debone the hocks, cut the shoulder into 5 pieces, slice the slab bacon and garlic sausage, and set aside to keep warm. Slice half of an onion and sauté it lightly with the slab bacon; adding the sautéed onion, with the cream back into the lentils. Dish the lentils into each plate; Arrange the meats onto the center of the lentils, and garnish the dish with slices of the cooked carrot and the chopped parsley.

188 Seven-Hour Leg of Lamb

Serves 8

For the lamb:
1 leg of lamb
Salt and pepper to taste
Fresh thyme
3 cloves garlic
6 shallots, peeled and chopped
1 onion, peeled and chopped
3 carrots, peeled and chopped
2 turnips, peeled and chopped
8 stalks celery, finely chopped
4 leeks, cleaned and chopped
4 ounces unsalted butter
¼ pound ham, finely chopped
1 ham bone
8 cups red wine
1 cup consommé

For the garnish:
Fresh herbs

To prepare the leg of lamb, remove the hip bone, the aitchbone and the center leg bone. Keep the hindshank bone attached for the presentation. Do not butter-fly the meat. Season the lamb with salt and pepper. In the hole left from the bone, place 2 sprigs of thyme and the garlic cloves. Tie the leg with butcher's twine. Sweat the remaining vegetables in the butter in a large dutch oven for 15 minutes. Add the ham and continue cooking. Meanwhile, roast the leg of lamb and lamb bone in a very hot oven until golden brown. Transfer to the dutch oven with the vegetables. Add the ham bone, red wine and consommé. Cover and set in a 175 degree oven for 7 hours.

After 7 hours, carefully remove the lamb from the braising liquid. Slice. Degrease the braising liquid and reduce on top of the stove until it is the consistency of a sauce. To serve, ladle the braised vegetables and sauce over the sliced lamb and garnish with the fresh herbs.

189 Lamb Tripe with Pancetta and Porcini

Serves 6

For the tripe:
2 pounds lamb tripe
½ pound carrots, peeled and roughly chopped
½ pound turnips, peeled and roughly chopped
4 leeks, cleaned and chopped
6 stalks celery, roughly chopped
3 onions, peeled and roughly chopped
5 shallots, peeled and roughly chopped
¼ pound ham, chopped
4 tablespoons olive oil
1 bottle red wine
2 bay leaves
3 sprigs fresh thyme
2 cups consommé
Salt and pepper to taste

For the pearl onions:
1 pound pearl onions, peeled
4 ounces unsalted butter
2 ounces sugar
Pinch of salt

For the pancetta:
¼ pound pancetta, julienned

For the porcini:
½ pound fresh porcini, cleaned and sliced
2 cloves garlic, peeled and minced
3 tablespoons olive oil

Soak the tripe in cold, running water for 24 hours. On the day of service, sweat the carrots, turnips, leeks, celery, onions, shallots, and ham in the olive oil in a large dutch oven for 15 to 20 minutes, until tender. Add the wine, bay leaves, and thyme. Continue cooking for 1 minute. Add the tripe and the consommé, cover and set in a 250 degree oven for 2½ hours. Once it has finished braising, remove the tripe and cut into large julienne. Set aside. Strain the sauce and reduce by half. Reserve.

Sauté the pearl onions in the butter with the sugar, salt and a few tablespoons of water. Cook for about 30 minutes until the onions are caramelized and tender. Set aside. Blanch the pancetta in boiling water to remove the salt. Sauté the porcini and garlic in the olive oil.

Combine the tripe, sauce, pearl onions, pancetta and porcini in a lañe pot. Bring to a boil and serve piping hot.

190 Lamb Loin with Ratatouille and Basil Oil

Serves 4

For the ratatouille:
2 onions, peeled and diced
1 red pepper, seeded and diced
1 yellow pepper, seeded and diced
1 cup olive oil
1 clove garlic, peeled and minced
Salt and pepper
Cayenne pepper
½ eggplant, finely diced
2 zucchini, finely diced
2 yellow squash, finely diced
15 tomatoes, peeled, seeded and chopped
1½ tablespoons tomato paste
2 bay leaves
Fresh thyme and parsley stems

For the basil oil:
4 ounces basil, blanched
3 cups vegetable oil

For the sauce:
1 small onion, peeled and diced
1 carrot, peeled and diced
1 cup mushroom stems, chopped
1 stalk celery, chopped
2 tablespoons olive oil
1 bay leaf
Fresh thyme
Whole black peppercorns
Parsley stems
6 cups lamb stock
1 head garlic, split in half

For the lamb:
2 boneless lamb loins
Salt and pepper
Olive oil

For the garnish:
Fried basil leaves

To prepare the ratatouille, sauté the onions and peppers in ½ cup of the olive oil for approximately 5 minutes, until the onions are translucent. Add the garlic and cook for an additional minute. Season with salt, pepper and cayenne. Drain off any excess oil. In the remaining olive oil, sauté the eggplant, zucchini and yellow squash for 4 to 5 minutes. Season with salt and pepper and drain.

In a medium-sized, oven-proof pot, combine all of the cooked vegetables, tomato paste and herbs. Bring to a boil. Cover with a sheet of buttered parchment and a lid and set in a 225 degree oven for 1½ to 2 hours. Adjust the seasoning.

For the basil oil, combine the basil and vegetable oil in a blender and process until smooth. Strain through a fine chinois and store in a covered glass jar.

To prepare the sauce, sauté the onion, carrot, mushroom stems and celery in the olive oil until tender. Add the herbs and spices. Pour in the lamb stock and add the garlic. Reduce until the sauce is thick enough to lightly coat the back of a spoon. Pass through a fine chinois and adjust the seasoning.

Just before service, season the lamb loins with salt and pepper. Heat some olive oil in a heavy skillet. Sear the lamb on all sides and cook until medium-rare. Using a metal ring, spoon the ratatouille in the center of each serving plate. Slice the lamb on the bias and arrange on top of the ratatouille. Drizzle the sauce and basil oil around the plates and garnish with the fried basil leaves.

191 Pork Tenderloin with Eggplant Terrine

Serves 4

For the pork tenderloin:
1 tablespoon Chinese rose wine
2 cloves garlic, peeled and minced
2 teaspoons chopped fresh ginger
Salt and freshly ground
black pepper to taste
1 cup soy sauce
1 tablespoon malt sugar
1 tablespoon sesame oil
2 pork tenderloins
Dark chicken stock

For the eggplant terrine:
4 to 6 Japanese eggplants, peeled
and thinly sliced, retain the peel
4 teaspoons chopped coriander
1 small red chili, seeded
2 cloves garlic, minced
1 tablespoon chopped ginger
2 eggs
Flour and breadcrumbs for breading
Peanut oil for frying

For the orange sauce:
4 tablespoons dark chicken stock
2 tablespoons orange marmalade
Vinegar to taste
Salt to taste

For the garnish:
Szechuan chili peppers
Fresh coriander

To prepare the tenderloins, begin 1 day in advance. Combine all of the ingredients except for the pork and the chicken stock. Set the tenderloins in a small, shallow dish and pour this marinade over top. Allow the pork to marinate, refrigerated, for at least 1 day. Turn the tenderloins frequently to ensure they marinate evenly.

On the day of service, prepare the eggplant terrine. Blanch the eggplant peel for 1 minute in salted boiling water to remove the bitterness. Shock in ice water. Line a small mold with this skin, shiny side facing out, leaving enough overhang to cover the top of the mold when filled. Combine the chili, coriander, garlic, ginger and eggs in a blender and blend until smooth. Dip the slices of eggplant first in the flour, then in the seasoned egg mixture, and finally in breadcrumbs. When all of the eggplant has been breaded, fry the slices in peanut oil until golden brown. Fill the mold lined with the eggplant peel with the fried eggplant. Fold the peel over the top and bake in a 350-degree oven for 30 minutes, or until the eggplant peel is tender. Remove from the oven and cool.

To prepare the orange sauce, combine all of the ingredients in a small sauce pan and heat until the marmalade is melted and the mixture has been well combined. Adjust the seasoning.

To serve, sear the marinated pork tenderloins in a hot saut pan until cooked. Meanwhile, reduce the marinade to the consistency of a thin sauce. Adjust the seasoning and strain. The sauce may have to be thinned down with chicken stock if the flavors are too strong. Spoon the sauce onto plates as shown. Slice the tenderloin and arrange. Unmold the eggplant terrine and slice it 1-inch thick. Garnish with the orange sauce, Szechuan chilies and fresh coriander.

191 Lamb Kidneys with Risotto

Serves 4

For the kidneys:
20 lamb kidneys
Caul fat
Salt and pepper to taste
Olive oil for sautéing

For the risotto:
½ white onion, peeled and diced
3 tablespoons butter
8 ounces arborio rice
1 cup chicken stock, heated
1 cup carrot juice, warmed
2 ears corn, shucked, blanched
and kernels removed
¾ cup fresh peas, blanched
½ small zucchini, diced
12 asparagus tips, blanched
2 tablespoons grated
Parmesan cheese
Salt and pepper to taste

For the garnish:
½ cup lamb glace
4 sprigs fresh savory
4 sprigs fresh thyme

To prepare the lamb kidneys, trim away any exterior fat and peel off the outer membranes. Lay out a large piece of caul fat on a flat surface. Place 3 kidneys on the edge of the fat, cleaned side facing up. Lay down 2 kidneys on top of the first three so that the cleaned sides are facing each other. Season with salt and pepper. Tightly roll the kidneys 2 or 3 times in the caul fat, keeping the edges of the fat tucked under the kidneys. Cut away any excess fat. Place in the refrigerator uncovered with the seam of the caul fat facing down.

For the risotto, sauté the diced onion until translucent in 2 tablespoons of the butter. Add the rice and sauté for an additional minute. Add ¼ cup of the hot chicken stock and stir with a wooden spoon until all of the stock has been absorbed by the rice. Add ¼ cup of the carrot juice and repeat the procedure. Continue adding the liquids, alternating ¼ cup at a time and stirring until absorbed after each addition.

When the rice is al dente, about 12 to 15 minutes, stir in the blanched vegetables, the remaining butter and the Parmesan cheese. Season with salt and pepper.

While the risotto is cooking, sauté the kidney rolls in olive oil, seam side first, until brown. Set in a preheated 450 degree oven for 8 to 10 minutes, or until medium-rare. Remove from the oven and let rest for 5 minutes. Heat the lamb glace.

To serve, place the risotto in the middle of a warm soup plate. Slice each kidney roll into 3 medallions and place on top of the risotto. Spoon 2 to 3 tablespoons of the lamb glace over the kidneys. Garnish with sprigs of savory and thyme.

192 Rack of Lamb with White Bean Ravioli

Serves 6

For the lamb:
20 cloves garlic, peeled and sliced
¾ cup olive oil
2 tablespoons black peppercorns, cracked
2 dried red chilies, crushed
3 tablespoons soy sauce
½ cup rosemary leaves
Grated rind and juice of 2 lemons
3 racks of lamb, trimmed

For the ravioli filling:
¾ cup dried cannellini beans, soaked overnight
3 cups light chicken stock
1 bay leaf
4 sprigs thyme
1 small onion, peeled and studded with 6 cloves
12 cloves garlic, peeled and finely chopped
¼ cup extra virgin olive oil
Lemon juice
Salt and freshly cracked pepper to taste

For the pasta:
1 egg
3 egg yolks
2 cups all-purpose flour
Light egg wash

For the chard:
18 stalks red chard
½ cup olive oil
4 shallots, peeled and sliced
1 tablespoon sugar
Salt and pepper
Freshly grated Parmesan cheese
½ cup clarified butter

For the Parmesan sauce:
1 cup chicken stock
¾ cup grated imported Parmesan cheese
1 tablespoon chopped parsley
2 tablespoons aïoli
1 tablespoon extra virgin olive oil
Salt and pepper to taste

For the lamb sauce:
2 cups lamb jus
Lamb marinade, from above
2 tablespoons butter

For the garnish:
Freshly shredded Parmesan cheese
Cracked black pepper

To prepare the marinade for the lamb, sauté the garlic in the olive oil. Add the black pepper, chilies, soy sauce, rosemary, lemon rind and juice. Rub this marinade over the lamb racks and let sit for 2 to 6 hours. Once marinated, wrap the bones with foil and grill the lamb over very high heat to char the outside. Set aside.

For the ravioli filling, cook the beans in the light chicken stock with the bay leaf, thyme and onion until tender. Drain. Mash the beans with a fork. Sauté the garlic in the olive oil. Add a squirt of lemon juice and season with salt and pepper.

For the pasta, combine the egg, egg yolks and flour in a small bowl or on a clean work surface. Knead until smooth and elastic, about 10 minutes. Let rest. Roll out the dough into thin sheets, using the last setting on the pasta machine. Cover the sheets of pasta with a damp towel so they do not dry out.

To form the ravioli, place 1 teaspoon of bean filling every 4 inches along a strip of pasta. Moisten a second sheet with a very light egg wash. Place this sheet on top of the filling, pressing out any air bubbles with the tips of your fingers. Cut the ravioli into 3-inch squares using a scalloped pastry wheel. At this point, the ravioli can be frozen for future use. If the ravioli are to be used soon, sprinkle with coarse semolina or cornmeal. Before service, boil the ravioli in salted water and drain. Brush with olive oil.

To prepare the chard, cut the leaves off of the stems. In a sauté pan, heat the olive oil and sauté the shallots. Add the red chard stems and sauté until colored on one side. Sprinkle with the sugar and season with salt and pepper. Do not overcook.

Blanch the leaves in salted water. Shock in ice water. Loosely wrap each ravioli in one of the blanched chard leaves, leaving one corner of each ravioli uncovered. Sprinkle with salt and pepper and some grated Parmesan cheese. Sauté the ravioli, upside down, in the clarified butter until slightly browned. Flip and keep warm.

To prepare the Parmesan sauce, combine the chicken stock with the Parmesan cheese, parsley, aïoli, olive oil, salt and pepper. Gently warm this mixture, but do not boil.

For the lamb sauce, combine the lamb jus with half of the marinade used to flavor the racks. Try not to remove any oil from the marinade. Reduce this mixture to a light sauce and finish with butter. Adjust the seasoning.

Roast the lamb racks at 400 degrees for approximately 12 minutes, until medium-rare. Remove from the oven and let rest. To serve, place 3 ravioli on each plate. Lay the red chard stems in a crisscross pattern over the ravioli. Slice each rack into 8 chops and lay 4 chops on each plate. Spoon a small amount of the Parmesan sauce over each chop. Ladle the lamb jus around the plate and sprinkle with more Parmesan and black pepper.

196 Braised Oxtail with Quinoa

Serves 4

For the broth:
3 tablespoons concentrated red wine reduction
½ cup wild mushroom consommé
2 ounces fresh foie gras
Salt and pepper to taste

For the quinoa:
1½ cups cooked quinoa
⅔ cup oxtail meat, braised
1 small leek, poached and chopped
1 handful fresh spinach, cleaned, blanched and chopped
¼ bulb fennel, roasted and finely chopped
Salt and pepper to taste

For the broth, heat the red wine reduction. In a separate saucepan, bring the consommé to a boil. Combine both liquids in a blender with the foie gras and blend until smooth. Season with salt and pepper.

For the quinoa, heat the cooked quinoa in the top of a double boiler. Add the braised oxtail meat, leeks, spinach and fennel. Season with salt and pepper. Shape this mixture into quenelles and arrange on soup plates. Pour approximately 3 tablespoons of the broth around each quenelle and serve piping hot.

197 Tenderloin of Beef in a Potato Crust

Serves 4

For the tenderloin:
12 ounces spinach, washed
Salt and pepper to taste
Olive oil
4 6-ounce pieces beef tenderloin, trimmed
3 Idaho potatoes, peeled

For the red wine sauce:
¾ cup Cabernet Sauvignon
2 shallots, peeled and chopped
1 sprig fresh thyme
3 whole black peppercorns
¾ cup veal stock
1 tablespoon butter

For the garnish:
1 medium carrot, turned
1 large turnip, turned
1 large celeriac, turned
½ pint pearl onions, peeled
1 cup olive oil
1 clove garlic, peeled and crushed
2 tablespoons assorted herbs, chopped
Salt and pepper to taste

To prepare the tenderloins, season the spinach with salt and pepper and wilt in olive oil. Cool and drain. Lay the tenderloin pieces on a work surface and top with the wilted spinach. Shred the potatoes on a mandoline. Season with salt and pepper. Squeeze dry. Lay a 12-inch square piece of parchment paper on the work surface. Down the center of the parchment place a thin layer of shredded potato. Lay a spinach-topped beef tenderloin on top of the potato and top with more shredded potato to cover. Pull up the parchment to completely envelope the tenderloin in the shredded potato. Repeat with remaining tenderloins. Remove the parchment and immediately place the tenderloins in a hot skillet. Brown on all sides. Set the beef in a 400 degree oven and cook to desired doneness. Remove from the oven and set aside.

For the sauce, combine the Cabernet Sauvignon, shallots, thyme and peppercorns in a small saucepan. Reduce by three-quarters. Add the veal stock and simmer. Strain and reserve. Just before service, whisk in the butter.

For the garnish, sauté the vegetables in olive oil with the garlic until tender. Season with salt and pepper and toss with fresh herbs.

To serve, arrange each tenderloin on a plate and garnish with the vegetables. Drizzle the Cabernet Sauvignon sauce around the plate and serve.

119 Sautéed Daurade with Sweet and Sour Sauce

Serves 4

For the sauce:
1 pound beef shank, cubed
2 tablespoons olive oil
2 tablespoons butter
¾ cup diced spring onion
¾ cup diced peeled carrot
1 teaspoon flour
1¼ cup red wine
1 cup veal stock
¼ bunch fresh thyme
1 bay leaf
2 oranges, zest reserved for garnish
Salt and fresh cracked pepper
1 tablespoon orange juice
1 teaspoon red wine vinegar
2 tablespoons butter

For the batter:
¼ cup rice flour
1 egg yolk
1 tablespoon olive oil
⅓ cup water, as needed

For the fish:
4 6 ounce fillets daurade or porgy
Salt and pepper to season
2 tablespoons olive oil

For the garnish:
8 large zucchini flowers
20 leaves young mixed greens
1 bunch Italian parsley
1 quart peanut oil for frying
2 tablespoons candied orange zest

For the sauce, one day in advance sear the beef shank in the olive oil and butter to a rich brown. Add in the onion and the carrot, continuing to brown for about 5 minutes. Bring up the juices and oil with the flour and deglaze the pan with the red wine. Reduce the wine by ¾ and pour in the veal stock. Skim the stock and add in the thyme, bay leaf, and oranges. Simmer for another 45 minutes until reduced to a light glaze and strain. When ready to serve, season with the salt and pepper, the orange juice and vinegar; reduce slightly and finish the sauce with the butter.

For the batter beat the egg yolk and olive oil into the rice flour until smooth. Blend in the water as needed to make a light liquid batter.

To serve, season the fish fillets and quickly sear in the olive oil, begining with the skin side down. Dredge the zucchini flower petals and the baby greens in the batter and fry in the 350 degree oil until crispy; fry the parsley in the oil without any batter. Arrange a bouquet of the fried herbs to the top of the plate, ladle a pool of the finished sauce in the center, and set the seared daurade fillets in the middle of the sauce with the skin side up. Garnish the fish with the candied orange zest.

198 Grilled Beef Brisket with Gratin of Salsify

Serves 4

For the salsify:
1 pound salsify
½ cup heavy cream, whipped
4 tablespoons freshly grated Parmesan cheese

For the spice mixture:
½ teaspoon black peppercorns, cracked
½ teaspoon white peppercorns, cracked
½ teaspoon pink peppercorns, cracked
¼ teaspoon allspice, cracked
¼ teaspoon coriander seeds, cracked
Zest of ½ a tangerine

For the brisket:
4 6-ounce cooked beef brisket steaks
2 tablespoons olive oil
Salt to taste

For the garnish:
2 cups mashed potatoes
1 carrot, peeled, julienned and blanched
½ leek, julienned and blanched

For the salsify, peel and cut it into ½-inch pieces. Blanch the salsify in lightly salted water until tender. Drain in a colander and rinse with cold water.

For the spice mixture, combine all the ingredients and mix well.

For the brisket, brush the brisket steaks with the olive oil on both sides. Sprinkle with salt and cover 1 side of the steaks with a generous amount of the spice mixture. Grill the steaks on a hot broiler until thoroughly hot.

To serve, arrange the salsify on plates. Spoon some whipped cream over each piece of salsify and sprinkle with the Parmesan cheese. Place the plates under a hot broiler and brown. Divide the mashed potatoes among the plates and top with the grilled brisket steaks. Garnish the dish with julienned carrots and leeks.

199 Spiced Beef Brisket in Bouillon

Serves 4

For the spice mixture:
½ teaspoon black peppercorns, cracked
½ teaspoon white peppercorns, cracked
½ teaspoon pink peppercorns, cracked
¼ teaspoon allspice, cracked
¼ teaspoon coriander seeds, cracked
Zest of ½ a tangerine

For the brisket:
4 6-ounce cooked beef brisket steaks
2 tablespoons olive oil
4 cups beef bouillon
Salt to taste

For the garnish:
1 leek, green part only, blanched
1 carrot, peeled, blanched and julienned
1 branch celery, blanched and julienned
4 thyme sprigs
4 rosemary sprigs
4 pieces dried tangerine peels
Chives
Chervil

For the spice mixture, combine all ingredients and mix well.

For the brisket, cover one side of each steak with a generous amount of the spice mixture. Sauté the brisket steaks in a skillet until thoroughly hot. Heat the bouillon, season to taste and keep hot.

For the garnish, roll the carrots sticks, celery, thyme, rosemary and dried tangerine peel in the blanched leek leaves and tie into bundles with the chives. Place the bundles in the bouillon and heat. To serve, pour the bouillon into soup bowls, place 1 brisket steak and 1 bundle of vegetables in each bowl, garnish with chervil sprigs and serve.

200 Roasted Veal Shank with Mint

Serves 4

For the shanks:
4 cross cut veal shanks
Seasoned flour for dredging
1 cup butter
1/3 cup chopped carrots
1/3 cup chopped onions
1/3 cup chopped celery
2 cloves garlic, minced
1/2 bunch mint
1 sprig parsley
1 sprig rosemary
1/2 cup coarsely chopped seeded tomatoes
1 cup white wine
Pinch of ground nutmeg
1/2 tablespoon grated lemon peel
4 cups veal stock
Salt and pepper to taste

For the rice:
6 tablespoons butter
1/2 cup finely minced onions
1 1/2 cups Arborio rice
1/2 cup white wine
5 cups lean veal broth
Pinch of saffron
1/2 teaspoon salt
6 tablespoons grated
Parmigiano-Reggiano cheese

For the garnish:
1/2 tablespoon grated lemon peel
1 teaspoon minced garlic
1/2 tablespoon finely chopped parsley leaves
1 tablespoon finely chopped mint leaves
4 sprigs fresh mint

For the shanks, dust the veal shanks in the seasoned flour. Melt the butter in a casserole or heavy sauté pan and brown the shanks evenly; adding the chopped carrots, onions, celery, the minced garlic, the mint, rosemary and parsley sprigs. When all the ingredients are lightly browned, add in the tomatoes and deglaze the pan with the white wine, allowing the alcohol to evaporate. Add in the grated nutmeg and lemon peel. Cover the shanks with the veal stock, reduce the heat, cover the casserole and braise until tender and the meat begins to come away from the bone. Remove the shanks and set them aside to keep warm; reduce the sauce to a light glaze, adjust the seasoning, and pass it through a fine sieve.

For the rice, brown 4 tablespoons of the butter in a saucepan and add in the chopped onions. When the onions begin to get tender, add in the rice and stir until it is lightly toasted and has absorbed the fat. Pour in the wine and let it evaporate. Add in a ladle of broth and continue to stir. Let the rice absorb it; continue to add more broth while stirring, one ladle at a time, allowing each ladleful to be absorbed before adding in the next one. Halfway through the cooking add in the saffron and the salt. When the rice is al dente, turn off the heat and mix in the remaining butter with the Parmigiano-Reggiano cheese. Stir the rice well with a wooden spoon until all the ingredients are blended thoroughly and the risotto is smooth-the rice grains should be fluffy, yet hold together and should not be too fluid.

To serve, remove the meat from the shanks, slice the meat thinly and arrange on each plate in a fan. Stand the marrow bones to the left of each fan and fill each bone with some of the gremolata mixture of finely minced lemon peel, garlic, parsley and mint. Make two quenelles of the saffron rice and set them off from the marrow bone. Glaze the sliced meat with a ladle of the sauce, allowing the sauce to flow onto the plate. Sprinkle the meat lightly with the remaining gremolata and finish the dish with a sprig of fresh mint.

201 Calves' Brain Sandwich

Serves 4

For the mayonnaise:
1 ounce calves' brain
1 tablespoon lemon zest
2 tablespoons capers
Salt and pepper
1/2 cup olive oil

For the sandwich:
2 calves' brains, cleaned
2 tablespoons brown butter
6 tablespoons butter
8 1/4-inch thick brioche rounds
4 slices rendered bacon, cut into strips

For the garnish:
1 cup baby salad greens
16 lotus root chips
2 tablespoons mustard oil
8 sandwich picks of onion, cornichon and tomato

For the mayonnaise, purée the 1 ounce of calves' brain and add in the lemon zest, capers, salt and pepper. Slowly pour the olive oil into the puréed brains to emulsify, the protein of the brains will act as the yolk of an egg.

For the sandwich, sauté the calves' brains in the brown butter, chill and cut into 4 equal portions with a cookie cutter. Butter both sides of the brioche rounds and build the sandwiches in each cutter or metal ring: first the brioche, then mayonnaise, bacon, a slice of brain, mayonnaise, bacon and brioche. Cook the sandwiches slowly on a griddle until they are warm throughout and toasted brown.

To serve, remove the sandwiches from the rings, cut in two and place in the middle of each plate. Garnish with a small salad of greens, the lotus chips, mustard oil and sandwich picks.

202 Smoked Fillet of Veal with Black-eyed Pea Chili

Serves 4

For the chili:
2 cups black eyed peas, presoaked
2 quarts veal stock
2 medium potatoes, peeled and cut in ½ inch dice
1 medium carrot, diced
3 cloves garlic, minced
1 medium jalapeño pepper, diced
2 tablespoons chili powder
1 tablespoon cumin seed, ground
2 tablespoons brown sugar

For the smoked veal:
4 6 ounce veal tenderloin
2 tablespoon barbecue spice
4 sticks cinnomon

For the Garnish:
2 cups spaghetti squash, blanched
1 head garlic, roasted whole
12 shallots, roasted and peeled
2 medium carrots, blanched and cut into 12 curly "Q"s
3 large beets, blanched and cut into 12 curly "Q"s
4 sprigs rosemary
16 sprigs cilantro, fried crisp

For the chili, bring the black eyed peas to a boil in the veal stock; reduce heat and simmer for 1 hour. Add the diced carrots, potatoes and jalapeño pepper with the minced garlic, chili powder, ground cumin and the brown sugar. Simmer the chili for 1 hour more, until the peas are tender. Adjust the seasoning.

To smoke the veal tenderloin, coat each piece with the barbecue spice and smoke until medium-rare in a hot smoker with the cinnomon sticks and hickory wood chips.

To serve, ladel ½ cup of the chili onto each plate. Sauté the spaghetti squash and spoon onto center of the plate. Slice the smoked tenderloin into medallions and fan them around the top of the spaghetti squash. Sauté the curly "Q" beets and the carrots; carefully arrange in the center of the tenderloin medallions. Garnish each dish with 3 whole roasted shallots, 3 cloves of roasted garlic, the sprigs of fried cilantro and fresh rosemary.

203 Roasted Veal Loin with Vegetables

Serves 4

For the veal roast:
2 pounds veal loin, trimmed
½ pound veal trimmings
Salt and pepper to taste
2 tablespoons olive oil
2 quarts white veal stock
1 cup peeled and sliced carrots
1 cup small pickling onions, peeled
1 cup turned new potatoes
⅓ cup butter

For the garnish:
1 tablespoon chopped parsley

For the veal, thoroughly brown the seasoned veal loin and the trimmings in the olive oil in a deep roasting pan. Roast in a 325 degree oven for 40 minutes. Remove the loin, cover it with foil and keep warm Deglaze the pan with 3 cups of the veal stock and reduce the liquid until almost dry. Add 3 more cups of veal stock and reduce again until ½ cup of liquid remains. Strain the sauce, season with salt and pepper and keep warm.

In a saucepan, sauté the carrots in half of the butter, deglazing the pan with a cup of veal stock. Simmer until the carrots are tender. In another saucepan, brown the onions and the potatoes in the remaining butter and deglaze with the last cup of stock. Simmer until the potatoes are cooked. Toss the potatoes, onions and carrots together.

To serve, place the vegetables in their sauce in a serving dish and top with the roasted veal loin. Garnish with the chopped parsley.

204 Calves' Liver with Red Currants

Serves 4

For the calves' liver:
4 tablespoons vegetable oil
2 tablespoons butter
4 6 ounce slices calves' liver
Seasoned flour for dredging
1 tablespoon port wine
1 tablespoon Guignolet cherry brandy
½ cup rich chicken stock
1 cup fresh red currants

For the garnish:
4 small clusters red currants

For the liver, heat the oil with 1 tablespoon of butter in a large skillet; dredge the calves' liver in the seasoned flour and sauté each piece until the liver is crisp on both sides, but still juicy and pink inside. Pour off the oil, deglaze the pan with the port and the cherry brandy, remove the liver and add in the chicken stock. Reduce the liquid to a light glaze; whisk in the remaining butter and toss the currants with the sauce for 1 minute.

To serve, place the crisp sauteed liver across eack of the warmed plates, spoon the currants over the liver, letting some fall to the bottom rim and pour the sauce over the liver and the currants. Garnish each dish with a cluster of currants.

205 Calves' Liver and Kidney Tartelette

Serves 6

For the kidney:
6 tablespoons kosher salt
1 teaspoon saltpeter
1 teaspoon white pepper
1½ teaspoons poultry seasoning
2 tablespoons honey
2 tablespoons molasses
1 veal kidney, trimmed

For the sauce:
½ cup sage vinegar
2 shallots, chopped fine
5 peppercorns
2 cups veal stock
Salt and pepper to taste
1 tablespoon fresh sage leaves

For the tartelette:
12 ounces pâte brisée
2 pounds of calves' liver, cut into 6 steaks
Flour for dredging
6 tablespoons butter
Reserved smoked kidney strips
2 tablespoons butter, clarified
2 shallots, diced
1 cups leeks, blanched and cut julienne
½ cup carrots, blanched and cut julienne
½ cup celery, blanched and cut julienne
Salt and pepper to taste
1½ cups potatoes, whipped

For the garnish:
12 shallots, roasted and peeled
24 pearl onions, peeled and blanched
Fresh sage leaves

For the smoked kidney, mix together all the ingredients for a marinade; lather onto the kidney and let it sit, refrigerate it for 24 to 36 hours. Drain off the marinade and rinse the kidney of any excess liquid. Cold smoke the kidney for 1 hour. The kidney should be cut into small strips and used as you would bacon for flavor.

For the sauce, reduce the sage vinegar with the shallots and the peppercorns until ½ cup of liquid remains. Add in the veal stock and continue to simmer until the liquid is reduced to a light sauce; adjust the seasoning, steep the fresh sage leaves and pass the sauce through a fine sieve just before serving.

For the tartelettes, roll the pâte brisée out into thin strips, wrap the dough bands around the inside of metal rings, and bake them at 350 degrees until golden brown and crisp. Dredge the liver steaks in the flour and sauté them in 4 tablespoons of butter until they are nicely browned. Finish cooking the liver in a 350 degree oven for 4-5 minutes and let the meat rest 1-2 minutes before serving. In the hot pan sear off the smoked kidney in clarified butter and caramelize with the shallots. Sauté the julienned celery, leek and carrots together in the remaining butter and season them with salt and pepper.

To serve, pipe a ring of warm potato purée in the center of each plate. Place the pâte brisée rings on top of the potato and fill the rings with the seasoned vegetables. Cut the liver into thin slices and fan them around the inside edge of the rings. Ladle the sauce into the tartelette, spilling some over onto the plate. Garnish the plate with the smoked kidney, the shallots and pearl onions. Top the tartelette with fresh sage leaves.

208 Classic Alsatian Kugelhopf

Yields 1 kugelhopf
For the kugelhopf:
1 ounce fresh yeast
1½ cups milk, warmed
2½ pounds all-purpose flour
6 ounces raisins
2 ounces Kirsch
½ teaspoon salt
3 eggs
10 ounces butter, room temperature
Whole almonds as needed

Begin by preparing the first dough. Combine the yeast with half of the milk and enough flour to make a dough. Place this dough in a bowl, cover and set in a warm place until double in bulk. Combine the raisins and the Kirsch and allow to steep.

In a separate bowl, prepare the second dough. Combine the remaining flour with the salt, eggs and the remaining milk. Knead energetically for about 15 minutes by hand until the dough is smooth and elastic. Knead in the butter until evenly incorporated. Combine the first dough, continuing to knead until blended. Set the dough into a bowl, cover with a cloth and allow to sit for an hour in a warm place.

After the dough has rested for an hour, transfer it to a lightly floured surface. Make a well in the center of the dough and place the pre-soaked raisins and their soaking liquid in the center of the well. Knead until well mixed. Grease a kugelhopf mold with butter and line the mold with the whole almonds. Set the kugelhopf in a 375 degree oven and bake for approximately 45 minutes until the bread sounds hollow when tapped. If the kugelhopf browns too quickly, cover with a sheet of parchment paper and continue baking until done.Serve at room temperature.

***Note:** Some aficionados prefer the kugelhopf after it has "matured" for at least one day.

209 Kugelhopf with Escargots

Yields 1 kugelhopf
For the kugelhopf:
2 pounds all-purpose flour
3 eggs
1½ ounces fresh yeast
¾ cup water, lukewarm
⅔ cup milk, lukewarm
½ pound garlic butter, cut into cubes and softened
1 tablespoon salt
2 cups escargots, sautéed in garlic butter and cooled to room temperature
½ cup sliced almonds
Egg wash

To prepare the kugelhopf, combine the flour, eggs, yeast, water and milk in the bowl of an electric mixer fitted with a dough hook. Knead for six or seven minutes until the dough is smooth and elastic. While the mixer is running, add the garlic butter and continue kneading until incorporated. Knead in the salt and the escargots. Turn the dough out onto a lightly floured surface and shape into a ball. Set in a deep bowl, cover and let rise until double in volume, approximately two to three hours. Return the dough to a floured surface and punch down.

Grease a kugelhopf mold with butter and sprinkle the inside of the mold with the sliced almonds. Set the dough into the mold, brush with egg wash, cover and let rise until the dough reaches the top of the mold. Bake in a 400 degree oven for approximately 50 minutes, until the bread sounds hollow when tapped. Remove from the mold and allow to cool on a wire rack. Serve at room temperature or slightly warmed.

210 Chocolate Cherry Kugelhopf

Yields 1 kugelhopf
For the kugelhopf:
2 cups dried cherries
Kirsch
1 pound all-purpose flour
1 ounce fresh yeast
⅔ cup milk, lukewarm
3 ounces unsweetened cocoa powder
½ teaspoon salt
2 eggs
3 tablespoons sugar
3 ounces butter, softened

To begin, place the dried cherries in a small bowl and pour in enough Kirsch to cover. Let soak overnight. Drain the cherries, reserving one ounce of the Kirsch. Prepare the first dough by combining the yeast with half of the milk and enough of the flour to form a soft dough. Set aside, in a warm separate bowl combine the remaining flour with the cocoa, salt, eggs, sugar and remaining milk. Knead energetically for 15 minutes until the dough is smooth and elastic. Add the butter and continue kneading until incorporated. Next, combine the two doughs and knead until blended. Make a well in the dough and pour in the soaked cherries and the Kirsch. Knead gently until combined.

Shape the dough into a ball and set in a warm place to double in a bowl. Punch down and set in a greased kugelhopf mold. Allow the dough to rise until it reaches the top of the mold. Bake in a 375 degree oven for approximately 45 minutes, or until the bread sounds hollow when tapped. Remove from the mold and cool on a wire rack.

211 Smoked Salmon Kugelhopf

Yields 1 kugelhopf

For the kugelhopf:

1 egg
1 pound all-purpose flour
1 pound baked potatoes, chilled, peeled and put through a food mill
1 ounce fresh yeast
½ cup milk, lukewarm
½ pound butter, cut into cubes
1 tablespoon salt
½ pound smoked salmon, cut into small pieces
1 bunch dill, chopped
3 tablespoons sesame seeds

To prepare the kugelhopf, mix together the flour, potato, egg, yeast and milk in the bowl of an electric mixer fitted with a dough hook. Knead for six or seven minutes until the dough is smooth and elastic. With the mixer still running, add the butter. Once the butter has been incorporated into the dough, add the salt. Knead in the smoked salmon and chopped dill. Turn the dough out onto a lightly floured surface and shape into a ball. Place in a deep bowl, cover and let rise until doubled in volume, two to three hours.

Return the dough to a floured surface and punch down. Lightly grease a kugelhopf mold with butter and sprinkle with the sesame seeds. Transfer the dough to the mold, cover with plastic and let rise until the dough has reached the top of the mold, Bake in a 400 degree oven for approximately 50 minutes until the bread sounds hollow when tapped. Remove from the mold and allow to cool on a wire rack.
Serve at room temperature or slightly warmed.

211 Cinnamon Pecan Kugelhopf

Yields 1 kugelhopf

For the kugelhopf:

4 eggs
1 ounce fresh yeast
2 cups milk, warmed
2 pounds all-purpose flour
¾ pound butter, cut into cubes and softened
1 tablespoon salt
6 ounces sugar
1 cup pecans, roughly chopped
3 tablespoons cinnamon

To prepare the kugelhopf, make a sponge by combining the yeast, milk and ⅓ of the flour in a large bowl of an electric mixer with a dough hook. Spoon the remaining flour on top of the sponge, but do not mix. Set the bowl in a warm place and allow the mixture to proof until deep cracks have formed in the surface of the flour. Set the bowl in the mixer and use the dough hook to blend in the flour. Add the eggs, one at a time. After the last egg has been fully incorporated, continue kneading for approximately six or seven minutes, until the dough is smooth and elastic. With the mixer running, add the butter. Once the butter is incorporated into the dough, add the salt and two ounces of the sugar. Mix until the dough pulls easily away from the side of the bowl.Turn the dough out onto a lightly floured surface and shape into a ball. Place the dough in a deep bowl, cover and let sit in a warm place until double in bulk. Punch down.

Divide the dough into eight pieces and let rest for five minutes. Grease the kugelhopf mold with butter and sprinkle with chopped pecans and a little sugar. Mix the remaining sugar with the cinnamon. Roll each piece of dough into the shape of a thick rope and then roll in the cinnamon-sugar mixture to coat. Arrange the pieces of dough in the kugelhopf mold. Cover and let rise until the dough reaches the top of the mold. Bake at 400 degrees for 45 minutes, or until the bread sounds hollow when tapped. Unmold and cool on a rack.

212 Vegetable Moussaka

Serves 6

For the moussaka:
2 medium eggplants, sliced ¼-inch thick
4 zucchini, sliced ¼-inch thick
4 yellow squash, sliced ¼-inch thick
1 cup virgin olive oil
2 red bell peppers, roasted, peeled and seeded
2 yellow peppers, roasted, peeled and seeded
White pepper to taste
½ cup grated Parmesan cheese
Salt

For the garnish:
1 yellow squash, cut into fine brunoise
1 zucchini, cut into fine brunoise
1 red pepper, cut into fine brunoise
1 yellow pepper, cut into fine brunoise
½ cup corn oil
Salt and pepper to taste
Balsamic vinegar
Chopped chives
Assorted fresh herbs

To prepare the moussaka, salt the eggplant slices and let sit for 1 hour. Rinse and pat dry. Lightly brush the eggplant, zucchini and yellow squash with olive oil. Grill until tender. In a small, rectangular baking dish, 4 inches wide by 6 inches long by 2 inches deep, begin layering the vegetables. Start with the eggplant. Sprinkle the eggplant with a dusting of Parmesan cheese. Layer the red pepper on top. Sprinkle with more cheese. Add another layer of eggplant, yellow squash, cheese, zucchini, cheese, and continue until the dish is filled to the top. End with a layer of egg-plant. Cover the dish with aluminum foil and bake in a 350-degree oven for 45 minutes. Cool.

For the garnish, lightly sauté the vegetable brunoise in the corn oil. Season with salt and pepper. Cut the moussaka into 6 even pieces. Carefully place 1 piece on each plate. Garnish with the vegetable brunoise, balsamic vinegar, chopped chives and assorted herbs.

213 Stuffed Eggplants

Serves 4

For the eggplant:
4 small eggplants
3 tablespoons virgin olive oil
3 onions, peeled and sliced
2 cloves garlic, minced
2 large ripe tomatoes, cored and roughly chopped
1 canned plum tomato, chopped
Salt and freshly ground black pepper
⅓ kefalotiri cheese*, cut into strips
½ bunch parsley, chopped

To prepare the eggplant, trim the stems and rub with oil. Cut 3 evenly spaced vertical wedges from each eggplant. Salt the exposed flesh and set aside.

Heat the olive oil in a small saucepan. Add the onions and garlic and sauté until golden brown. Add the fresh and canned tomatoes, parsley, salt and pepper and continue cooking until the onions are soft. Adjust the seasoning. Rinse the eggplant. Stuff the tomato and onion mixture into the open wedges of the eggplant and force a piece of kefalotiri cheese in to hold everything in place. Set the remaining onion and tomato mixture in the bottom of a small baking dish. Lay the stuffed eggplant on top and bake in a 425-degree oven until the eggplant are tender and the cheese has browned. Sprinkle with chopped parsley before serving.

*__Note__: Kefalotiri is a hard cheese made from a mixture of sheep's milk and cow's milk. Any hard, strong cheese (i.e. Sardinian pecorino) can be substituted.

214 Rolled Soufflé with Spinach and Cheese

Serves 8

For the soufflé:
5 large eggs
1½ cups half and half
4 tablespoons butter
5 tablespoons flour
1½ teaspoons salt
½ teaspoon white pepper
¼ teaspoon freshly grated nutmeg
½ cup freshly grated Parmesan cheese

For the spinach filling:
3 tablespoons olive oil
3 red onions, peeled and chopped
2 small cloves garlic, peeled and minced
2 leeks, washed and sliced
¾ cup dry white wine
1 teaspoon minced tarragon
1 pound young spinach leaves, stems removed

2 cups grated Gruyère cheese
1¼ cups grated asiago cheese
Salt and freshly ground black pepper to taste

For the red pepper sauce:
2 tablespoons butter
3 onions, peeled and minced
8 red bell peppers, seeded and chopped
1 cup dry white wine
1 cup rich vegetable stock
1 teaspoon honey
Salt and freshly ground white pepper to taste

For the garnish:
Shaved fennel
Curry oil
Flowering rosemary

To prepare the soufflé, separate the eggs. Lightly beat the yolks and set aside. In a small saucepan, scald the half and half. In a separate pan, make a roux with the butter and flour and cook for 3 minutes without browning. Whisk in the scalded half and half and cook, stirring constantly, for another 3 minutes until thick. Remove from the heat and stir in the salt, pepper and nutmeg. Gradually whisk the hot mixture into the egg yolks and set aside.

Beat the egg whites until they form stiff peaks. Stir a quarter of the beaten whites along with half of the cheese into the egg mixture to lighten it. Gently fold in the rest of the whites. Butter a 10 inch by 15 inch baking sheet and line with parchment. Lightly butter the parchment and dust with flour. Pour the soufflé mixture onto the prepared sheet, spread it evenly to the corners of the pan and sprinkle the remaining Parmesan over top. Bake in a preheated 400-degree oven for 15 minutes, until the top is browned and puffed. When the soufflé is done, remove from the oven and cool.

For the spinach filling, heat the olive oil and sauté the onions until lightly caramelized. Add the leeks and garlic and cook 3 minutes longer until soft. Pour in the wine. Add the herbs and cook until most of the liquid is evaporated. Add the spinach and cook 1 minute longer to partially wilt. Set aside and cool. Lightly toss the mixture with cheeses and season to taste with salt and pepper.

Spread the spinach filling evenly over the soufflé and carefully roll up lengthwise like a jelly-roll. Place the rolled soufflé in a preheated 350-degree oven for 8 to 10 minutes, just to heat through and melt the cheese.

For the red pepper sauce, place the butter in a saucepan and sauté the onions and peppers until soft, not brown. Add the wine, stock and honey and reduce over moderate heat until only half of the liquid remains. Remove from the pan and purée in a blender or food processor. Strain. Correct the seasoning and thin if necessary with additional stock.

To serve, ladle the sauce on the bottom of the plates. Slice the rolled soufflé and arrange the slices on the sauce. Garnish with the shaved fennel, curry oil and flowering rosemary as shown.

214 Artichokes in Champagne Sauce

Serves 5

For the artichokes:
4 cups finely chopped mirepoix
1 bouquet garni, with basil stems from garnish
4 tablespoons olive oil
5 large artichokes, trimmed with stalks left on
½ bottle champagne
Salt

For the sauce:
4 egg yolks
½ bottle champagne
1 cup extra virgin olive oil
Salt and pepper

For the garnish:
1 large tomato, peeled, seeded and finely chopped
1 small bunch basil, chopped and stems reserved for bouquet garni
3 tablespoons extra virgin olive oil
Salt and pepper
Edible flowers

To prepare the artichokes, sweat the mirepoix and bouquet garni in 2 tablespoons olive oil in a covered saucepan for 20 minutes. Do not allow the mirepoix to brown.

Place the artichokes in a deep pan with their stalks pointing up and pour the sweated mirepoix over them. Sprinkle the artichokes with salt and remaining 2 tablespoons of olive oil. Cover and sweat for an additional 20 minutes. Add the champagne, cover and cook until the artichokes are tender.

Remove the artichokes and set aside. Pass the mirepoix through a sieve and retain the juices. Reduce the liquid to ½ cup. Cool.

For the champagne sauce, whisk some of the reduced artichoke cooking liquid into the egg yolks. Add the champagne. Continue beating in a double boiler until the sauce is thick and ribbony. Remove from the heat and set the bowl over ice. Slowly beat in the extra virgin olive oil. Season with salt and pepper.

For the garnish, combine the diced tomato and the chopped basil. Stir in the olive oil and some of the artichoke cooking liquid and season with salt and pepper.

To serve, position the artichokes on a platter. Garnish with the tomato salad and spoon on the champagne sauce. Decorate with edible flowers.

215 Wild Mushrooms with Fennel Sauce

Serves 8

For the red pepper custard:
1 large red bell pepper, roasted, peeled, seeded and chopped
¼ cup light cream
3 large eggs
½ cup vegetable stock
1 teaspoon salt
1 teaspoon white wine
Worcestershire sauce

For the fennel sauce:
6 shallots, peeled and minced
½ cup chopped mushrooms
4 tablespoons butter
1 tablespoon fennel seed
2 cups rich vegetable stock
1 cup dry white wine
¾ cup heavy cream
2 tablespoons dry sherry
2 tablespoons Dijon mustard
Juice of 1 lemon
Salt and freshly ground white pepper to taste
2 teaspoons mustard seeds, toasted
1 tablespoon minced chives

For the mushrooms:
1½ pounds fresh wild mushrooms
1 large fennel bulb, sliced
Olive oil
Salt and pepper to taste

For the garnish:
Roasted and grilled baby vegetables
Parsnip chips
Toasted mustard seeds
Bronze fennel sprigs

For the red pepper custard, combine the pepper with the light cream in a blender and purée until smooth, scraping down the sides of the blender as needed. Add the remaining ingredients and blend until completely combined. Strain. Fill 8 buttered 2-ounce ramekins. Place them in a shallow baking dish and fill the dish with boiling water halfway up the sides of the ramekins. Bake in a preheated 350-degree oven for 20 minutes. Remove the ramekins from the water bath and allow to cool slightly. Run a knife around the inside of the ramekins to unmold.

To prepare the fennel sauce, in a saucepan, sauté the shallots and mushrooms in 2 tablespoons of the butter until lightly browned. Add the fennel seed, stock, wine and reduce over high heat by half. Add the cream and reduce again to a light sauce consistency. Stir in the sherry and mustard and reduce slightly. Remove the pan from the heat and whisk in the remaining 2 tablespoons of butter. Strain and correct the seasoning with the lemon juice, salt and pepper. Stir in the mustard seeds and chives. Hold the sauce in a warm place until ready to use.

To prepare the mushrooms, clean and trim the mushrooms and set aside. Lightly oil the fennel slices, season with salt and pepper and grill or broil for 1 to 2 minutes on each side. Do not overcook. Set aside and keep warm. Lightly oil the mushrooms and quickly roast or grill them until tender. Be careful not to overcook them; they should retain a chewy texture.

To serve, arrange the mushrooms, fennel slices and red pepper custard on warm plates. Spoon the sauce around and garnish with baby vegetables, parsnip chips, mustard seeds and fennel sprigs.

217 Mushroom Tamales

Yields 10 tamales

For the filling:
2 portobellos, sliced
4 fresh shiitakes, stems removed and sliced
4 creminis, sliced
4 morels, sliced
Olive oil for sautéing
2 shallots, peeled and diced
3 teaspoons chopped thyme
7 ounces unsalted butter
Salt and pepper to taste
10 ounces cuitlacoche*
2¼ cups poultry stock
Zest of 1 lemon
2 teaspoons kosher salt
½ pound masa harina
1 Anaheim chile pepper, roasted, peeled, seeded and finely julienned

For the wrapping:
20 corn husks, soaked
Corn husk strips for tying

To prepare the filling, sauté the portobellos, shiitakes, creminis and morels separately in olive oil. Combine the mushrooms in one sauté pan. Add the shallots, 1 teaspoon of the chopped thyme, and half of the butter. Season with salt and pepper.

Purée the cuitlacoche in a blender until smooth. Pass through a fine chinois. In a 2 quart saucepan, combine the poultry stock, cuitlacoche purée, the remaining thyme, lemon zest and kosher salt. Bring to a boil. Reduce to a simmer. Sifting the masa harina through your fingers, whisk it into the simmering liquid. Continue whisking while the masa cooks. The dough is done when it has tightened and does not stick to your fingers.

Transfer the cooked masa to a bowl and stir in the sautéed mushrooms and the roasted, julienned Anaheim chile. Cool. Lay out the reconstituted corn husks and place 3 ounces of the filling in the middle of each. Roll and tie. Steam the tamales for 20 minutes on high heat. Cool. To serve, untie and pull back the corn husk.

*__Note:__ Cuitlacoche is a flavorful fungus, which grows on the inside of corn husks. It can be purchased flash-frozen in specialty food stores.

216 Fresh Corn Tamales

Yields 8 tamales

For the filling:
4 ounces lard
2 cups fresh corn kernels, puréed
1 teaspoon salt
½ teaspoon chile caribe flakes
½ teaspoon finely ground black pepper
1½ teaspoons baking powder
4 ounces aged goat cheese, crumbled
8 Anaheim chilies, roasted, peeled, seeded and finely julienned

For the wrapping:
16 corn husks, soaked
Corn husk strips for tying

To prepare the filling, beat the lard in an electric mixer until very light in texture, about 1 minute. Add the corn purée, salt, spices and baking powder and continue beating until smooth and light. Fold in the crumbled goat cheese and the julienned chilies. Lay out the corn husks and place 3 ounces of the filling in the center of the husks. Roll and tie. Steam until the filling has pulled away from the husks, approximately 30 minutes. Serve.

217 Greek Tamales

Yields 6 tamales

For the masa:
1½ cups water
¼ cup corn oil
2 cups masa harina
½ teaspoon baking powder
Salt and pepper to taste

For the filling:
1 pound feta cheese, crumbled
1 cup calamata olives, pitted

For the wrapping:
6 corn husks, soaked
Corn husk strips for tying

For the sauce:
1 pound basil leaves
½ cup pine nuts
1½ cups clam juice
¼ cup fresh lime juice
1 cup olive oil

For the garnish:
6 corn husks
Feta cheese
Calamata olives
Fresh oregano

To prepare the masa, bring the water and oil to a boil in a medium-sized saucepan. Sift the masa harina through your fingers into the boiling water and whisk until smooth. Add the baking powder, salt and pepper and continue stirring until the masa has become shiny and it pulls away from the sides of the pot. Cool. Spread the masa on the reconstituted corn husks. Place 2 tablespoons of feta and 3 or 4 olives in the center and roll and tie. Steam the tamales for 8 to 12 minutes, until the corn husks easily pull away from the filling.

To prepare the sauce, purée all of the ingredients except for the olive oil in a blender. Slowly drizzle in the oil while the blender is still running to form an emulsion.

To serve, unwrap the tamales. Place them on the plates and ladle the sauce over top. Garnish with corn husks, feta, olives and fresh oregano.

218 Vegetarian Tamales

Yields 6 tamales

For the masa:
1½ cups water
¼ cup corn oil
2 cups masa harina
½ teaspoon baking powder
Salt and pepper to taste

For the filling:
3 carrots, peeled and finely diced
2 potatoes, peeled and finely diced
2 zucchini, finely diced
1 clove garlic, peeled and minced
Olive oil for sautéing
Salt and pepper to taste

For the wrapping:
6 corn husks, soaked
Corn husk strips for tying

For the sauce:
4 cups carrot juice
¼ cup butter, cut into cubes and chilled
Salt and pepper to taste

For the garnish:
6 corn husks
Fresh chilies
Fresh cilantro

To prepare the masa, bring the water and oil to a boil in a medium-sized saucepan. Sift the masa harina through your fingers into the boiling water and whisk until smooth. Add the baking powder, salt and pepper and continue stirring until the masa has become shiny and it pulls away from the sides of the pot. Cool.

For the filling, blanch the vegetables for 1 to 2 minutes in boiling, salted water. Sauté with the garlic in olive oil until tender. Season with salt and pepper.

To form the tamales, spread the masa on the reconstituted corn husks. Spoon the sautéed vegetables in the middle and roll and tie them. Steam for 10 to 15 minutes, until the masa has stiffened.

To prepare the sauce, place the carrot juice in a small, non-reactive saucepan and set over low heat. Slowly reduce the juice by half. Whisk in the butter until blended. Adjust the seasoning with salt and pepper.

To serve, unwrap the tamales and set on the plates with corn husks. Spoon the carrot sauce over the tamales and garnish with chili peppers and fresh cilantro.

219 Stuffed Artichoke Hearts with Pesto Broth

Serves 4

For the artichokes:
4 medium-sized artichokes
1 lemon
5 tablespoons virgin olive oil
1 onion, peeled and sliced
1 carrot, peeled and sliced
1 leek, white part only, julienned
1 cup dry white wine
2 bay leaves
1 sprig fresh thyme
2 cloves garlic, peeled
Salt and freshly ground black pepper
2 cloves garlic, peeled and finely chopped
6 leaves basil, finely chopped
1 teaspoon chopped parsley
1 teaspoon chopped chives
1 tomato, peeled, seeded and diced
12 asparagus tips, blanched
12 snow peas, blanched

For the stuffing:
2 russet potatoes, peeled, boiled and mashed
¼ pound spinach, cleaned and wilted in olive oil
2 tablespoons freshly grated Parmesan cheese
Salt and pepper to taste

To prepare the artichokes, cut off the stems and trim away all of the outer leaves. Remove the choke and trim the bottoms so that none of the hard green skin remains. As you work, keep dipping the cut edges of the artichoke bottoms into a bowl of water mixed with lemon juice to keep them from turning brown. Hold the trimmed artichokes in the acidulated water. Heat the olive oil in a medium-sized saucepan.

Add the sliced onion, carrot and julienned leek and sauté them over high heat for 5 minutes. Deglaze the pan with the white wine. Add the artichoke hearts, bay leaves, thyme, whole garlic cloves, salt and freshly ground pepper. Pour in just enough water to cover the vegetables and bring to a boil. Lower the heat to a very slow simmer and continue cooking for 20 to 25 minutes. Carefully transfer the artichokes to a warm serving platter and cover with aluminum foil.

For the stuffing, combine all of the ingredients and adjust the seasoning. Stuff the cooked artichokes with this mixture, handling them gently so they do not fall apart. Set the stuffed artichokes on a sheet pan and brown under a broiler. Meanwhile, finish the broth. Add the chopped garlic, basil, parsley, chives, diced tomato, asparagus tips and snow peas to the vegetables that cooked with the artichokes. Bring to a boil over high heat and stir gently. Adjust the seasoning with salt and pepper. Gently spoon the vegetables and broth onto serving plates. Position the stuffed artichokes in the center of each plate and serve.

222 Swedish Punch and Raisin Ice Cream

Serves 4

For the ice cream:
8 egg yolks
4 to 6 whole eggs
9 ounces sugar
2 cups milk
2 cups heavy cream
5 whole vanilla beans
2½ ounces fruit punch
3½ ounces raisins
1¼ ounces rum

For the pancakes:
6 whole eggs
5½ ounces flour
2 cups milk
3½ ounces melted butter
Sugar
Salt to taste
Melted butter for frying pancakes

For garnish:
Powdered sugar
Orange peel
Shaved white and dark chocolates

For the ice cream, combine 8 egg yolks and 4-6 whole eggs, mix with sugar and whip until fluffy. Boil milk and cream together, cut the vanilla sticks and let them soak in the milk-cream mixture for about 20 minutes. Strain liquid into the egg mixture, continue to stir, add punch to taste and freeze in an ice-cream machine as usual. Boil raisins in run until they plump up. When the ice cream is almost ready, add the raisins and put the ice cream in the freezer.

For the pancakes, mix eggs and flour into a gluey dough, stir in milk a little at a time and finally add the melted butter. Let rest 30 minutes. Fry thin pancakes in melted butter. Sprinkle with powdered sugar

To serve, garnish plate of pancakes and ice cream with lemon peel and shaved chocolate.

223 Tarragon and White Chocolate Terrine

Serves 12

For the sweet pastry dough:
½ pound all-purpose flour
¼ cup cocoa
⅓ cup sugar
5 ounces unsalted butter, cubed and chilled
2 egg yolks
3 tablespoons ice water

For the wild cranberry sauce:
2 cups wild cranberries, stems removed
1 cup apple juice
¼ cup honey
1½ cups late harvest, botrytized wine

For the truffle mixture:
21 ounces white chocolate
3 ounces heavy cream
2 ounces clarified butter
3 ounces crème de cacao liqueur
4 sprigs fresh tarragon, stems removed and chopped

For the garnish:
Fresh mint

To prepare the dough, combine the flour, cocoa and sugar in a medium-sized mixing bowl or in the bowl of a large food processor. Add the butter and blend. In a small bowl whisk together the egg yolks and chilled water. Add the egg yolk mixture to the flour mixture and blend to form a soft dough. Knead for approximately 2 minutes. Wrap the dough in plastic wrap and let rest in the refrigerator for one hour.

Meanwhile, prepare the sauce. Place all of the ingredients except for 1 cup of the cranberries, in a small saucepan. Simmer for 30 minutes. Strain the liquid from the berries into another pot. Discard the cooked berries. Reduce the liquid by half over high heat, approximately 10 minutes. Pour the hot liquid over the reserved berries and let sit. Transfer to a sealed container and refrigerate until needed.

To prepare the white chocolate truffle mixture, chop the white chocolate into very small pieces. Combine it with the cream, butter and crème de cacao in a medium-sized metal bowl. Melt the mixture over a pot of simmering water, stirring continuously until everything has melted into a smooth, amalgamated mixture. Remove from the heat. Stir in the chopped tarragon and set aside.

To finish the terrine, roll out the dough to ⅛-inch thick. Line a triangular terrine mold with the dough. Place a sheet of parchment paper inside the terrine and fill with dried beans. Bake the crust for 25 minutes in a convection oven set to 340 degrees. Remove the terrine from the oven. Remove the beans and parchment paper, return the terrine to the oven and continue baking an additional 5 minutes. Cool.

Pour the white chocolate truffle mixture into the cooled crust. If the chocolate has hardened, it can be remelted over simmering water until pourable. Chill the terrine in the refrigerator for at least four hours. Remove from the refrigerator and slice with a very sharp knife. Fan out the slices and arrange on the plates. Ladle the wild cranberry sauce around the terrine and garnish with the sprigs of fresh mint.

224 Gin Bavarian in Ginger Tulip

Serves 20

For the gin bavarian:
¾ cup milk
1 tablespoon plus
2 teaspoons unflavored gelatin
1¼ cups milk
4 ounces sugar
8 egg yolks
3 egg whites
2 ounces sugar
5 ounces gin
2 cups heavy cream,
whipped to soft peaks

For marinated citrus sections:
40 each pink, red and white grapefruit sections
40 orange sections
1 tablespoon finely chopped orange zest, poached lightly
1 tablespoon finely chopped grapefruit zest, poached lightly
2 cups wild clover or orange blossom honey
1 cup gin*

For the ginger tulip cups:
6 ounces sugar
4 ounces egg whites
4 ounces butter
2½ ounces all-purpose flour
4 teaspoons ground ginger

For the garnish:
Chocolate butterfly
Whipped cream
Pulled sugar strand

For the gin cream, combine milk and gelatin and let rest 10 minutes to bloom. Meanwhile, bring milk to a boil in saucepan. Temper egg yolks and sugar, add to milk mixture, and stir and cook until thickened and nappés a spoon. Pour into gelatin mixture to dissolve it, and cool to room temperature. Beat egg whites and sugar to stiff peaks. Fold into cooled egg yolk mixture. Fold in gin and whipped cream. Pour mixture into molds and let chill 3 hours.

For the marinated citrus sections, combine fruits and zests in glass bowl. Combine honey and gin and pour over. Chill overnight.

For the ginger tuiles, in mixing bowl beat sugar, egg whites and butter. Add flour and ginger. Let set 2 hours at room temperature. Spread over tulip-shaped stencil and bake at 325 degrees for 10 minutes, or until lightly brown. Remove from oven and while still warm mold over cups to form 20 tulip shaps.

For the garnish of chocolate butterfly, place a pattern of a butterfly under a sheet of acetate or cellophane. Pipe in dark tempered chocolate and make the outline of the butterfly. Let set. Fill in details with white chocolate glaze, part white and part colored yellow. Let this set. Remove acetate. Secure two wings to dark chocolate body.

To serve, unmold gin bavarians. Place in tuile cups and set on a plate. Arrange citrus sections around cup and spoon marinade over sections. Set butterfly on timbale, securing with a small amount of whipped cream. Garnish with pulled sugar strand.

*__Note:__ If gin is not desirable, substitute another liquor or liqueur like Grand Marnier or Grand Passion.

225 Peach Napoleon with Honey Pecan Ice Cream

Serves 10

For the peach filling:
8 peaches, peeled and sliced
½ cup sugar
½ teaspoon cinnamon
1 tablespoon Amaretto
½ teaspoon lemon juice
Cornstarch to thicken

For the Amaretto pastry cream:
2 tablespoons butter
2 cups milk
⅓ cup plus 1 tablespoon sugar
2 egg yolks
¼ cup cornstarch
1 teaspoon vanilla
2 tablespoons Amaretto

For the napoleon assembly:
6 sheets phyllo pastry
Clarified butter
Powdered sugar

For the honey pecan ice cream:
2 cups milk
3 cups heavy cream
1⅓ cups orange blossom honey
7 egg yolks
4 ounces chopped, toasted pecans

For the tuile leaf cookies:
2 ounces butter
3 ounces sugar
2 ounces egg whites
1¼ ounces all-purpose flour

For the chocolate bee ornament:
Tempered couveture chocolate, melted
Tempered white chocolate tinted with yellow food coloring, melted

For the garnish:
Cocoa powder

For the peach filling, combine half of the peaches, sugar, cinnamon, Amaretto and lemon juice. Bring to a boil. Thicken with cornstarch so filling will not run. Add remaining peaches. Bring back to a boil, and check consistency.

For the Amaretto pastry cream, bring butter and milk to a boil. Combine sugar, egg yolks and cornstarch. Temper with hot milk and then add mixture to milk. Bring back to a boil. Cook 1 minute. Add vanilla and Amaretto. Let cool.

For the napoleon assembly, layer 6 sheets of phyllo dough with clarified butter brushed between layers. Cut into 10 3½- by 1½-inch rectangles. Place between two sheet pans and bake until brown. Store until time to serve between the pans.

For the honey pecan ice cream, combine milk, cream and honey. Bring to a boil. Temper yolks and combine with milk mixture. Cook, stirring, until mixture thickens and naps a spoon. Cool. If mixture appears to curdle, run in blender when cool. Freeze in ice cream freezer. Fold in chopped roasted pecans.

For the tuile leaf cookies, melt butter and combine with sugar, egg whites and flour. Let rest 1 hour. On greased and floured sheet pan, spread mixture over leaf stencil. Remove stencil and bake at 325 degrees for 8 to 10 minutes. Form curve in leaf while still warm.

To prepare plates, cut a cardboard stencil in the shape of a peach. Place over plate and dust with cocoa. Secure tuile leaf to plate with chocolate. Store plates until serving time.

To make chocolate bee, first make two wings. Pipe melted dark chocolate over a stencil or freeform into wings. Let set. For body, alternate, dark and yellow-tinted white chocolate in sections. Just before chocolate has set, attach wings.

To complete napoleon, layer warm peach filling with about 1 tablespoon pastry cream between 3 pieces of phyllo. Dust top layer with powdered sugar and caramelize this with torch.

To serve, place napoleon and ice cream atop cocoa peach. Top ice cream with chocolate bee.

225 Sabayon of Fruit au Gratin

Serves 5

For the sorbet's sugar syrup:
8½ ounces water
11 ounces sugar
3½ ounces glucose

For the sorbet:
10 ounces sugar syrup
22 ounces fresh orange juice
Juice of ½ lemon
1½ ounces campari

For the lemon tuiles:
1½ ounces sugar
1 ounce egg whites
1 ounce butter
¾ ounce all-purpose flour
1 teaspoon grated lemon rind

For the sabayon:
4 egg yolks
2 ounces sugar
1 ounce champagne
Grated zest of ½ orange
2 ounces heavy cream

For the fruit:
Sliced strawberries
Raspberries
Sliced mango
Sliced melon
Orange sections
Grapefruit sections

For the garnish:
Spirals of pulled sugar

For the sorbet's sugar syrup, combine water, sugar and glucose in a saucepan. Bring to a boil.

For the sorbet, chill 10 ounces of sugar syrup to 28 degrees. Combine with orange juice, lemon juice and campari and freeze in ice cream freezer according to manufacturer's directions. Keep frozen. This makes 1 quart. You will not need all of this for five servings.

For the tuiles, in mixing bowl, beat sugar, egg whites and butter. Add flour and lemon zest. Let rest 2 hours at room temperature. Spread over shallow cups and bake at 325 degrees for about 8 to 10 minutes, or until lightly browned. Remove tuiles from pan, and while still warm, press into cup shape.

For the sabayon, combine egg yolks, sugar, champagne and orange zest in bowl set over simmering water. Whip until thickened. Then, whip over ice until cooled. Fold in cream.

For the fruit, prepare fruits and arrange in a circle on plates, leaving the center of plates clear. Spoon sabayon over fruits and brown under broiler.

Place lemon tuiles filled with sorbet in center of plates. Garnish with spirals of pulled sugar.

226 Chocolate Napoleon with Mint Sauce

Serves 20

For dark and white chocolate layers:
8 ounces semi-sweet couveture chocolate, melted
8 ounces high-quality white chocolate, melted

For white chocolate mousse filling:
7 ounces sugar
2 ounces water
2 teaspoons unflavored gelatin
2 tablespoons water
2 tablespoons creme de cocoa
5 egg yolks, beaten
1 pound white chocolate, melted
1 quart heavy cream, whipped to soft peaks

For the mint sauce:
2 cups milk
2 cups heavy cream
1 tablespoon chopped fresh mint
6 ounces sugar
10 egg yolks
2 ounces creme de menthe

For the garnish:
Gold leaf
Cocoa powder
Chocolate ganache or melted chocolate for lines on plate
Chocolate ornament made of tempered couveture chocolate

For the dark and white chocolate layers, spread melted chocolate onto flat sheets pans that have been chilled in freezer. Layers should be almost paper thin. Immediately cut out rectangles and loosen chocolate from pan by running a paring knife under rectangles. Return to refrigerator to set chocolate firmly. Rectangles can also be prepared from tempered chocolate on parchment paper.

For the white chocolate mousse filling, combine sugar and water in saucepan. Cook to 240 degrees. Mix gelatin with water and creme de cocoa. Let bloom 5 minutes, and then heat to dissolve gelatin. Beat egg yolks, adding sugar mixture and whip to full volume and cool. Mix in dissolved gelatin mixture. Fold in melted white chocolate and whipped cream. Chill.

For the mint sauce, bring milk, cream and mint to a boil. In a mixing bowl over low heat combine and temper sugar and egg yolks. Add this to cream mixture and stir until it coats a spoon. Do not boil. Cool. Add creme de menthe and strain out fresh mint.

For the assembly, for each napoleon prepare two white chocolate and two dark chocolate layers. Pipe white chocolate mousse between layers, with two white chocolate layers placed in center.

For the garnish, top half with gold leaf and other half with dusting of cocoa powder.

To serve, pipe chocolate ganache or melted chocolate onto plate. Pour sauce between lines and top with napoleon. Garnish with chocolate ornament.

227 Chocolate Medley

Serves 10

For the Praline Basket with Mocha Sherbet:
Praline Basket:
7 ounces glucose
7 ounces sugar
7 ounces sliced almonds
7 ounces unsalted butter

Mocha Sherbet:
1 cup brewed coffee
2½ ounces sugar
¼ ounce cocoa powder
4 ounces semi-sweet chocolate
Vanilla extract to taste
Dark rum to taste

For the Hot Chocolate Macaroon Truffles:
10 Chocolate truffles in chocolate shell
10 almond macaroon cookies
40 squares phyllo pastry

For the Hazelnut Success with Marsala White Chocolate Mousse and Caramel Sauce:
For the mousse:
1¼ teaspoons unflavored gelatin
1½ teaspoons water
2½ tablespoons dry marsala
3½ ounces granulated sugar
2 tablespoons water

3 egg yolks
8 ounces white chocolate, melted
2 cups heavy cream, whipped to soft peaks

For the hazelnut success:
6 ounces granulated sugar
3 ounces confectioners' sugar
4 ounces hazelnut flour
2 ounces all-purpose flour
5 ounces egg whites
1 ounce granulated sugar
1/4 cup milk

Caramel Sauce:
1 pound sugar
2 ounces glucose
1 cup water
1/2 cup heavy cream
2 ounces butter
2 teaspoons vanilla

For the Pate a Choux Basket with Berries and Fruit:
6 ounces milk
2 ounces butter
4 ounces flour
4 eggs
Seasonal berries and fruit

For the Chocolate Tuile Teaspoon with Fresh Cream:
3 1/2 ounces all-purpose flour
1/2 ounce cocoa powder
4 ounces egg whites
4 ounces sugar
3 ounces melted butter
Whipped cream

For the praline basket, heat glucose in saucepan. Add sugar and almonds, then butter. Heat until butter has absorbed. Turn out mixture onto parchment paper, and turn paper over and roll thin with a rolling pin. Remove top paper and bake at 325 degrees until caramel colored, about 10-15 minutes. While still warm, cut circle out for basket and form into a cup. Cut out handles and form these while still warm. Set aside to cool.

For the mocha sherbet, bring coffee, sugar and milk to a boil in a saucepan. Remove from heat and add cocoa and chocolate. Stir to melt. Add flavorings to taste. Let cool, and then freeze in an ice cream freezer according to manufacturer's directions.

To serve, spoon sherbet into praline basket and garnish with a white chocolate rose or other ornament.

For the chocolate truffle, place chocolate truffle on top of almond macaroon cookie. Wrap this in four squares of phyllo pastry. Twist top to secure. Place on pan in freezer until ready to serve. When ready, bake at 375 degrees in a convection oven or 400 degrees in a conventional oven until lightly browned, about 10 minutes.

For the hazelnut success' marsala and white chocolate mousse, place gelatin in water and marsala and let bloom. In saucepan, boil sugar and water together until 240 degrees or soft-ball stage. Place egg yolks in an electric mixer and add sugar mixture while machine is running. Whip at high speed until cool. Warm bloomed gelatin to dissolve. Add to yolk mixture. Add melted white chocolate and whipped cream. Set aside.

For the cake layers, combine granulated sugar, confectioners' sugar, hazelnut and all-purpose flours in a mixing bowl. Sift if needed. In separate bowl, whip egg whites with sugar until stiff. Add milk to flour mixture, followed by egg whites. Pipe mixture onto greased and floured parchment paper. Bake at 350 for 15 minutes. Let cool. Cut sheet in half. Layer with mousse and chill overnight.

For the caramel sauce, cook sugar, glucose and water to a deep caramel color. Carefully stir in cream. Remove from heat. (Mixture will boil violently). Whip in butter and vanilla to finish. This is a thick consistency for designs or serve warm. If served cold, thin further with cream to desired consistency.

To finish, cut success into slices. Garnish with a marbleized white and dark chocolate effect on top, or a wood grain look, or as you like. Serve atop caramel sauce.

For the choux pastry basket with fruit, boil milk with butter in saucepan. Add flour and cook until mixture balls up. Transfer this to a mixer. Add eggs, one at a time, while mixer is running. Pour over 10 curved molds. Bake at 325 degrees for 10 to 15 minutes, or until lightly browned. You will have extra choux pastry.

Let cool and then fill with fruits and berries.

For the chocolate teaspoon, sift flour and cocoa. Combine with egg whites, sugar and melted butter to make a smooth paste. Let set 1 hour. Grease and flour a sheet pan and spread mixture over teaspoon. Bake at 325 degrees for 8 to 10 minutes. While still warm, press into spoon to form indentation. Let cool and serve with cream.

227 Cappuccino Bavarian with Carmel Sauce

Serves 20

For the bavarian:
1 tablespoon plus 1½ teaspoons unflavored gelatin
⅔ cup milk
1⅓ cups milk
5 egg yolks
2 ounces sugar
3 egg whites
2 ounces sugar
2 cups soft whipped cream
1 teaspoon ground cinnamon
2 ounces coffee extract paste
2 ounces coffee liqueur
20 rounds chocolate sponge cake to fit mold

For the tuile saucer:
3½ ounces all-purpose flour
½ ounce cocoa powder
4 ounces egg whites
4 ounces sugar
3 ounces melted butter

For the vanilla sauce:
1 cup milk
1 cup heavy cream
6 egg yolks
3 ounces sugar
Vanilla extract to taste
Brandy to taste

For the caramel sauce:
1 pound sugar
2 ounces glucose
1 cup water
½ cup heavy cream
2 ounces butter
2 teaspoons vanilla

For the chocolate cups:
Covering chocolate
Chocolate ornaments

For garnish:
Cocoa powder

For the bavarian, bloom gelatin in ⅔ cup milk. Bring 1⅓ cups milk to a boil in saucepan. Combine sugar and egg yolks and temper. Add milk, and stir and cook as you would for custard sauce. Remove from heat. Combine with gelatin mixture and cool to room temperature. Whip egg whites with sugar until stiff peaks form. Fold into yolk mixture. Fold in whipped cream. Reserve about 2½ cups of bavarian and flavor with cinnamon. Flavor the remaining mixture with coffee extract paste and liqueur. Cut 20 PVC pipe molds 2 inches in diameter and 1½ inches long. Oil inside of pipe mold. Dip in powdered sugar. Line with sponge cake rounds. Pipe coffee mixture into mold. Then pipe cinnamon bavarian into center of coffee bavarian. Let chill 2 to 3 hours.

For the tuile saucers, sift flour and cocoa. Combine with egg whites, sugar and melted butter to make a smooth paste. Let set 1 hour. Grease and flour a sheet pan and spread mixture over stencil cut from cardboard in the shape of a saucer. Bake at 325 degrees for 8 to 10 minutes. While still warm, press into saucer to form indention.

For the vanilla sauce, bring milk and cream to a boil. Combine egg yolks and sugar and temper. Add to milk and cream. Cook, stirring, until thickened and naps a spoon. Flavor with vanilla and brandy. Chill overnight.

For the caramel sauce, cook sugar, glucose and water to a deep caramel color. Carefully stir in cream. Remove from heat. (Mixture will boil violently). Whip in butter and vanilla to finish. If the sauce is to be served cold, thin further with more cream.

For the chocolate cup wrapping, place a clean sheet pan in freezer to chill. Melt covering chocolate. While pan is ice cold, spread chocolate in a paper-thin layer on pan. Cut a strip to wrap around bavarian, immediately remove strip from pan and wrap bavarian as chocolate softens. Return pan to freezer to set chocolate and continue with remaining cups. Make a chocolate handle out of chocolate and attach to side. Garnish with chocolate ornament.

To assemble, place spoon on serving plate and dust around it with cocoa. Remove spoon. Place chocolate cup atop tuile saucer. Serve vanilla sauce to the side with caramel sauce swirled in.

228 Chocolate Crêpe with Mocha Cream Sauce

Serves 6

For the filling:
1 cup milk
4 teaspoons coffee extract
3 egg yolks
4 teaspoons sugar
4 teaspoons cornstarch
2 sheets gelatin, softened
4½ tablespoons sugar
4 teaspoons water
4 egg whites, room temperature

For the mocha cream sauce:
1 cup milk
½ cup heavy cream
2 ounces sugar
1 tablespoon coffee extract
3 egg yolks

For the garnish:
6 chocolatae crêpes
2 cups mocha cream sauce
¼ cup candied orange peel, julienned

For the filling, bring the milk and the coffee extract to a boil; mix the egg yolks, the sugar and the cornstarch together; whisk the scalded milk into the egg yolk mixture, return it to the heat and slowly cook in to a thickened pastry cream; add in the softened sheets of gelatin and keep the pastry cream hot. Boil the 4½ tablespoons of sugar with the 4 teaspoons of water to the soft-ball stage, 241 degrees; whisk the egg whites in a stainless mixing bowl and slowly pour the hot sugar syrup into the egg whites while beating vigorously; continue beating the veringue until stiff peakes are formed. Gently fold the hot pastry cream into the meringue; fill the crêpes immediately and refrigerate them.

For the mocha cream sauce, heat the milk, cream, sugar and coffee extract in a saucepan. Bring to a simmer and remove from the heat. In a mixing bowl, beat the egg yolks. Pour ⅓ of the milk mixture into the egg yolks, while constantly stirring. Pour this mixture back into the saucepan and stir over low heat with a wooden spoon until the back of the spoon is coated. Remove from heat and let cool.

To serve, warm the crêpes in a 325 degree oven for 5 minutes. Ladle a pool of mocha cream sauce over the entire plate, set 1 crêpe in the middle of each plate and garnish each crêpe with candied orange peel.

229 Tiramisu with Espresso Sauce

Serves 20 Makes half a sheet pan

For the flourless chocolate layers:
14 ounces egg yolks
14 ounces granulated sugar
18 ounces egg whites
9 ounces granulated sugar
6 ounces cocoa powder

For the chocolate and white sponge cake layer:
8 egg whites
7 ounces sugar
8 egg yolks
2 tablespoons vanilla extract
6½ ounces cake flour
½ ounce cocoa powder

For the chocolate mousse filling:
13 ounces semi-sweet chocolate
7 ounces sugar
2 ounces water
5 egg yolks
1 quart heavy cream, whipped to soft peaks
1 teaspoon vanilla extract
1 tablespoon dark rum

For the marsala sugar syrup:
1½ cups water
1 cup sugar
½ dry marsala

For the marscapone cheese filling:
1 pound cream cheese
7 ounces confectioners' sugar
1 cup heavy cream
9 ounces marscapone cheese

For the topping:
2 cups crushed macaroon cookies
Cocoa powder for dusting

For the espresso sauce:
1 cup milk
1 cup heavy cream
6 egg yolks
3 ounces sugar
Vanilla extract to taste
1 tablespoon coffee extract
1 tablespoon coffee liqueur

For the garnish:
Semi-sweet coverture chocolate melted, for ribbons
Semi-sweet writing chocolate, melted, for border

For the chocolate layers, beat yolks with sugar until thickened and mixture no longer increases in volume. In separate bowl, whip egg whites with sugar to a stiff meringue. Fold whites into batter. Turn batter into a pastry bag fitted with a No. 2 plain tip, and pipe mixture onto a sheet pan that has been lined with greased parchment paper. Bake at 350 degrees for 15 to 20 minutes. Remove from oven and cool.

For the chocolate and white sponge cake layer, whip egg whites. Add sugar in thirds, and whip until stiff. Fold in beaten egg yolks. Divide batter into two parts. Add vanilla extract and half cake flour to one half. Add remaining flour and cocoa to remaining mixture. Fill two pastry bags fitted with No. 6 plain tips with each mixture. Pipe alternating lines on greased parchment paper. Bake at 350 for 15 minutes. Remove from oven and cool

For the chocolate mousse filling, chop and melt chocolate and set aside. In saucepan, combine sugar and water. Bring to a boil and cook until syrup reaches the soft-ball stage, 240 degrees. Place egg yolks in mixer and while they are whipping, pour in sugar mixture. Whip until mixture is cool. Fold melted chocolate into yolk mixture. Fold the whipped cream, vanilla extract and rum in briskly to yield a smooth mixture. Now fold in remaining cream, vanilla and rum. Chill.

For the marsala sugar syrup, combine water and sugar. bring to a boil so that sugar may dissolve. Stir in marsala.

For the marscapone cheese filling, beat cream cheese and sugar until smooth. Slowly fold in cream and then marscapone.

For assembly, trim flourless chocolate layer to half sheet pan size. Layer on chocolate mousse filling. Top with half sheet pan size of chocolate and white sponge cake. Soak sponge cake heavily with marsala sugar syrup. Chill or freeze until mousse is set. When mousse is firm, spread on a layer of cheese filling about ¼-inch thick. Top with second layer of chocolate cake. Freeze until firm. Spread top of chocolate layer with a thin layer of cheese filling. Chill or freeze until firm.

For serving, slice cake into desired portions. Cover top with crushed macaroon cookies and dust with cocoa powder.

For the espresso sauce, bring milk and cream to a boil. Combine egg yolks and sugar and temper. Add to milk and cream. Cook, stirring, until thickened and mixture naps a spoon. Flavor with chocolate extract and chocolate liqueur.

For the chocolate ribbons, freeze a sheet pan until ice cold. Pour on a thin layer of melted chocolate. When hardened, cut into ribbons, and when the chocolate melts slightly you will be able to curl it as you desire. Return sheet pan to freezer and continue cutting out ribbons and curling them until all chocolate is used. Keep ribbons cold.

To serve, pipe a border of writing chocolate around plate. Pour in sauce so that it stays within borders. Place tiramisu atop sauce and garnish with chocolate ribbons.

230 Ginger Soufflé Glacé with Poached Apples

Serves 8

For the ginger syrup:
½ cup sugar
½ cup water
2 tablespoons fresh ginger

For the soufflé:
3 eggs yolks
½ cup sugar
¾ cup ginger syrup
3 egg whites
1½ cups heavy cream, whipped to soft peaks

For the sesame tuiles:
¾ cup plus 1 tablespoon butter
¾ cup sugar
1 cup honey
½ cup all-purpose flour
1 teaspoon ground ginger
6 tablespoons sesame seeds

For the poached fruit:
2 cups plum wine
2 cups sugar
½ cup sliced plums
½ cup sliced apples
½ cup candied apricots
½ cup orange segments
¼ cup blanched almonds

For the garnish:
24 mint leaves

For the ginger syrup, bring the sugar, water and fresh ginger to a boil. Reduce it to a thick syrup, strain and allow to cool.

For the soufflé, warm the egg yolks, and ¼ cup of the sugar slightly in a mixing bowl and whip them to full volume. Add in the ginger syrup. In another mixing bowl whip the egg whites to full volume, adding the remaining sugar a bit at a time and fold the whites into the yolks very gently; to this fold in the whipped cream and freeze.

For the tuiles, in a saucepan combine the butter, the sugar and the honey, heating over a medium flame until all the sugar is dissolved. In a small mixer with a paddle beat the flour and the ginger into the sugar mixture; continue to mix on medium speed until the batter is cool. Add in the sesame seeds and refrigerate for 2 hours. Place small scoops of the dough on a silpat-lined sheet pan and bake at 375 degrees until the cookies are golden brown. While they are still warm cut the tuiles into perfect rounds and cool on a flat surface.

For the poached fruit, bring the plum wine and the sugar to a boil and reduce it to a light syrup. Pour this liquid over the fruits and almonds and let the fruit steep until it is plump and tender.

To serve, spoon the poached fruit and plum syrup onto each plate; place three scoops of the frozen soufflé in the middle of the compote and two to the side; set one sesame tuile on top of the three scoops in the middle and garnish the dish with fresh mint leaves.

231 Caramelized Apple and Wheat Torte

Serves 8

For the ice cream:
2 cups half and half
¾ cup sugar
8 egg yolks
1 cup sour cream

For the sour cream anglaise:
1½ cups milk
6 egg yolks
½ cup sugar
1 cup sour cream

For the wheat tortes:
12 ounces Kadaifi dough
(may be found in any Greek market)
2 tablespoons clarified butter
2 tablespoons superfine sugar

For the apples:
8 Granny Smith apples
1 cup superfine sugar

For the ice cream, mix together the half and half with half of the sugar in a saucepan and bring it to boil. In a stainless mixing bowl, combine the egg yolks with the remaining half of the sugar. Whisk in the scalded half and half and cook to a light custard over a double boiler. Remove the custard from the heat, allow it to cool until tepid and blend in the sour cream. Freeze in an ice cream machine.

For the sour cream anglaise, scald the milk in a saucepan. Mix together the egg yolks with the sugar in a stainless bowl, whisk in the scalded milk and cook over a double boiler until it is thick enough to not run when dished. Cool the sauce to room temperature and blend in the sour cream.

For the wheat tortes, carefully loosen and separate the strands of the Kadaifi dough and coat them with the clarified butter. Mold the buttered strands into 8 2½-inch and 8 4½-inch cakes that are ½ inch thick; sprinkle the tops of the Kadaifi cakes with superfine sugar and bake on a parchment-lined sheet pan in a 350 degree oven until they are golden brown. Dust the warm cakes with superfine sugar.

For the baked apples, place each peeled and cored apple inside a metal ring on a parchment-lined sheet pan and sprinkle them with the superfine sugar. Bake in a 350 degree oven for approximately 20 minutes, until knife tender. Remove them from the oven and allow them to cool.

For the clear caramel, place the sugar and water in a small pot and bring to a boil over a high flame. Reduce to a light caramel stage. Remove from heat and shock in ice water.

To serve, sandwich each baked apple with a dollop of sour cream anglaise, between a 2½ inch and a 4½ inch Kadaifi cake. Place the wheat tortes to the top right of each plate; around the surface of the dish splash puddles of the sour cream anglaise and the caramel. Finish the dish with three small scoops of sour cream ice cream, diced roasted apple, a tuile ribbon and fresh mint leaves.

230 Apple and Toasted Pistachio Terrine with Apple Strudel

Serves 10

For the crêpes:
8 ounces all-purpose flour
3 ounces sugar
5 eggs
½ cup heavy cream
1 cup milk
1 vanilla bean

For the apples:
4 apples, peeled and cored
1½ cups sugar

For the pistachio paste:
2 cups pistachios
1 cup sugar

For the pistachio mascarpone:
1½ cups mascarpone cheese
½ cup pistachio paste

For the strudel:
4 sheets strudel dough
½ cup clarified butter
2 cups diced apples
¼ cup sugar

For the applejack sabayon:
4 egg yolks
½ cup sugar
¼ cup applejack brandy
1 vanilla bean
½ cup heavy cream, whipped

For the garnish:
10 quenelles of vanilla ice cream
10 scoops of vanilla ice cream
20 fresh mint leaves
⅓ cup caramel sauce
20 long threads of candied sugar

For the crêpes, sift together the flour and the sugar in a mixing bowl; in a separate bowl combine the eggs, the heavy cream, milk and the seeds from the vanilla bean. Beat this into the dry ingredients for a smooth batter. Using a warm crêpe pan, pour a thin layer of the batter to cover the entire surface and cook until golden brown.

For the caramelized apples, cut the apples into thin wedges. In a sauté pan,sprinkle the bottom of the pan with sugar over a high heat; once the sugar starts to caramelize place the apples in the pan and toss them to caramelize both sides. Set the apples aside to cool.

For the pistachio paste, roast the pistachios on a sheet pan in a hot oven until they are nicely toasted. Remove from the heat and transfer to the bowl of a food processor fitted with the metal blade attachment. Add the sugar and process until smooth. Set ½ cup aside for the pistachio mascarpone and place the remaining pistachio paste in a pastry bag fitted with a medium round tip. Set aside.

For the pistachio mascarpone, beat the mascarpone together with the pistachio paste until they are completely incorporated and smooth.

To assemble the terrine, line a terrine mold with plastic wrap. Place a layer of crêpes down first, going up the sides just slightly; then a layer of pistachio mascarpone; followed with another layer of crêpes; a layer of caramelized apples; followed by another layer of crêpes; then a layer of pistachio mascarpone and pipe some pistachio paste; followed by another layer of crêpes. Repeat the layers until the terrine is full. Press the terrine down just a bit and refrigerate overnight. Slice the terrine and keep cool until ready to use.

For the strudel, layer the sheets of strudel dough with the clarified butter and cut out 5 inch circles. In a hot sauté pan caramelize the apples with the sugar. Place a small amount of the caramelized apples in the center of each strudel dough round and fold the sides over to create a pouch. Bake the strudels with the seam side down on a parchment-lined sheet pan in a hot oven until golden brown.

For the sabayon, whisk together the egg yolks, the sugar, the applejack and the vanilla bean over a double boiler until thick and frothy. Remove the vanilla bean, allow the sabayon to cool to room temperature and fold in the whipped cream.

To serve, set 1 slice of the terrine in the center of each plate; to each side spoon a small pool of the sabayon. On the left side set a piece of apple strudel together with a quenelle of vanilla ice cream; to the right a small scoop of vanilla ice cream. Garnish the dish with fresh mint leaves, caramel sauce and threads of candied sugar.

232 Mascarpone Sherbet with Wild Strawberries

Serves 6

For the sorbet:
1 cup water
3½ tablespoons corn syrup
½ cup sugar
2 tablespoons lemon juice
9 ounces mascarpone cheese

For the warm juice:
¼ cup strawberries, cleaned
¼ cup raspberries
¼ cup sour white cherries, pitted
¼ cup black berries
¼ cup sugar
1 teaspoon water

For the garnish:
8 wild strawberries, stems on

For the sorbet, make a simple syrup with the water, corn syrup, sugar and the lemon juice. Cool the syrup to room temperature and blend it into the mascarpone. Freeze in an ice cream machine according to the manufactuer's instructions.

For the warm juice, mix together the fresh fruits with the sugar and the water in a plastic covered stainless bowl; cook for 2 hours in a water bath. Remove from the heat and pass the juice through a fine sieve; keep warm.

To serve, make quenelles from the sorbet and place 1 in each well chilled dessert bowl. At the monemt of service ladle the warm juice into the bowl and garnish the sorbet with wild strawberries.

232 Apple Beignets with Pistachio Ice Cream

Serves 12

For the ice cream:
4 cups milk
1 cup pistachios
1 cup sugar
12 egg yolks

For the beignet batter:
1½ cups flour
Pinch of salt
1 tablespoon sugar
2 tablespoons oil
1¼ cups beer
2 egg whites

For the beignets:
8 apples
3½ tablespoons sugar
½ cup rum
4 cups oil for frying
Beignet batter
6 tablespoons cinnamon-sugar for dusting

For the garnish:
1 cup blackberry coulis
1 cup whole blackberries
½ cup whole pistachios
3 tablespoons candied lemon zest
12 strawberry fans

For the ice cream, scald the milk; crush the pistachios and mix them together with the sugar and the egg yolks in a stainless bowl, whisk the scalded milk into the egg mixture and thicken to a light custard over a double boiler. Allow the custard to cool and infuse overnight, then strain out the pistachios and freeze in an ice cream machine.

For the beignet batter, mix together the flour, salt, sugar and oil; slowly blend in the beer without working it too much. Let the batter stand for 2 hours. Whip the egg whites to a firm peak and fold the whites into the beer batter.

For the beignets, slice the apples about ½ inch thick and marinate them for 1 hour in the sugar and rum. Heat the oil to 200 degrees, dip the apple slices in the batter and fry the beignets for 3 minutes on each side. Blot the beignets on a clean towel and sprinkle them with the cinnamon-sugar.

To serve, pour the blackberry coulis into a large pool on each plate. Place 2 beignets just to the top of the coulis and garnish them with whole blackberries. Finish the dish with an oval scoop of pistachio ice cream, sprinkle with whole pistachios and candied lemon zest and a strawberry fan.

233 Chilled Golden Delicious Apple Mousse

Serves 8

For the cashew nougat:
½ cup water
1½ cups sugar
6 tablespoons butter
1 cup coarsely chopped toasted cashews

For the frozen apple mousse:
¾ cup sugar
½ cup water
2 drops lemon juice
2 egg whites
2 cups mascarpone cheese
¾ cup Golden Delicious apple purée
2 cups cashew nougat

For the cashew anglaise:
1 cup milk
¼ cup toasted cashews
4 tablespoons sugar
4 egg yolks

For the dark sugar syrup:
½ cup dark brown sugar
½ cup water
1 drop lemon juice
¼ cup apple peels

For the phyllo waves:
6 sheets phyllo dough
¼ cup clarified butter
¼ cup powdered sugar

For the garnish:
8 tuile or phyllo rings
8 quenelles mascarpone cheese
8 nougat baskets
4 tablespoons diced caramelized apple
4 tablespoons whole caramelized cashews
24 mint leaves

For the nougat, bring the water and the sugar to a boil in a heavy stainless pot. While the sugar is boiling, brush the sides of the pan with water to eliminate sugar crystal formation. Cook the sugar syrup to an amber color, or 300 degrees. Add in small pieces of the butter and incorporate by shifting the pot back and forth. Do not stir as it will cause crystal formation. Once the butter is incorporated add in the chopped cashews and pour the nougat onto a greased sheet pan or marble. Cool the nougat and chop it into small pieces.

For the mousse, line a loaf pan with parchment paper and set aside. In a small saucepan bring the sugar, water and the lemon juice to a boil. Reduce to a syrup consistency, remove from the heat and set aside. In the bowl of an electric mixer fitted with the whip attachment, whip the egg whites to soft peaks. Slowly add the sugar syrup while continuing to whip. Whip until the egg whites are completely cooled and set aside. In the bowl of a food processor fitted with the metal blade attachment combine the mascarpone cheese and the apple purée. Pulse until the mixture is well combined and smooth. Fold the mascarpone mixture into the egg whites and add the chopped nougat. Pour the mousse into the prepared loaf pan and place in the freezer until firm.

For the cashew anglaise, slowly scald the milk with the toasted cashews and 2 tablespoons of the sugar. Steep over a low flame until the cashew flavor is present in the milk. In a stainless bowl mix together the egg yolks with the remaining sugar; whisk in the scalded milk and thicken the sauce over a double boiler. Strain out the cashews and cool in an ice water bath.

For the dark sugar syrup, mix the sugar, water, the lemon juice and the apple peels together in a saucepan and bring this to a boil. Reduce the liquid to a thick syrup and strain out the apple peels.

For the phyllo waves, layer the phyllo sheets with the clarified butter and cut it into 1 by 7 inch long strips. Place the strips between pieces of parchment paper dusted with powdered sugar. Place the parchment covered phyllo strips between two crimped pieces of stainless steel and bake them to a golden brown in a 350 degree oven.

To serve, form a pool of the cashew anglaise. Drizzle the dark sugar syrup over the plate and set a tuile or phyllo ring in the middle of the plate. In the ring, place a slice of the apple mousse, a quenelle of mascarpone cheese, a nougat basket overflowing with caramelized apple, cashews and 2 phyllo strips. Finish the dish with fresh mint leaves.

234 Caramel Flan

Serves 4

For the flan:
3½ tablespoons sugar
½ cup heavy cream
½ cup half and half
3 egg yolks
1¾ tablespoons grated bittersweet chocolate
1¾ tablespoons chopped toasted almonds

For the chocolate sauce:
3 ounces semi-sweet chocolate
3 tablespoons water
1 tablespoon butter
6 tablespoons heavy cream

For the caramel sauce:
4 tablespoons water
1 cup sugar
10 tablespoons heavy cream
Lemon juice to taste

For the garnish:
Caramel that has been broken into pieces

For the flan, cook sugar moistened with a little water in a heavy saucepan over medium heat. Cook to a dark caramel. Add cream, then half and half and simmer for 1 minute. Lightly whisk egg yolks and then whisk caramel cream mixture into yolks. Pour this into a shallow pan lined with buttered aluminum foil. The mixture should be no more than ½ inch deep. Sprinkle top with grated chocolate and toasted almonds. Bake at 350 degrees until set, about 25 minutes. Cool and refrigerate.

For the chocolate sauce, break chocolate into small pieces and melt them with water and butter in a small, heavy saucepan over low heat. Stir in cream until smooth. Set aside.

For the caramel sauce, place water in a small, heavy saucepan and add sugar. When sugar has moistened, cook over medium heat, until sugar turns golden brown. Remove from heat and pour in cream carefully. Return to heat and cook until thickened and sugar has dissolved. Add lemon juice to cut the sweetmess, if desired. Set aside.

To serve, cut three successive rounds of the flan with a 2 inch cutter, leaving each round in the cutter so that the layers are stacked. Press out onto plates and serve with chocolate and caramel sauces swirled in decorative pattern. Garnish with caramel pieces.

Sweet Potato Sorbet

Serves 4

For the sorbet:
1½ pounds sweet potatoes, peeled and quartered
2 quarts water
¾ cup sugar
1½ cups water
2 tablespoons corn syrup
Juice of 2 lemons

For the sauce:
½ pound sweet potatoes, peeled and quartered
½ quart water
1 cup sugar
½ cup cream
1 vanilla bean, split

For the garnish:
Powdered sugar
Shoestring-fried sweet potatoes

For the sorbet, place the sweet potatoes in 2 quarts of boiling water and cook over high heat for approximately 20 minutes or until very tender. Strain the cooked potatoes and purée with a hand-held mixer. Pass the purée through a fine sieve, and mix in the lemon juice. Chill.

Prepare a simple syrup with the sugar, water and light corn syrup. Cool. Add the simple syrup to the chilled sweet potato purée. Place this mixture in a sorbet machine and freeze according to manufacturer's instructions.

For the sauce, cook the sweet potatoes in ½ quart of boiling water for 10 minutes. Strain the potatoes and dice. In a heavy-bottomed sauce pan, caramelize the sugar. Add the cream and vanilla bean, stirring until smooth. Add the diced sweet potatoes, remove the vanilla bean and set aside to cool.

To serve, place sauce on each plate and top with a quenelle of sorbet. Garnish with shoestring-fried sweet potatoes dusted with powdered sugar.

Key Lime Tortilla with Tropical Fruit Salsa

Serves 4

For the natilla:
2 eggs
2 egg yolks
⅔ cup minus 1 tablespoon sugar
½ cup Key lime juice
4 ounces sweet butter, cut into small pieces and softened
2 cups heavy cream

For the tortilla:
8 sheets phyllo pastry
¼ cup melted butter
6 tablespoons sugar
¼ teaspoon cayenne pepper

For the salsa:
2 mangoes
Simple sugar syrup
½ pineapple
1 papaya

For the cilantro syrup:
1 bunch cilantro, with stems, washed
¼ cup simple sugar syrup

To prepare the natilla, combine the whole eggs, yolks, sugar and lime juice in a large mixing bowl. Whisk vigorously over simmering water until the mixture is ribbony and pale in color. Remove from the heat and whisk in the softened butter. Scrape down the sides of the bowl and cover with plastic wrap. Refrigerate for at least two hours. Whip the cream until stiff. Whisk approximately ¼ of the cream into the Key lime mixture to lighten it. Carefully fold in the remaining cream with a rubber spatula. Cover and refrigerate.

For the tortilla, brush one sheet of phyllo liberally with melted butter. Sprinkle on a thin, even layer of sugar. Repeat with each sheet, stacking them as you go. Sprinkle the second sheet with cayenne pepper. Refrigerate the stacked phyllo to chill the butter and for easier handling.

Remove the phyllo from the refrigerator and cut into circles that are 5 inches in diameter. Cut each of these circles in half and place the halves on a parchment-lined sheet pan. Top with another sheet of parchment and sit another sheet pan on top of that. Bake at 350 degrees until the sugar caramelizes, approximately 15 to 20 minutes. Let cool.

To prepare the fruit salsa, purée one of the mangoes with enough sugar syrup to obtain a smooth consistency. Dice the papaya, pineapple and remaining mango into very small pieces and stir them into the mango purée. The mixture should have a very thick, salsa-like consistency. Chill.

For the cilantro syrup, blanch the cilantro in boiling water for approximately 20 seconds. Immediately plunge the cilantro into ice water. This will intensify the flavor and color of the cilantro. Purée the cilantro with the sugar syrup and pass through a fine strainer. Reserve. To serve, place one semi-circle of phyllo on each plate. Spoon the Key lime and cream mixture on top of the phyllo and position another semi-circle on top of that. Spoon the salsa around the mock tortilla and decorate with the cilantro syrup.

237 Chestnut Fritters with Zabaglione

Serves 6

For the fritters:
1 cup milk
2 ounces butter
Pinch of salt
½ cup sugar
4 ounces sifted flour
5 eggs
1 cup chestnut purée
½ cup raisins
1 tablespoon kirschwasser

For the zabaglione:
4 egg yolks
¼ cup sugar
½ cup Marsala

For the garnish:
Powdered sugar
Whole chestnuts

For the chestnut purée, shell, peel and simmer the chestnuts in milk and flavor them with vanilla bean. Then grate and work them into a smooth purée.

For the fritters, place the milk, butter, salt and sugar in a pot and bring to a boil. Add the flour and stir vigorously with a wooden spoon until the mixture no longer clings to the pot or spoon. Remove from the heat and let cool for 10 minutes. Beat in the eggs one after the other, stirring thoroughly. Add the chestnut purée, raisins and kirschwasser and blend well. Put the paste into a pastry bag and drop 2 to 3 inch pieces of the fritter batter into a deep fryer. Turn the fritters gently several times until they are golden brown. Remove from the oil and blot on paper towels.

For the zabaglione, place the egg yolks and sugar in the top part of a double boiler and beat with a wire whisk until pale yellow. Add the wine and place the mixture over boiling water. Whisk constantly until it becomes frothy. Do not overcook. Remove from heat. To serve, dust the fritters with powdered sugar and put on plates. Garnish with the whole chestnuts and serve with the zabaglione.

237 Peche Haeberlin

Serves 8

For the pistachio ice cream:
2 cups milk
2 cups cream
1½ cups sugar
1 vanilla bean
10 egg yolks
5 ounces pistachios, freshly
  hulled and crushed
2 drops bitter almond extract

For the Champagne sabayon:
16 egg yolks
1⅔ cups sugar
1 bottle Champagne

For the final presentation:
8 peaches poached
  in a simple syrup
Whipped cream for decoration

For the pistachio ice cream, bring the milk and cream to a boil with the vanilla bean and half of the sugar. In a bowl, beat the egg yolks with the remaining sugar until pale yellow. Add the hot milk to the yolks while continuing to beat. Place the mixture over a low flame and stir constantly until it begins to thicken. Add the pistachios and the bitter almond extract. Pass through a chinois and place in an ice cream maker to freeze.

For the Champagne sabayon, combine the egg yolks and sugar in the top of a double boiler. Whisk until the mixture becomes pale yellow and thick. Add the bottle of Champagne. Place the sauce over gently simmering water and continue beating until the sauce begins to thicken. Remove from the heat and whisk until cool.

On a large, fairly deep plate place one of the poached peaches and a scoop of the pistachio ice cream. Ladle the sabayon over the top and decorate with whipped cream.

236 Filled Apple Crêpes

Serves 4

For the crêpes:
2 cups flour
3 eggs
2 cups milk
Pinch of salt
1 tablespoon melted butter

For the filling:
4 dessert apples
4 tablespoons butter
4 tablespoons sugar
4 tablespoons Calvados

For the caramel sauce:
3 tablespoons sugar
1 tablespoon water
½ cup heavy cream

For the garnish:
1 cup raspberry coulis
½ cup caramel sauce

For the crêpes, prepare a batter by mixing the flour, eggs, milk, salt and butter into a smooth mixture. Let the batter stand for 2 hours at room temperature. Pour a small amount of batter into a non-stick pan and cook the crêpes on both sides until golden brown. Make at least 8 crêpes.

For the filling, peel and core the apples and cut into thin wedges. Heat the butter in a heavy pan and add the sugar and apples. Cook until the sugar caramelizes. Deglaze the pan with the Calvados. Set aside and keep warm.

For the carmel sauce, put the sugar and water in a thick-bottomed pot and cook until the sugar melts and turns into a dark caramel. Remove the pot from the heat and carefully add the cream. Simmer until all the sugar has dissolved, them cool.

To serve, sandwich the cooked apples between 2 crêpes, cut the crêpes into quarters and place on plates. Drizzle the plates with the raspberry coulis and caramel sauce. Garish with mint leaves.

238 Warm Rhubarb Tart with Saffron Sauce

Serves 4
For the tarts:
½ pound puff pastry
1 pound rhubarb
1 cup pastry cream
2 tablespoons butter, melted
Zest of ½ orange
½ cup sugar

For the sauce:
2 cups milk
¼ cup sugar
5 egg yolks
12 strands saffron

For the garnish:
Fresh mint sprigs

For the tarts, roll the puff pastry to a thickness of ⅛ inch, cut 4 3-inch circles from it and place the circles onto a sheet pan. Prick the dough with a fork and let the dough rest for ½ hour in the refrigerator. In the meantime, peel the rhubarb and slice diagonally about ⅛ inch thick. Spread a thin layer of pastry cream onto each pastry circle, arrange the rhubarb pieces so they overlap each other, drizzle each tart with the butter and sprinkle with the orange zest and sugar. Bake the tarts in a preheated oven at 375 degrees for 20 minutes.

For the sauce, scald the milk in the top of a double boiler. In a bowl, mix the remaining ingredients. Slowly add half of the hot milk and whisk vigorously. Add the egg yolk mixture to the remaining milk in the double boiler. Stir the sauce constantly with a wooden spoon until it covers the back of the spoon. Remove from heat and stir occasionally to release the steam.

To serve, pour pools of the cooled sauce on plates. Top with the hot tarts and garnish with mint sprigs.

239 Chilled Apple Soupe with Apple Granité

Serves 4
For the soup and granité:
8 Winesap apples
2 cinnamon sticks
1 quart water
Sugar to taste

For the garnish:
1 apple, cored and thinly sliced
½ cup apple pearls
(made with small melon baller)
Confectioners' sugar
Tuile cookies
2 ounces chopped pistachios

For the maple syrup:
½ cup maple syrup
½ vanilla bean

For the soup and granité, core and quarter the apples. Place in a pot with the cinnamon sticks and water. Add sugar to taste and simmer for 45 minutes. Let the soup cool and strain through a cheesecloth. Freeze ¼ of the soup in a shallow pan. Refrigerate the remaining soup.

For the maple syrup, heat the syrup over medium heat. Add the vanilla bean, which has been cut in half lengthwise. Keep the syrup warm. To serve, scrape the frozen apple soup with a fork to from crystals. Pour the soup into chilled plates. Add the sliced and scooped apples. Top each plate with a tuile cookie, place the granité in the center, and sprinkle with confectioners' sugar and chopped pistachios. Serve with warm maple syrup.

239 Fried Cannolis

Serves 4

For the dough:
¾ cup warm white wine (110 degrees)
1½ ounces compressed yeast
1 tablespoon olive oil
Pinch of ground anise seeds
Pinch of salt
2 cups flour
1 cup granulated sugar

For the rice pudding:
¼ cup short-grain rice
1½ cups hot milk
Pinch of salt
1 teaspoon butter
1 teaspoon sugar
½ teaspoon vanilla extract

For the filling:
2 cups rice pudding
1 cup applesauce
1 cup pastry cream

For the garnish:
2 cups chocolate sauce
Cooked sugar spirals

For the dough, place the warm white wine in a food processor bowl and add the yeast. After 5 minutes, the yeast will dissolve and begin to foam. Add the oil, anise salt and 1 cup of the flour. Whirl for 1 minute. Add the remaining flour and whirl until a smooth ball forms. Turn the dough out into an oiled bowl. Roll the dough over so it is coated with oil. Cover the bowl with a cloth, put in a warm place and let the dough rise to double its size. Punch the dough down, place on a floured surface and roll to a ⅛ inch thick sheet. Cut the sheet into 5 by 6 inch rectangle. Wrap each sheet around a metal tube and fry in 350 degree oil until crisp and golden brown. Blot the cannolis on paper towels and remove the metal tubes. Roll the cannoli shells in granulated sugar.

For the rice pudding, cook the rice, milk and salt in the top of a double boiler for 1 hour. Stir frequently and watch that the water in the bottom pan does not boil off. When the rice is tender, cool slightly and add the butter, sugar and vanilla.

To assemble the cannolis, fill each shell with half rice pudding and half applesauce. Top with the pastry cream.

To serve, pour pools of chocolate sauce and arrange some cannolis in the center on plates. Garnish with the sugar spirals.

240 Spiced Peaches

Serves 2

For the peaches:
4 ripe peaches
1 quart water
1 pound sugar

For the sauce:
1 piece star anise
3 cloves
8 black peppercorns
1 tablespoon caraway seeds
1 cinnamon stick
2 tablespoons butter
2 tablespoons honey
Juice of 1 lemon
Juice of 1 orange
1 vanilla bean, cut in half lengthwise

For the garnish:
Fennel sprigs

For the peaches, drop the peaches in boiling water and simmer for 30 seconds. Plunge the peaches in ice water to stop the cooking process. When the peaches have cooled, peel and set aside. Bring the water and the sugar to a boil, add the peaches and simmer until they become tender. Remove the peaches from the heat and let them cool in their own liquid.

For the sauce, grind the dry spices in a coffee grinder into a coarse powder. Melt the butter in a heavy skillet, add the honey and let caramelize. Deglaze the pan with the lemon and orange juices and add the ground spices and the split vanilla bean. Add the peaches and simmer for 4 to 5 minutes.

To serve, remove 2 peaches from the sauce and cut into wedges. Pour pools of sauce onto the plate, arrange the wedges and whole peaches and garnish with fennel sprigs.

241 Peach Dumplings

Serves 8

For the dumplings:
½ ounce fresh yeast
3 tablespoons sugar
9 ounces all-purpose flour
⅝ cup whole milk (110 degrees)
1½ ounces unsalted butter, melted
Pinch of salt
1 egg
4 peaches, boiled, peeled, pitted and diced
1 ounce granulated sugar plus
½ cup granulated sugar

For the sauce:
2 peaches, peeled and pits removed
⅓ cup sugar
½ cup water
Juice of ½ lemon

For the garnish:
Crème fraîche
Cooked peach wedges
Mint leaves
Confectioners' sugar

For the dumplings, in a medium bowl combine the yeast and milk. Set aside until dissolved, about 10 minutes. Add the flour, butter, one ounce of sugar and egg. Milt to combine, cover with plastic wrap and set aside in a warm place until doubled in volume, about 1 hour. Punch down the dough, add the peaches, and mix to combine. Form the dough into 8 rounds and place on a parchment-lined shee pan. Bring a saucepan of lightly salted water to a simmer and add the dumplings. Simmer until tender in the center, about 45 minutes. Remove from the heat and plae on a paper towel-lined sheet pan to drain. Set aside until cooled. Place the remaining sugar in a small bowl and roll the dumpling in the sugar. Place on a parchment-lined sheet pan and set aside.

For the sauce, cut the peaches into small chunks and place in a pot. Add the sugar, water and lemon juice. Cover and simmer until the peaches are completely soft. Pour into a blender cup and purée until smooth. Let the sauce cool.

To serve, remove the dumplings from the water and blot on paper towels. Sprinkle with the granulated sugar and place on plates. Pour a ring of sauce around each dumpling and drizzle with the crème fraîche. Garnish the dish with the peach wedges and mint leaves. Sprinkle the rims of the plates with confectioners' sugar.

242 Cherry Strudel

Serves 6

For the strudel:
4 phyllo dough leaves
2 pounds pitted cherries
¼ cup finely chopped pistachios
½ cup sugar
1 tablespoon kirschwasser
4 tablespoons melted butter
Confectioners' sugar

For the garnish:
Vanilla ice cream
Coffee ice cream
Cherries
¼ cup finely chopped pistachios
Confectioners' sugar

For the strudel, stack the phyllo leaves on top of each other on a clean cloth. Sprinkle with the cherries, chopped pistachios and sugar. Drizzle with the kirschwasser, and with the help of the cloth, roll the phyllo into a cylinder. Slide the strudel onto a well greased baking sheet. Brush the strudel with the melted butter. Bake the strudel in a preheated oven at 350 degrees for 20 minutes, then lower the temperature to 325. Brush with remaining butter bake for 10 minutes, until golden brown. Remove the strudel from the oven and dust with confectioners' sugar. Cut into 1-inch wide diagonal slices.

To serve, arrange the strudel slices on plates along with 1 scoop of each of the ice creams. Garnish the dish with a cluster of cherries and chopped pistachios and sprinkle with confectioners' sugar.

243 Mandarin Ice with Fortune Cookies

Serves 4

For the ice:
3 cups mandarin orange juice,
freshly squeezed and strained
½ cup simple sugar syrup

For the candied zest:
Zest of 2 oranges
Zest of 2 lemons
Zest of 2 limes
⅓ cup simple sugar syrup

For the fortune cookies:
7 ounces all-purpose flour
10 ounces powdered sugar
1 cup egg whites
10 ounces butter, melted and warmed
1 teaspoon vanilla extract
Fortunes

For the mandarin ice, combine the juice with the syrup, place in ice cream maker and process according to manufacturer's instructions, or use classical sorbet technique.

To candy the zests, place all zests in a metal strainer and blanch them in boiling water for approximately 20 seconds. Plunge them immediately into ice water to stop the cooking.

Bring the simple syrup to a boil and drop in the zests. Allow them to boil 1 to 2 minutes, until the syrup thickens slightly. Drain the syrup and lightly dust the zests in granulated sugar. Separate the strands and allow them to cool.

For the fortune cookies, combine the flour and sugar in the bowl of an electric mixer that has a paddle attachment. Add the egg whites and mix until smooth. Add the butter in a steady stream until it is fully incorporated. Add the vanilla and chill the mixture for at least two hours or overnight.

Preheat the oven to 300 degrees. Using a spatula, spread the chilled cookie batter very thinly into circles, 5 inches in diameter, on a non-stick sheet pan. Spread out only three or four cookies at a time because they harden quickly and will become unworkable. Bake the cookies for approximately 10 minutes or until they are golden brown. A second oven set at warm will help keep the cookies pliable while you are working with them.

Remove only one cookie at a time from the sheet pan in order for you to shape them before they harden. Place the fortune across the center of the cookie and fold in the two outside edges so they overlap. Immediately grasp the two long ends and fold them backwards, away from the other folded sides. Set the cookies aside to cool. Store in an airtight container until ready to serve.

To serve, fill a shallow soup plate with finely crushed ice. Arrange scoops of the mandarin sorbet on the ice and garnish with the candied zest and fortune cookies. Serve.

243 Apple Pudding with Caramel Sauce

Serves 20

For the vanilla ice cream:
4 cups heavy cream
Pinch salt
1 cup sugar
½ vanilla bean, split and scraped
10 egg yolks

For the frangipan:
1¾ pounds almond paste
1 tablespoon vanilla extract
2 cups sugar
Pinch salt
3 cups flour
12 eggs
¾ pound butter

For the apple mixture:
10 Golden Delicious apples, peeled, cored and thinly sliced
4 tablespoons freshly grated nutmeg
1 to 1½ cups sugar, depending on sweetness of apples
Grated zest of 1 orange
¼ cup apple brandy
5 tablespoons orange flour water

For the streusel:
1 cup brown sugar
1 cup butter
4 cups flour
5 tablespoons ground cinnamon
1 cup chopped pecans

For the pudding:
6 egg yolks
½ cup sugar
1 tablespoon vanilla extract
Pinch salt
Grated zest of 1 orange
8 ounces frangipan
6 egg whites
½ cup sugar
1 pound hazelnut or almond flour

For the caramel sauce:
6 cups sugar
3 cups water
10 ounces unsalted butter, cut into pieces
4 cups heavy cream

For the garnish:
Mint leaves

For the vanilla ice cream, scald heavy cream with salt, sugar and vanilla bean in a heavy stainless steel saucepot. When scalded pour a quarter of the mixture into mixing bowl with egg yolks. Whisk continuously so as not to cook eggs. Pour egg mixture back into remaining cream in pot. Whisk continuously until thickened. Chill. Freeze mixture in an ice cream freezer according to manufacturer's instructions.

For the frangipan, cream butter and almond paste in mixing bowl. Add sugar and salt and cream until fluffy. Scrape down bowl and add eggs and vanilla alternately with flour, beginning and ending with flour. Scrape almond mixture into a clean bowl and reserve for use in this recipe and others. This is best made 1 day ahead.

For the apples, toss sliced apples with remaining ingredients and set aside.

For the streusel topping, cut butter into sugar and flour in mixing bowl. Mix with a paddle until mixture looks like small nuggets. Add cinnamon and pecans and mix 1 minute.
Set aside.

For the pudding, preheat oven to 350 degrees. In mixing bowl whip egg yolks with sugar, vanilla, salt and orange zest until light and fluffy. Mix in frangipan and set aside. In another mixing bowl, whip egg whites with sugar until stiff but not dry. Fold a quarter of the egg whites into yolk mixture to lighten. Fold in remaining whites along with nut flour. Turn batter into a greased 9- by 12-inch baking pan and top with apple mixture.Top with streusel mixture and bake for 35 to 45 minutes or until a skewer inserted in center comes out clean. Remove from oven and set aside to firm up.

For the sauce, place sugar and water in a heavy-bottomed stainless steel saucepan over medium heat. Wash down sides of pan with a pastry brush dipped in water to dissolve crystals on side of pot. Cook until dark amber in color. Add pieces of butter, one by one, stirring after each addition. Be careful, as butter will spatter. Add cream. Simmer 2 minutes or until thickened.

To serve, ladle 2 tablespoons caramel sauce onto each plate. Cut apple pudding into 20 pieces and place one on top of caramel sauce. Place scoop of ice cream alongside pudding and garnish with mint leaf.

244 Lemon Verbena Sorbet

Serves 8

For the sorbet:
6 cups water
3 cups sugar
1 pound lemon verbena
1 cup seltzer water
1¾ cups lemon juice

For the garnish:
8 white chocolate fan cups
Lemon coulis
Lemon rind
White chocolate orchid flowers
Champagne grapes

For the sorbet, combine the water and sugar to make a simple syrup. Cook the lemon verbena in this syrup for approximately 30 minutes and allow to steep for one hour. Strain. Add the seltzer and lemon juice, and freeze in an ice cream machine according to manufacturer's instructions. Scoop the sorbet into the white chocolate fan cups and freeze until service.

To serve, garnish the plates with lemon coulis and fresh lemon rind. Place a sorbet fan cup in the center of each plate and decorate with white chocolate orchids and champagne grapes.

245 Brandy Snap with Glazed Citrus

Serves 8

For the brandy snap basket:
½ cup butter
⅔ cup sugar
¾ cup flour
2 tablespoons brandy
½ cup Kayro syrup
¼ teaspoon cardamom

For the orange pound cake:
¾ cup butter
1½ cups sugar
2 eggs
1¾ cups flour
½ teaspoon cream of tartar
¾ teaspoon baking powder
⅛ teaspoon salt
7 tablespoons milk
2 tablespoons orange juice
1 teaspoon vanilla
Grated rind of 1 orange

For the tangerine sabayon:
4 egg yolks
½ cup sugar
1 cup heavy cream
½ cup tangerine purée

For the garnish:
¼ cup Grand Marnier
Brown sugar
4 grapefruits, peeled and sectioned
2 oranges, peeled and sectioned
2 tangerines, peeled and sectioned
½ cup tangerine purée

Caramelized sugar designs

For the brandy snap, cream the butter and sugar until light, and then add all of the other ingredients in the order listed. Scrape down the bowl well after mixing. Line a sheet pan with parchment paper and grease with butter. At 3-inch intervals down the center of the pan place approximately two tablespoons of batter. Spread the batter evenly into long, thin strips. Bake at 350 degrees until golden brown. Remove from the oven and trim the edges. While the cookies are still warm, wrap each around a circular metal cutter to form a basket. Cool.

For the orange pound cake, cream the butter and sugar. Add the eggs. Combine the dry ingredients and the wet ingredients in separate bowls. Add the dry ingredients alternately with the wet ingredients to the creamed butter mixture, blending well after each addition. Pour into a greased and floured cake pan and bake at 350 degrees until set.

For the sabayon, heat the yolks and sugar in a metal bowl over simmering water until they are warm to touch and the sugar has begun to dissolve. In a separate bowl, whip the heavy cream to soft peaks. Remove the warmed yolks from the heat and whip until pale yellow and cool. Fold in the cream and the tangerine purée.

To serve, cut the orange pound cake to fit inside the brandy snap baskets. Soak the cake with Grand Marnier. Combine the brown sugar with just enough water to dissolve and heat until the sugar has melted and caramelized. Add the citrus to the caramel and toss gently to coat. Place the cake-filled baskets on serving plates. Spoon one tablespoon of sabayon on top of each cake and decorate with the caramel-glazed citrus. Finish the plates with tangerine sabayon and tangerine purée. Garnish with caramelized sugar designs.

245 Orange Blossom

Serves 4

For the mousseline:
2 cups milk
Zest of 2 oranges
8 egg yolks
4 ounces sugar
1¼ ounces cornstarch
8 ounces butter, softened

For the sponge cake:
5 egg yolks
1½ cups sugar
Juice of ½ orange
Zest of 1 lemon
½ teaspoon vanilla
1 cup flour
3 egg whites

For the garnish:
White chocolate petals and leaves
Orange purée
Cocoa powder
Powdered sugar

For the mousseline, scald the milk with the orange zest. Mix the egg yolks, sugar and cornstarch together. Temper this egg yolk mixture with the scalded milk and return the mixture to the stove. Cook, stirring constantly until thickened. Cool to room temperature. Place the mousseline in the bowl of an electric mixer fitted with the paddle attached. Slowly add the butter and mix until fully combined. Fill metal ladles with mixture and freeze until set.

For the sponge cake, beat the egg yolks with all but 1 tablespoon of the sugar on high speed until thick and ribbony. Lower the speed of the mixer and add the orange juice, lemon zest and vanilla. Sift the flour over this yolk mixture. Beat the egg whites until stiff, but not dry. Fold the whites into the yolk mixture along with the sifted flour in two additions. Pour the batter onto a hot sheet pan and sprinkle with the remaining tablespoon of sugar. Bake for 35 to 40 minutes at 350 degrees. Cool. With a cookie cutter, cut the cake into four 3-inch rounds.

To serve, arrange the white chocolate petals in the center of the plates. Place a round of sponge cake in the center of each blossom. Heat the ladles to unmold the frozen mousseline and place one mousseline on top of each sponge cake. Garnish the plates with the orange purée, and dust with cocoa powder and powdered sugar.

246 Citronelle Brûlée on Warm Berry Compote

Serves 8

For the passion fruit curd:
1½ cups heavy cream
7 egg yolks
1 tablespoon cornstarch
¾ cup sugar
⅔ cup passion fruit purée
Zest of 5 lemons

For the citronelle brûlée:
1½ cups heavy cream
2 teaspoons gelatin
Juice of 1 large lemon
1 teaspoon sugar

For the berry compote:
¼ cup passion fruit purée
Juice of 1 lemon
½ cup sugar
½ cup blackberries
½ cup raspberries
½ cup strawberries, sliced
¼ cup blueberries
¼ cup butter, softened
and cut into small pieces

For the garnish:
Black and white chocolate cigars

For the passion fruit curd, bring the heavy cream to a boil. Combine the egg yolks, cornstarch, sugar and passion fruit purée. Temper this mixture with the hot cream. Return to a saucepan, add the lemon zest and cook over medium heat stirring constantly until thickened. Strain and let cool.

For the citronelle brûlée, whip the heavy cream until it forms soft peaks. Chill. Dissolve the gelatin in lemon juice, heating gently over simmering water until the gelatin is thoroughly dissolved. Whisk the passion fruit curd into the gelatin until well blended. Whisk ⅓ of the whipped cream into the gelatin mixture to lighten, and then fold in the remaining ⅔ of the whipped cream. Fill individual, round, metal molds with this mixture and freeze until set, approximately three hours. Remove from the freezer and unmold by applying heat to the sides. Sprinkle sugar over the top and caramelize with a blow torch. Garnish with chocolate cigars and refrigerate until service.

For the berry compote, heat the passion fruit purée, lemon juice and sugar until boiling. Reduce the heat, toss in the berries and add the butter. Toss the pan until the butter is melted. Turn off the heat and spoon the berry compote onto plates. Arrange a citronelle brûlée in the center of each plate and serve.

247 Blood Orange Sherbet on Almond Gratinée

Serves 8

For the sherbet:
¾ cup water
3 ounces sugar
2 tablespoons glucose
1 cup blood orange juice
½ tablespoon créme fraîche

For the almond cream:
2¼ ounces unsalted butter
2¼ ounces sugar
2¼ ounces almond flour
½ ounce all-purpose flour
1 tablespoon dark rum
1 egg

For the garnish:
Blood orange zest
Fresh mint

To prepare the sherbet, combine the water, sugar and glucose in a small saucepan and boil for 1 minute. Cool. Mix the blood orange juice with the sugar syrup and process in an ice cream maker according to the manufacturer's instructions. Just as the churning is complete, add the créme fraîche and continue churning for an additional minute. Remove from the ice cream machine and freeze for at least 4 hours before serving.

For the almond cream, cream the butter and sugar together in the bowl of an electric mixer. Add the egg and continue beating. Add the flours and rum and beat on high for 1 minute until light. To plate the dessert, spread a thin layer of almond cream on the bottom of an ovenproof plate. Set under a preheated broiler until golden brown. Arrange the blood orange segments in a circle in the center of the almond cream. Place a scoop of the sherbet in the middle of the orange sections. Garnish with the orange zest and fresh mint. Serve while the almond cream is still hot.

248 Chocolate Mousse with Popcorn

Serves 8 to 10

For the popcorn:
1 tablespoon vegetable oil
¼ cup popcorn
12 ounces sugar
3 ounces corn syrup
4 tablespoons honey
3½ ounces water

For the chocolate mousse:
14 ounces milk chocolate
¼ cup cocoa butter, melted
2¼ cups heavy cream,
whipped to stiff peaks

For the caramel sauce:
4 tablespoons water
1 cup sugar
10 tablespoons heavy cream
Lemon juice to taste

For the garnish:
Leftover caramelized popcorn
Dark chocolate shapes
Melted chocolate
Caramel sauce

For the popcorn, pop corn in oil in a saucepan. Set aside. In a separate pan cook sugar with corn syrup and honey until mixture reaches 160 degrees. Add water and let boil. Add popcorn. Mix well and pour onto a cool surface to dry. When hardened, separate popcorn kernels.

For the chocolate mousse, warm milk chocolate and cocoa butter in a double boiler. Remove from heat and quickly fold this into whipped cream. Add half of the popcorn mixture. Mix well and turn into 8 to 10½-cup sized molds. Chill 3 hours or freeze for 1 hour.

For the caramel sauce, place water in a small, heavy saucepan and add sugar. When sugar has moistened, cook over medium heat, until sugar turns golden brown. Remove from heat and pour in cream carefully. Return to heat and cook until thickened and sugar has dissolved. Add lemon juice to cut the sweetness, if desired. Set aside.

To serve, turn out popcorn mixture from molds. Decorate with remaining popcorn, dark chocolate shapes and melted chocolate and caramel sauce swirled on plate.

249 Ginger and Plum Ice Cream with Lavender Bread Pudding

Serves 8 to 10

For the ice cream:
2 cups heavy cream
2 cups milk
1 vanilla bean, split
8 egg yolks
1 cup sugar
6 ripe plums, pitted and diced
2 ounces candied ginger, chopped

For the bread pudding:
2 loaves stale brioche, cut into uneven slices
6 plums, pitted and sliced
1 bunch fresh lavender
20 egg yolks
½ cup honey
1 cup sugar
1 tablespoon vanilla extract
1 quart light cream
Pinch of salt
Pinch of cinnamon

For the garnish:
Cinnamon sugar
Caramel shapes
Fresh lavender honey
Powdered sugar

To prepare the ice cream, combine the cream and milk in a small saucepan. Add the vanilla bean and steep over low heat for 10 minutes. Meanwhile, whip the egg yolks with the sugar until light and fluffy. Temper the yolks with the warm cream and add back to the saucepan with the remaining cream. Cook over low heat, stirring constantly, until the mixture has thickened to the point that it coats the back of a spoon. Strain and chill. Stir in the diced plums and candied ginger and freeze in an ice cream machine according to the manufacturer's directions.

For the bread pudding, layer the brioche with the plums and fresh lavender in a large baking dish. In a mixing bowl, whisk together the egg yolks, honey, sugar, vanilla, cream, salt and cinnamon. Pour this mixture over the bread. If necessary, add more cream so that all of the bread is moistened. Bake in a 350 degree oven until the custard has set and browned, about 1 hour. Remove from the oven and cool.

To serve, scoop the ice cream and bread pudding onto plates. Sprinkle the bread pudding with cinnamon sugar. Garnish with the caramel shapes, lavender, honey and powdered sugar.

249 Mississippi Mud Pie

Serves 10

For the white chocolate ice cream:
2 cups heavy cream
2 cups milk
1 vanilla bean, split
8 ounces white chocolate, chopped
8 egg yolks
1 cup sugar

For the cappuccino ice cream:
2 cups heavy cream
2 cups milk
1 vanilla bean, split
5 ounces semi-sweet chocolate, roughly chopped
½ teaspoon cinnamon
4 tablespoons instant espresso powder

For the chocolate tuiles:
¼ cup egg whites
½ teaspoon vanilla extract
1 teaspoon crème de cacao
Pinch of salt
⅓ cup all-purpose flour
2 tablespoons cocoa powder
¾ cup powdered sugar
5 tablespoons butter, softened
Chopped Oreo cookies

For the chocolate sauce:
¾ pound butter
¾ pound semi-sweet chocolate
1½ cups sugar
1½ cups cocoa powder
½ cup strong coffee
1 cup light corn syrup
2 cups heavy cream
Pinch of cinnamon
Pinch of salt

For the garnish:
Honey
Choux pastry shapes
Whipped cream
Fresh raspberries
Oreo cookies
Cocoa powder
Powdered sugar

To prepare the white chocolate ice cream, combine the cream and milk in a small saucepan with the vanilla bean and white chocolate. Place over a medium flame until the cream is scalded and the white chocolate has melted. Meanwhile, beat the egg yolks with the sugar in a mixing bowl until light and fluffy. Temper the yolks with the warm cream and return to the saucepan. Slowly bring to a boil over low heat, stirring constantly, until thick. Remove from the heat and cool. Freeze in an ice-cream machine according to the manufacturer's directions.

Repeat this process to make the cappuccino ice cream. Scald the cream and milk together with the vanilla, chocolate, cinnamon and espresso powder. Beat the egg yolks with the sugar. Temper the yolks, add back to the remaining cream and continue cooking until thick. Freeze in an ice cream machine.

To prepare the chocolate tuiles, whisk the whites with the vanilla extract, crème de cacao and salt in a mixing bowl. Sift together the flour, cocoa powder and powdered sugar. Add to the whites and whisk until smooth. Spoon this batter onto parchment-lined sheet pans, thinly spreading out the cookies with the back of a spoon. Sprinkle the cookies with the chopped Oreos. Bake at 350 degrees for 5 to 7 minutes. Cool slightly, remove from the pan and, using a small bowl, shape into cups.

To prepare the chocolate sauce, melt the butter and chocolate in the top of a double boiler. In a separate saucepan, whisk together the sugar, cocoa powder and coffee over low heat. Add the melted chocolate along with the corn syrup, heavy cream, cinnamon and salt. Whisk over low heat until the sugar has dissolved and the sauce has a smooth consistency.

To assemble the dessert, line a dish with plastic wrap. Layer the white chocolate and cappuccino ice cream inside the dish and freeze until firm. Unmold the ice cream and slice into desired shapes. Place the ice cream inside the chocolate tuile cups. Drizzle the plate with the chocolate sauce and honey. Also drizzle chocolate sauce over the baked choux pastry shapes. Set the cookie cup on the plate. Garnish with whipped cream, fresh raspberries, Oreo cookies, cocoa powder and powdered sugar.

250 Buttermilk Ice Cream with Rosemary Biscuits

Serves 8 to 10

For the ice cream:
4 cups buttermilk
1½ cups light corn syrup
Juice and zest of 4 lemons
½ cup sugar

For the biscuits:
2 pounds all-purpose flour
5 ounces baking powder
½ ounce salt
4 ounces sugar
⅛ cup chopped fresh rosemary
1 pound butter, chilled
Light cream

For the blueberry sauce:
1 pint fresh blueberries
Sugar to taste
Juice of 3 oranges
2 cinnamon sticks

For the garnish:
Fresh blueberries
Fresh mint
Fresh rosemary
Caramel sticks

To prepare the ice cream, combine all of the ingredients and freeze in an ice cream machine according to the manufacturer's directions.

For the biscuits, combine the flour, baking powder, salt, sugar and rosemary. Mix well. Cut in the butter until the mixture resembles coarse crumbs. Add enough light cream to form a soft, smooth dough. Do not overwork. Pat out the dough until it is ¾-inch thick. Cut out biscuits and set them on an ungreased baking sheet. Bake at 350 degrees for 12 to 15 minutes, until the biscuits have risen and turned golden brown. Remove from the oven and cool.

To prepare the blueberry sauce, combine all of the ingredients in a small saucepan. Bring to a boil, reduce to a simmer and cook for 5 minutes. Remove from the heat. Remove the cinnamon sticks and cool.

To serve, split the biscuits in half. Scoop the buttermilk ice cream onto the biscuits. Spoon the blueberry sauce around the plate. Garnish with the fresh blueberries, mint, rosemary and caramel sticks.

251 Frozen Tahitian Vanilla Soufflé

Serves 8 to 10

For the white chocolate cones:
6 ounces dark chocolate, tempered
1 pound white chocolate, tempered

For the vanilla syrup:
½ cup sugar
½ cup water
2 Tahitian vanilla beans

For the frozen soufflé:
3 egg yolks
½ cup sugar
¾ cup vanilla syrup, from above
3 egg whites
2 cups heavy cream

For the almond tuiles:
7½ ounces unsalted butter
15 ounces granulated sugar
15 ounces blanched almonds, finely ground
5 ounces flour
1 ounce vodka
7 ounces warm water

For the citrus sauce:
4 cups tangerine juice
2 cups granulated sugar

For the tangerine sorbet:
4 cups tangerine juice
1 cup simple syrup

For the cinnamon toast bread:
8 ounces light brown sugar
4 ounces dark brown sugar
4 ounces unsalted butter
1 egg
¾ teaspoon ground cloves
1 tablespoon cinnamon
½ teaspoon baking powder
½ teaspoon baking soda
3 cups all-purpose flour
¼ cup milk
½ cup sour cream
Powdered sugar

For the phyllo wings:
4 sheets phyllo pastry
Clarified butter
Superfine sugar

For the garnish:
Orange segments
Sliced grapes
Candied apricots
Bing cherries
Fresh mint

To prepare the white chocolate cones, form triangles of parchment paper into 3-inch cones, securing the edges with tape. Drizzle the tempered dark chocolate in an abstract pattern on the inside of the cone. Cool until set. Fill the cones with the tempered white chocolate and let sit for 2 minutes. Invert the cone to drain out the excess white chocolate. Revert to an upright position and cool until hardened. Peel off the paper and set aside.

Prepare the vanilla syrup by boiling all of the ingredients in a small saucepan until thick and syrupy. Remove the vanilla beans. Keep hot.

To prepare the frozen soufflé, beat the egg yolks with ¼ cup of the sugar in the bowl of an electric mixer set over warm water. When the yolks are room temperature, beat with the electric mixer on high speed until light in color and triple in volume, approximately 8 minutes. Pour the hot vanilla syrup down the side of the bowl and continue beating until cool, an additional 15 minutes. In another bowl, whip the egg whites to stiff peaks, adding the remaining ¼ cup of sugar just before the beating is finished. Gently fold the egg whites into the egg yolk mixture, being careful not to deflate. Beat the heavy cream to soft peaks and fold into the egg mixture. Fill the white chocolate cones with this soufflé mixture and freeze until set, approximately 2 hours.

To prepare the tuiles, cream the butter and sugar until smooth. Add the remaining ingredients except for the warm water and mix until well incorporated. Add the warm water and mix until smooth. Spread a very thin layer of this batter on a non-stick sheet pan. Bake in a 325 degree oven until golden brown. Cut into 3-inch squares and shape into small dishes. Cool.

For the citrus sauce, combine the tangerine juice and granulated sugar in a stainless steel saucepan and boil until slightly thick and syrupy. Cool in an ice bath.

For the tangerine sorbet, combine the tangerine juice and simple syrup. Freeze in an ice-cream machine according to the manufacturer's directions.

To prepare the cinnamon toast bread, cream the brown sugars with the butter until smooth. Incorporate the eggs. Sift together all of the remaining dry ingredients except for the powdered sugar and add to the egg mixture, alternating with the milk and sour cream. Mix until smooth, scraping down the sides of the bowl. Pour into a greased loaf pan and bake at 300 degrees until firm in the center. Once done, freeze the cake. Slice into thin slices and cut the slices into 3-inch triangles. Toast the triangles and dust with powdered sugar.

To prepare the phyllo wings, layer the four sheets of phyllo pastry, liberally brushing each sheet with the clarified butter. Cover the top sheet with more butter. Cut the phyllo into 8-inch wing shapes, punching a small hole in the center of each wing. Dredge both sides of the wings in superfine sugar. Lay on a parchment-lined sheet pan. Cover with another sheet of parchment and set another sheet pan on top to weigh down the dough. Bake in a 325 degree oven until golden brown. Remove from the oven and cool.

To serve, place the frozen soufflé in the chocolate cone in the middle of each plate. Balance a phyllo wing on top of each soufflé. Garnish the plate with orange segments, sliced grapes, candied apricots and cherries. Scoop three balls of the tangerine sorbet into each tuile and set on the plate. Garnish with mint and drizzle with the citrus sauce. Serve.

251 Frozen Pine Nut Nougat with Banana

Serves 8 to 10

For the pine nut nougatine:
1½ cups granulated sugar
Lemon juice
1 cup toasted pine nuts
3 tablespoons unsalted butter

For the frozen banana mousse:
¾ cups sugar
5 egg whites
1¾ cups mascarpone, softened
3 large, ripe bananas, puréed

For puff pastry discs:
1 pound puff pastry
1½ cups powdered sugar

For the tuiles:
½ pound unsalted butter
2 cups powdered sugar
½ cup egg whites
1½ cups honey
2 cups all-purpose flour

For the sautéed bananas:
2 tablespoons butter
6 ripe bananas
¼ cup hazelnut liqueur
½ cup simple syrup
¼ cup pine nuts

For the garnish:
Hazelnut-flavored whipped cream
Caramel shapes
Banana chips
Fresh mint

To prepare the pine nut nougatine, dissolve the sugar in a stainless steel saucepan with enough water to make a wet sand. Add a couple of drops of lemon juice and place over a high flame. Bring to a boil, washing the sugar crystals off the sides of the pan with a clean brush dipped in cold water. When the sugar begins to turn amber remove from the fire and add the unsalted butter and pine nuts. Stir until well incorporated. Turn out onto a greased half sheet pan and cool. Once hardened, chop into small pieces.

For the banana mousse, dissolve the sugar in a stainless steel saucepan with enough water to make a wet sand. Boil over a high flame until the medium-ball stage is reached. Meanwhile, begin whipping the egg whites in an electric mixer set on high speed. When the whites begin to form stiff peaks, slowly pour the hot sugar syrup down the side of the bowl. Continue beating on high speed until the meringue is completely cool. In a separate bowl, beat the mascarpone until smooth. Add the banana purée. Fold the meringue into this mixture. Once incorporated, stir in the chopped pine nut nougatine. Line 2½-inch ring molds with plastic wrap and fill with the banana mousse mixture. Freeze until firm.

To prepare the puff pastry discs, roll out the pastry on a flat surface dusted with powdered sugar until it is 1/16-inch thick. Cut the pastry into 5-inch discs and set in the freezer until firm. Once chilled, cut a 1-inch hole in the center of each disc. Cut 2 triangular notches out of the sides of each disc. Dredge the discs in more powdered sugar and set on parchment paper. Place the parchment on the backside of an inverted sheet pan. Lay another piece of parchment on top to prevent the dough from rising. Bake in a 350 degree oven until the discs are golden brown. Remove from the oven and cool on a flat surface.

To prepare the tuiles, combine the butter and sugar in the bowl of an electric mixer. Whip this mixture with a paddle until fluffy, scraping down the sides of the bowl. Add the egg whites, honey, flour and cream until smooth. Refrigerate. Spread this mixture into long, thin strips and bake in a 300 degree oven until golden brown. Remove from the oven, and while still hot, bend the tuiles over a slightly convex surface to cool.

Just before service, prepare the sautéed bananas. Melt the butter in a large sauté pan and add the bananas. Sauté until slightly brown. Add the hazelnut liqueur and the simple syrup, reducing the liquid to form a thick syrup. Remove from the flame and toss in the toasted pine nuts. Divide the bananas among the plates, spooning some of the excess sauce on top. Unmold the frozen banana mousse and set in the center of the plate. Place a quenelle of whipped cream on top and rest the puff pastry disc on top of the cream. Arrange the tuiles on the sides of the pastry disc and garnish with caramel shapes, banana chips and fresh mint.

252 Peking-Style Banana Fritters

Serves 4

For the mousse:
1 cup coconut milk
½ cup sugar
Heavy cream
Pinch of salt
2 teaspoons sambuca
1½ sheets gelatin, softened in cold water
1¼ cups heavy cream, whipped

For the fritters:
½ cup dried red mung beans
3 tablespoons sugar
2 teaspoons water
1 teaspoon vanilla
2 ripe bananas
Flour for dredging

For the batter:
4 egg whites
1 heaping tablespoon flour
1 heaping tablespoon cornstarch
Pinch of salt
Oil for deep frying
Cocoa powder
Powdered sugar

For the garnish:
Apricot preserves
Crème anglaise mixed with berry purée
White chocolate brittle
Caramel shapes
Fresh mint
Powdered sugar

For the coconut caramel mousse, reduce the coconut milk by half in a small saucepan set over medium heat. Place the sugar in another small saucepan and add just enough water to make a wet sand. Caramelize the sugar until very dark. Add the reduced coconut milk and just enough heavy cream to smooth out the mixture. Add the salt, sambuca and gelatin and stir over low heat until dissolved. Remove from the heat and cool completely. Fold in the whipped cream and transfer the mixture to a small terrine. Chill until set.

For the fritters, begin by preparing the red bean paste. Boil the mung beans in water until very soft. Drain and purée until smooth. Melt the sugar and water together in a small saucepan. Add the vanilla and the bean purée. Continue cooking over low heat until the mixture takes on a deep red color. Adjust the sweetness with more sugar if necessary and cool. Peel the bananas and slice into rounds approximately ½-inch thick. Spread the red bean paste on 1 slice of banana and make a sandwich with another slice. Repeat this procedure until all of the bananas have been used. Dredge these banana sandwiches in flour. Meanwhile, preheat the oil to 375 degrees. Beat the egg whites to soft peaks. Fold in the flour, cornstarch and salt to form a light batter. Depending on the volume of the whites, it may be necessary to add additional flour and cornstarch, in equal parts, to the batter.

Dip the floured banana sandwiches into the batter and deep fry until golden brown. Drain on paper towels and dust with cocoa and powdered sugar. To serve, unmold the mousse and cut into 1-inch thick slices. Spoon the berry crème anglaise onto the plates and lay the mousse on top. Arrange the banana fritters on the plates. Garnish with white chocolate brittle, caramel shapes, fresh mint and powdered sugar

253 Sheep's Milk Ice Cream

Yields 1½ quarts
For the cream sauce:
1 quart fresh sheep's milk
1 tablespoon sugar
1 tablespoon armagnac

For the ice cream:
3 cups skimmed sheep's milk
(reserved from the cream sauce preparation)
6 ounces sugar
4 grams ice-cream stabilizer
1 pound soft, fresh sheep's
milk cheese

For the sauce:
1 cup huckleberries
2 tablespoons simple syrup
Lemon juice

For the garnish:
Toasted brioche
Fresh mint

To prepare the cream sauce, boil the sheep's milk in a small saucepan. As the milk boils, skim off the cream that floats to the top. Transfer this cream to a small bowl. Add the sugar and armagnac and set aside until service. Reserve the skimmed milk to make the ice cream.

To prepare the ice cream, boil the skimmed sheep's milk with the sugar. Cool slightly. Add the stabilizer and fold in the soft cheese, stirring until smooth. Strain through a fine sieve and process in an ice-cream machine according to the manufacturer's directions. Freeze.

For the sauce, purée half of the huckleberries and pass through a fine chinois. Add the simple syrup and a few drops of lemon juice. Boil in a small saucepan over medium heat until thick. Save the remaining huckleberries for garnish.

To serve, pool a small portion of the flavored cream on the bottom of the serving plates. Garnish the plate with a ring of huckleberries. Form quenelles of the sheep's milk ice cream and place on top of the cream. Drizzle the huckleberry syrup around the plate, garnish with toasted brioche and fresh mint.

247 Rice Pudding

Serves 6 to 8
For the pudding:
4 cups milk
1 thick strip lemon peel
½ cup long-grain white rice
1 egg yolk
¾ cup sugar
½ cup heavy cream
½ teaspoon vanilla extract
Ground cinnamon

To prepare the pudding, place the milk, lemon peel and rice in the top of a heavy, 4-quart saucepan. Cook, uncovered, for about 1 hour, or until the rice is soft to the bite but still retains its shape. It is important to stir the mixture almost constantly to prevent the rice from clumping and to prevent a skin from forming on the surface.

In a small bowl, mix the egg yolk with the sugar until crumbly. Remove the rice from the heat. Rapidly stir a spoonful of the hot rice mixture into the yolk mixture to temper the yolk, then stir the yolk mixture into the rice, mixing steadily to prevent the yolk from cooking too quickly and forming solid particles. Return to low heat and continue to cook, stirring almost constantly, for several minutes. Add the cream and cook, stirring, until the mixture is steaming. Remove from the heat and stir in the vanilla. Continue to stir the pudding until it has cooled slightly, then press a piece of plastic wrap directly onto the surface to prevent a skin from forming.

Although traditionally served chilled, this rice pudding may also be served warm or at room temperature. Dust servings with ground cinnamon.

254 Dried Cherry and Pistachio Baklava

Serves 6

For the filling:
11 ounces shelled pistachios, roughly chopped
5 ounces dried cherries, roughly chopped
2 ounces granulated sugar
2 ounces pasteurized egg yolk

For the pastry:
9 sheets phyllo dough
½ pound butter, melted and cooled

For the syrup:
¾ cup simple syrup
6 sprigs fresh mint
18 dried cherries, cut in half

To prepare the filling, combine all of the ingredients in a medium-sized bowl and mix well. Set aside.

To form the baklava, stack 3 sheets of phyllo on top of each other, brushing liberally with butter between each sheet and on top. Cut the stack in half, crosswise, to create 2 smaller rectangles. Spread each rectangle with filling, leaving a 1-inch border of dough around the edge. Fold the border along the longer sides of the rectangle in toward the center to hold the filling. Tightly roll the pastry like a jelly roll, beginning at the short side. Set on baking sheets and brush with butter. Repeat this procedure to form 6 baklava. Bake the baklava at 350 degrees until golden brown. Cool.

To prepare the syrup, boil the simple syrup with the mint and dried cherries until the cherries are tender. Lightly brush the baked baklava with this syrup. Slice the baklava in half and plate and serve with additional syrup.

255 Upside-Down Corn Cakes

Serves 12

For the corn cakes:
14 ounces butter
⅔ cup sugar
8 eggs
1 tablespoon vanilla
2¼ cups flour
⅓ cup cornmeal
2 teaspoons baking powder
4 tablespoons light brown sugar
3 pints fresh raspberries
3 tablespoons brandy
1 cup simple syrup

For the raspberry purée:
2 pints fresh raspberries
Simple syrup to taste

For the garnish:
Whipped cream
Fresh raspberries
Powdered sugar for dusting
Fresh mint sprigs

For the corn cakes, cream butter and sugar in a mixing bowl. Add eggs, one at a time, to incorporate. Add vanilla. Sift flour, cornmeal and baking powder together and fold into egg and butter mixture. Mix just to form a smooth batter.

Preheat oven to 375 degrees. Butter 24 3-inch ramekins. Sprinkle 1½ teaspoons brown sugar and about 8 raspberries on the bottom of each. Fill with batter halfway full. Bake until firm, about 10 minutes. Let cool in ramekins and then remove. Combine brandy and simple syrup and brush the tops-fruit side up-of the corn cakes.

For the raspberry purée, purée fresh raspberries in blender and add simple syrup to taste. Strain and set aside.

To serve, place 2 cakes on each plate, fruit-side up. Surround with whipped cream, a pool of raspberry purée and several raspberries on each plate. Swirl a little of the whipped cream into raspberry sauce, if desired. Sprinkle all with powdered sugar and garnish whipped cream with a sprig of mint.

255 Dark Chocolate Tamales

Yields 12 tamales

For the filling:
1½ cups white masa harina
1¼ cups hot water
4 ounces unsalted butter
1 cup sugar
½ cup milk
½ cup cocoa powder
3 ounces semi-sweet chocolate, finely chopped
1 teaspoon baking powder
1¼ cups raisins, soaked overnight in rum

For the wrapping:
24 corn husks, soaked
Corn husk strips for tying

For the garnish:
Fudge swirl ice cream chantilly
Toasted pine nuts

To prepare the filling, combine the masa harina with the hot water and mix to form a slightly sticky, but firm dough. Cream the butter and sugar in the bowl of an electric mixer until light and fluffy. Heat the milk and cocoa powder over medium heat until boiling, whisking to prevent the formation of lumps. Add the chopped chocolate and stir until melted. Cool to room temperature.

Alternating the reconstituted masa and the chocolate mixture, add them to the creamed butter and sugar, incorporating well after each addition. Add the baking powder and beat on high speed for 5 minutes until the texture is very light and smooth.

Transfer this chocolate and masa mixture to a heavy-bottomed saucepan and cook over medium heat, stirring constantly until the mixture darkens and develops a glossy finish, about 5 minutes. To test for doneness, touch the mixture with your fingertips. It should not be sticky. At this point, fold in the soaked raisins.

Spoon 3 ounces of the tamale filling into the center of the reconstituted corn husks. Roll and tie the tamales. Steam for 20 minutes, or until the filling no longer sticks to the corn husk when it is peeled away. Serve with ice cream and crème chantilly and garnish with toasted pine nuts.

257 Petit Déjeuner

Serves 8

For the petit pain au chocolat:
7½ ounces white chocolate
9⅓ tablespoons cream
3 sheets gelatin, softened
2 cups heavy cream, whipped
2 tablespoons coffee extract

For the coffee bavarian:
3 cups milk
6 egg yolks
9⅓ tablespoons sugar
4 sheets gelatin, softened
4½ tablespoons coffee extract
2 cups heavy cream, whipped
8 molded white chocolate
coffee cups
8 molded white chocolate coffee spoons
½ cup heavy cream, whipped
6 teaspoons fine ground coffee powder

For the chocolate croissants:
2 pounds gianduja
(a super-fine blending of pulverized hazelnuts and milk chocolate)
2 tablespoons coffee extract

For the petit pain, chop the white chocolate in a food processor. Bring the cream to a boil, pour it into the white chocolate and purée until the chocolate is smooth. Blend in the softened gelatin, cool and fold in the whipped cream. Pour the white chocolate mousse into a trough made of aluminum foil, molding it with your hands and freeze. While the pain au chocolat is hard, remove the foil, cut it into 3-inch sections and spray each piece with coffee extract. Defrost before serving.

For the bavarian cream coffee cups, bring the milk to a boil; mix together the egg yolks and the sugar; slowly pour the scalded milk into the yolks and cook to a light custard over a double boiler. Remove the custard from the heat, mix in the gelatin and the coffee extract, cool and fold in the whipped cream. Fill the white chocolate coffee cups with the coffee bavarian, top with a dollop of whipped cream and dust each one with coffee powder.

For the chocolate croissants, soften the gianduja and knead it until it is smooth. Roll it out between two sheets of plastic wrap and cut it into 5½ by 3-inch triangles. Roll each triangle into a croissant and spray with coffee extract.

256 Chocolate Tamales

Yields 32 tamales

For the tamales:
2½ pounds semisweet chocolate, roughly chopped
4 cups heavy cream
16 corn husks

For the caramel lime sauce:
1 cup sugar
¾ cup heavy cream
½ cup fresh lime juice

For the garnish:
Cocoa powder
Corn husks
Edible gold leaf
Spun sugar

To prepare the filling, set the chocolate in a large mixing bowl. Bring the cream to a boil in a small saucepan. Pour the hot cream over the chocolate and stir until melted. Refrigerate to set. Using a pastry bag, pipe approximately 2 ounces of the ganache mixture into the center of 5-inch squares of plastic wrap. Shape the ganache into rectangles, roughly 1½ inches wide by 3 inches long. Cut the corn husks into rectangles that are the same size as the ganache.

Lay the husks on top of the ganache. Wrap the ganache in the plastic wrap, gently pressing the corn husk into the chocolate to imprint the texture. Refrigerate until set. For the sauce, in a small saucpan combine the sugar with just enough water to moisten. Boil the sugar until it turns into a light amber caramel. Remove from the heat and add the cream. Return to the heat and stir until the caramel is dissolved. Add the lime juice and cool.

To serve, unwrap the tamales and peel off the corn husks. Dust with cocoa powder. Ladle the sauce onto the plates and position the tamale on top. Garnish with whole corn husks, gold leaf and spun sugar.

257 Trio of Sweet Tamales

Serves 6 to 8

For the wrapping:
36 to 48 corn husks
Mango purée
Raspberry purée
Corn husk strips for tying

For the chocolate masa:
1 cup water
2 tablespoons cocoa powder
2 tablespoons honey
1 cup masa harina
1 tablespoon butter
Lemon juice

For the cajeta caramel:
4 cups evaporated goat's milk
2 cups milk
5 teaspoons cornstarch
½ teaspoon baking soda
1½ cups sugar
6 tablespoons water
Juice of ½ lemon

For the mango masa:
1 cup mango purée
2 tablespoons honey
1 cup masa harina
1 tablespoon butter
Lemon juice

For the pineapple filling:
2 cups milk
5 ounces unsweetened coconut
1 vanilla bean
5 ounces fresh pineapple, finely diced
2 eggs
4 tablespoons sugar
2 tablespoons all-purpose flour

For the apple cinnamon masa:
1 cup apple purée
2 tablespoons honey
1 teaspoon cinnamon
1 cup masa harina
1 tablespoon butter
Lemon juice

For the apple cinnamon filling:
4 large apples, peeled, cored and diced
2 tablespoons butter
4 tablespoons brown sugar
1 teaspoon cinnamon
½ teaspoon nutmeg
Juice of ½ lemon
½ cup crushed pecans

For the assembly:
1 fresh mango, peeled and cut into strips
1 pint fresh raspberries

For the garnish:
Mango purée
Raspberry purée
Apple purée
Spun sugar

To prepare the wrapping, soak half of the corn husks in mango purée and the other half in raspberry purée for at least 24 hours.

For the chocolate masa, combine the water, cocoa powder and honey in a small saucepan. Bring to a boil and whisk in the masa. Reduce the heat and cook for 10 minutes, stirring frequently. Remove from the heat and stir in the butter and a squirt of fresh lemon juice. Cool and store in an airtight container until ready to use.

To prepare the cajeta caramel, combine both milks in a small saucepan and bring to a boil. Reduce to a simmer. Mix together the corn-starch and baking soda. Add enough hot milk to form a smooth paste then whisk this paste into the remaining milk. Continue simmering. Combine the sugar, water and lemon juice in another small saucepan. Cook over high heat to caramelize the sugar. When golden brown, remove from the heat and slowly add half of the hot milk mixture to the caramelized sugar. Pour this mixture back into the remaining milk and continue to cook at a low boil until the caramel is thick and dark, approximately 1 hour. Remove from the heat and cool.

To prepare the mango masa, combine the mango purée and honey in a small saucepan. Bring to a boil and whisk in the masa. Reduce the heat and cook for 10 minutes, stirring frequently. Remove from the heat and stir in the butter and a squirt of fresh lemon juice. Cool and store in an airtight container until ready to use.

For the pineapple coconut filling, combine the milk, coconut, vanilla bean and pineapple in a small saucepan. Steep for 10 minutes over a low flame. In a separate bowl, combine the eggs and sugar and whisk until light in color and ribbony. Whisk in the flour. Temper the egg mixture with some of the warm milk and whisk together. Return to the heat and slowly bring to a boil, stirring constantly. When thick, remove from the heat and cool.

To prepare the apple cinnamon masa, combine the apple purée, honey and cinnamon in a small saucepan. Bring to a boil and whisk in the masa. Reduce the heat and cook for 10 minutes, stirring frequently. Remove from the heat and stir in the butter and a squirt of fresh lemon juice. Cool and store in an airtight container until ready to use.

For the apple cinnamon filling, sauté the apples in the butter and brown sugar until tender. Add the cinnamon, nutmeg and lemon juice and mix thoroughly. Remove from the heat and stir in the pecans.

To assemble the tamales, wipe any excess fruit purée off of the reconstituted corn husks. For the mango chocolate tamales, spread the chocolate masa on ⅓ of the mango-soaked corn husks. Spoon some of the cajeta caramel in the center. Lay 2 to 3 strips of fresh mango in the center, top with another mango-soaked husk and roll them. For the pineapple coconut tamales, spread the mango masa over ⅓ of the raspberry-soaked corn husks. Spoon some of the pineapple coconut filling on top and place 3 or 4 raspberries in a line down the center. Top with another raspberry-soaked corn husk and roll and tie. For the cinnamon apple tamales, spread the cinnamon apple masa on the remaining mango-soaked corn husks. Spoon the cinnamon mango filling in the center. Top with the remaining raspberry-soaked corn husks and roll and tie them.

To serve, steam the tamales for 12 minutes, until the filling pulls away from the husk. Garnish with the fruit purées and spun sugar.

258 Dessert Medley

Serves 8

For the crème brûlée:
2 cups heavy cream
2 cups milk
1 vanilla bean
1 cinnamon stick
5 ounces sugar
9 egg yolks

For the lemon triangles:
1 pound Linzer dough
1½ pounds unsalted butter, melted
32 egg yolks
28 ounces sugar
3 cups lemon juice

For the banana soufflé:
2 cups milk
3 ounces sugar
3 ounces flour
6 eggs, separated
1 very ripe banana

For the hot chocolate obsession:
6 ounces butter, softened
4 ounces sugar
3 eggs
6 ounces semisweet chocolate
4 ounces flour
1 tablespoon cocoa
1 tablespoon baking powder

For the strawberry shortcake:
1 quart fresh strawberries
Sugar
Raspberry purée
Champagne
Shortcake

For the dish:
Chocolate ice cream
Vanilla ice cream
Macerated cherries
Caramelized bananas

For the garnish:
Chocolate and caramel shapes
mint sprigs

To prepare the crème brûlée, bring the cream and milk to a boil with the vanilla bean, cinnamon stick and half of the sugar. Beat the remaining sugar with the egg yolks until light and fluffy. Temper the yolk mixture with some of the hot milk. Add the remaining warm liquid. Pour into ramekins and bake in a water bath in a 300 degree oven until set.

For the lemon triangles, line a half sheet pan with Linzer dough and prebake the crust. Combine the melted butter, egg yolks, sugar and lemon juice and cook over a bain-marie until thick. Pour into the prebaked crust and chill. Cut into triangles.

For the banana soufflé, heat the milk until boiling. Combine the sugar, flour and egg yolks. Beat until ribbony and light in color. Temper the yolks with some of the hot milk and add this mixture back to the remaining milk. Cook, stirring constantly, until thick. Cool. Purée the ripe banana and add it to the cooled soufflé base. Whip the egg whites to stiff peaks and fold into the banana mixture. Butter and sugar 8 soufflé molds and fill with the soufflé mixture. Bake at 375 degrees for approximately 15 minutes.

To prepare the chocolate obsession, cream the butter and sugar. Add the eggs and continue beating until light and fluffy. Add the melted chocolate. Combine the dry ingredients and add to the chocolate mixture, being careful not to overmix. Pipe the mixture into eight ring molds and freeze. Bake, frozen, in a 375 degree oven until just cooked around the edges.

For the strawberry shortcake, hull and slice the berries. Macerate the strawberries in the sugar, raspberry purée and champagne. Spoon on top of shortcake to serve.

To assemble the dessert, arrange one portion of each dessert on plates. Garnish with chocolate and caramel shapes.

258 White Peach Soup with Berries

Serves 4

For the peach soup:
4 firm ripe white peaches
1 tablespoon lemon juice
1 cup strong Bergamot orange tea
4 tablespoons kirsch
4 tablespoons honey
¼ cup wild strawberries
¼ cup raspberries
¼ cup blackberries
¼ cup blueberries
2 tablespoons sugared red currants

For the garnish:
4 sprigs citronella
4 small clusters sugared red currants

For the peach soup, plunge the peaches into scalding hot water for 10 seconds, followed by ice water, to loosen the skin and peel; sprinkle the peeled peaches with lemon juice to keep them from turning brown. Combine the Bergamot tea with the kirsch and the honey; bring to a simmer, poach the peeled peaches for 10 minutes and cool. Reduce the poaching syrup to 1 cup and chill.

To serve, set the poached peaches, stem side down, in the center of the soup plates; pour the poaching syrup into the plates, with the mixed berries scattered around the peaches. Garnish the dish with the citronella sprigs and red currant clusters.

Chef Contributors

John Ash
Mark Baker
Paul Bartolotta
Jan Birnbaum
David Blom
Daniel Boulud
Charles Bowman
Peter Bührer
David Burke
Michael Chiarello
Cheung Kam Chuen
Gianni Cosetti
Michel Cousin
Roberto Cozzarolo
Christian Delouvrier
Jody Denton
Francis Drillien
Alain Ducasse
Alain Dutournier
Jonathan Fox
Amy Ferguson-Ota
Dennis Foy
David Fye
Toni Giacomini
Paul Haberlin
Yiorgos Hatzyiannakis
Christopher Hawver
Tomas Herranz
Ken Hom
Paul Ingenito
Inaki Izaguirre
André Jager
Jean Joho
Hubert Keller
Karl-Heinz Krücken
Gray Kunz
Emeril Lagasse
Christer Larsson
Pedro Larumbe
Richard Leach
Gilbert LeCoze
Suser Lee
Stephen Levine
Roland Liccioni
Jill Light
Christer Lingström
George Mahaffey
Nobuyuki Matsushisa
George Mavrothalassitis
George Morrone
Chris Northmore
Patrick O'Connell
Jean-Louis Palladin
Gérard Pangaud
Mark Peel
Jörgen Persson
Debra Ponzek
Ron Pickarski
Sinclair Philip
Philippe Reininger
Michel Richard
Richard Riehm
Douglass Rodriguez
Michel Rostang
Dan Rundell
Roland Sager
Jean Schillinger
Jimmy Schmidt
John Sedlar
Julian Serrano
Lydia Shire
Sim Siik
Lam Kam Shing
Joachim Splichal
Frank Stitt
Allen Susser
Makoto Tanaka
Elizabeth Terry
Bruno Tison
Jacques Torres
Jeremiah Tower
Charlie Trotter
David Walzog
Antoine Westermann
Brian Whitmer
Joan Winters
Martin Woesle
Don Woods
Norman Van Aken
Christoforos Veneris
Jean-Georges Vongerichten
Roy Yamaguchi

Notes

Index

The rebellions of the belly are the worst.

Francis Bacon